The Student's Catullus

Oklahoma Series in Classical Culture

Oklahoma Series in Classical Culture

Series Editor

Susan Ford Wiltshire, *Vanderbilt University*

The Student's

CATULLUS

Second Edition

By

Daniel H. Garrison

Department of Classics,
Northwestern University

University of Oklahoma Press: Norman

Catullus, Gaius Valerius.
   [Works. 1995]
   The student's Catullus / by Daniel H. Garrison.—2nd ed.
     p. cm—(Oklahoma series in classical culture; v. 5)
   Complete poems of Catullus in Latin; commentary in English.
   Includes bibliographical references.
   ISBN 0–8061–2763–5 (alk. paper)
   1. Love poetry, Latin. 2. Epigrams, Latin. 3. Rome—Poetry.
  I. Garrison, Daniel H. II. Title. III. Series
PA6274.A2 1995
874'.01—dc20   95–1280
                                                                                                          CIP

The Student's Catullus is Volume 5 in the Oklahoma Series in Classical Culture.

The paper in this book meets the guidelines for permanence and durability of the Committee on Production Guidelines for Book Longevity of the Council on Library Resources, Inc.

Front-cover illustration is from Horace Gregory, The Poems of Catullus, illustrated by Zhenya Gray, by permission of Random House, Inc./Crown Publishers, Inc.

Maps I-IV courtesy of The Cleveland Museum of Art.

Copyright © 1989, 1995 by Daniel H. Garrison. Published by the University of Oklahoma Press, Norman, Publishing Division of the University. All rights reserved. Manufactured in the U.S.A. First edition, 1989. First paperback printing, 1991. First printing of the Second Edition, 1995.

6 7 8 9 10 11 12 13 14

CONTENTS

MAPS

PREFACE

This edition is specifically designed for students who are studying Catullus for the first time. The text is therefore a reading text (not a strictly conservative scholar's version), with readings that will interfere as little as possible with the poetry as a whole. The commentary is the result of my own encounters with the Latin text, enlightened by my students, the commentaries of Ellis, Merrill, Fordyce, and Quinn, and as much of the current scholarship as I could review in the past year. Like the text, this commentary is meant to interfere as little as possible with the reading of the poems. It does not as a rule call attention to parallels in other authors, participate in scholarly controversies, or promote specific judgments of literary value. Its chief purpose is to help readers over difficulties with the Latin, and to offer such help as unobtrusively as possible. To assist the reader further, the commentary is supplemented by end materials: a list of Catullan persons (appendix A), a guide to Catullan meters (appendix B), a glossary of rhetorical and other classical terminology (appendix C), a guide to Catullan usage (appendix D), six maps, and a comprehensive lexicon of Catullan Latin. This package should allow any reader familiar with Latin basics to read Catullus with good understanding and to make reasonably informed judgments about the poetry he wrote.

For the conception of the book as a whole as well as a thoughtful critique that saved it from many errors before it went to press, I am much indebted to Marilyn Skinner; for numerous corrections and improvements, the anonymous referees of the University of Oklahoma Press; T. P. Wiseman; and Arthur Robinson. Professor Robinson also supplied the materials for appendix D. For funding to prepare the earliest version of this book, I am indebted to a grant from the President's Fund for Educational Excellence.

Daniel H. Garrison

Northwestern University
January 1989

PREFACE TO THE SECOND EDITION

In the six years that have passed since completing the first edition, I have made numerous additions and corrections, most of them suggested by my continuing classroom experience, some by the comments of reviewers and colleagues, and others by scholarly work that has appeared. In several instances, I have changed my mind about the interpretation of Catullus' language; in others, I have corrected errors, clarified my language, and added new aids to the reader. This edition, while keeping to the same assumptions as the first, should be more useful to the student of Catullus, clearer, and more prescient in anticipating difficulties. Among the many people who have suggested improvements, I owe special thanks to Don Fowler, Arthur Robinson, David Traill, P. Walcot, and John Yardley. I am also indebted to Anne Garrison, who came out of editorial retirement to scrutinize the entire book sentence by sentence.

D.H.G.

January 1995

INTRODUCTION

Most of what is important about Catullus is in the poems he wrote. Chronology, identifications of persons, and other biographical details are often conjectural, and so open to dispute that all reconstructions of his life (including the one that follows) must be taken *cum grano salis*. It is generally believed that he was born about 84 B.C. and died young, in about 54. He came from a prominent family based in Verona, in what was then Cisalpine Gaul. Suetonius says his father was a frequent host of Julius Caesar, a relationship that may have begun during the latter's governorship of that province. Though Catullus went to Rome at an early age, his poems show a continued attachment to his first home.

Catullus' poems are so vividly emotional that critics since antiquity have tended to read them as a record of his personal life. Though this biographical tendency is probably justified to some extent, the tradition in which Catullus wrote called instead for the artful projection of an image or *persona*, literally a mask behind which the poet manipulates the tools of poetic rhetoric. Catullus' achievement lies in his seamless transformation of actual experience into poetic fiction that is at once audacious and believable. No one reading his poems today can tell where self-revelation gives way to invention.

His wealth and social position gave him the independence that this audacity required. He openly mocked Caesar himself in verse; other poems attacking prominent Romans made scurrilous, often obscene, and no doubt grossly libelous accusations, apparently with impunity. Though more an observer than a participant in politics, he moved among highly public figures and enjoyed provoking scandal.

Audacity in Catullus sometimes includes exuberant obscenity. One recent scholarly edition omits no fewer than 32 of the 113 poems—a seventh of the surviving lines of Catullus—"which do not lend themselves to comment in English." But whoever chooses to avoid this side may also miss "the lightning-quick, sneering, out-of-doors manner" that Virginia Woolf heard in the lines of Sophocles' Electra. Catullus can be pretty, but his style does not confine itself to prettiness.

Some of Catullus' contemporaries may have read him for the scandal, but long after his enemies were dead, he continued to be read for his eloquence as a poet. He has been identified with a coterie of poets whom Cicero called *poetae novi* or *neoteroi*. Though the coherence and even the existence of such a "school" is more allegation than established fact, it appears that some poets were, like Catullus, impatient with Latin poetry's dependence on Greek conventions and the dry bookishness of Hellenistic poetry in which poems were chiefly imitations of other poems rather than immediate experience intensified by the disciplines of poetic craft. Another Neoteric belief seems to have been that Latin had a native vigor of its own which was stifled by imitation of Greek models. The vernacular color of Catullus' language gives it a racy freshness (like that of Plautus on the stage) that we can still feel.

The immediacy of fresh, even vulgar language is tempered by some traditional virtues. Hellenistic literary values demanded both learning and discipline. Later Roman poets honored Catullus' learning by according him the epithet *doctus*. But like the best of the Hellenistic poets, Catullus and his circle disliked long, rambling poems that made up in bulk what they lacked in workmanship. From the bookish Alexandrians, the *neoteroi* learned the virtues of economy, craftsmanship, and the wit whose soul is brevity. Words like *lepidus* and *venustus* describe the stylish crispness of the best Catullan diction; we find them often when he is praising a person or a poem. Another traditional feature is the iambic rhythm inherited from the earliest Greek iambic poets: rapid and colloquial but more difficult to use in Latin than in Greek, its association with irreverent mockery (including self-mockery) served Catullus well.

The mixture of street language and learned craft gives Catullus a classic style of his own that is particularly distinctive in the polymetric poems (nos. 1–60). Another, more traditional, style is epic, occurring in a middle group of long poems of various subjects and meters (61–68). Sometimes he uses the high language of epic to emphasize an ironic view of the heroic past, but he was not immune to the lure of the grand style for its own sake. Many readers consider poem 64, the mini-epic about the wedding of Peleus and Thetis and Theseus' abandonment of Ariadne, one of Catullus' greatest achievements. Catullus rose to challenges: poem 63 is a tour de force in the nearly impossible Galliambic metre as well as a chilling (and mostly believable) account of religious fanaticism. Marriage and marriage hymns also attracted him.

A third style appears in the short elegiac poems (nos. 69–116), where Catullus employs a more literary than colloquial manner, both in his choice of words and in their arrangement. These poems had an influence on the satirical epigrams of Martial as well as the love elegies of Gallus, Propertius, Tibullus, and Ovid a generation later. Though the subject matter is similar to that of the polymetric poems, the manner is more traditional, growing out of the elegant artifice of the Hellenistic epigram.

Although sexual excess, perversion, corruption, betrayal, and despair figure prominently in Catullus' poetry, he remains emotionally sympathetic and morally earnest, more traditional than decadent in his beliefs. Catullus enjoys what is twisted only to expose it to ridicule. Sexual love and the love of friends are both taken seriously, though he is not above the light-hearted amusements that Rome had to offer and he is anything but self-righteous. He is as ready to expose his own awkwardness as he is to mock that of others.

Because he was a young writer and an innovator who took poetic risks as readily as emotional ones, Catullus suffered poetic as well as emotional disasters. No one who loves Catullus admires all his poems equally, and every reader should feel challenged to make judgments of literary value with respect to particular poems, lines, and words. The overall achievement of this remarkable poet is beyond criticism in detail; his contributions to the art of Latin poetry made the achievements of the Augustan age and the early Empire possible, and they have inspired poets in other languages as well. Catullus' poems have a special appeal to modern readers who accept rough language, unseemly subjects, and personal obsessions in the literature they read. An age that has absorbed the madness of Ezra Pound and Virginia Woolf, the obsessiveness of James Joyce and Samuel Beckett, and the wacky humor of Andy Warhol will find common ground with the paradoxical character of Catullus.

Three biographical events mark the work of Catullus as we have it. The first and undoubtedly the most important was his love affair with a married woman he calls Lesbia. Apuleius says her real name was Clodia, and it is generally believed she was a woman ten years his senior, sister of Cicero's enemy P. Clodius Pulcher and wife (later the widow) of Q. Metellus Celer, who governed Cisalpine Gaul between 64 and 62 B.C. For her, it was a casual affair, one of many. For Catullus it was the cause of both euphoria and anguish, with little middle ground. Some twenty-five poems chronicle the ups and downs of this relationship, which ran on from perhaps 60 or 59 (before the death of Metellus in 59) to 55 or 54. The Lesbia poems are the best-known of Catullus' work.

A second event reflected in Catullus' poetry is his year in Asia Minor, on the southern coast of the Black Sea, where he was on the staff of C. Memmius, Roman governor of Bithynia, from 57 to 56. It was his only experience of the tasks of empire that young men of his class were supposed to undertake, and though he appears to have enjoyed it little, this year away sharpened his love of Rome and Verona and undoubtedly gave him the time for reading and writing that his life in Roman high society made scarce. The steep forests of the north Anatolian coast, transplanted to the Troad, contribute a sinister effect to his poem about Attis (no. 63, one of his longer masterpieces).

Some time before this foreign sojourn, the death of his brother struck Catullus with an impact that is reflected in several poems: 101, commemorating a visit to his tomb in the Troad during or just after his tour of duty in Bithynia, and passages in 65 (5–14) and 68 (19–26, 91–100). The poetic record that we have may have been written in its entirety during or after the trip to Bithynia. The deep grief that these passages describe may have kept the poet from giving immediate literary expression to his feelings.

Catullus reacted to personalities as much as events. Besides Lesbia, there was the young Juventius, with whom Catullus was jealously infatuated. Furius and Aurelius are alternately his rivals for Juventius and friendly intercessors with Lesbia. His wrath calls scandalous attention to many personal enemies: Lesbia's notorious brother, the politician P. Clodius Pulcher; Mamurra, the corrupt billionaire protegé of Caesar and Pompey, whom Catullus dubs Mentula, the "Prick"; Caesar himself, who seems to have liked Catullus in spite of his offensive attacks. Friendships are also celebrated in the poems: Cornelius Nepos, the historian and biographer to whom Catullus dedicates a book of poems (not necessarily our own collection); and

Licinius Calvus, an outstanding orator and poet, Catullus' closest friend. A full account of friends, enemies, and other personalities will be found in appendix A.

The collection of 113 poems which has come down to us is arranged in three sections:

1–60 are the polymetric poems, written in a variety of meters. Variants of the iambic rhythm prevail, the favorites being the hendecasyllabic (about two thirds of this section) and the choliambic "limping iambics" or scazons, especially effective in mockery (self-mockery in poem 8).

A second group of seven long poems (61–68) in other meters includes glyconic stanzas, common dactylic hexameters (the meter of Homer as well as Virgil), and elegiac couplets.

The third and final section is entirely in elegiac couplets, a meter associated with Greek epigram and after Catullus with the Augustan love elegy of Propertius, Tibullus, and Ovid. These are usually short: epigrams in the usual sense of the word, with characteristic wit and brevity of statement. Their intent, however, is not always humorous. All of Catullus' metres are explained in appendix B.

Though these poems survived the end of antiquity in only one manuscript, Catullus himself was much read and talked about in the century following his death, and he made a considerable impression on the great Augustan poets Horace, Virgil, and Ovid. Later neglect of his work—partly because it was not in the educatiõnal mainstream of medieval schools and monasteries—contributed to the near-disappearance of his writing. Therefore the text, having derived at one critical point from a single copy, is often corrupt. The version presented in this book represents the best current consensus, but no two editors of Catullus agree on all points, and there is no standard version.

FURTHER READING

Of the many books about Catullus and his poetry, line-by-line commentaries provide the fastest answers to questions about a specific piece of text. The standard modern commentary is by C. J. Fordyce (Oxford, 1961, reissued in soft covers 1990), flawed chiefly by its omission of some 32 poems he considers indecent. The commentary of Kenneth Quinn (2d ed., St. Martin's, 1973) covers all the poems, but a bit more concisely, with useful references to learned articles about specific poems. Phyllis Young Forsyth's "Teaching Text" (Univ. Press of America, 1986) is sound and concise, with many aids to translation. Still valuable older commentaries are by Robinson Ellis (2d ed., Oxford, 1889) and E. T. Merrill (Harvard, 1893). For those who read German, Wilhelm Kroll's *Catull* (Leipzig and Berlin, 1922) can also be helpful; Hans Peter Syndikus' three-volume *Catull* (Darmstadt, 1984–87) provides valuable short discussions of each poem.

Sometimes the best commentary is a translation. G.P. Goold's *Catullus* (Duckworth, 1983) has facing Latin and English pages with a general introduction and brief notes on each poem. Guy Lee's translation (*The Poems of Catullus*, Oxford, 1990) is also accompanied by facing Latin text. See also Charles Martin's translation, similarly titled (Hopkins, 1990).

Of the discursive books about Catullus and his poetry, John Ferguson's *Catullus* (Oxford, 1988) is a concise (50 pp.) handbook, with a survey of critical views and a select bibliography. A fuller appraisal, written by a poet, is Charles Martin's *Catullus* (Yale, 1992). Stuart G. P. Small's *Catullus. A Reader's Guide to the Poems* (Univ. Press of America, 1983) is a judicious guide to Catullus' poetry, arranged by topic. T. P. Wiseman has written extensively on Catullus; his most recent book, *Catullus and his World: A Reappraisal*, is a readable and stimulating account of the social and literary world in which Catullus wrote. Kenneth Quinn, whose commentary has already been cited, has collected some of the best Catullan scholarship from the years 1947–1968 in *Approaches to Catullus* (Barnes & Noble, 1972). Two other studies by Quinn, *The Catullan Revolution* (Heffer, 1959, 1969) and *Catullus: An Interpretation* (Batsford, 1972), are also valuable. Marilyn B. Skinner's *Catullus' Passer* (Arno, 1981) studies the arrangement of poems 1–51, and concludes that these were arranged as we have them by Catullus himself. Whether or not this is right, her monograph offers valuable insights into relations between the poems in our collection.

This commentary makes occasional reference to Allen and Greenough's *New Latin Grammar* (1888, revised 1903, 1916, 1931), reprinted many times, most recently by Caratzas (New Rochelle, NY, 1992). This book is indispensible to any serious student of the Latin language.

Historical novels can be a good way to bring a writer to life in one's imagination. The classic novel about Catullus and his contemporaries is Thornton Wilder's *The Ides Of March* (Harper, 1948). Benita Kane Jaro's *The Key* (Dodd, Mead, 1988) sees Catullus through the eyes of his friend M. Caelius Rufus (about whom see appendix A).

THE POEMS

1

DEDICATION TO CORNELIUS

Cui dono lepidum novum libellum
arida modo pumice expolitum?
Corneli, tibi: namque tu solebas
meas esse aliquid putare nugas
iam tum cum ausus es unus Italorum   5
omne aevum tribus explicare cartis
doctis, Iuppiter, et laboriosis!
Quare habe tibi quidquid hoc libelli
qualecumque; quod, o patrona virgo,
plus uno maneat perenne saeclo.   10

2

TO HER SPARROW

Passer, deliciae meae puellae,
quicum ludere, quem in sinu tenere,
cui primum digitum dare appetenti
et acris solet incitare morsus,
cum desiderio meo nitenti   5
carum nescio quid lubet iocari,
et solaciolum sui doloris,
credo, ut tum gravis acquiescat ardor:
tecum ludere sicut ipsa possem
et tristis animi levare curas!   10
. . .
tam gratum est mihi quam ferunt puellae
pernici aureolum fuisse malum,
quod zonam soluit diu ligatam.

3

LAMENT FOR A SPARROW

Lugete, o Veneres Cupidinesque,
et quantum est hominum venustiorum:
passer mortuus est meae puellae,
passer, deliciae meae puellae,
quem plus illa oculis suis amabat—   5
nam mellitus erat suamque norat
ipsam tam bene quam puella matrem,
nec sese a gremio illius movebat,
sed circumsiliens modo huc modo illuc
ad solam dominam usque pipiabat: 10
qui nunc it per iter tenebricosum
illud, unde negant redire quemquam.
At vobis male sit, malae tenebrae
Orci, quae omnia bella devoratis:
tam bellum mihi passerem abstulistis.   15
O factum male! O miselle passer!
Tua nunc opera meae puellae
flendo turgiduli rubent ocelli.

ↄ 4

A BARK'S DEDICATION

Phaselus ille quem videtis, hospites,
ait fuisse navium celerrimus,
neque ullius natantis impetum trabis
nequisse praeterire, sive palmulis
opus foret volare sive linteo. 5
Et hoc negat minacis Hadriatici
negare litus insulasve Cycladas
Rhodumque nobilem horridamque Thraciam
Propontida trucemve Ponticum sinum
(ubi iste post phaselus antea fuit 10
comata silva—nam Cytorio in iugo
loquente saepe sibilum edidit coma).
Amastri Pontica et Cytore buxifer,
tibi haec fuisse et esse cognitissima
ait phaselus, ultima ex origine 15
tuo stetisse dicit in cacumine,
tuo imbuisse palmulas in aequore;
et inde tot per impotentia freta
erum tulisse, laeva sive dextera
vocaret aura, sive utrumque Iuppiter 20
simul secundus incidisset in pedem;
neque ulla vota litoralibus deis
sibi esse facta, cum veniret a mari
novissimo hunc ad usque limpidum lacum.
Sed haec prius fuere; nunc recondita 25
senet quiete seque dedicat tibi,
gemelle Castor et gemelle Castoris.

5

TO LESBIA, ABOUT KISSES

Vivamus, mea Lesbia, atque amemus
rumoresque senum severiorum
omnes unius aestimemus assis!
Soles occidere et redire possunt;
nobis cum semel occidit brevis lux,   5
nox est perpetua una dormienda.
Da mi basia mille, deinde centum;
dein mille altera, dein secunda centum;
deinde usque altera mille, deinde centum.
Dein, cum milia multa fecerimus,   10
conturbabimus illa, ne sciamus,
aut ne quis malus invidere possit,
cum tantum sciat esse basiorum.

6

WHO'S THE NEW GIRL, FLAVIUS?

Flavi, delicias tuas Catullo,
ni sint illepidae atque inelegantes,
velles dicere nec tacere posses.
Verum nescio quid febriculosi
scorti diligis: hoc pudet fateri.   5
Nam te non viduas iacere noctes
nequiquam tacitum cubile clamat
sertis ac Syrio fragrans olivo,
pulvinusque peraeque et hic et ille
attritus, tremulique quassa lecti   10
argutatio inambulatioque.
Nam nil stupra valet, nihil tacere.
Cur? Non tam latera ecfututa pandas,
ni tu quid facias ineptiarum.
Quare, quidquid habes boni malique,   15
dic nobis. Volo te ac tuos amores
ad caelum lepido vocare versu.

7

HOW MANY KISSES

Quaeris quot mihi basiationes
tuae, Lesbia, sint satis superque.
·Quam magnus numerus Libyssae harenae
lasarpiciferis iacet Cyrenis
oraclum Iovis inter aestuosi   5
et Batti veteris sacrum sepulcrum;
aut quam sidera multa, cum tacet nox,
furtivos hominum vident amores:
tam te basia multa basiare
vesano satis et super Catullo est,   10
quae nec pernumerare curiosi
possint nec mala fascinare lingua.

8

BE DONE WITH HER, CATULLUS!

Miser Catulle, desinas ineptire,
et quod vides perisse perditum ducas.
Fulsere quondam candidi tibi soles,
cum ventitabas quo puella ducebat
amata nobis quantum amabitur nulla;   5
ibi illa multa cum iocosa fiebant
quae tu volebas nec puella nolebat,
fulsere vere candidi tibi soles.
Nunc iam illa non volt: tu quoque, impotens, noli,
nec quae fugit sectare, nec miser vive,   10
sed obstinata mente perfer, obdura.
Vale, puella! Iam Catullus obdurat,
nec te requiret, nec rogabit invitam.
At tu dolebis, cum rogaberis nulla.
Scelesta, vae te! Quae tibi manet vita?   15
Quis nunc te adibit? Cui videberis bella?
Quem nunc amabis? Cuius esse diceris?
Quem basiabis? Cui labella mordebis?
At tu, Catulle, destinatus obdura.

9

WELCOME HOME, VERANIUS!

Verani, omnibus e meis amicis
antistans mihi milibus trecentis,
venistine domum ad tuos penates
fratresque unanimos anumque matrem?
Venisti. O mihi nuntii beati!   5
Visam te incolumem audiamque Hiberum
narrantem loca, facta, nationes,
ut mos est tuus, applicansque collum
iucundum os oculosque suaviabor.
O quantum est hominum beatiorum,   10
quid me laetius est beatiusve?

10

A BAD MOMENT WITH VARUS AND HIS GIRL

Varus me meus ad suos amores
visum duxerat e foro otiosum:
scortillum (ut mihi tum repente visum est)
non sane illepidum neque invenustum;
huc ut venimus, incidere nobis   5
sermones varii, in quibus quid esset
iam Bithynia, quo modo se haberet,
et quonam mihi profuisset aere.
Respondi id quod erat: nihil neque ipsis
nec praetoribus esse nec cohorti,   10
cur quisquam caput unctius referret:
praesertim quibus esset irrumator
praetor, nec faceret pili cohortem.
"At certe tamen," inquiunt "quod illic
natum dicitur esse, comparasti   15
ad lecticam homines." Ego (ut puellae
unum me facerem beatiorem)
"Non" inquam "mihi tam fuit maligne,
ut, provincia quod mala incidisset,
non possem octo homines parare rectos."   20
(At mi nullus erat nec hic neque illic
fractum qui veteris pedem grabati
in collo sibi collocare posset.)
Hic illa, ut decuit cinaediorem,
"Quaeso," inquit "mihi, mi Catulle, paulum   25
istos commoda: nam volo ad Serapim
deferri." "Mane," inquii puellae,
"istud quod modo dixeram me habere ...
fugit me ratio: meus sodalis—
Cinna est Gaius—is sibi paravit.   30
Verum utrum illius an mei, quid ad me?
Utor tam bene quam mihi pararim.
Sed tu insulsa male et molesta vivis,
per quam non licet esse neglegentem!"

11

A MESSAGE FOR LESBIA

Furi et Aureli, comites Catulli,
sive in extremos penetrabit Indos,
litus ut longe resonante Eoä
    tunditur unda,

sive in Hyrcanos Arabasve molles,   5
seu Sagas sagittiferosve Parthos,
sive quae septemgeminus colorat
    aequora Nilus,

sive trans altas gradietur Alpes,
Caesaris visens monimenta magni,   10
Gallicum Rhenum, horribile aequor ulti-
    mosque Britannos,

omnia haec, quaecumque feret voluntas
caelitum, temptare simul parati,
pauca nuntiate meae puellae   15
    non bona dicta:

cum suis vivat valeatque moechis,
quos simul complexa tenet trecentos,
nullum amans vere, sed identidem omnium
    ilia rumpens;   20

nec meum respectet, ut ante, amorem,
qui illius culpa cecidit velut prati
ultimi flos, praetereunte postquam
    tactus aratro est.

12

TO A NAPKIN THIEF

Marrucine Asini, manu sinistra
non belle uteris, in ioco atque vino:
tollis lintea neglegentiorum.
Hoc salsum esse putas? Fugit te, inepte:
quamvis sordida res et invenusta est.   5
Non credis mihi? Crede Pollioni
fratri, qui tua furta vel talento
mutari velit; est enim leporum
differtus puer ac facetiarum.
Quare aut hendecasyllabos trecentos   10
exspecta, aut mihi linteum remitte,
quod non me movet aestimatione,
verum est mnemosynum mei sodalis.
Nam sudaria Saetaba ex Hiberis
miserunt mihi muneri Fabullus   15
et Veranius; haec amem necesse est
ut Veraniolum meum et Fabullum.

13

INVITATION

Cenabis bene, mi Fabulle, apud me
paucis, si tibi di favent, diebus —
si tecum attuleris bonam atque magnam
cenam, non sine candida puella
et vino et sale et omnibus cachinnis;   5
haec si, inquam, attuleris, venuste noster,
cenabis bene; nam tui Catulli
plenus sacculus est aranearum.
Sed contra accipies meros amores,
seu quid suavius elegantiusve est: 10
nam unguentum dabo, quod meae puellae
donarunt Veneres Cupidinesque;
quod tu cum olfacies, deos rogabis,
totum ut te faciant, Fabulle, nasum.

14

ON A VILE BOOK OF POEMS

Ni te plus oculis meis amarem,
iucundissime Calve, munere isto
odissem te odio Vatiniano:
nam quid feci ego quidve sum locutus,
cur me tot male perderes poetis?   5
Isti di mala multa dent clienti,
qui tantum tibi misit impiorum.
Quod si, ut suspicor, hoc novum ac repertum
munus dat tibi Sulla litterator,
non est mi male, sed bene ac beate,   10
quod non dispereunt tui labores.
Di magni, horribilem et sacrum libellum!
Quem tu scilicet ad tuum Catullum
misti, continuo ut die periret,
Saturnalibus, optimo dierum!   15
Non non hoc tibi, salse, sic abibit.
Nam, si luxerit, ad librariorum
curram scrinia, Caesios, Aquinos,
Suffenum, omnia colligam venena,
ac te his suppliciis remunerabor.   20
Vos hinc interea valete abite
illuc, unde malum pedem attulistis,
saecli incommoda, pessimi poetae.

14b

Si qui forte mearum ineptiarum
lectores eritis manusque vestras
non horrebitis admovere nobis . . .

15

A WARNING TO AURELIUS

Commendo tibi me ac meos amores,
Aureli. Veniam peto pudentem,
ut, si quicquam animo tuo cupisti,
quod castum expeteres et integellum,
conserves puerum mihi pudice,   5
non dico a populo—nihil veremur
istos, qui in platea modo huc modo illuc
in re praetereunt sua occupati—
verum a te metuo tuoque pene
infesto pueris bonis malisque.   10
Quem tu qua lubet, ut lubet, moveto
quantum vis, ubi erit foris paratum:
hunc unum excipio, ut puto, pudenter.
quod si te mala mens furorque vecors
in tantam impulerit, sceleste, culpam,   15
ut nostrum insidiis caput lacessas,
a tum te miserum malique fati!
Quem attractis pedibus patente porta
percurrent raphanique mugilesque.

16

A REPLY TO MY CRITICS

Pedicabo ego vos et irrumabo,
Aureli pathice et cinaede Furi,
qui me ex versiculis meis putastis,
quod sunt molliculi, parum pudicum.
Nam castum esse decet pium poetam   5
ipsum, versiculos nihil necesse est;
qui tum denique habent salem ac leporem,
si sunt molliculi ac parum pudici,
et quod pruriat incitare possunt,
non dico pueris, sed his pilosis   10
qui duros nequeunt movere lumbos.
Vos, quod milia multa basiorum
legistis, male me marem putatis?
Pedicabo ego vos et irrumabo.

⚘ 17

A VICTIM FOR THE BRIDGE

O Colonia, quae cupis ponte ludere longo,
et salire paratum habes, sed vereris inepta
crura ponticuli axulis stantis in redivivis,
ne supinus eat cavaque in palude recumbat:
sic tibi bonus ex tua pons libidine fiat,   5
in quo vel Salisubsali sacra suscipiantur,
munus hoc mihi maximi da, Colonia, risus.
Quendam municipem meum de tuo volo ponte
ire praecipitem in lutum per caputque pedesque,
verum totius ut lacus putidaeque paludis   10
lividissima maximeque est profunda vorago.
Insulsissimus est homo, nec sapit pueri instar
bimuli tremula patris dormientis in ulna.
Cui cum sit viridissimo nupta flore puella
(et puella tenellulo delicatior haedo,   15
adservanda nigerrimis diligentius uvis),
ludere hanc sinit ut lubet, nec pili facit uni,
nec se sublevat ex sua parte; sed velut alnus
in fossa Liguri iacet suppernata securi,
tantundem omnia sentiens quam si nulla sit usquam,   20
talis iste meus stupor nil videt, nihil audit,
ipse qui sit, utrum sit an non sit, id quoque nescit.
Nunc eum volo de tuo ponte mittere pronum,
si pote stolidum repente excitare veternum,
et supinum animum in gravi derelinquere caeno,   25
ferream ut soleam tenaci in voragine mula.

21

A SECOND WARNING TO AURELIUS

Aureli, pater esuritionum,
non harum modo, sed quot aut fuerunt
aut sunt aut aliis erunt in annis,
pedicare cupis meos amores.
nec clam: nam simul es, iocaris una, 5
haerens ad latus omnia experiris.
Frustra: nam insidias mihi instruentem
tangam te prior irrumatione.
Atque id si faceres satur, tacerem:
nunc ipsum id doleo, quod esurire 10
meus iam puer et sitire discet.
Quare desine, dum licet pudico,
ne finem facias, sed irrumatus.

22

A STYLISH POET'S AWKWARD POEMS

Suffenus iste, Vare, quem probe nosti,
homo est venustus et dicax et urbanus,
idemque longe plurimos facit versus.
Puto esse ego illi milia aut decem aut plura
perscripta, nec sic ut fit in palimpsesto   5
relata: cartae regiae, novi libri,
novi umbilici, lora rubra, membranae,
derecta plumbo et pumice omnia aequata.
Haec cum legas tu, bellus ille et urbanus
Suffenus unus caprimulgus aut fossor   10
rursus videtur: tantum abhorret ac mutat.
Hoc quid putemus esse? Qui modo scurra
aut si quid hac re scitius videbatur,
idem infaceto est infacetior rure,
simul poëmata attigit, neque idem umquam   15
aeque est beatus ac poëma cum scribit:
tam gaudet in se tamque se ipse miratur.
Nimirum idem omnes fallimur, neque est quisquam
quem non in aliqua re videre Suffenum
possis. Suus cuique attributus est error;   20
sed non videmus manticae quod in tergo est.

23

NO LOAN FOR FURIUS

Furi, cui neque servus est neque arca
nec cimex neque araneus neque ignis,
verum est et pater et noverca, quorum
dentes vel silicem comesse possunt:
est pulcre tibi cum tuo parente   5
et cum coniuge lignea parentis.
Nec mirum: bene nam valetis omnes,
pulcre concoquitis, nihil timetis,
non incendia, non graves ruinas,
non facta impia, non dolos veneni,   10
non casus alios periculorum.
Atqui corpora sicciora cornu
aut siquid magis aridum est habetis
sole et frigore et esuritione.
Quare non tibi sit bene ac beate?   15
A te sudor abest, abest saliva,
mucusque et mala pituita nasi.
Hanc ad munditiem adde mundiorem,
quod culus tibi purior salillo est,
nec toto decies cacas in anno,   20
atque id durius est faba et lapillis,
quod tu si manibus teras fricesque,
non umquam digitum inquinare posses.
Haec tu commoda tam beata, Furi,
noli spernere nec putare parvi,   25
et scstertia quae soles precari
centum desine: nam sat es beatus.

24

TO JUVENTIUS, ON HIS FRIENDSHIP WITH FURIUS

O qui flosculus es Iuventiorum,
non horum modo, sed quot aut fuerunt
aut post hac aliis erunt in annis,
mallem divitias Midae dedisses
isti, cui neque servus est neque arca,   5
quam sic te sineres ab illo amari.
"Qui? Non est homo bellus?" inquies. Est.
Sed bello huic neque servus est neque arca.
Hoc tu quam lubet abice elevaque:
nec servum tamen ille habet neque arcam.   10

25

TO THALLUS THE THIEF

Cinaede Thalle, mollior cuniculi capillo
vel anseris medullula vel imula oricilla
vel pene languido senis situque araneoso,
idemque, Thalle, turbida rapacior procella,
cum diva Murcia arbitros ostendit oscitantes,   5
remitte pallium mihi meum, quod involasti,
sudariumque Saetabum catagraphosque Thynos,
inepte, quae palam soles habere tamquam avita.
Quae nunc tuis ab unguibus reglutina et remitte,
ne laneum latusculum manusque mollicellas   10
inusta turpiter tibi flagella conscribillent,
et insolenter aestues, velut minuta magno
deprensa navis in mari, vesaniente vento.

26

AN EXPOSED HOUSE

Furi, villula vestra non ad Austri
flatus opposita est neque ad Favoni
nec saevi Boreae aut Apheliotae,
verum ad milia quindecim et ducentos.
O ventum horribilem atque pestilentem!   5

27

DRINKING ORDERS

Minister vetuli puer Falerni,
inger mi calices amariores,
ut lex Postumiae iubet magistrae
ebrioso acino ebriosioris.
At vos quo lubet hinc abite, lymphae,   5
vini pernicies, et ad severos
migrate. Hic merus est Thyonianus.

28

BAD PICKINGS IN THE PROVINCES

Pisonis comites, cohors inanis,
aptis sarcinulis et expeditis,
Verani optime tuque mi Fabulle,
quid rerum geritis? Satisne cum isto
vappa frigoraque et famem tulistis?   5
Ecquidnam in tabulis patet lucelli
expensum, ut mihi, qui meum secutus
praetorem refero datum lucello?
O Memmi, bene me ac diu supinum
tota ista trabe lentus irrumasti.   10
Sed, quantum video, pari fuistis
casu: nam nihilo minore verpa
farti estis. Pete nobiles amicos!
At vobis mala multa di deaeque
dent, opprobria Romuli Remique.   15

29

MAMURRA'S GREED

Quis hoc potest videre, quis potest pati,
nisi impudicus et vorax et aleo,
Mamurram habere quod comata Gallia
habebat ante et ultima Britannia?
Cinaede Romule, haec videbis et feres?   5
Et ille nunc superbus et superfluens
perambulabit omnium cubilia,
ut albulus columbus aut Adoneus?
Cinaede Romule, haec videbis et feres?
Es impudicus et vorax et aleo.   10
Eone nomine, imperator unice,
fuisti in ultima occidentis insula,
ut ista vestra diffututa mentula
ducenties comesset et trecenties?
Quid est alid sinistra liberalitas?   15
Parum expatravit an parum elluatus est?
Paterna prima lancinata sunt bona,
secunda praeda Pontica, inde tertia
Hibera, quam scit amnis aurifer Tagus:
nunc Galliae timetur et Britanniae.   20
Quid hunc malum fovetis? Aut quid hic potest
nisi uncta devorare patrimonia?
Eone nomine urbis o piissimi
socer generque, perdidistis omnia?

30

SOME FRIEND

Alfene immemor atque unanimis false sodalibus,
iam te nil miseret, dure, tui dulcis amiculi?
Iam me prodere, iam non dubitas fallere, perfide?
Nec facta impia fallacum hominum caelicolis placent.
Quae tu neglegis ac me miserum deseris in malis.   5
Eheu quid faciant, dic, homines cuive habeant fidem?
Certe tute iubebas animam tradere, inique, me
inducens in amorem, quasi tuta omnia mi forent.
Idem nunc retrahis te ac tua dicta omnia factaque
ventos irrita ferre ac nebulas aëreas sinis.   10
Si tu oblitus es, at di meminerunt, meminit Fides,
quae te ut paeniteat postmodo facti faciet tui.

31

BACK HOME AGAIN IN SIRMIO

Paene insularum, Sirmio, insularumque
ocelle, quascumque in liquentibus stagnis
marique vasto fert uterque Neptunus,
quam te libenter quamque laetus inviso,
vix mi ipse credens Thyniam atque Bithynos   5
liquisse campos et videre te in tuto.
O quid solutis est beatius curis,
cum mens onus reponit, ac peregrino
labore fessi venimus larem ad nostrum,
desideratoque acquiescimus lecto?   10
Hoc est quod unum est pro laboribus tantis.
Salve, o venusta Sirmio, atque ero gaude
gaudente; vosque, o Lydiae lacus undae,
ridete quidquid est domi cachinnorum.

32

A MODEST PROPOSAL

Amabo, mea dulcis Ipsitilla,
meae deliciae, mei lepores,
iube ad te veniam meridiatum.
et si iusseris, illud adiuvato,
ne quis liminis obseret tabellam,   5
neu tibi lubeat foras abire,
sed domi maneas paresque nobis
novem continuas fututiones.
Verum si quid ages, statim iubeto:
nam pransus iaceo et satur supinus   10
pertundo tunicamque palliumque.

33

TO TWO CREEPS

O furum optime balneariorum
Vibenni pater et cinaede fili
(nam dextra pater inquinatiore),
culo filius est voraciore),
cur non exilium malasque in oras   5
itis, quandoquidem patris rapinae
notae sunt populo, et natis pilosas,
fili, non potes asse venditare?

34

HYMN TO DIANA

Dianae sumus in fide
puellae et pueri integri:
Dianam pueri integri
  puellaeque canamus.

O Latonia, maximi   5
magna progenies Iovis,
quam mater prope Deliam
  deposivit olivam,

montium domina ut fores
silvarumque virentium   10
saltuumque reconditorum
  amniumque sonantum:

tu Lucina dolentibus
Iuno dicta puerperis,
tu potens Trivia et notho es   15
  dicta lumine Luna.

Tu cursu, dea, menstruo
metiens iter annuum,
rustica agricolae bonis
  tecta frugibus exples.   20

Sis quocumque tibi placet
sancta nomine, Romulique,
antique ut solita es, bona
  sospites ope gentem.

35

AN INVITATION TO CAECILIUS

Poetae tenero, meo sodali,
velim Caecilio, papyre, dicas
Veronam veniat, Novi relinquens
Comi moenia Lariumque litus.
Nam quasdam volo cogitationes   5
amici accipiat sui meique.
Quare si sapiet viam vorabit,
quamvis candida milies puella
euntem revocet, manusque collo
ambas iniciens roget morari.   10
Quae nunc, si mihi vera nuntiantur,
illum deperit impotente amore.
Nam quo tempore legit incohatam
Dindymi dominam, ex eo misellae
ignes interiorem edunt medullam.   15
Ignosco tibi, Sapphica puella
musa doctior; est enim venuste
Magna Caecilio incohata Mater.

36

A BOOK FIT FOR BURNING

Annales Volusi, cacata carta,
votum solvite pro mea puella.
Nam sanctae Veneri Cupidinique
vovit, si sibi restitutus essem
desissemque truces vibrare iambos,   5
electissima pessimi poetae
scripta tardipedi deo daturam
infelicibus ustulanda lignis.
Et hoc pessima se puella vidit
iocosis lepide vovere divis.   10
Nunc o caeruleo creata ponto,
quae sanctum Idalium Uriosque apertos
quaeque Ancona Cnidumque harundinosam
colis quaeque Amathunta quaeque Golgos
quaeque Durrachium Hadriae tabernam,   15
acceptum face redditumque votum,
si non illepidum neque invenustum est.
At vos interea venite in ignem,
pleni ruris et infacetiarum
annales Volusi, cacata carta.   20

37

BARFLIES

Salax taberna vosque contubernales,
a pilleatis nona fratribus pila,
solis putatis esse mentulas vobis,
solis licere, quidquid est puellarum,
confutuere et putare ceteros hircos?   5
An, continenter quod sedetis insulsi
centum (an ducenti?) non putatis ausurum
me una ducentos irrumare sessores?
Atqui putate: namque totius vobis
frontem tabernae sopionibus scribam.   10
Puella nam mi, quae meo sinu fugit,
amata tantum quantum amabitur nulla,
pro qua mihi sunt magna bella pugnata,
consedit istic. Hanc boni beatique
omnes amatis, et quidem, quod indignum est,   15
omnes pusilli et semitarii moechi;
tu praeter omnes une de capillatis,
cuniculosae Celtiberiae fili,
Egnati, opaca quem bonum facit barba
et dens Hibera defricatus urina.   20

38

IN DISTRESS, TO CORNIFICIUS

Malest, Cornifici, tuo Catullo,
malest, me hercule, et laboriose,
et magis magis in dies et horas.
Quem tu, quod minimum facillimumque est,
qua solatus es allocutione?   5
Irascor tibi. Sic meos amores?
Paulum quid lubet allocutionis,
maestius lacrimis Simonideis.

39

THE SMILING SPANIARD

Egnatius, quod candidos habet dentes,
renidet usquequaque. Si ad rei ventum est
subsellium, cum orator excitat fletum,
renidet ille; si ad pii rogum fili
lugetur, orba cum flet unicum mater,   5
renidet ille. Quidquid est, ubicumque est,
quodcumque agit, renidet: hunc habet morbum,
neque elegantem, ut arbitror, neque urbanum.
Quare monendum est te mihi, bone Egnati.
Si urbanus esses aut Sabinus aut Tiburs   10
aut parcus Umber aut obesus Etruscus
aut Lanuvinus ater atque dentatus
aut Transpadanus, ut meos quoque attingam,
aut quilubet, qui puriter lavit dentes,
tamen renidere usquequaque te nollem: 15
nam risu inepto res ineptior nulla est.
Nunc Celtiber es: Celtiberia in terra,
quod quisque minxit, hoc sibi solet mane
dentem atque russam defricare gingivam,
ut, quo iste vester expolitior dens est,   20
hoc te amplius bibisse praedicet loti.

40

FAIR WARNING TO RAVIDUS

Quaenam te mala mens, miselle Ravide,
agit praecipitem in meos iambos?
Quis deus tibi non bene advocatus
vecordem parat excitare rixam?
An ut pervenias in ora vulgi?   5
Quid vis? Qualubet esse notus optas?
Eris, quandoquidem meos amores
cum longa voluisti amare poena.

41

MAMURRA'S PRICEY GIRL FRIEND

Ameana puella defututa
tota milia me decem poposcit
ista turpiculo puella naso,
decoctoris amica Formiani.
Propinqui, quibus est puella curae,   5
amicos medicosque convocate:
non est sana puella, nec rogare
qualis sit solet aes imaginosum.

42

TO A STREET GANG

Adeste, hendecasyllabi, quot estis
omnes undique, quotquot estis omnes.
Iocum me putat esse moecha turpis,
et negat mihi vestra redditturam
pugillaria, si pati potestis.   5
Persequamur eam et reflagitemus.
Quae sit, quaeritis? Illa, quam videtis
turpe incedere, mimice ac moleste
ridentem catuli ore Gallicani.
Circumsistite eam, et reflagitate: 10
"Moecha putida, redde codicillos!
Redde, putida moecha, codicillos!"
Non assis facis? O lutum, lupanar,
aut si perditius potest quid esse.
Sed non est tamen hoc satis putandum.   15
Quod si non aliud potest, ruborem
ferreo canis exprimamus ore.
Conclamate iterum altiore voce
"Moecha putida, redde codicillos,
redde, putida moecha, codicillos!"   20
Sed nil proficimus, nihil movetur.
Mutanda est ratio modusque vobis,
siquid proficere amplius potestis:
"Pudica et proba, redde codicillos!"

43

MAMURRA'S UGLY GIRL FRIEND

Salve, nec minimo puella naso
nec bello pede nec nigris ocellis
nec longis digitis nec ore sicco
nec sane nimis elegante lingua,
decoctoris amica Formiani.   5
Ten provincia narrat esse bellam?
Tecum Lesbia nostra comparatur?
O saeclum insapiens et infacetum!

44

THANKS TO MY VILLA, NONE TO SESTIUS

O funde noster, seu Sabine seu Tiburs
(nam te esse Tiburtem autumant, quibus non est
cordi Catullum laedere; at quibus cordi est,
quovis Sabinum pignore esse contendunt),
sed seu Sabine sive verius Tiburs,   5
fui libenter in tua suburbana
villa, malamque pectore expuli tussim,
non inmerenti quam mihi meus venter,
dum sumptuosas appeto, dedit, cenas.
Nam Sestianus dum volo esse conviva,   10
orationem in Antium petitorem
plenam veneni et pestilentiae legi.
Hic me gravedo frigida et frequens tussis
quassavit usque, dum in tuum sinum fugi,
et me recuravi otioque et urtica.   15
Quare refectus maximas tibi grates
ago, meum quod non es ulta peccatum.
Nec deprecor iam, si nefaria scripta
Sesti recepso, quin gravedinem et tussim
non mi, sed ipsi Sestio ferat frigus,   20
qui tunc vocat me, cum malum librum legi.

45

A LOVE-IDYLL

Acmen Septimius suos amores
tenens in gremio "mea" inquit "Acme,
ni te perdite amo atque amare porro
omnes sum assidue paratus annos,
quantum qui pote plurimum perire,   5
solus in Libya Indiaque tosta
caesio veniam obvius leoni."
Hoc ut dixit, Amor sinistra ut ante
dextra sternuit approbationem.
At Acme leviter caput reflectens   10
et dulcis pueri ebrios ocellos
illo purpureo ore suaviata,
"Sic" inquit "mea vita Septimille,
huic uni domino usque serviamus,
ut multo mihi maior acriorque   15
ignis mollibus ardet in medullis."
Hoc ut dixit, Amor sinistra ut ante
dextra sternuit approbationem.
Nunc ab auspicio bono profecti
mutuis animis amant amantur.   20
Unam Septimius misellus Acmen
mavult quam Syrias Britanniasque:
uno in Septimio fidelis Acme
facit delicias libidinesque.
Quis ullos homines beatiores   25
vidit, quis Venerem auspicatiorem?

46

SPRING TRAVEL

Iam ver egelidos refert tepores,
iam caeli furor aequinoctialis
iucundis Zephyri silescit auris.
Linquantur Phrygii, Catulle, campi
Nicaeaeque ager uber aestuosae: 5
ad claras Asiae volemus urbes.
Iam mens praetrepidans avet vagari,
iam laeti studio pedes vigescunt.
O dulces comitum valete coetus,
longe quos simul a domo profectos   10
diversae varie viae reportant.

sense of immediacy

redundancy

47

PISO'S PUNKS

Porci et Socration, duae sinistrae
Pisonis, scabies famesque mundi,
vos Veraniolo meo et Fabullo
verpus praeposuit Priapus ille?
Vos convivia lauta sumptuose   5
de die facitis, mei sodales
quaerunt in trivio vocationes?

48

KISSES FOR JUVENTIUS

Mellitos oculos tuos, Iuventi,
si quis me sinat usque basiare,
usque ad milia basiem trecenta
nec numquam videar satur futurus,
non si densior aridis aristis   5
sit nostrae seges osculationis.

33

49

THANKS TO CICERO

Disertissime Romuli nepotum,
quot sunt quotque fuere, Marce Tulli,
quotque post aliis erunt in annis,
gratias tibi maximas Catullus
agit pessimus omnium poeta,   5
tanto pessimus omnium poeta
quanto tu optimus omnium patronus.

50

SOUVENIR OF A PERFECT DAY

Hesterno, Licini, die otiosi
multum lusimus in meis tabellis,
ut convenerat esse delicatos:
scribens versiculos uterque nostrum
ludebat numero modo hoc modo illoc,   5
reddens mutua per iocum atque vinum.
Atque illinc abii tuo lepore
incensus, Licini, facetiisque,
ut nec me miserum cibus iuvaret
nec somnus tegeret quiete ocellos,   10
sed toto indomitus furore lecto
versarer, cupiens videre lucem,
ut tecum loquerer simulque ut essem.
At defessa labore membra postquam
semimortua lectulo iacebant,   15
hoc, iucunde, tibi poëma feci,
ex quo perspiceres meum dolorem.
Nunc audax cave sis, precesque nostras,
oramus, cave despuas, ocelle,
ne poenas Nemesis reposcat a te;   20
est vemens dea: laedere hanc caveto.

51

FROM SAPPHO

Ille mi par esse deo videtur,
ille, si fas est, superare divos,
qui sedens adversus identidem te
    spectat et audit

dulce ridentem, misero quod omnis   5
eripit sensus mihi: nam simul te,
Lesbia, aspexi, nihil est super mi
    vocis in ore

lingua sed torpet, tenuis sub artus
flamma demanat, sonitu suopte   10
tintinant aures, gemina teguntur
    lumina nocte.

Otium, Catulle, tibi molestum est:
otio exsultas nimiumque gestis:
otium et reges prius et beatas   15
    perdidit urbes.

52

SCOUNDRELS IN OFFICE

Quid est, Catulle? Quid moraris emori?
Sella in curuli struma Nonius sedet,
per consulatum peierat Vatinius:
quid est Catulle? Quid moraris emori?

53

THE BEST SHOW IN TOWN

Risi nescio quem modo e corona,
qui, cum mirifice Vatiniana
meus crimina Calvos explicasset,
admirans ait haec manusque tollens,
"Di magni, salaputium disertum!"   5

54

CAESAR'S HACKS

Othonis caput oppido est pusillum;
Hirri rustica, semilauta crura,
subtile et leve peditum Libonis,
si non omnia; displicere vellem
tibi et Fufidio seni recocto . . .   5
irascere iterum meis iambis
inmerentibus, unice imperator.

55

WHERE ARE YOU, CAMERIUS?

Oramus, si forte non molestum est,
demonstres ubi sint tuae tenebrae.
Te Campo quaesivimus minore,
te in Circo, te in omnibus libellis,
te in templo summi Iovis sacrato.   5
In Magni simul ambulatione
femellas omnes, amice, prendi,
quas vultu vidi tamen sereno.
†aveltet†, sic ipse flagitabam,
"Camerium mihi, pessimae puellae!"   10
Quaedam inquit, nudum reclusa pectus,
"En hic in roseis latet papillis."
Sed te iam ferre Herculi labos est;
tanto te in fastu negas, amice.
Dic nobis ubi sis futurus, ede   15
audacter, committe, crede luci.
Nunc te lacteolae tenent puellae?
Si linguam clauso tenes in ore,
fructus proicies amoris omnes.
Verbosa gaudet Venus loquella.   20
Vel, si vis, licet obseres palatum,
dum vestri sim particeps amoris.

56

SOMETHING FUNNY FOR CATO

O rem ridiculam, Cato, et iocosam,
dignamque auribus et tuo cachinno!
Ride quidquid amas, Cato, Catullum:
res est ridicula et nimis iocosa.
Deprendi modo pupulum puellae   5
trusantem; hunc ego, si placet Dionae,
pro telo rigida mea cecidi.

57

SEX OFFENDERS

Pulcre convenit improbis cinaedis,
Mamurrae pathicoque Caesarique.
Nec mirum: maculae pares utrisque,
urbana altera et illa Formiana,
impressae resident nec eluentur: 5
morbosi pariter, gemelli utrique,
uno in lecticulo erudituli ambo,
non hic quam ille magis vorax adulter,
rivales socii et puellularum.
Pulcre convenit improbis cinaedis.   10

58

LESBIA'S DISGRACE

Caeli, Lesbia nostra, Lesbia illa,
illa Lesbia, quam Catullus unam
plus quam se atque suos amavit omnes,
nunc in quadriviis et angiportis
glubit magnanimi Remi nepotes.   5

58b

LOOKING FOR CAMERIUS

Non custos si fingar ille Cretum,
non si Pegaseo ferar volatu,
non Ladas ego pinnipesve Perseus,
non Rhesi niveae citaeque bigae;
adde huc plumipedas volatilesque,⠀⠀⠀⠀⠀⠀⠀⠀5
ventorumque simul require cursum,
quos iunctos, Cameri, mihi dicares:
defessus tamen omnibus medullis
et multis languoribus peresus
essem te mihi, amice, quaeritando.⠀⠀⠀⠀⠀⠀10

59

LINES FOR A TOILET WALL

Bononiensis Rufa Rufulum fellat,
uxor Meneni, saepe quam in sepulcretis
vidistis ipso rapere de rogo cenam,
cum devolutum ex igne prosequens panem
ab semiraso tunderetur ustore.⠀⠀⠀⠀⠀⠀⠀5

60

NO HUMAN HEART

Num te leaena montibus Libystinis
aut Scylla latrans infima inguinum parte
tam mente dura procreavit ac taetra,
ut supplicis vocem in novissimo casu
contemptam haberes, a nimis fero corde?⠀⠀⠀5

61

A MARRIAGE HYMN

Collis o Heliconii
cultor, Uraniae genus,
qui rapis teneram ad virum
virginem, o Hymenaee Hymen,
   o Hymen Hymenaee;   5

cinge tempora floribus
suave olentis amaraci,
flammeum cape laetus, huc
huc veni, niveo gerens
   luteum pede soccum;   10

excitusque hilari die,
nuptialia concinens
voce carmina tinnula,
pelle humum pedibus, manu
   pineam quate taedam.   15

Namque Iunia Manlio,
qualis Idalium colens
venit ad Phrygium Venus
iudicem, bona cum bona
   nubet alite virgo,   20

floridis velut enitens
myrtus Asia ramulis
quos Hamadryades deae
ludicrum sibi roscido
   nutriunt umore.   25

Quare age, huc aditum ferens,
perge linquere Thespiae
rupis Aonios specus,
nympha quos super irrigat
   frigerans Aganippe.   30

Ac domum dominam voca
coniugis cupidam novi,
mentem amore revinciens,
ut tenax hedera huc et huc
  arborem implicat errans.   35

Vosque item simul, integrae
virgines, quibus advenit
par dies, agite in modum
dicite, o Hymenaee Hymen,
  o Hymen Hymenaee.   40

Ut lubentius, audiens
se citarier ad suum
munus, huc aditum ferat
dux bonae Veneris, boni
  coniugator amoris.   45

Quis deus magis est ama-
tis petendus amantibus?
Quem colent homines magis
caelitum, o Hymenaee Hymen,
  o Hymen Hymenaee?   50

Te suis tremulus parens
invocat, tibi virgines
zonula soluunt sinus,
te timens cupida novos
  captat aure maritus.   55

Tu fero iuveni in manus
floridam ipse puellulam
dedis a gremio suae
matris, o Hymenaee Hymen,
  o Hymen Hymenaee.   60

Nil potest sine te Venus,
fama quod bona comprobet,
commodi capere, at potest
te volente. Quis huic deo
  compararier ausit?   65

Nulla quit sine te domus
liberos dare, nec parens
stirpe nitier; at potest
te volente. Quis huic deo
  compararier ausit?   70

Quae tuis careat sacris,
non queat dare praesides
terra finibus: at queat
te volente. Quis huic deo
  compararier ausit?   75

Claustra pandite ianuae.
Virgo adest. Viden ut faces
splendidas quatiunt comas?
· · · · · · · · ·
 · · · · · · · ·

 · · · · · · · · ·
· · · · · · · · ·
tardet ingenuus pudor.
Quem tamen magis audiens,   80
  flet quod ire necesse est.

Flere desine. Non tibi Au-
runculeia periculum est,
ne qua femina pulcrior
clarum ab Oceano diem   85
  viderit venientem.

Talis in vario solet
divitis domini hortulo
stare flos hyacinthinus.
Sed moraris, abit dies.   90
  Prodeas nova nupta.

Prodeas nova nupta, si
iam videtur, et audias
nostra verba. Viden? Faces
aureas quatiunt comas: 95
  prodeas nova nupta.

Non tuus levis in mala
deditus vir adultera,
probra turpia persequens,
a tuis teneris volet   100
  secubare papillis,

lenta sed velut adsitas
vitis implicat arbores,
implicabitur in tuum
complexum. Sed abit dies: 105
  prodeas nova nupta.

O cubile, quod omnibus
· · · · · · ·
· · · · · · ·
· · · · · · ·
  candido pede lecti,

quae tuo veniunt ero,
quanta gaudia, quae vaga   110
nocte, quae medio die
gaudeat! Sed abit dies:
  prodeas nova nupta.

Tollite, o pueri, faces:
flammeum video venire.   115
Ite concinite in modum
"Io Hymen Hymenaee io,
  io Hymen Hymenaee."

Ne diu taceat procax
Fescennina iocatio,   120
nec nuces pueris neget
desertum domini audiens
  concubinus amorem.

Da nuces pueris, iners
concubine! Satis diu   125
lusisti nucibus: lubet
iam servire Talasio.
  Concubine, nuces da.

Sordebant tibi vilicae,
concubine, hodie atque heri: 130
nunc tuum cinerarius
tondet os. Miser a miser
  concubine, nuces da.

Diceris male te a tuis
unguentate glabris marite   135
abstinere, sed abstine.
Io Hymen Hymenaee io,
  io Hymen Hymenaee.

Scimus haec tibi quae licent
sola cognita, sed marito   140
ista non eadem licent.
Io Hymen Hymenaee io,
  io Hymen Hymenaee.

Nupta, tu quoque quae tuus
vir petet cave ne neges,   145
ni petitum aliunde eat.
Io Hymen Hymenaee io,
  io Hymen Hymenaee.

En tibi domus ut potens
et beata viri tui,   150
quae tibi sine serviat
(io Hymen Hymenaee io,
  io Hymen Hymenaee)

usque dum tremulum movens
cana tempus anilitas   155
omnia omnibus annuit.
Io Hymen Hymenaee io,
  io Hymen Hymenaee.

Transfer omine cum bono
limen aureolos pedes,   160
rasilemque subi forem.
Io Hymen Hymenaee io,
  io Hymen Hymenaee.

Aspice intus ut accubans
vir tuus Tyrio in toro   165
totus immineat tibi.
Io Hymen Hymenaee io,
    io Hymen Hymenaee.

Illi non minus ac tibi
pectore uritur intimo   170
flamma, sed penite magis.
Io Hymen Hymenaee io,
    io Hymen Hymenaee.

Mitte brachiolum teres,
praetextate, puellulae: 175
iam cubile adeat viri.
Io Hymen Hymenaee io,
    io Hymen Hymenaee.

Vos bonae senibus viris
cognitae bene feminae   180
collocate puellulam.
Io Hymen Hymenaee io,
    io Hymen Hymenaee.

Iam licet venias, marite:
uxor in thalamo tibi est,   185
ore floridulo nitens,
alba parthenice velut
    luteumve papaver.

At marite, ita me iuvent
caelites, nihilo minus   190
pulcer es, neque te Venus
neglegit. Sed abit dies:
    perge, ne remorare.

Non diu remoratus es:
iam venis. Bona te Venus   195
iuverit, quoniam palam
quod cupis cupis, et bonum
    non abscondis amorem.

Ille pulveris Africi
siderumque micantium   200
subducat numerum prius,
qui vestri numerare volt
    multa milia ludi.

Ludite ut lubet, et brevi
liberos date. Non decet   205
tam vetus sine liberis
nomen esse, sed indidem
    semper ingenerari.

Torquatus volo parvulus
matris e gremio suae   210
porrigens teneras manus
dulce rideat ad patrem
    semihiante labello.

Sit suo similis patri
Manlio et facile insciis   215
noscitetur ab omnibus,
et pudicitiam suae
    matris indicet ore.

Talis illius a bona
matre laus genus approbet,   220
qualis unica ab optima
matre Telemacho manet
    fama Penelopeo.

Claudite ostia, virgines:
lusimus satis. At boni   225
coniuges, bene vivite et
munere assiduo valentem
    exercete iuventam.

62

AN AMOEBEAN MARRIAGE HYMN

Vesper adest, iuvenes, consurgite: Vesper Olympo
exspectata diu vix tandem lumina tollit.
Surgere iam tempus, iam pinguis linquere mensas,
iam veniet virgo, iam dicetur hymenaeus.
Hymen o Hymenaee, Hymen ades o Hymenaee!   5

Cernitis, innuptae, iuvenes? Consurgite contra;
nimirum Oetaeos ostendit Noctifer ignes.
Sic certest; viden ut perniciter exsiluere?
Non temere exsiluere, canent quod vincere par est.
Hymen o Hymenaee, Hymen ades o Hymenaee!   10

Non facilis nobis, aequales, palma parata est;
aspicite, innuptae secum ut meditata requirunt.
Non frustra meditantur: habent memorabile quod sit;
nec mirum, penitus quae tota mente laborant.
Nos alio mentes, alio divisimus aures;   15
Iure igitur vincemur: amat victoria curam.
Quare nunc animos saltem convertite vestros;
dicere iam incipient, iam respondere decebit.
Hymen o Hymenaee, Hymen ades o Hymenaee!

Hespere, quis caelo fertur crudelior ignis?   20
Qui natam possis complexu avellere matris,
complexu matris retinentem avellere natam,
et iuveni ardenti castam donare puellam.
Quid faciunt hostes capta crudelius urbe?
Hymen o Hymenaee, Hymen ades o Hymenaee!   25

Hespere, quis caelo lucet iucundior ignis?
Qui desponsa tua firmes conubia flamma,
quae pepigere viri, pepigerunt ante parentes,
nec iunxere prius quam se tuus extulit ardor.
Quid datur a divis felici optatius hora?   30
Hymen o Hymenaee, Hymen ades o Hymenaee!

Hesperus e nobis, aequales, abstulit unam.
. . .
. . .

namque tuo adventu vigilat custodia semper;
nocte latent fures, quos idem saepe revertens,
Hespere, mutato comprendis nomine Eous.   35
At lubet innuptis ficto te carpere questu.
Quid tum, si carpunt, tacita quem mente requirunt?
Hymen o Hymenaee, Hymen ades o Hymenaee!

Ut flos in saeptis secretus nascitur hortis,
ignotus pecori, nullo convolsus aratro,   40
quem mulcent aurae, firmat sol, educat imber;
multi illum pueri, multae optavere puellae:
idem cum tenui carptus defloruit ungui,
nulli illum pueri, nullae optavere puellae:
sic virgo, dum intacta manet, dum cara suis est;   45
cum castum amisit polluto corpore florem,
nec pueris iucunda manet, nec cara puellis.
Hymen o Hymenaee, Hymen ades o Hymenaee!

Ut vidua in nudo vitis quae nascitur arvo,
numquam se extollit, numquam mitem educat uvam,   50
sed tenerum prono deflectens pondere corpus
iam iam contingit summum radice flagellum;
hanc nulli agricolae, nulli coluere iuvenci:
at si forte eadem est ulmo coniuncta marito,
multi illam agricolae, multi coluere iuvenci;   55
sic virgo dum intacta manet, dum inculta senescit;
cum par conubium maturo tempore adepta est,
cara viro magis et minus est invisa parenti.

Et tu ne pugna cum tali coniuge, virgo.
Non aequom est pugnare, pater cui tradidit ipse,   60
ipse pater cum matre, quibus parere necesse est.
Virginitas non tota tua est, ex parte parentum est,
tertia pars patrist, pars est data tertia matri,
tertia sola tua est: noli pugnare duobus,
qui genero sua iura simul cum dote dederunt.   65
Hymen o Hymenaee, Hymen ades o Hymenaee!

63

THE STORY OF ATTIS

Super alta vectus Attis celeri rate maria,
Phrygium ut nemus citato cupide pede tetigit
adiitque opaca silvis redimita loca deae,
stimulatus ibi furente rabie, vagus animis,
devolsit ili acuto sibi pondera silice,   5
itaque ut relicta sensit sibi membra sine viro,
etiam recente terrae sola sanguine maculans,
niveis citata cepit manibus leve typanum,
typanum tuum, Cybebe, tua, mater, initia,
quatiensque terga tauri teneris cava digitis   10
canere haec suis adorta est tremebunda comitibus.
"Agite ite ad alta, Gallae, Cybeles nemora simul,
simul ite, Dindymenae dominae vaga pecora,
aliena quae petentes velut exules loca
sectam meam exsecutae duce me mihi comites   15
rapidum salum tulistis truculentaque pelagi,
et corpus evirastis Veneris nimio odio;
hilarate erae citatis erroribus animum.
Mora tarda mente cedat: simul ite, sequimini
Phrygiam ad domum Cybebes, Phrygia ad nemora deae, 20
ubi cymbalum sonat vox, ubi tympana reboant,
tibicen ubi canit Phryx curvo grave calamo,
ubi capita Maenades vi iaciunt hederigerae,
ubi sacra sancta acutis ululatibus agitant,
ubi suevit illa divae volitare vaga cohors,   25
quo nos decet citatis celerare tripudiis."
Simul haec comitibus Attis cecinit notha mulier,
thiasus repente linguis trepidantibus ululat,
leve tympanum remugit, cava cymbala recrepant,
viridem citus adit Idam properante pede chorus.   30
Furibunda simul anhelans vaga vadit animam agens
comitata tympano Attis per opaca nemora dux,
veluti iuvenca vitans onus indomita iugi,
rapidae ducem sequuntur Gallae properipedem.
Itaque ut domum Cybebes tetigere lassulae,   35
nimio e labore somnum capiunt sine Cerere.
Piger his labante languore oculos sopor operit;
abit in quiete molli rabidus furor animi.
Sed ubi oris aurei Sol radiantibus oculis

lustravit aethera album, sola dura, mare ferum,   40
pepulitque noctis umbras vegetis sonipedibus,
ibi Somnus excitam Attin fugiens citus abiit;
trepidante eum recepit dea Pasithea sinu.
Ita de quiete molli rapida sine rabie
simul ipsa pectore Attis sua facta recoluit,   45
liquidaque mente vidit sine quis ubique foret,
animo aestuante rusum reditum ad vada tetulit.
Ibi maria vasta visens lacrimantibus oculis,
patriam allocuta maesta est ita voce miseriter.
"Patria o mei creatrix, patria o mea genetrix,   50
ego quam miser relinquens, dominos ut erifugae
famuli solent, ad Idae tetuli nemora pedem,
ut aput nivem et ferarum gelida stabula forem,
et earum opaca adirem furibunda latibula,
ubinam aut quibus locis te positam, patria, reor?   55
Cupit ipsa pupula ad te sibi derigere aciem,
rabie fera carens dum breve tempus animus est.
Egone a mea remota haec ferar in nemora domo?
Patria, bonis, amicis, genitoribus abero?
Abero foro, palaestra, stadio et gymnasiis?   60
Miser a miser, querendum est etiam atque etiam, anime.
Quod enim genus figuraest, ego non quod obierim?
Ego mulier, ego adolescens, ego ephebus, ego puer,
ego gymnasi fui flos, ego eram decus olei:
mihi ianuae frequentes, mihi limina tepida,   65
mihi floridis corollis redimita domus erat,
linquendum ubi esset orto mihi Sole cubiculum.
Ego nunc deum ministra et Cybeles famula ferar?
Ego Maenas, ego mei pars, ego vir sterilis ero?
Ego viridis algida Idae nive amicta loca colam?   70
Ego vitam agam sub altis Phrygiae columinibus,
ubi cerva silvicultrix, ubi aper nemorivagus?
Iam iam dolet quod egi, iam iamque paenitet."
Roseis ut huic labellis sonitus citus abiit,
geminas deorum ad aures nova nuntia referens,   75
ibi iuncta iuga resolvens Cybele leonibus
laevumque pecoris hostem stimulans ita loquitur.
"Agedum," inquit "age ferox i, fac ut hunc furor agitet,
fac uti furoris ictu reditum in nemora ferat,
mea libere nimis qui fugere imperia cupit.   80
Age caede terga cauda, tua verbera patere,

fac cuncta mugienti fremitu loca retonent,
rutilam ferox torosa cervice quate iubam."
Ait haec minax Cybebe religatque iuga manu.
Ferus ipse sese adhortans rapidum incitat animo,   85
vadit, fremit, refringit virgulta pede vago.
At ubi umida albicantis loca litoris adiit,
teneramque vidit Attin prope marmora pelagi,
facit impetum. Illa demens fugit in nemora fera;
ibi semper omne vitae spatium famula fuit.   90
Dea, magna dea, Cybebe, dea domina Dindymi,
procul a mea tuos sit furor omnis, era, domo:
alios age incitatos, alios age rabidos.

64

A LITTLE WEDDING EPIC

Peliaco quondam prognatae vertice pinus
dicuntur liquidas Neptuni nasse per undas
Phasidos ad fluctus et fines Aeëteos,
cum lecti iuvenes, Argivae robora pubis,
auratam optantes Colchis avertere pellem   5
ausi sunt vada salsa cita decurrere puppi,
caerula verrentes abiegnis aequora palmis.
Diva quibus retinens in summis urbibus arces
ipsa levi fecit volitantem flamine currum,
pinea coniungens inflexae texta carinae.   10
Illa rudem cursu prima imbuit Amphitriten;
quae simul ac rostro ventosum proscidit aequor
tortaque remigio spumis incanuit unda,
emersere freti candenti e gurgite vultus
aequoreae monstrum Nereïdes admirantes.   15
Illa, atque haud alia, viderunt luce marinas
mortales oculis nudato corpore Nymphas
nutricum tenus exstantes e gurgite cano.
Tum Thetidis Peleus incensus fertur amore,
tum Thetis humanos non despexit hymenaeos,   20
tum Thetidi pater ipse iugandum Pelea sensit.
O nimis optato saeclorum tempore nati
heroes, salvete, deum genus! O bona matrum
progenies, salvete iter<um, salvete bonarum!>   23b
vos ego saepe, meo vos carmine compellabo.
Teque adeo eximie taedis felicibus aucte,   25
Thessaliae columen Peleu, cui Iuppiter ipse,
ipse suos divum genitor concessit amores;
tene Thetis tenuit pulcerrima Nereïne?
Tene suam Tethys concessit ducere neptem,
Oceanusque, mari totum qui amplectitur orbem?   30
Quae simul optatae finito tempore luces
advenere, domum conventu tota frequentat
Thessalia, oppletur laetanti regia coetu:
dona ferunt prae se, declarant gaudia vultu.
Deseritur Cieros, linquunt Pthiotica Tempe   35
Crannonisque domos ac moenia Larisaea,
Pharsalum coeunt, Pharsalia tecta frequentant.
Rura colit nemo, mollescunt colla iuvencis,

non humilis curvis purgatur vinea rastris,
non glebam prono convellit vomere taurus,   40
non falx attenuat frondatorum arboris umbram,
squalida desertis rubigo infertur aratris.
Ipsius at sedes, quacumque opulenta recessit
regia, fulgenti splendent auro atque argento.
Candet ebur soliis, collucent pocula mensae,   45
tota domus gaudet regali splendida gaza.
Pulvinar vero divae geniale locatur
sedibus in mediis, Indo quod dente politum
tincta tegit roseo conchyli purpura fuco.
Haec vestis priscis hominum variata figuris   50
heroum mira virtutes indicat arte.
Namque fluentisono prospectans litore Diae,
Thesea cedentem celeri cum classe tuetur
indomitos in corde gerens Ariadna furores,
necdum etiam sese quae visit visere credit,   55
utpote fallaci quae tum primum excita somno
desertam in sola miseram se cernat harena.
Immemor at iuvenis fugiens pellit vada remis,
irrita ventosae linquens promissa procellae.
Quem procul ex alga maestis Minoïs ocellis,   60
saxea ut effigies bacchantis, prospicit, eheu,
prospicit et magnis curarum fluctuat undis,
non flavo retinens subtilem vertice mitram,
non contecta levi velatum pectus amictu,
non tereti strophio lactentis vincta papillas,   65
omnia quae toto delapsa e corpore passim
ipsius ante pedes fluctus salis alludebant.
Sed neque tum mitrae neque tum fluitantis amictus
illa vicem curans toto ex te pectore, Theseu,
toto animo, tota pendebat perdita mente.   70
A misera, assiduis quam luctibus externavit
spinosas Erycina serens in pectore curas,
illa tempestate, ferox quo ex tempore Theseus
egressus curvis e litoribus Piraeï
attigit iniusti regis Gortynia templa.   75
Nam perhibent olim crudeli peste coactam
Androgeoneae poenas exsolvere caedis
electos iuvenes simul et decus innuptarum
Cecropiam solitam esse dapem dare Minotauro.
Quis angusta malis cum moenia vexarentur,   80

ipse suum Theseus pro caris corpus Athenis
proicere optavit potius quam talia Cretam
funera Cecropiae nec funera portarentur.
Atque ita nave levi nitens ac lenibus auris
magnanimum ad Minoa venit sedesque superbas.   85
Hunc simul ac cupido conspexit lumine virgo
regia, quam suavis exspirans castus odores
lectulus in molli complexu matris alebat,
quales Eurotae praecingunt flumina myrtus
aurave distinctos educit verna colores,   90
non prius ex illo flagrantia declinavit
lumina, quam cuncto concepit corpore flammam
funditus atque imis exarsit tota medullis.
Heu misere exagitans immiti corde furores
sancte puer, curis hominum qui gaudia misces,   95
quaeque regis Golgos quaeque Idalium frondosum,
qualibus incensam iactastis mente puellam
fluctibus, in flavo saepe hospite suspirantem!
Quantos illa tulit languenti corde timores!
Quanto saepe magis fulgore expalluit auri,   100
cum saevum cupiens contra contendere monstrum
aut mortem appeteret Theseus aut praemia laudis!
Non ingrata tamen frustra munuscula divis
promittens tacito succepit vota labello.
Nam velut in summo quatientem brachia Tauro   105
quercum aut conigeram sudanti cortice pinum
indomitus turbo contorquens flamine robur,
eruit (illa procul radicitus exturbata
prona cadit, late quaevis cumque obvia frangens),
sic domito saevum prostravit corpore Theseus   110
nequiquam vanis iactantem cornua ventis.
Inde pedem sospes multa cum laude reflexit
errabunda regens tenui vestigia filo,
ne labyrintheis e flexibus egredientem
tecti frustraretur inobservabilis error.   115
Sed quid ego a primo digressus carmine plura
commemorem, ut linquens genitoris filia vultum,
ut consanguineae complexum, ut denique matris,
quae misera in gnata deperdita laetabatur,
omnibus his Thesei dulcem praeoptarit amorem: 120
aut ut vecta rati spumosa ad litora Diae
venerit, aut ut eam devinctam lumina somno

liquerit immemori discedens pectore coniunx?
Saepe illam perhibent ardenti corde furentem
clarisonas imo fudisse e pectore voces,   125
ac tum praeruptos tristem conscendere montes,
unde aciem in pelagi vastos protenderet aestus,
tum tremuli salis adversas procurrere in undas
mollia nudatae tollentem tegmina surae,
atque haec extremis maestam dixisse querellis,   130
frigidulos udo singultus ore cientem:

"Sicine me patriis avectam, perfide, ab aris,
perfide, deserto liquisti in litore, Theseu?
Sicine discedens neglecto numine divum,
immemor a! devota domum periuria portas?   135
Nullane res potuit crudelis flectere mentis
consilium? Tibi nulla fuit clementia praesto,
immite ut nostri vellet miserescere pectus?
At non haec quondam blanda promissa dedisti
voce mihi, non haec miserae sperare iubebas,   140
sed conubia laeta, sed optatos hymenaeos,
quae cuncta aërii discerpunt irrita venti.
Nunc iam nulla viro iuranti femina credat,
nulla viri speret sermones esse fideles;
quis dum aliquid cupiens animus praegestit apisci,   145
nil metuunt iurare, nihil promittere parcunt:
sed simul ac cupidae mentis satiata libido est,
dicta nihil metuere, nihil periuria curant.
Certe ego te in medio versantem turbine leti
eripui, et potius germanum amittere crevi,   150
quam tibi fallaci supremo in tempore dessem.
Pro quo dilaceranda feris dabor alitibusque
praeda, neque iniacta tumulabor mortua terra.
Quaenam te genuit sola sub rupe leaena,
quod mare conceptum spumantibus exspuit undis,   155
quae Syrtis, quae Scylla rapax, quae vasta Charybdis,
talia qui reddis pro dulci praemia vita?
Si tibi non cordi fuerant conubia nostra,
saeva quod horrebas prisci praecepta parentis,
attamen in vestras potuisti ducere sedes,   160
quae tibi iucundo famularer serva labore,
candida permulcens liquidis vestigia lymphis,
purpureave tuum consternens veste cubile.
Sed quid ego ignaris nequiquam conquerar auris,

externata malo, quae nullis sensibus auctae   165
nec missas audire queunt nec reddere voces?
Ille autem prope iam mediis versatur in undis,
nec quisquam apparet vacua mortalis in alga.
Sic nimis insultans extremo tempore saeva
fors etiam nostris invidit questibus auris.   170
Iuppiter omnipotens, utinam ne tempore primo
Cnosia Cecropiae tetigissent litora puppes,
indomito nec dira ferens stipendia tauro
perfidus in Cretam religasset navita funem,
nec malus hic celans dulci crudelia forma   175
consilia in nostris requiesset sedibus hospes!
Nam quo me referam? Quali spe perdita nitor?
Idaeosne petam montes? At gurgite lato
discernens ponti truculentum dividit aequor.
An patris auxilium sperem? Quemne ipsa reliqui   180
respersum iuvenem fraterna caede secuta?
Coniugis an fido consoler memet amore?
Quine fugit lentos incurvans gurgite remos?
Praeterea nullo colitur sola insula tecto,
nec patet egressus pelagi cingentibus undis.   185
Nulla fugae ratio, nulla spes: omnia muta,
omnia sunt deserta, ostentant omnia letum.
Non tamen ante mihi languescent lumina morte,
nec prius a fesso secedent corpore sensus,
quam iustam a divis exposcam prodita multam   190
caelestumque fidem postrema comprecer hora.
Quare facta virum multantes vindice poena
Eumenides, quibus anguino redimita capillo
frons exspirantes praeportat pectoris iras,
huc huc adventate, meas audite querellas,   195
quas ego vae misera, extremis proferre medullis
cogor inops, ardens, amenti caeca furore.
Quae quoniam verae nascuntur pectore ab imo,
vos nolite pati nostrum vanescere luctum,
sed quali solam Theseus me mente reliquit,   200
tali mente, deae, funestet seque suosque."

Has postquam maesto profudit pectore voces,
supplicium saevis exposcens anxia factis,
annuit invicto caelestum numine rector;
quo motu tellus atque horrida contremuerunt   205
aequora concussitque micantia sidera mundus.

Ipse autem caeca mentem caligine Theseus
consitus oblito dimisit pectore cuncta,
quae mandata prius constanti mente tenebat,
dulcia nec maesto sustollens signa parenti   210
sospitem Erechtheum se ostendit visere portum.
Namque ferunt olim, classi cum moenia divae
linquentem gnatum ventis concrederet Aegeus,
talia complexum iuveni mandata dedisse:
"Gnate mihi longa iucundior unice vita,   215
gnate, ego quem in dubios cogor dimittere casus,
reddite in extrema nuper mihi fine senectae,
quandoquidem fortuna mea ac tua fervida virtus
eripit invito mihi te, cui languida nondum
lumina sunt gnati cara saturata figura,   220
non ego te gaudens laetanti pectore mittam,
nec te ferre sinam fortunae signa secundae,
sed primum multas expromam mente querellas,
canitiem terra atque infuso pulvere foedans,
inde infecta vago suspendam lintea malo,   225
nostros ut luctus nostraeque incendia mentis
carbasus obscurata dicet ferrugine Hibera.
Quod tibi si sancti concesserit incola Itoni,
quae nostrum genus ac sedes defendere Erecthei
annuit, ut tauri respergas sanguine dextram,   230
tum vero facito ut memori tibi condita corde
haec vigeant mandata, nec ulla oblitteret aetas;
ut simul ac nostros invisent lumina collis,
funestam antennae deponant undique vestem,
candidaque intorti sustollant vela rudentes,   235
quam primum cernens ut laeta gaudia mente
agnoscam, cum te reducem aetas prospera sistet."
Haec mandata prius constanti mente tenentem
Thesea ceu pulsae ventorum flamine nubes
aereum nivei montis liquere cacumen.   240
At pater, ut summa prospectum ex arce petebat,
anxia in assiduos absumens lumina fletus,
cum primum infecti conspexit lintea veli,
praecipitem sese scopulorum e vertice iecit,
amissum credens immiti Thesea fato.   245
Sic funesta domus ingressus tecta paterna
morte ferox Theseus, qualem Minoïdi luctum
obtulerat mente immemori, talem ipse recepit.

Quae tum prospectans cedentem maesta carinam
multiplices animo volvebat saucia curas.   250

At parte ex alia florens volitabat Iacchus
cum thiaso Satyrorum et Nysigenis Silenis,
te quaerens, Ariadna, tuoque incensus amore.
Cui Thyades passim lymphata mente furebant
euhoe bacchantes, euhoe capita inflectentes.   255
Harum pars tecta quatiebant cuspide thyrsos,
pars e divolso iactabant membra iuvenco,
pars sese tortis serpentibus incingebant,
pars obscura cavis celebrabant orgia cistis,
orgia quae frustra cupiunt audire profani;   260
plangebant aliae proceris tympana palmis,
aut tereti tenuis tinnitus aere ciebant;
multis raucisonos efflabant cornua bombos
barbaraque horribili stridebat tibia cantu.

Talibus amplifice vestis decorata figuris   265
pulvinar complexa suo velabat amictu.
Quae postquam cupide spectando Thessala pubes
expleta est, sanctis coepit decedere divis.
Hic, qualis flatu placidum mare matutino
horrificans Zephyrus proclivas incitat undas,   270
Aurora exoriente vagi sub limina Solis,
quae tarde primum clementi flamine pulsae
procedunt leviterque sonant plangore cachinni,
post vento crescente magis magis increbescunt,
purpureaque procul nantes ab luce refulgent: 275
sic tum vestibuli linquentes regia tecta
ad se quisque vago passim pede discedebant.
Quorum post abitum princeps e vertice Pelei
advenit Chiron portans silvestria dona:
nam quoscumque ferunt campi, quos Thessala magnis   280
montibus ora creat, quos propter fluminis undas
aura parit flores tepidi fecunda Favoni,
hos indistinctis plexos tulit ipse corollis,
quo permulsa domus iucundo risit odore.
Confestim Penios adest, viridantia Tempe,   285
Tempe, quae silvae cingunt super impendentes,
†Minosim linquens †doris celebranda choreis,
non vacuos: namque ille tulit radicitus altas
fagos ac recto proceras stipite laurus,

non sine nutanti platano lentaque sorore   290
flammati Phaëthontis et aërea cupressu.
Haec circum sedes late contexta locavit,
vestibulum ut molli velatum fronde vireret.
Post hunc consequitur sollerti corde Prometheus,
extenuata gerens veteris vestigia poenae,   295
quam quondam silici restrictus membra catena
persolvit pendens e verticibus praeruptis.
Inde pater divum sancta cum coniuge natisque
advenit caelo, te solum, Phoebe, relinquens
unigenamque simul cultricem montibus Idri: 300
Pelea nam tecum pariter soror aspernata est,
nec Thetidis taedas voluit celebrare iugalis.

Qui postquam niveis flexerunt sedibus artus,
large multiplici constructae sunt dape mensae,
cum interea infirmo quatientes corpora motu   305
veridicos Parcae coeperunt edere cantus.
His corpus tremulum complectens undique vestis
candida purpurea talos incinxerat ora,
at roseae niveo residebant vertice vittae,
aeternumque manus carpebant rite laborem.   310
Laeva colum molli lana retinebat amictum,
dextera tum leviter deducens fila supinis
formabat digitis, tum prono in pollice torquens
libratum tereti versabat turbine fusum,
atque ita decerpens aequabat semper opus dens,   315
laneaque aridulis haerebant morsa labellis,
quae prius in levi fuerant exstantia filo:
ante pedes autem candentis mollia lanae
vellera virgati custodibant calathisci.
Haec tum clarisona pellentes vellera voce   320
talia divino fuderunt carmine fata,
carmine, perfidiae quod post nulla arguet aetas.

O decus eximium magnis virtutibus augens,
Emathiae tutamen, Opis carissime nato,
accipe, quod laeta tibi pandunt luce sorores,   325
veridicum oraclum: sed vos, quae fata sequuntur,
  currite ducentes subtegmina, currite, fusi.

Adveniet tibi iam portans optata maritis
Hesperus, adveniet fausto cum sidere coniunx,
quae tibi flexanimo mentem perfundat amore,   330

languidulosque paret tecum coniungere somnos,
levia substernens robusto brachia collo.
Currite ducentes subtegmina, currite, fusi.

Nulla domus tales umquam contexit amores,
nullus amor tali coniunxit foedere amantes,   335
qualis adest Thetidi, qualis concordia Peleo.
Currite ducentes subtegmina, currite, fusi.

Nascetur vobis expers terroris Achilles,
hostibus haud tergo, sed forti pectore notus,
qui persaepe vago victor certamine cursus   340
flammea praevertet celeris vestigia cervae.
Currite ducentes subtegmina, currite, fusi.

Non illi quisquam bello se conferet heros,
cum Phrygii Teucro manabunt sanguine campi,
Troicaque obsidens longinquo moenia bello,   345
periuri Pelopis vastabit tertius heres.
Currite ducentes subtegmina, currite, fusi.

Illius egregias virtutes claraque facta
saepe fatebuntur gnatorum in funere matres,
cum incultum cano solvent a vertice crinem,   350
putridaque infirmis variabunt pectora palmis.
Currite ducentes subtegmina, currite, fusi.

Namque velut densas praecerpens messor aristas
sole sub ardenti flaventia demetit arva,
Troiugenum infesto prosternet corpora ferro.   355
Currite ducentes subtegmina, currite, fusi.

Testis erit magnis virtutibus unda Scamandri,
quae passim rapido diffunditur Hellesponto,
cuius iter caesis angustans corporum acervis
alta tepefaciet permixta flumina caede.   360
Currite ducentes subtegmina, currite, fusi.

Denique testis erit morti quoque reddita praeda,
cum teres excelso coacervatum aggere bustum
excipiet niveos perculsae virginis artus.
Currite ducentes subtegmina, currite, fusi.   365

Nam simul ac fessis dederit fors copiam Achivis
urbis Dardaniae Neptunia solvere vincla,
alta Polyxenia madefient caede sepulcra;

quae, velut ancipiti succumbens victima ferro,
proiciet truncum summiso poplite corpus.   370
  Currite ducentes subtegmina, currite, fusi.

Quare agite optatos animi coniungite amores.
Accipiat coniunx felici foedere divam,
dedatur cupido iam dudum nupta marito.
  Currite ducentes subtegmina, currite, fusi.   375

Non illam nutrix orienti luce revisens
hesterno collum poterit circumdare filo,   377
anxia nec mater discordis maesta puellae   379
secubitu caros mittet sperare nepotes.   380
  Currite ducentes subtegmina, currite, fusi.

Talia praefantes quondam felicia Pelei
carmina divino cecinerunt pectore Parcae.
Praesentes namque ante domos invisere castas
heroum, et sese mortali ostendere coetu,   385
caelicolae nondum spreta pietate solebant.
Saepe pater divum templo in fulgente revisens,
annua cum festis venissent sacra diebus,
conspexit terra centum procumbere tauros.
Saepe vagus Liber Parnasi vertice summo   390
Thyiadas effusis euantis crinibus egit,
cum Delphi tota certatim ex urbe ruentes
acciperent laeti divum fumantibus aris.
Saepe in letifero belli certamine Mavors
aut rapidi Tritonis era aut Amarunsia virgo   395
armatas hominum est praesens hortata catervas.
Sed postquam tellus scelere est imbuta nefando
iustitiamque omnes cupida de mente fugarunt,
perfudere manus fraterno sanguine fratres,
destitit extinctos gnatus lugere parentes,   400
optavit genitor primaevi funera nati,
liber ut innuptae poteretur flore novercae,
ignaro mater substernens se impia nato
impia non verita est divos scelerare penates.
Omnia fanda nefanda malo permixta furore   405
iustificam nobis mentem avertere deorum.
Quare nec talis dignantur visere coetus,
nec se contingi patiuntur lumine claro.

65

LINES SENT WITH A TRANSLATION OF CALLIMACHUS

Etsi me assiduo confectum cura dolore
  sevocat a doctis, Ortale, virginibus,
nec potis est dulcis Musarum expromere fetus
  mens animi, tantis fluctuat ipsa malis—
namque mei nuper Lethaeo gurgite fratris   5
  pallidulum manans alluit unda pedem,
Troia Rhoeteo quem subter litore tellus
  ereptum nostris obterit ex oculis.
. . .
  numquam ego te, vita frater amabilior,   10
aspiciam posthac? At certe semper amabo,
  semper maesta tua carmina morte canam,
qualia sub densis ramorum concinit umbris
  Daulias, absumpti fata gemens Ityli.—
Sed tamen in tantis maeroribus, Ortale, mitto   15
  haec expressa tibi carmina Battiadae,
ne tua dicta vagis nequiquam credita ventis
  effluxisse meo forte putes animo,
ut missum sponsi furtivo munere malum
  procurrit casto virginis e gremio,   20
quod miserae oblitae molli sub veste locatum,
  dum adventu matris prosilit, excutitur,
atque illud prono praeceps agitur decursu,
  huic manat tristi conscius ore rubor.

66

THE LOCK OF BERENICE

Omnia qui magni dispexit lumina mundi,
  qui stellarum ortus comperit atque obitus,
flammeus ut rapidi solis nitor obscuretur,
  ut cedant certis sidera temporibus,
ut Triviam furtim sub Latmia saxa relegans   5
  dulcis amor gyro devocet aëreo:
idem me ille Conon caelesti in lumine vidit
  e Beroniceo vertice caesariem
fulgentem clare, quam multis illa dearum
  levia protendens brachia pollicita est,   10
qua rex tempestate novo auctus hymenaeo
  vastatum finis iverat Assyrios,
dulcia nocturnae portans vestigia rixae,
  quam de virgineis gesserat exuviis.
Estne novis nuptis odio Venus? Anne parentum   15
  frustrantur falsis gaudia lacrimulis,
ubertim thalami quas intra limina fundunt?
  non, ita me divi, vera gemunt, iverint.
Id mea me multis docuit regina querellis
  invisente novo proelia torva viro.   20
Et tu non orbum luxti deserta cubile,
  sed fratris cari flebile discidium?
Quam penitus maestas exedit cura medullas!
  Ut tibi tunc toto pectore sollicitae
sensibus ereptis mens excidit! At te ego certe   25
  cognoram a parva virgine magnanimam.
Anne bonum oblita es facinus, quo regium adepta es
  coniugium, quod non fortior ausit alis?
Sed tum maesta virum mittens quae verba locuta es!
  Iuppiter, ut tristi lumina saepe manu!   30
Quis te mutavit tantus deus? An quod amantes
  non longe a caro corpore abesse volunt?
Atque ibi me cunctis pro dulci coniuge divis
  non sine taurino sanguine pollicita es,
si reditum tetulisset. Is haut in tempore longo   35
  captam Asiam Aegypti finibus addiderat.
Quis ego pro factis caelesti reddita coetu
  pristina vota novo munere dissoluö.
Invita, regina, tuo de vertice cessi,

invita: adiuro teque tuumque caput,   40
digna ferat quod si quis inaniter adiurarit:
  sed qui se ferro postulet esse parem?
Ille quoque eversus mons est, quem maximum in oris
  progenies Thiae clara supervehitur,
cum Medi peperere novum mare, cumque iuventus   45
  per medium classi barbara navit Athon.
Quid facient crines, cum ferro talia cedant?
  Iuppiter, ut Chalybon omne genus pereat,
et qui principio sub terra quaerere venas
  institit ac ferri stringere duritiem!   50
abiunctae paulo ante comae mea fata sorores
  lugebant, cum se Memnonis Aethiopis
unigena impellens nutantibus aëra pennis
  obtulit Arsinoës Locridos ales equos,
isque per aetherias me tollens avolat umbras   55
  et Veneris casto collocat in gremio.
Ipsa suum Zephyritis eo famulum legarat,
  Graïa Canopitis incola litoribus.
Inde Venus vario ne solum in lumine caeli
  ex Ariadnaeis aurea temporibus   60
fixa corona foret, sed nos quoque fulgeremus
  devotae flavi verticis exuviae,
uvidulam a fluctu cedentem ad templa deum me
  sidus in antiquis diva novum posuit.
Virginis et saevi contingens namque Leonis   65
  lumina, Callisto iuncta Lycaoniae,
vertor in occasum, tardum dux ante Boöten,
  qui vix sero alto mergitur Oceano.
Sed quamquam me nocte premunt vestigia divum,
  lux autem canae Tethyï restituit,   70
(pace tua fari hic liceat, Ramnusia virgo,
  namque ego non ullo vera timore tegam,
nec si me infestis discerpent sidera dictis,
  condita quin veri pectoris evoluam)
non his tam laetor rebus, quam me afore semper, 75
  afore me a dominae vertice discrucior,
quicum ego, dum virgo quondam fuit omnibus expers
  unguentis, una milia multa bibi.
Nunc vos, optato quas iunxit lumine taeda,
  non prius unanimis corpora coniugibus   80
tradite nudantes reiecta veste papillas,

quam iucunda mihi munera libet onyx,
vester onyx, casto colitis quae iura cubili.
  Sed quae se impuro dedit adulterio,
illius a mala dona levis bibat irrita pulvis: 85
  namque ego ab indignis praemia nulla peto.
Sed magis, o nuptae, semper concordia vestras,
  semper amor sedes incolat assiduus.
Tu vero, regina, tuens cum sidera divam
  placabis festis luminibus Venerem,   90
unguinis expertem non siris esse tuam me,
  sed potius largis affice muneribus.
Sidera corruerint utinam! Coma regia fiam,
  proximus Hydrochoï fulgeret Oarion!

67

FRONT DOOR BARES ALL

O dulci iucunda viro, iucunda parenti,
  salve, teque bona Iuppiter auctet ope,
ianua, quam Balbo dicunt servisse benigne
  olim, cum sedes ipse senex tenuit,
quamque ferunt rursus gnato servisse maligne,   5
  postquam es porrecto facta marita sene.
Dic agedum nobis, quare mutata feraris
  in dominum veterem deseruisse fidem.
"Non (ita Caecilio placeam, cui tradita nunc sum)
  culpa mea est, quamquam dicitur esse mea,   10
nec peccatum a me quisquam pote dicere quicquam:
  verum est ius populi: ianua quicque facit,
qui, quacumque aliquid reperitur non bene factum,
  ad me omnes clamant: 'ianua, culpa tua est.' "
Non istuc satis est uno te dicere verbo,   15
  sed facere ut quivis sentiat et videat.
"Qui possum? Nemo quaerit nec scire laborat."
  Nos volumus: nobis dicere ne dubita.
"Primum igitur, virgo quod fertur tradita nobis,
  falsum est. Non illam vir prior attigerit,   20
languidior tenera cui pendens sicula beta
  numquam se mediam sustulit ad tunicam;
sed pater illius gnati violasse cubile
  dicitur et miseram conscelerasse domum,
sive quod impia mens caeco flagrabat amore,   25
  seu quod iners sterili semine natus erat,
ut quaerendum unde unde foret nervosius illud,
  quod posset zonam solvere virgineam."
Egregium narras mira pietate parentem,
  qui ipse sui gnati minxerit in gremium.   30
"Atqui non solum hoc dicit se cognitum habere
  Brixia Cycneae supposita speculae,
flavus quam molli praecurrit flumine Mella,
  Brixia Veronae mater amata meae,
sed de Postumio et Corneli narrat amore,   35
  cum quibus illa malum fecit adulterium.
Dixerit hic aliquis: 'Quid? Tu istaec, ianua, nosti,
  cui numquam domini limine abesse licet,
nec populum auscultare, sed hic suffixa tigillo

tantum operire soles aut aperire domum?'   40
Saepe illam audivi furtiva voce loquentem
  solam cum ancillis haec sua flagitia,
nomine dicentem quos diximus, utpote quae mi
  speraret nec linguam esse nec auriculam.
Praeterea addebat quendam, quem dicere nolo   45
  nomine, ne tollat rubra supercilia.
Longus homo est, magnas cui lites intulit olim
  falsum mendaci ventre puerperium."

68

A LETTER AND A POEM

Quod mihi fortuna casuque oppressus acerbo
  conscriptum hoc lacrimis mittis epistolium,
naufragum ut eiectum spumantibus aequoris undis
  sublevem et a mortis limine restituam,
quem neque sancta Venus molli requiescere somno   5
  desertum in lecto caelibe perpetitur,
nec veterum dulci scriptorum carmine Musae
  oblectant, cum mens anxia pervigilat:
id gratum est mihi, me quoniam tibi dicis amicum,
  muneraque et Musarum hinc petis et Veneris.   10
Sed tibi ne mea sint ignota incommoda, Mani,
  neu me odisse putes hospitis officium,
accipe, quis merser fortunae fluctibus ipse,
  ne amplius a misero dona beata petas.
Tempore quo primum vestis mihi tradita pura est,   15
  iucundum cum aetas florida ver ageret,
multa satis lusi: non est dea nescia nostri,
  quae dulcem curis miscet amaritiem.
Sed totum hoc studium luctu fraterna mihi mors
  abstulit. O misero frater adempte mihi,   20
tu mea tu moriens fregisti commoda, frater,
  tecum una tota est nostra sepulta domus,
omnia tecum una perierunt gaudia nostra,
  quae tuus in vita dulcis alebat amor.
Cuius ego interitu tota de mente fugavi   25
  haec studia atque omnes delicias animi.
Quare quod scribis Veronae turpe Catullo

esse, quod hic quisquis de meliore nota
frigida deserto tepefactet membra cubili,
   id, Mani, non est turpe, magis miserum est.   30
Ignosces igitur si, quae mihi luctus ademit,
   haec tibi non tribuo munera, cum nequeo.
Nam, quod scriptorum non magna est copia apud me,
   hoc fit, quod Romae vivimus: illa domus,
illa mihi sedes, illic mea carpitur aetas;   35
   huc una ex multis capsula me sequitur.
Quod cum ita sit, nolim statuas nos mente maligna
   id facere aut animo non satis ingenuo,
quod tibi non utriusque petenti copia posta est:
   ultro ego deferrem, copia siqua foret.   40
Non possum reticere, deae, qua me Allius in re
   iuverit aut quantis iuverit officiis,
ne fugiens saeclis obliviscentibus aetas
   illius hoc caeca nocte tegat studium:
sed dicam vobis, vos porro dicite multis   45
   milibus et facite haec carta loquatur anus.
. . .
   notescatque magis mortuus atque magis,
nec tenuem texens sublimis aranea telam
   in deserto Alli nomine opus faciat.   50
Nam, mihi quam dederit duplex Amathusia curam,
   scitis, et in quo me torruerit genere,
cum tantum arderem quantum Trinacria rupes
   lymphaque in Oetaeis Malia Thermopylis,
maesta neque assiduo tabescere lumina fletu   55
   cessarent tristique imbre madere genae.
Qualis in aërii perlucens vertice montis
   rivus muscoso prosilit e lapide,
qui cum de prona praeceps est valle volutus,
   per medium densi transit iter populi,   60
dulce viatori lasso in sudore levamen,
   cum gravis exustos aestus hiulcat agros,
ac velut in nigro iactatis turbine nautis
   lenius aspirans aura secunda venit
iam prece Pollucis, iam Castoris implorata,   65
   tale fuit nobis Allius auxilium.
Is clausum lato patefecit limite campum,
   isque domum nobis isque dedit dominae,
ad quam communes exerceremus amores.

Quo mea se molli candida diva pede   70
intulit et trito fulgentem in limine plantam
innixa arguta constituit solea,
coniugis ut quondam flagrans advenit amore
    Protesilaëam Laüdamia domum
inceptam frustra, nondum cum sanguine sacro   75
    hostia caelestis pacificasset eros.
Nil mihi tam valde placeat, Ramnusia virgo,
    quod temere invitis suscipiatur eris.
Quam ieiuna pium desideret ara cruorem,
    docta est amisso Laüdamia viro,   80
coniugis ante coacta novi dimittere collum,
    quam veniens una atque altera rursus hiems
noctibus in longis avidum saturasset amorem,
    posset ut abrupto vivere coniugio,
quod scibant Parcae non longo tempore abesse,   85
    si miles muros isset ad Iliacos.
Nam tum Helenae raptu primores Argivorum
    coeperat ad sese Troia ciere viros,
Troia (nefas!) commune sepulcrum Asiae Europaeque,
    Troia virum et virtutum omnium acerba cinis,   90
quaene etiam nostro letum miserabile fratri
    attulit. Ei misero frater adempte mihi,
ei misero fratri iucundum lumen ademptum,
    tecum una tota est nostra sepulta domus,
omnia tecum una perierunt gaudia nostra,   95
    quae tuus in vita dulcis alebat amor.
Quem nunc tam longe non inter nota sepulcra
    nec prope cognatos compositum cineres,
sed Troia obscena, Troia infelice sepultum
    detinet extremo terra aliena solo.   100
Ad quam tum properans fertur lecta undique pubes
    Graeca penetralis deseruisse focos,
ne Paris abducta gavisus libera moecha
    otia pacato degeret in thalamo.
Quo tibi tum casu, pulcerrima Laüdamia,   105
    ereptum est vita dulcius atque anima
coniugium: tanto te absorbens vertice amoris
    aestus in abruptum detulerat barathrum,
quale ferunt Graï Pheneum prope Cyllenaeum
    siccare emulsa pingue palude solum,   110
quod quondam caesis montis fodisse medullis

audit falsiparens Amphitryoniades,
tempore quo certa Stymphalia monstra sagitta
   perculit imperio deterioris eri,
pluribus ut caeli tereretur ianua divis,   115
   Hebe nec longa virginitate foret.
Sed tuus altus amor barathro fuit altior illo,
   qui tamen indomitam ferre iugum docuit.
Nam nec tam carum confecto aetate parenti
   una caput seri nata nepotis alit,   120
qui, cum divitiis vix tandem inventus avitis
   nomen testatas intulit in tabulas,
impia derisi gentilis gaudia tollens
   suscitat a cano volturium capiti:
nec tantum niveo gavisa est ulla columbo   125
   compar, quae multo dicitur improbius
oscula mordenti semper decerpere rostro,
   quam quae praecipue multivola est mulier.
Sed tu horum magnos vicisti sola furores,
   ut semel es flavo conciliata viro.   130
Aut nihil aut paulo cui tum concedere digna
   lux mea se nostrum contulit in gremium,
quam circumcursans hinc illinc saepe Cupido
   fulgebat crocina candidus in tunica.
Quae tamen etsi uno non est contenta Catullo,   135
   rara verecundae furta feremus erae,
ne nimium simus stultorum more molesti.
   Saepe etiam Iuno, maxima caelicolum,
coniugis in culpa flagrantem concoquit iram,
   noscens omnivoli plurima furta Iovis.   140
Atqui nec divis homines componier aequum est,
   . . .

   . . .
   ingratum tremuli tolle parentis onus.
Nec tamen illa mihi dextra deducta paterna
   fragrantem Assyrio venit odore domum,
sed furtiva dedit mira munuscula nocte,   145
   ipsius ex ipso dempta viri gremio.
Quare illud satis est, si nobis is datur unis
   quem lapide illa dies candidiore notat.
Hoc tibi, quod potui, confectum carmine munus
   pro multis, Alli, redditur officiis,   150
ne vestrum scabra tangat rubigine nomen

haec atque illa dies atque alia atque alia.
Huc addent divi quam plurima, quae Themis olim
    antiquis solita est munera ferre piis.
Sitis felices et tu simul et tua vita,   155
    et domus ipsa in qua lusimus et domina,
et qui principio nobis †terram dedit aufert†,
    a quo sunt primo omnia nata bona,
et longe ante omnes mihi quae me carior ipso est,
    lux mea, qua viva vivere dulce mihi est.   160

69

WHAT'S WRONG WITH RUFUS

Noli admirari, quare tibi femina nulla,
    Rufe, velit tenerum supposuisse femur,
non si illam rarae labefactes munere vestis
    aut perluciduli deliciis lapidis.
Laedit te quaedam mala fabula, qua tibi fertur   5
    valle sub alarum trux habitare caper.
Hunc metuunt omnes, neque mirum: nam mala valde est
    bestia, nec quicum bella puella cubet.
Quare aut crudelem nasorum interfice pestem,
    aut admirari desine cur fugiunt.   10

70

FORGOTTEN VOWS

Nulli se dicit mulier mea nubere malle
    quam mihi, non si se Iuppiter ipse petat.
Dicit: sed mulier cupido quod dicit amanti,
    in vento et rapida scribere oportet aqua.

71

RUFUS' UNLUCKY RIVAL

Si cui iure bono sacer alarum obstitit hircus,
  aut si quem merito tarda podagra secat,
aemulus iste tuus, qui vestrum exercet amorem,
  mirifice est a te nactus utrumque malum.
Nam quotiens futuit, totiens ulciscitur ambos: 5
  illam affligit odore, ipse perit podagra.

72

LOVE AND RESENTMENT

Dicebas quondam solum te nosse Catullum,
  Lesbia, nec prae me velle tenere Iovem.
Dilexi tum te non tantum ut vulgus amicam,
  sed pater ut gnatos diligit et generos.
Nunc te cognovi: quare etsi impensius uror,   5
  multo mi tamen es vilior et levior.
Qui potis est, inquis? Quod amantem iniuria talis
  cogit amare magis, sed bene velle minus.

73

INGRATITUDE

Desine de quoquam quicquam bene velle mereri
  aut aliquem fieri posse putare pium.
Omnia sunt ingrata, nihil fecisse benigne
  prodest, immo etiam taedet obestque magis;
ut mihi, quem nemo gravius nec acerbius urget,   5
  quam modo qui me unum atque unicum amicum habuit.

74

KEEPING UNCLE QUIET

Gellius audierat patruum obiurgare solere,
  si quis delicias diceret aut faceret.
Hoc ne ipsi accideret, patrui perdepsuit ipsam
  uxorem et patruum reddidit Arpocratem.
Quod voluit fecit: nam, quamvis irrumet ipsum   5
  nunc patruum, verbum non faciet patruus.

75

LOVE WITHOUT CHOICE

Huc est mens deducta tua mea, Lesbia, culpa,
  atque ita se officio perdidit ipsa suo,
ut iam nec bene velle queat tibi, si optima fias,
  nec desistere amare, omnia si facias.

76

A PRAYER FOR HEALTH

Siqua recordanti benefacta priora voluptas
  est homini, cum se cogitat esse pium,
nec sanctam violasse fidem, nec foedere nullo
  divum ad fallendos numine abusum homines,
multa parata manent in longa aetate, Catulle,   5
  ex hoc ingrato gaudia amore tibi.
Nam quaecumque homines bene cuiquam aut dicere possunt
  aut facere, haec a te dictaque factaque sunt:
omnia quae ingratae perierunt credita menti.
  Quare iam te cur amplius excrucies?   10
Quin tu animo offirmas atque istinc teque reducis,
  et dis invitis desinis esse miser?
Difficile est longum subito deponere amorem;
  difficile est, verum hoc qua lubet efficias.
Una salus haec est, hoc est tibi pervincendum;   15
  hoc facias, sive id non pote sive pote.
O di, si vestrum est misereri, aut si quibus umquam
  extremam iam ipsa in morte tulistis opem,
me miserum aspicite et, si vitam puriter egi,
  eripite hanc pestem perniciemque mihi,   20
quae mihi subrepens imos ut torpor in artus
  expulit ex omni pectore laetitias.
Non iam illud quaero, contra me ut diligat illa,
  aut, quod non potis est, esse pudica velit:
ipse valere opto et taetrum hunc deponere morbum.   25
  O di, reddite mi hoc pro pietate mea.

77

TO A TREACHEROUS FRIEND

Rufe mihi frustra ac nequiquam credite amice
  (frustra? immo magno cum pretio atque malo),
sicine subrepsti mi, atque intestina perurens
  ei misero eripuisti omnia nostra bona?
Eripuisti, heu heu nostrae crudele venenum   5
  vitae, heu heu nostrae pestis amicitiae.

78

RISKY PANDERING

Gallus habet fratres, quorum est lepidissima coniunx
  alterius, lepidus filius alterius.
Gallus homo est bellus: nam dulces iungit amores,
  cum puero ut bello bella puella cubet.
Gallus homo est stultus, nec se videt esse maritum,   5
  qui patruus patrui monstret adulterium.

78b

A LECHER'S FAME

. . .

. . .

Sed nunc id doleo, quod purae pura puellae
  suavia comminxit spurca saliva tua.
Verum id non impune feres: nam te omnia saecla
  noscent et, qui sis, fama loquetur anus.

79

PRETTY BOY

Lesbius est pulcer. Quid ni? Quem Lesbia malit
  quam te cum tota gente, Catulle, tua.
Sed tamen hic pulcer vendat cum gente Catullum,
  si tria notorum suavia reppererit.

80

GELLIUS' LIPS

Quid dicam, Gelli, quare rosea ista labella
  hiberna fiant candidiora nive,
mane domo cum exis et cum te octava quiete
  e molli longo suscitat hora die?
Nescio quid certe est: an vere fama susurrat   5
  grandia te medii tenta vorare viri?
Sic certe est: clamant Victoris rupta miselli
  ilia, et emulso labra notata sero.

81

JUVENTIUS' OFF-COLOR FRIEND

Nemone in tanto potuit populo esse, Iuventi,
  bellus homo, quem tu diligere inciperes,
praeterquam iste tuus moribunda ab sede Pisauri
  hospes inaurata pallidior statua,
qui tibi nunc cordi est, quem tu praeponere nobis   5
  audes, et nescis quod facinus facias?

82

A PLEA TO QUINTIUS

Quinti, si tibi vis oculos debere Catullum
  aut aliud si quid carius est oculis,
eripere ei noli, multo quod carius illi
  est oculis seu quid carius est oculis.

83

LESBIA'S WRATH

Lesbia mi praesente viro mala plurima dicit:
  haec illi fatuo maxima laetitia est.
Mule, nihil sentis? Si nostri oblita taceret,
  sana esset: nunc quod gannit et obloquitur,
non solum meminit, sed, quae multo acrior est res,   5
  irata est. Hoc est, uritur et loquitur.

84

ARRIUS' PHONY HACCENT

Chommoda dicebat, si quando commoda vellet
  dicere, et insidias Arrius hinsidias,
et tum mirifice sperabat se esse locutum,
  cum quantum poterat dixerat hinsidias.
Credo, sic mater, sic liber avunculus eius,   5
  sic maternus avus dixerat atque avia.
Hoc misso in Syriam requierant omnibus aures:
  audibant eadem haec leniter et leviter,
nec sibi postilla metuebant talia verba,
  cum subito affertur nuntius horribilis,   10
Ionios fluctus, postquam illuc Arrius isset,
  iam non Ionios esse sed Hionios.

85

ODI ET AMO

Odi et amo. Quare id faciam, fortasse requiris.
Nescio, sed fieri sentio et excrucior.

86

QUINTIA VS. LESBIA

Quintia formosa est multis. Mihi candida, longa,
  recta est: haec ego sic singula confiteor.
Totum illud formosa nego: nam nulla venustas,
  nulla in tam magno est corpore mica salis.
Lesbia formosa est, quae cum pulcerrima tota est,   5
  tum omnibus una omnis surripuit Veneres.

87

SUPREME LOVE

Nulla potest mulier tantum se dicere amatam
  vere, quantum a me Lesbia amata mea est.
Nulla fides ullo fuit umquam foedere tanta,
  quanta in amore tuo ex parte reperta mea est.

88

SUPREME PERVERSION

Quid facit is, Gelli, qui cum matre atque sorore
   prurit et abiectis pervigilat tunicis?
Quid facit is, patruum qui non sinit esse maritum?
   Ecquid scis quantum suscipiat sceleris?
Suscipit, o Gelli, quantum non ultima Tethys   5
   nec genitor Nympharum abluit Oceanus:
nam nihil est quicquam sceleris, quo prodeat ultra,
   non si demisso se ipse voret capite.

89

OVERWORKED

Gellius est tenuis: quid ni? Cui tam bona mater
   tamque valens vivat tamque venusta soror
tamque bonus patruus tamque omnia plena puellis
   cognatis, quare is desinat esse macer?
Qui ut nihil attingat, nisi quod fas tangere non est,   5
   quantumvis quare sit macer invenies.

90

BIRTH OF A MAGUS

Nascatur magus ex Gelli matrisque nefando
   coniugio et discat Persicum aruspicium:
nam magus ex matre et gnato gignatur oportet,
   si vera est Persarum impia religio,
gratus ut accepto veneretur carmine divos   5
   omentum in flamma pingue liquefaciens.

91

TO GELLIUS

Non ideo, Gelli, sperabam te mihi fidum
  in misero hoc nostro, hoc perdito amore fore,
quod te cognossem bene constantemve putarem
  aut posse a turpi mentem inhibere probro;
sed neque quod matrem nec germanam esse videbam 5
  hanc tibi, cuius me magnus edebat amor.
Et quamvis tecum multo coniungerer usu,
  non satis id causae credideram esse tibi.
Tu satis id duxti: tantum tibi gaudium in omni
  culpa est, in quacumque est aliquid sceleris.   10

92

LESBIA'S ABUSE

Lesbia mi dicit semper male nec tacet umquam
  de me: Lesbia me dispeream nisi amat.
Quo signo? Quia sunt totidem mea: deprecor illam
  assidue, verum dispeream nisi amo.

93

TO HELL WITH CAESAR

Nil nimium studeo, Caesar, tibi velle placere,
  nec scire utrum sis albus an ater homo.

94

MENTULA THE PRICK

Mentula moechatur. Moechatur mentula? Certe.
  Hoc est quod dicunt: ipsa olera olla legit.

95

ON CINNA'S *ZMYRNA*

Zmyrna mei Cinnae nonam post denique messem
   quam coepta est nonamque edita post hiemem,
milia cum interea quingenta Hortensius uno
   . . .
Zmyrna cavas Satrachi penitus mittetur ad undas,   5
   Zmyrnam cana diu saecula pervoluent.
At Volusi annales Paduam morientur ad ipsam
   et laxas scombris saepe dabunt tunicas.
Parva mei mihi sint cordi monimenta sodalis:
   at populus tumido gaudeat Antimacho.   10

96

TO CALVUS, ON THE DEATH OF QUINTILIA

Si quicquam mutis gratum acceptumve sepulcris
   accidere a nostro, Calve, dolore potest,
quo desiderio veteres renovamus amores
   atque olim missas flemus amicitias,
certe non tanto mors immatura dolori est   5
   Quintiliae, quantum gaudet amore tuo.

97

THE FOUL MOUTH OF AEMILIUS

Non (ita me di ament) quicquam referre putavi,
  utrumne os an culum olfacerem Aemilio.
Nilo mundius hoc, nihiloque immundius illud,
  verum etiam culus mundior et melior:
nam sine dentibus est. Hoc dentis sesquipedalis,   5
  gingivas vero ploxeni habet veteris,
praeterea rictum qualem diffissus in aestu
  meientis mulae cunnus habere solet.
Hic futuit multas et se facit esse venustum,
  et non pistrino traditur atque asino?   10
Quem siqua attingit, non illam posse putemus
  aegroti culum lingere carnificis?

98

THE FOUL TONGUE OF VICTIUS

In te, si in quemquam, dici pote, putide Victi,
  id quod verbosis dicitur et fatuis.
Ista cum lingua, si usus veniat tibi, possis
  culos et crepidas lingere carpatinas.
Si nos omnino vis omnes perdere, Victi,   5
  hiscas: omnino quod cupis efficies.

99

A STOLEN KISS

Surripui tibi, dum ludis, mellite Iuventi,
  suaviolum dulci dulcius ambrosia.
Verum id non impune tuli: namque amplius horam
  suffixum in summa me memini esse cruce,
dum tibi me purgo nec possum fletibus ullis   5
  tantillum vestrae demere saevitiae.
Nam simul id factum est, multis diluta labella
  guttis abstersisti omnibus articulis,
ne quicquam nostro contractum ex ore maneret,
  tamquam commictae spurca saliva lupae.   10
Praeterea infesto miserum me tradere amori
  non cessasti omnique excruciare modo,
ut mi ex ambrosia mutatum iam foret illud
  suaviolum tristi tristius elleboro.
Quam quoniam poenam misero proponis amori,   15
  numquam iam posthac basia surripiam.

100

BROTHERS IN LOVE

Caelius Aufillenum et Quintius Aufillenam
  flos Veronensum depereunt iuvenum,
hic fratrem, ille sororem. Hoc est, quod dicitur, illud
  fraternum vere dulce sodalicium.
Cui faveam potius? Caeli, tibi: nam tua nobis   5
  perspecta est igni tum unica amicitia,
cum vesana meas torreret flamma medullas.
  Sis felix, Caeli, sis in amore potens.

101

A FINAL OFFERING AT A DISTANT GRAVE

Multas per gentes et multa per aequora vectus
  advenio has miseras, frater, ad inferias,
ut te postremo donarem munere mortis
  et mutam nequiquam alloquerer cinerem.
Quandoquidem fortuna mihi tete abstulit ipsum,   5
  heu miser indigne frater adempte mihi,
nunc tamen interea haec, prisco quae more parentum
  tradita sunt tristi munere ad inferias,
accipe fraterno multum manantia fletu,
  atque in perpetuum, frater, ave atque vale.   10

102

TRUST ME

Si quicquam tacito commissum est fido ab amico,
  cuius sit penitus nota fides animi,
meque esse invenies illorum iure sacratum,
  Corneli, et factum me esse puta Arpocratem.

103

SILO'S CHOICE

Aut sodes mihi redde decem sestertia, Silo,
  deinde esto quamvis saevus et indomitus:
aut, si te nummi delectant, desine quaeso
  leno esse atque idem saevus et indomitus.

104

ON SPEAKING HARSHLY TO LESBIA

Credis me potuisse meae maledicere vitae,
  ambobus mihi quae carior est oculis?
Non potui, nec, si possem, tam perdite amarem:
  sed tu cum Tappone omnia monstra facis.

105

NO POET

Mentula conatur Pipleium scandere montem:
  Musae furcillis praecipitem eiciunt.

106

READY FOR BUSINESS

Cum puero bello praeconem qui videt esse,
  quid credat, nisi se vendere discupere?

107

BACK WITH LESBIA

Si quicquam cupido optantique optigit umquam
  insperanti, hoc est gratum animo proprie.
Quare hoc est gratum nobisque hoc carius auro,
  quod te restituis, Lesbia, mi cupido,
restituis cupido atque insperanti, ipsa refers te   5
  nobis. O lucem candidiore nota!
Quis me uno vivit felicior, aut magis hac rem
  optandam in vita dicere quis poterit?

108

A SCOUNDREL'S CORPSE

Si, Comini, populi arbitrio tua cana senectus
  spurcata impuris moribus intereat,
non equidem dubito quin primum inimica bonorum
  lingua exsecta avido sit data vulturio,
effossos oculos voret atro gutture corvus,   5
  intestina canes, cetera membra lupi.

109

IF IT COULD ONLY BE

Iucundum, mea vita, mihi proponis amorem
  hunc nostrum inter nos perpetuumque fore.
Di magni, facite ut vere promittere possit,
  atque id sincere dicat et ex animo,
ut liceat nobis tota perducere vita   5
  aeternum hoc sanctae foedus amicitiae.

110

TO A CHEAT

Aufillena, bonae semper laudantur amicae:
  accipiunt pretium, quae facere instituunt.
Tu, quod promisti, mihi quod mentita inimica es,
  quod nec das et fers saepe, facis facinus.
Aut facere ingenuae est, aut non promisse pudicae,   5
  Aufillena, fuit: sed data corripere
fraudando officiis, plus quam meretricis avarae est
  quae sese toto corpore prostituit.

111

WORSE THAN A CHEAT

Aufillena, viro contentam vivere solo,
  nuptarum laus ex laudibus eximiis:
sed cuivis quamvis potius succumbere par est,
  quam matrem fratres concipere ex patruo.

112

A LOT OF MAN

Multus homo es, Naso, neque tecum multus homo est quin
  te scindat: Naso, multus es et pathicus.

113

A LOT OF MEN

Consule Pompeio primum duo, Cinna, solebant
  Maeciliam: facto consule nunc iterum
manserunt duo, sed creverunt milia in unum
  singula. Fecundum semen adulterio.

114

MENTULA'S ESTATE

Firmano saltu non falso Mentula dives
  fertur, qui tot res in se habet egregias,
aucupium omne genus, piscis, prata, arva ferasque.
  nequiquam: fructus sumptibus exsuperat.
Quare concedo sit dives, dum omnia desint.   5
  Saltum laudemus, dum modo ipse egeat.

115

RICH AS CROESUS

Mentula habet instar triginta iugera prati,
  quadraginta arvi: cetera sunt maria.
Cur non divitiis Croesum superare potis sit,
  uno qui in saltu tot bona possideat,
prata arva ingentes silvas saltusque paludesque   5
  usque ad Hyperboreos et mare ad Oceanum?
omnia magna haec sunt, tamen ipsest maximus ultro,
  non homo, sed vero mentula magna minax.

116

WAR ON GELLIUS

Saepe tibi studioso animo venante requirens
  carmina uti possem vertere Battiadae,
qui te lenirem nobis, neu conarere
  tela infesta meum mittere in usque caput,
hunc video mihi nunc frustra sumptum esse laborem,   5
  Gelli, nec nostras hic valuisse preces.
Contra nos tela ista tua evitabimus acta:
  at fixus nostris tu dabi' supplicium.

REFERENCE MAPS

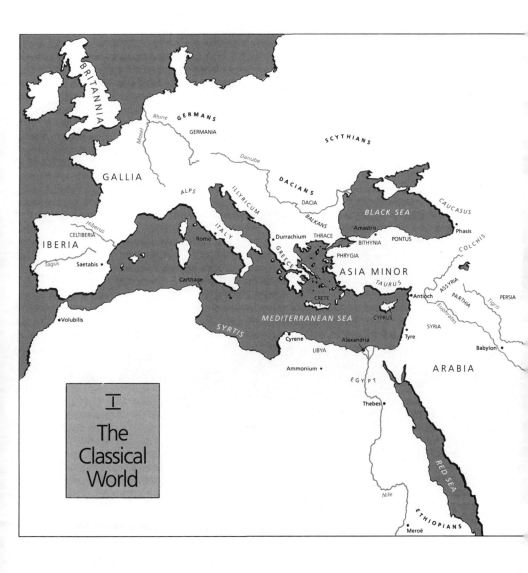

BRITANNIA

GERMANS

Rhine

GERMANIA

SCYTHIANS

Mosel

Danube

GALLIA

DACIANS

DACIA

ALPS

ILLYRICUM

BALKANS

BLACK SEA

CAUCASUS

Hiberus

ITALY

Amastris

Phasis

CELTIBERIA

Rome

Durrachium

THRACE

PONTUS

COLCHIS

IBERIA

GREECE

BITHYNIA

Tagus

Saetabis •

PHRYGIA

Carthage

ASIA MINOR

TAURUS

ASSYRIA

PARTHIA

PERSIA

CRETE

Antioch

Euphrates

Tigris

• Volubilis

MEDITERRANEAN SEA

CYPRUS

SYRIA

Babylon •

SYRTIS

Cyrene

Alexandria

Tyre

LIBYA

ARABIA

Ammonium •

EGYPT

Thebes •

RED SEA

Nile

☰
The
Classical
World

ETHIOPIANS

Meroë •

ALPS

GALLIA
TRANSPADANA

*LACUS
LARIUS*

Comum

Brixia

*LACUS
BENACUS*

Sirmio

Verona

Po

LIGURIA

Piacenza

Bologna

Arno

ETRURIA

Florentia

Volterra
Siena

UMBRIA

Arezzo
(Arretium)

Perugia
(Perusia)

Ombrone

Orcia

ELBA

Vulci

Tiber

SABINA

Rome

Ostia

Tibur

Lanuvium

Esino

Potenza

Ariminum
Pisaurum

Ancona

Firmum

PICENUM

APENNINES

LATIUM

Formiae

CAMPANIA

Cumae

Naples

Mt. Vesuvius

Pompeii

Paestum

*BAY
OF NAPLES*

ADRIATIC SEA

Urium

APULIA

Uria

Brundisium

Tarentum

LUCANIA

Thurii

CORSICA

SARDINIA

TYRRHENIAN SEA

STRAIT OF MESSINA

Riace

Locri
Rhegium

MAGNA GRAECIA

Himera

SICILY
(TRINACRIA)

Syracuse

Tunis
(Carthage)

II

Italy

III

Greece

THRACE

MACEDONIA

EMATHIA
Pella •

• Thessalonica

CHALCIDICE

Vergina
(Aegae) •

Abdera •

• Mt. Athos

LEMNOS

PIERIA
• Mt. Olympus

Peneus

TEMPE

EPIRUS

• Dodona

Larisa •
• Crannon

CORFU

THESSALY
• Pharsalus

• Mt. Pelion

AEGEAN SEA

PAXOS ISLANDS

PHTHIOTIS

• Artemisium

Actium •

GULF OF MALIA

AETOLIA

Mt. Oeta •
Thermopylae •

EUBOEA

• Mt. Parnassus

Delphi •
• Daulis

Chalcis •
• Eretria

BOEOTIA
• Mt. Helicon

GULF OF CORINTH

Thebes •

ATTICA

IONIAN ISLANDS

ACHAEA

• Mt. Cyllene

Marathon •

• Elis

Pheneus •

Athens •
Piraeus •

PELOPONNESE

Corinth •

ELIS

ARCADIA

AEGINA

Olympia •

• Mycenae

Alpheus

ARGOLIS
Argos •

CYCLADES

DELOS

MESSENIA

Eurotas

Sparta •

LACONIA

Phylakopi •

MELOS

IONIAN SEA

• Anticythera

THRACE

BLACK SEA

BOSPORUS

PROPONTIS

BITHYNIA

• Nicaea

Mt. Dindymus

HELLESPONT

PHRYGIA

Troy
(Ilium)

TROAD

Scamander

• Mt. Ida

LESBOS

Mytilene

• Pergamum

LYDIA

• Myrina

• Cyme

CHIOS

• Sardis

Smyrna

Cayster

Apamea •

AEGEAN SEA

• Ephesus

SAMOS

• Priene

• Laodicea

• Mt. Latmus

• Aphrodisias

Miletus

CARIA

Halicarnassus

COS

LYCIA

Cnidus

RHODES

MEDITERRANEAN SEA

IV

Asia
Minor

NOTES

An opening tribute to Cornelius Nepos, fellow northerner and poet, a well-known biographer and historian (see appendix A). Though independently wealthy and therefore free of the necessity of flattering a patron, Catullus is fulsome in his praise of Nepos' *magnum opus* (a three-roll synopsis of universal history) and deprecatory of his own one-roll publication (probably an early collection of short poems). This is playful irony, but not necessarily unfriendly to Cornelius.
Meter: hendecasyllabics (see appendix B).
1 **lepidum**: a key term for Catullus and the *poetae novi*, emphasizing the charm and wit of their ideal rather than its impressiveness and weight. **libellum**: the use of the diminutive instead of *librum* sets a tone of self-deprecation, and adds the colloquial note that Catullus liked.
2 **arida ... pumice expolitum** refers to the smoothing-off of the ends of the rolled *volumen*—and perhaps metaphorically to the literary polish inside. *Pumex*, normally masculine, is feminine here, as shown by *arida*.
3 **esse aliquid**: amount to something. **nugas**: trifles, compared to the weighty work of Cornelius.
8 **quidquid ... libelli**: partitive gen. with the indefinite pronoun, followed by *qualecumque* (such as it is) for optimum modesty. The rhetorical technique is called meiosis.
9 **virgo**: the real patron is the muse, invoked as usual at the beginning of a literary enterprise.
10 **perenne saeclo**: a surprise at the end. Having rhetorically minimized his little booklet, he now prays for its immortality. A *saeclum* is any long period of time: generation, century or age.

2

This apostrophe to Lesbia's pet bird is used as an occasion for Catullus to comment on his feelings about Lesbia. It has been implausibly argued that the *passer* here and in poem 3 represents the poet's phallus. This poem is one of many damaged in transmission, with a lacuna after line 10.
Meter: hendecasyllabics.
1 **passer** is vocative, as becomes clear with *tecum* (9). Though the sparrow is a bad pet, the name *passer* was also commonly given to the blue rock-

thrush, which is easily tamed and is still a popular pet in Italy. **deliciae** occurs five times in Catullus with a singular meaning: pet or darling.
2 **quicum**: an old alternative for the ablative *quocum*. **sinu**: any hollow or fold, such as her lap or the fold of the garment above her breasts.
3 **primum digitum**: her fingertip rather than her first finger. **cui appetenti**: because English uses participles less freely, we might paraphrase *to whose attack* to avoid the awkwardness of *to whom attacking*.
5 **cum**: the conjunction (when) rather than the preposition (with).
6 **nescio quid**: the idiomatic indefinite (cf. 6.4, 53.1, 80.5), sometimes written as a single word. As usual in poetry, *nescio* scans as a dactyl. With *carum*, it is an accus. of specification with *iocari*: to make some dear joke.
7 The text of the poem becomes disturbed from about this point. It is unclear whether **solaciolum** is a subject or object because it lacks a verb. Quinn understands it as an extension of *carum nescio quid*. The diminutive *-olum* is colloquial, giving a sense of intimacy, as often in Catullus.
8–10 **ardor ... curas**: the point of these lines is that Lesbia's *gravis ardor* (her sexual tension) is relieved by as little a thing as playing with her pet bird while Catullus' *tristis curas* (his desire for Lesbia) cannot be as easily forgotten.
9 **possem**: optative subjunctive, expressing the poet's wish.
11 **gratum**: the reference is unclear because of the missing line or lines: some verb or neuter noun is as pleasing to Catullus as the golden apple was to Atalanta in the story about how Milanion or Hippomenes won her hand. When an oracle warned the athletic Atalanta not to marry, she made winning a footrace with her a requirement for her many suitors, who would be killed if they lost. Venus gave Milanion a golden apple to place in Atalanta's path to distract her while he ran on ahead. Being already in love with him, Atalanta was happy enough to have this occasion for losing. The story is retold with interesting details in Ovid's *Metamorphoses*, 10.610 ff.
12 **pernici**: *pernix* comes from *perna*, leg. Atalanta is leggy, hence swift. The word is unrelated to the root of pernicious, just as the apple (**malum**) is

unrelated to the adjective *malus, -a -um.* **aureolum:** the diminutive again, untranslatably attached to an adjective.

13 **quod** is the relative pronoun (which), not the conjunction. **soluit:** trisyllabic. **zonam:** by conventional metonymy, a woman's belt being untied means she loses her virginity.

tive diminutives bring Catullus dangerously close to baby talk in commiserating with Lesbia (for *misellus* in an erotic sense, cf. 35.14 and 45.21). The hiatus in the middle of 16 adds to the mock-tragic effect. 17 Both meter and syntax require that **opera** is the abl. of *opera, -ae,* f., work, rather than the plural of *opus.*

3

A mock threnody or dirge for Lesbia's bird, filled with good-humored overstatement meant to tease her out of her grief. Lines 8–10 of the preceding poem suggest that Lesbia is perhaps more attached to her pet than to Catullus, who ingratiates himself here by sharing her sorrow. The literary pedigree of this poem includes Hellenistic laments for a dead pet.

Meter: hendecasyllabics.

2 **quantum est hominum:** after the high-sounding opening, a colloquial usage, the first of many in this poem: all the *homines venustiores* there are, referring to the "beautiful people" of Roman high society. The genitive is partitive. For variants of this construction, cf. 9.10, 31.14, 37.4

3–4 **passer ... meae puellae:** anaphora raises the rhetorical tone again, but Catullus is particularly fond of repetitions in many contexts.

6 **mellitus:** he was honey-sweet to her. **norat** is a syncopated form of *noverat,* from *nosco.*

7 **ipsam:** in the vernacular, "herself" meant the mistress of the house. The Irish have a similar usage: Don't look now, but herself just walked in. **norat** is the syncopated form of *noverat,* plupf. of *nosco.*

8 **illius** has a short second *i,* as usual in Catullus and is not the deictic "of that one" but the simple pronominal "her."

9 With its elisions, **modo huc modo illuc** imitates the little bird's hopping-around (*circumsiliens*) action, as *pipiabat* imitates its voice.

11 **iter tenebricosum,** etc.: even at his lightest, Catullus sees little but darkness after life.

13–15 **male ... malae, bella ... bellum:** more repetitions, with a colloquial flavor; *bellus* is a popular diminutive of *bonus.* One of the guiding ideas of Catullus and the *novi poetae* was that poetry should be able to use the vernacular as freely as the lofty language of tragedy and epic.

16–18 **miselle:** dim. of *miser,* as **ocelli** is the dim. of *oculi* and **turgiduli** the dim. of *turgidi.* These affec-

4

The small ship that brought Catullus back from his year in Bithynia in the spring of 56 B.C. tells its story. The manner is that of the dedicatory inscriptions that became literary epigrams in Hellenistic poetry. Such epigrams told the story of a worker's career and retirement, with the dedication of his or her implements of trade. Catullus playfully adapts his model to a personified bark and expands its usual length. The syntactic structures are unusually complex for Catullus; he may, in fact, be making fun of epigrams in this style.

Meter: iambic senarii (see appendix B).

1 **Phaselus:** a light passenger ship, named after the Greek bean pod (φάσηλος) and built for speed. Catullus implies that he bought this bark or even had it built, since he calls himself its *erus* (19) and tells of its construction and retirement after a single uneventful journey. **hospites** corresponds to the Greek epigram's address to the passing stranger, thus indicating how we are to take the poem that follows.

2 **ait** sets up the indirect statement that will dominate all but the last three lines of the poem. It is renewed by **negat** (6), **ait** (15), and **dicit** (16). **celerrimus** would in regular Latin usage be *celerrimum* in indirect statement. The copyist regularized his text accordingly, but we know from an ancient parody of this line that Catullus wrote *celerrimus,* following a usage that is rare in classical Latin. The gender of the adjective follows that of *phaselus.*

3–4 **neque ... nequisse,** like **negat ... negare** (6–7), is litotic, expressing the positive idea forcefully, viz. the hyperbolic boast that it was the fastest little ship in the world, surpassing the rush of any floating boat. A *trabs* is any tree trunk or timber, by metonymy (from the keel timber) a boat. **nequisse:** perf. infinitive of *nequeo,* completed by **praeterire;** it was not incapable of surpassing. **palmulis:** virtually a *hapax legomenon,* occurring only here and in line 17; dim. for *palma,* an oar-blade. With its play

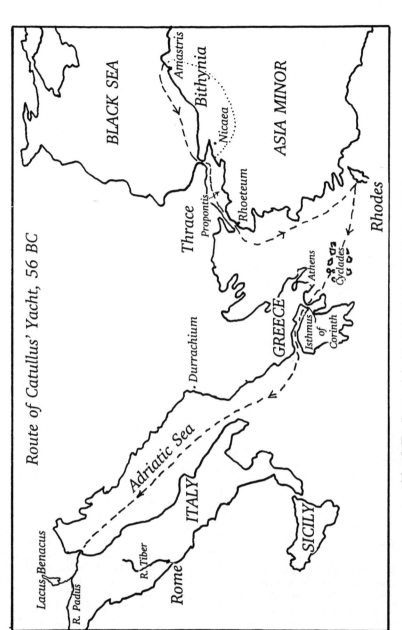

Map 5. The Route of Catullus' *phaselus* as described in poem 4.

on "palm" of the hand, the word choice (instead of *remis*) fits the personification of the bark.

5 **foret** is generally used instead of *futurus esset* in verse. **linteo:** linen cloth, here a canvas sail.

6 **hoc** refers to the speed claimed in the preceding sentence; it is the object of **negare** in the next line. The ship denies (**negat**) that a list of five places on its itinerary—the Adriatic coast, the Cycladic islands, Rhodes, Thracian Propontis, and the Pontic coast—deny (**negare**) its speed. Catalogues of place-names have been a favorite topic of poetry since Homer's Catalogue of Ships and their places of origin in the Iliad.

8 **Thraciam** is adjectival, agreeing with the Greek accusative **Propontida**. The reference is to the Sea of Marmora between the Black Sea (**Ponticum sinum**) and the Aegean.

10 **iste post phaselus:** this future bark. **post** is not the preposition but the adverb, used as an adjective. Previously it was leafy forest, afterwards a boat.

11 **Cytorio:** adjectival again, like **Thraciam** (8). The ridge south of Cytorus that runs along the southern coast was well-forested in antiquity and provided lumber for shipbuilding. For Catullus, its dark forests, transferred to the Troad, provided the sinister atmosphere in which he set his story of Attis (poem 63).

12 **loquente ... coma:** instrumental abl. The "speaking" of rustling leaves was a traditional metaphor.

13 **Amastri:** vocative. The third sentence is an apostrophe to the ports where the bark grew up (as trees) and became a boat. Amastris was the capital of Paphlagonia, part of Bithynia. **buxifer:** Catullus usually avoids such epic compounds except in his long poems. Cytorus, famous for its boxwood, is so mentioned by Virgil, Pliny, and Strabo.

18 **impotentia:** wild; the seas are helpless to restrain their own violence. Cf. 35.12, *impotente amore.*

19 **erum:** Catullus is not just a passenger, but the ship's master, as if it were a living servant.

20–21 **Iuppiter ... pedem.** Poetic language calls weather "Jupiter"; a **Iuppiter secundus** (from *sequor*) is a following wind that falls equally on either sheet (**utrumque pedem** refers to the lines or sheets that secure the lower corners of a square sail). The ancient ship, like all square-riggers, could sail a beam reach or a broad reach, but it could not tack upwind like a modern sailboat. **incidisset:** from *íncido* fall upon, not *incído* cut into.

22 **vota:** The bark was so seaworthy that no frightened vows were made to the shore gods during heavy weather. Survivors of storm or shipwreck made votive offerings at seaside shrines, sometimes with epigrams telling about the crisis they escaped.

23 **sibi:** dative of advantage, on its behalf.

23–24 **mari novissimo:** the journey's final sea on the journey from Bithynia to the Po valley would be the Adriatic. See map. **hunc ... lacum** may be the Lago di Garda near Catullus' home.

27 **gemelle:** dim. of *gemine*. A final apostrophe to the Dioscuri, patrons of mariners and twin stars. Castor's twin Pollux was the lesser of the two.

5

Love's euphoria, defiant of scandal and envy but a bit superstitious. Composed of three triads and a final quatrain, it is said to reflect the careless joy of Catullus' first fling with Lesbia.

Meter: hendecasyllabics.

3 **omnes unius:** strictly speaking, oxymoron is the juxtaposition of opposite words applied to the same thing, e.g. loveless love. The term is sometimes applied loosely to any emphatic juxtaposition of opposites whether or not they state a paradox, as here. **unius assis:** gen. of value with **aestimemus**, introducing a bookkeeping theme to be resumed in lines 10–11. The *i* of *unius*, normally long, may be short in verse (as here). An *as* is a coin of negligible value, like a penny.

4–6 The you-only-live-once argument was already an old favorite in love poetry. **soles ... lux** there are many days but only one brief "light" for us; the monosyllabic line ending is rare and emphatic. **dormienda** with **nox est** expresses ineluctable necessity; the periphrastic construction takes the dative of agent *nobis*. Passive in Latin, it is best paraphrased as an active in English, We must sleep.

7–10 Close repetitions of words are a hallmark of Catullus' style. **mille, deinde** (or **dein**), and **centum** are the elements of a playful sequence where form imitates content.

10 **fecerimus:** the future perfect indicative with a long ī, normal in Cicero, occurs here in verse for the first time.

11 **conturbabimus:** throw [the accounts] into confusion: borrowed (like **fecerimus** above) from bookkeeping jargon, this introduces a touch of superstition: what we don't know won't hurt us and can't be used against us.

12 **invidere**: more superstition. *In-video* in its original sense means to "look upon" with the evil eye and thus bewitch.

6

Like Catullus in poem 5, Flavius is up to his ears in some hot new affair. The poet uses cynical banter to provoke his friend into telling all. The poem's coarseness makes fun of Hellenistic love epigrams in which a guest at a symposium is discovered to be in love (Asclepiades GP 18, Callimachus GP 12–13).
Meter: hendecasyllabics.
1 **Flavi**: calling him by his family name adds a note of mock solemnity. **delicias tuas**, like **tuos amores** at the end (16), refers to a single girlfriend; cf. *deliciae* in 2.1 and 3.4.
2–3 **ni sint ... velles**: unless she were hopelessly gauche, you'd be willing to talk. The mixture of subjunctive tenses is unorthodox.
4–5 **Verum**: but in fact. **nescio quid ... scorti**: partitive gen., some kind of bimbo; for the idiom, see note on 2.6. A *scortum* is a "skin," slang for anyone available for a price. Moreover, she is *febriculosa*, feverish, not the cool and fashionable type one would introduce socially. The personal ending of *nescio* is short in poetry.
6 **non viduas**: not celibate. The ironic understatement (litotes) highlights the way Flavius has been spending his nights.
7 **nequiquam tacitum**: the bed is a vainly tacit witness because although it cannot speak it squeaks loudly. See appendix C, conceit. As often in poetry, the singular *clamat* has several subjects, including *cubile, pulvinus, argutatio, inambulatio*. 80.7f., *clamant ... ilia et ... labra*, is more grammatically correct.
8 **sertis**: *serta, -orum*, n (from *sero*) are woven festoons of flowers; Flavius has spared no effort to make things perfect with garlands of fresh flowers and aromatic olive oil from Syria. This contrasts with the noisy bed and tousled pillow.
9 **peraeque**: each pillow has been equally mussed, indicating (a) two occupants in the bed and (b) wide-ranging amatory activities.
10 **tremuli**: the feeble bed is no match for its occupants.
11 **inambulatio** renews the personification of **clamat** (7): the bed wiggles so violently it actually seems to walk around the bedroom.

12 **nil stupra ... tacere** = *nil valet stupra tacere*: mock righteousness about Flavius' "abominations." The belief that evil always comes to light is widespread: "Foul deeds will rise, though all the earth o'erwhelm them, to men's eyes." *Ham.* I ii 257f.
13 **latera ecfututa**: loosely, a body exhausted by sexual excess.
pandas, from *pando, -ere*: spread out or display.
13–14 **pandas ... facias**: use of the present instead of the imperfect subjunctive in a contrary-to-fact condition is an archaizing poetic usage.
14 **quid ... ineptiarum**: some kind of hanky-panky; another indefinite partitive gen. (cf. 4). The phrase is comic anticlimax: these orgies are worse than immoral, they are inept—but Catullus' final words on the matter (15–17) make it clear that the affair itself will be perfectly acceptable as soon as Flavius opens up about it.
16 **volo**: the short final vowel is the result of iambic shortening, a feature of colloquial Latin that pronounced an iambic disyllable (vŏlō) as a pyrrhic (vŏlŏ).
17 **ad caelum ... vocare**: that is, to immortalize.

7

A sequel to poem 5, this measures Lesbia's kisses not by the decimal system but by grains of sand and stars, which as traditional metaphors of infinitude make his love less vulnerable to evil spells.
Meter: hendecasyllabics.
1 **basiationes** are mock-pompous kissifications.
2 **tuae**: subjective. As in 5.7 *da mi basia mille*, Lesbia is doing the kissing.
4 **lasarpiciferis ... Cyrenis** is more magniloquence, making fun of the learned Hellenistic allusiveness of his sand metaphor. The fancy-sounding compound (see note on 4.13 **buxifer**) refers to silphium or *laserpicium*, a fennel-like plant whose resin was exported from Cyrene. According to ancient authorities, this "Cyrenaic juice" was an effective contraceptive. The case is locative; the plural **Cyrenis** refers to the territory around Cyrene, i.e. Cyrenaica.
5 **oraclum** (=*oraculum*): the oracular temple of Egyptian Ammon, whom the Romans identified with Jove. The god, once consulted by Alexander the Great, is sweltering (**aestuosi**) in the desert heat on the southern frontier of Cyrenaica.
6 **Batti ... sepulcrum**: the tomb of the first king of Cyrene was in the middle of this North African

capital, more than 300 miles from the oracle mentioned in line 5.

9 te: accus. subject of *basiare*. As in lines 1–2, Catullus is calling for kisses from Lesbia.

11–12 quae ... possint: subjunctive in a relative clause of purpose: so that busybodies (**curiosi** are worse than curious, they are meddlesome) won't be able to count them out. **mala ... lingua** with a short final **a** is the second subject of **possint. fascinare** is to put a *fascinum* or spell on somebody; one was thought especially vulnerable to a *fascinum* during moments of great happiness (cf. note on 61.120). A common rule of magic is that if you have exact information about a person you can inflict a curse. When Odysseus reveals his name to Polyphemus in Homer's *Odyssey*, the Cyclops is able to ask his father Poseidon for revenge.

8

Lesbia has broken off her affair with Catullus, who considers his foolishness and urges himself to tough it out (**obdura**, 11, cf. 12, 19). The firm position he is determined to adopt contrasts with the prevalent mood of humiliation and pathos. One of Catullus' masterpieces.

Meter: limping iambics (see appendix B) reinforce the grief and awkwardness (**ineptire**, 1) expressed by the language. Punctuation at the end of all but two of the poem's nineteen lines follows the heavy end-stopping of Catullus' phrasing; the lines come haltingly. This poem's conversational quality benefits from the correspondence of prose accent and metrical emphasis at the end of each line: ineptíre, dúcas, sóles, ducébat, etc.

1 miser: a favorite word of Catullus, occurring (with its cognates) 42 times in the poems. Besides general wretchedness, it connotes intense erotic love (51.5, 99.11 and 15, 64.71 and 140; cf. *misellus* at 35.14, 45.21). Its position here is emphatic, its meaning complex.

1–2 desinas, ducas: the jussive subjunctive is less blunt than the imperative. Catullus is remonstrating with himself: you must stop being a jerk, and realize that it's all over. **ducas**, consider, governs the indirect statement **perditum [esse]**, the subject of which is **quod vides perisse**. The juxtaposition *perisse perditum* emphasizes the perceived finality of the breakup.

4 ventitabas iterative form of *veniebas* to emphasize the frequency with which Lesbia led Catullus

around; Catullus has been a bit of a puppy, which must have been boring for Lesbia. **quo** is the adverb: where, to what place, whither.

5 amata ... quantum amabitur nulla is repeated in 37.12, paraphrased in 58.3. Catullus freely admits the obsessive quality of his love, which renders him more vulnerable than philosophic.

9 Nunc iam: the redundancy has a once-and-for-all finality. **impotens**: self-reproachful, "helpless," unable to control his despair.

10 quae: sc. *illam.* **sectare** is the imperative of the deponent *sector*, iterative of *sequor*. As in line 4 (the iterative *ventitabas*), Catullus berates his puppy instinct: Don't keep following her around! Catullus needs to regain his self-respect.

12 Vale: a defiant apostrophe to Lesbia that continues to 18, where the poet tries to persuade himself that the loss will be Lesbia's more than his own.

14 rogaberis nulla is a colloquial emphatic negative: you will not be asked out at all.

15 Scelesta mixes scorn and pity: You wretch!

16–18 Quis ... cui: the obsession takes over as Catullus imagines what she won't be doing with him.

19 destinatus: adverbial, from *destino*: determined, stubborn. **obdura**: having started with a jussive subjunctive (**desinas**), Catullus ends with a blunt imperative.

9

Veranius (see appendix A) has just returned from a tour of duty in Spain, much to the delight of Catullus. The triple repetition of *beatus* (lines 5, 10, 11) helps establish the mood.

Meter: hendecasyllabics.

1 omnibus: dat. ind. object of *antistans*; **meis amicis**: abl. object of prep. **e**: surpassing all my friends.

2 milibus trecentis: best taken with **amicis** as extravagant hyperbole: even if Catullus had 300,000 friends, Veranius would still be number one.

5 nuntii beati: a nom. pl. exclamation, like the exclamatory accusative.

8 mos ... tuus: Catullus fondly remembers his friend's interest in people and places, and his lively talk. **applicans**: with middle or reflexive force, attaching myself to.

9 suaviabor: the deponent *suavior*, kiss, is related to *suavis, persuadeo*, and our *sweet*. Among the physically demonstrative Romans, Catullus is particularly enthusiastic. This is more than the usual Mediterranean peck on the cheek.

10 **quantum ... beatiorum**: as in 3.2 (see note).

11 **quid** is colloquial, like the preceding phrase, and more sweeping than *quis*: not "who" but "what [of all possible people or things]?" Cf. the hyperbole with which the poem began.

10

Catullus' folly gets the better of him once again (as in poem 8), this time with more comic. results. The time is spring or summer of 56 B.C.; Catullus is just back from his administrative tour of duty in Bithynia (line 7); Varus, finding him in the Forum with time on his hands, invites him up to see his new mistress. When conversation turns to Bithynia and the graft that provincial officials were expected to extort from the natives, Catullus tries to save face with Varus' foxy mistress by claiming to have brought back eight of the litter bearers for which the region was famous. With feigned innocence, the unnamed lady (Fraenkel calls her "a drawing-room Nemesis") asks to borrow them for a visit to a local temple—thereby exposing his bluff and causing Catullus great annoyance.

Meter: hendecasyllabics.

1 **amores**: plural for singular, like *deliciae* in 2.1 and 3.4.

2 **visum**: supine in *-um*, expressing purpose.

3 **scortillum**: dim. of *scortum* (see 6.5). His exasperation rises when he thinks of her: a chippie or bimbette, but classy enough (line 4) that he tells a flimsy lie to impress her.

4 **non ... illepidum, invenustum**: the double negatives lend litotic emphasis, making Catullus' subsequent blunder all the more embarrasing. *Lepidus* and *venustus* are standard jargon for whatever Catullus and his circle considered elegant.

5 **incidere**: perfect indicative; the **sermones** (topics of conversation) came up casually.

6–8 **esset, haberet, profuisset**, subjunctives in indirect question, progress from the general to the particular, viz. what was in it for Catullus. **quonam ... aere**: the suffix -**nam** indicates that this, last but not least, was the point of the subject.

9 **ipsis** (dat. of reference with **nihil ... esse**) are the natives themselves. Nobody was getting rich in Bithynia.

10 **praetoribus**: governors sent to administer (and loot) Bithynia, the latest of whom was C. Memmius, under whom Catullus served. **cohorti**: the

staff on which Catullus served.

11 **cur ... referret**: indirect question, loosely dependent on *nihil ... esse* above: there was no reason why, etc. **caput unctius**: a better oiled head (like an oiled palm) belongs to someone who has made a profit. Heads were oiled on holidays and celebrations, hence a second meaning: nobody had anything to celebrate about.

12 **quibus** is dat. of possession with **esset**; it is compressed from *eis quibus*, continuing the datives of reference *ipsis ... praetoribus ... cohorti* in lines 9–10. **irrumator**: someone who forces others to give him oral sex, hence one who treats people with contempt. The obscene epithet is substituted for the name of C. Memmius. See also 28.10 (to Memmius), *tota ista trabe lentus irrumasti*.

13 **pili** is gen. of value with **faceret**: Memmius reckoned his cohort as worth less than a hair. This figure of speech plays off an earlier figure, *caput unctius* (11).

14 **quod** refers to the use of **ad lecticam homines** (16).

14–27 **inquiunt, inquam** (18), and **inquit** (25) are historical presents for dramatic effect; the perfect **inquii** (27) puts a stop to this embarrassing series of questions and answers.

17 **unum** has adverbial force: particularly.

19 **quod**: the adverb with concessive force, granted that. **incidisset**: fell to my lot.

22 **grabati**: cot. Catullus assumes the role of the penniless poet. He not only lacks litter bearers, but the only bed he claims to own is a crippled little pallet with a broken foot. This is, of course, nonsense coming from a man of Catullus' wealth, but poverty is the usual pose of anyone who assumes the mantle of the poet.

24 **hic**: at this point; Varus' girlfriend gets a bright idea, for which she is rewarded with the epithet **cinaediorem**, comp. of the adj. *cinaedus*, usually applied to a passive homosexual male or catamite. Here loosely used, meaning that her remark is what you would expect of a more unsavory type. **decuit**: perfect of the impersonal *decet*.

26–7 **commoda** and **mane**, imperatives with short final vowel, reflect colloquial usage, as does the dramatizing hiatus after **mane** (Wait...). **ad Serapim**: i.e., to the temple of the Egyptian god Serapis in Rome, where people went to be cured of their ailments. Whatever ails Varus' mistress, she wants to go across town in style. The reference helps to characterize her as a working girl: there had been popular agitation in 58 B.C. for shrines of Isis and Serapis on the Capitoline hill, which the Senate resisted.

28–30 Like the hiatus after **mane**, the short, broken phrases reflect the embarrassed Catullus groping for an excuse why he cannot produce the eight litter bearers.

28 **istud**: acc. of specification, antecedent of **quod**, as for that which.... The eight (imaginary) litter bearers are compressed into a neuter singular.

29 **fugit me ratio**: I made a mistake, it slipped my mind.

30 **Cinna est Gaius**: *Gaius* is trisyllabic here; Catullus stammers out the name backwards: Cinna—Gaius Cinna, that is—, a poet and politician who seems from this passage to have served with Catullus in Bithynia. See appendix A.

32 **tam bene quam**: sc. *si*. The feeble lie is that Catullus uses these litter bearers as readily as if he had gotten them for himself. **para(ve)rim**: for subjunctive in clauses of comparison, see Allen & Greenough §524.

33 **insulsa male ... vivis** is colloquial and idiomatic: you're stupid, nasty, and a pain in the neck. For *vivis* = *es*, cf. 89.2 *vivat*, 107.7 *vivit*. The compound *in-sulsa* (from *sal-*, salt) associates salt with wit. This floozy is supposedly too stupid to understand a joke—but of course the joke is on Catullus.

11

Catullus asks Furius and Aurelius to tell "my girl"—undoubtedly Lesbia—that he will have nothing more to do with her: she is promiscuous, and careless of his love. The poem is usually understood as a final repudiation of Lesbia. A persistent problem in its analysis has been the relation of the first three stanzas to the final two: what does the elaborate catalog of places have to do with the message for Lesbia?

Meter: Sapphic strophe (see appendix B).

1 **comites** is ironic, to judge from the poet's treatment of Furius and Aurelius in other poems (see appendix A). They are despised errand boys (like Hamlet's Rosenkrantz and Guildenstern), addressed with elaborate civility in four stanzas.

2 **sive** begins a romantic catalogue of places where Furius and Aurelius will be his **comites**: whether he goes to India, or Hyrcania, or Arabia, etc. **penetrabit**: Catullus refers to himself in the third person.

3 **ut**: where (as in 17.10). **Eoä** is the adjective, with

unda: the Eastern wave, named after the dawn goddess Eos.

5 **Hyrcanos**: the Hyrcani lived along the south shore of the Caspian Sea. The **Arabas** (acc. pl.) are **molles** by virtue of their luxurious exports.

6 **Sagas** are the nomadic Sacae of northern Iran. The Parthians bordered the Roman Empire on the east in Asia Minor; their archery rendered them especially dangerous to the Romans.

7 The Nile is called **septemgeminus** because of its seven mouths, which colored the nearby sea with its muddy waters.

10 **visens** is the iterative (*video* + -*to* = *vidto* > *viso*), going to see the **monimenta** of Caesar's recent exploits in Gaul and Britain: the Rhine, the *horribile aequor* of the English Channel, and the Britons. Since these incursions happened in 55 B.C., we have a *terminus post quem* for this poem. This is the only passage where Catullus makes honorific mention of Caesar, whom he had formerly lampooned. See appendix A, Caesar.

11 **horribile aequor**: asyndeton and two elisions speed up Catullus' catalogue near its end.

11–12 **ulti-mosque** is hypermetric (see appendix C), perhaps to add more haste to the end of the catalogue. But the Latin text of line 11 is uncertain.

13 **omnia haec**, obj. of *temptare*, closes off the catalogue which occupied the first half of the poem.

14 **caelitum** (gen. pl. of *caeles*) is stately and archaic, like "the heavenly host."

15 **meae puellae** recalls the happier days of 2.1 and 3.3–4.

17 **moechis**, adulterers, breaks the pattern of lofty language set in the first four stanzas.

18–19 **simul trecentos ... identidem**: disgusted exaggeration. She not only embraces 300 at a time, but she exhausts them, "breaking" their **ilia** or loins again and again. For the use of 300 as formulaic for any large number, cf. 12.10, 29.14, 48.3. The last syllable of *omnium* is hypermetric.

20 **ilia rumpens**: cf. 80.7f., *rupta ... ilia*.

21 **respectet**: hortatory or jussive subjunctive, as on line 17. She is not to count on his love any longer.

22 **qui**, etc: his love is compared to a wildflower casually uprooted by a passing plow. **cecidit**: pf. of *cado*. **prati ultimi**: gen., at the edge of a field; the elision of **prati** is hypermetric.

24 **tactus** emphasizes how easily Lesbia's callous promiscuity has destroyed his feelings of love: just a touch was enough. Her **culpa** has all the compassion of an iron plow.

12

A piece of occasional verse, ostensibly to embarrass Asinius Marrucinus (see appendix A) for filching a napkin of sentimental value. The main purpose, though, may have been to pay compliments to Pollio (6–9), Fabullus, and Veranius, and the napkin thief gets off with a lighter rebuke than the one served up to Thallus in poem 25.

Meter: hendecasyllabics.

1 **sinistra**: the hand used in dirty work.

2 **belle**: the dim. again, as in 3.14.

3 **tollis**: lift, a thinly veiled euphemism for "steal"; **lintea**: any linens, identifiable from the preceding line as table napkins. All Europeans ate with their fingers until the introduction of forks in the 15th century.

4 **salsum**: in 10.33 Varus' lady friend is rebuked as *insulsa*, stupid. Its opposite here is "clever." **Fugit te** leaves the subject unexpressed; cf. 10.29 *fugit me ratio* and the colloquial ellipsis "You're out of it."

5 **quamvis sordida** is compressed from *[tam] sordida quam vis*: as tacky as can be, extremely shabby or base. **invenusta** (cf. Eng. "uncool") was likely a popular term with Catullus and his circle of Roman sophisticates: it appears three times in Catullus, *venustus* seven times.

8 **mutari velit**: Pollio would like (potential subj.) his brother's **furta** changed or undone even by means of a talent, which is a lot of Greek money; he would pay plenty to change his ways.

9 **facetiarum**: gen. with word of plenty, **differtus** (stuffed). Pollio is a man of real wit (**facetiae**), who knows that swiping napkins is a poor excuse for a joke.

10 **hendecasyllabos**, the satirical policemen of high society, nearly personified here, are fully personified in poem 42.

12 **aestimatione**: value, as regularly in legal Latin. Before machine looms, any woven fabric was quite expensive. Cf. introductory notes on poems 25 and 33.

12–13 **non ... verum**: the conjunction is stronger than *sed*: To the contrary, it's a souvenir.... **mnemosynum**, a Greek word found only here in Latin, was no doubt a fashionable loan word in Catullus' circle. Catullus and the *poetae novi* generally avoided language borrowed from Greek.

14 **sudaria** applies to any napkins or handkerchiefs used to wipe away sweat (*sudor*). **Saetaba**, the adjective, from Saetabis (mod. Jativa) in Tarraconensis (cf. mod. Tarragon), where the Spanish produced the best linen in Europe.

15 **muneri**, for a gift, is a dative of purpose.

15–17 **Fabullus et Veranius, Veraniolum**: See appendix A. Catullus repeats the names with affectionate emphasis, altering the order for variety and adding a diminutive suffix, Veranius baby. Fabullus is the dim. of Fabius.

13

Catullus half-jokingly invites Fabullus, perhaps recently returned from Spain (see poem 12 and appendix A), to bring a date to a dinner party. Pleading poverty, he promises to supply everything but food, wine, and a *candida puella* to provide entertainment.

Meter: hendecasyllabics.

1 **apud me**, like French *chez moi*, is idiomatic: at my place.

2 **paucis ... diebus**: the vagueness of the invitation is part of the joke, as is the parenthetical qualification **si tibi di favent**. The hyperbaton or artificial separation of **paucis** from **diebus** adds to the humor.

4 The separation of **cenam** from **magnam** by line end has an effect similar to the hyperbaton in line 2. The close syntactical relation of two words separated by line ending is enjambment; contrast the strong end-stopping of lines 2 and 5, and the slight end-stopping of 1 and 4. The double negative (litotes) of **non sine** is slightly poetical, and more emphatic than if he had written *cum*. **candida**: a pale skin was considered a mark of great beauty—and a privileged life style that did not require exposure to the elements.

5 **sale** plays on two meanings, salt and wit; cf. 10.33 *insulsa* and 12.4 *salsum*. Besides food, Fabullus will have to bring everything else that makes a dinner party successful.

8 **plenus ... aranearum**: hyperbaton again. For the gen. construction, cf. 12.9 *leporum differtus*.

9 **meros amores**: in return (**contra**) for the fixings, Fabullus will receive something he will absolutely love. *Amores* in Catullus usually means girlfriend (e.g. 6.16, 10.1), but Fabullus will already have a *candida puella*, so this word raises a new expectation. There is another pun in **meros**: wine unmixed with water was called *merum*.

10 **seu quid**, like *aut si quid* in 22.13 and 82.2, is a breezy wave of the hand: you'll get **meros amores** or whatever (indef. pron. **quid**) is even better.

11 **nam** explains what Catullus is promising.

12 **donarunt**: for *donaverunt*; syncope of verb forms is common in Latin poetry. **Veneres Cupidinesque**, as in 3.1, are everything that makes Lesbia attractive. The idea is that the spirits of love conferred this aromatic oil on Lesbia as a special boon. The use of scents by men and women at a dinner party was a part of dressing up.

14 **totum ... nasum**: a final hyperbaton. The last word of a poem, especially a short one, is a position of special emphasis.

14

Catullus' friend Licinius Calvus has sent a book of bad poetry as a joke on the eve of the Saturnalia, when gifts were traditionally given. Since books were not mass produced but copied out by hand, one can infer that Calvus made an anthology of the worst current poems he could find. Catullus uses the occasion to make fun of the scribblers of the moment.

Meter: hendecasyllabics.

1–3 **amarem ... odissem**: imperfect subjunctive, as usual in present contrary-to-fact conditions. **Calve**: see appendix A. **Vatiniano**: as in 53.2. I would hate you as much as Vatinius does—an oblique compliment to Calvus for his celebrated prosecution of Vatinius (see appendix A).

5 **tot** modifies **poetis**, **male** intensifies **perderes**.

6 **isti ... clienti**, that *cliens* of yours, implies that Calvus enclosed a note with the book purporting to explain how he had come by it in the first place: it was a thank-you gift from a client whom Calvus had defended in court. Catullus goes on to accuse *Sulla litterator* (line 9), perhaps a self-styled connoisseur known to them both, as the source of this literary white elephant.

7 **tantum ... impiorum**: partitive gen., so many scoundrels (the poets represented in the collection).

8 **novum ac repertum**: hendiadys, newly discovered.

10–11: an ironic comment, made with friendly malice: Catullus professes to be happy that Calvus' efforts on behalf of his *cliens* have not gone unrewarded.

12 **sacrum**: exclamatory acc.; this bad meaning of *sacer* derives from the forfeiture to a god of anything that offends divine law. The line may be a playfully ironic echo of the tribute to Calvus in 53.5: *Di magni, salaputium disertum!*

14 **mis(is)ti ... ut periret**: comic overstatement.

continuo: without delay, on the same day you receive the gift. **die** is best understood with *optimo dierum*.

16 **hoc** refers to Calvus' joke on Catullus. **salse**: you joker! **sic**: that is, as a trick entirely at Catullus' expense. The sense of the idiomatic **tibi ... abibit** is: you won't get away with a joke like this.

17 **si luxerit**: a formula of pious caution (when, God willing), used with a touch of comic irony, implying that Calvus' waggish gift was such an atrocity that the sun might not even rise the next day.

17–18 **librariorum ... scrinia**: the bookdealers' cylindrical cases in which the book scrolls were kept.

18 **Caesios, Aquinos**: generalizing plurals, contemptuously referring to such poets as those named.

19 **Suffenum**: see poem 22 and appendix A.

22 **pedem attulistis**: a common idiom for "came," with a pun on the metrical foot in poetry.

23 **saecli incommoda**: more comic overstatement: misfortunes of our age.

14b

An unattached fragment placed here in the manuscripts, perhaps part of a prefatory poem in an earlier collection.

Meter: hendecasyllabics.

1 **ineptiarum**: a self-deprecating reference to his poems, like *nugae* in 1.4. There is perhaps also a reference to the theme of *ineptiae* (instances of folly) in the poems which follow, 15–26.

3 **nobis**: i.e., to my poems

15

Catullus entrusts his young boyfriend to Aurelius, but with comic misgivings that Aurelius will play fast and loose with him. The boy is probably Juventius (see appendix A). Like the Greeks, urban, Hellenized Romans saw nothing wrong with recreational sex of either type. There is some irony, however, in the repetition of *pudentem, pudice*, and *pudenter* (2, 5, 13) in a poem that has so much fun with abuse and indecency.

Meter: hendecasyllabics.

1 **meos amores**: my boyfriend, as we learn from *puerum* in line 5. For this idiom cf. *tuos amores* (6.16) and *suos amores* (10.1), both in those cases referring to a girlfriend.

2 **Aureli**: see appendix A.

3 **cupi(vi)sti**: the usual syncopation.

4 **castum** ... **et integellum** overstates the innocence of the boy for comic effect. **expeteres**: subjunctive in a relative clause of characteristic. The thought is: if you have ever wanted to keep something pure and inviolate for yourself, do the same for me.

6 **nihil**: an emphatic variant of *non*, as in 16.6.

8 **in re sua** ... **occupati**: minding their own business.

9 **a te metuo**: I fear danger from you.

11 **Quem** refers to *tuo ... pene* (9). **moveto**: fut. imperative, ply.

12 **paratum**: ready for business. We are invited to picture Aurelius as a satyr-like figure with a constant and insatiable erection. **foris** is emphatic: he is to indulge his lust only when he is outside, a safe distance from Catullus' boy.

13 **hunc** is the boy Catullus wants kept safe.

16 **nostrum** ... **caput**: emphatic for *me*, with overtones of "my rights" and perhaps "my darling."

17 **te miserum**: exclamatory acc. with **mali** ... **fati**: exclamatory gen. The style is comic bombast.

18–19: echoes of coarse Aristophanic humor. An adulterer caught in the act could be punished by having cruel and unusual objects thrust into his rectum.

16

Catullus aims a blizzard of obscenity at Furius and Aurelius (see appendix A), who have accused him of living indecently because he writes erotic poetry. The foul language has a point: there is a difference between the poet and the poetry he or she writes. The same argument was used on behalf of Philaenis in *A.P.* 7.345, later by Ovid in protesting his exile by Augustus, and later still by Martial: *lasciva est nobis pagina, vita proba* (*Ep* 1.4.8).

Meter: hendecasyllabics.

1 **pedicabo** ... **irrumabo**: inflict anal and oral sex upon. Both are ancient and primitive forms of humiliation, still in practice as forms of rape. *Pedicare* means to bugger; *irrumare* means to force a person to perform oral sex (fellatio). In 10.12 Catullus calls Memmius an *irrumator* for abusing his subordinates as governor of Bithynia.

2 **pathice** ... **cinaede**: a pathic is a person who willingly submits to anal sex, as does also a *cinaedus* or catamite, a boy kept for sexual purposes by a pederast. The words are combined again in 57.1–2. The idea is that (though it was acceptable for a

man to have a younger male boyfriend, like Catullus' Juventius) males who submit to sexual dominance by other males are contemptible.

3–4 **versiculis** ... **molliculi**: the diminutives minimize the verses in question and the degree of their erotic content. *Mollis*, soft, may also mean voluptuous or erotic; with the diminutive, a bit sexy. **putastis** is a syncopated form of *putavistis*. **parum pudicum**, insufficiently chaste (again in line 8), alliterates *p*-sounds for scornful effect—as does the poem as a whole.

6 **ipsum, versiculos**: adversative asyndeton: the poet should be pure, *but* not necessarily his verses. The English conjunction *but* specifies what the Latin only implies. The idea is repeated in Ovid (*Tristia* 2.354), Martial (1.4.8), and Pliny (*Epist.* 4.14.5). **nihil** is adverbial: not at all, as in 15.6.

7 **tum denique**: in the last analysis.

9 **pruriat**: the potential subjunctive with **incitare possunt** indicates that sexual excitement is a possible result of his erotic verse rather than its object; *prurire* is to itch or have a sexual craving.

10 **pueris**: dat. of reference. Erotic poetry is not for adolescents, who already have **quod pruriat**. **pilosis** is substantive, the shaggy ones.

11 **lumbos**: hips or loins (as the seat of sexual excitement).

12–13 **milia multa basiorum** may refer only to the language of poem 48, which is homosexual, but we are left guessing whether Lesbia poems like 5 and 7 are also meant. The *m* sounds in these two lines have the same effect as the *p* sounds. **male** is adverbial with the omitted *esse* and **marem** (from *mas, maris*, male): Do you think I am no proper male (just because I have written a homosexual poem)?

17

Roman marriages often joined women with men twice their age (and older). Here Catullus makes fun of an old man who is blind to the wild ways of his young wife. The scene is in the northern provinces, probably somewhere near Catullus' Verona, where the poet suggests the negligent husband be thrown into the swamp off a rickety bridge as a kind of propitiatory offering to keep the bridge from collapsing during an impending holiday. The bridge is as decrepit as the old man, and though it is unlikely the rite will do much to save the bridge timbers, Catullus hopes it will alert the victim to his husbandly responsibilities.

Meter: Priapean (see appendix B).

1 **Colonia**: a generic-sounding town name like River City. There is a Cologna Veneta about twenty miles east of Verona where locals point out a "Ponte di Catullo" to anyone who will believe them, but in all likelihood Catullus is being deliberately vague.

2 **salire paratum habes**: are ready to jump around on the bridge (in holiday dancing). **vereris**: you are wary (same root).

4 **cavaque in**: elision crosses the caesura here and in 11, 24, 26.

5–7 **sic ... fiat - munus ... da**: a prayer formula wherein the person with a wish to be granted expresses a corresponding wish for the entity prayed to. Catullus hopes that the bridge will perform as desired, in exchange for his wish that the townsmen throw the old man in the swamp. For the same formula in Horace, see *Odes* I 3.1ff. The Latin formula places the *sic* first where we would attach it to the second element: may the bridge turn out as you wish (*ex tua libidine*); so grant me this *munus*. **bonus** is predicate adjective with **fiat**: may the bridge be made good.

6 **Salisubsali**, etc.: alliteration for comic effect, imitating the shuffle of dancing feet. **suscipiantur** is a potential subjunctive with **vel**: even the rites of Salisubsalus (an unknown local deity) might be undertaken, etc.

7 **maximi risus**: gen. of description with **munus**.

8 **municipem meum** need not be taken literally, as if Catullus had a particular real person in mind, or a particular *municipium* such as Verona. Catullus could be highly personal in his attacks when he chose, but that is probably not his game in this poem, where his target is a comic type. **volo**: for the iambic shortening here and in line 23, see appendix C.

9 **per caputque pedesque**: head over heels.

10 **verum**, etc.: not just in the mud, but in the ugliest and deepest place has to offer. **ut**: where (as in 11.3).

12f. **pueri instar bimuli**: as much as a two-year-old.

13 **tremula**: rocking or shaking with the movements of one comforting an infant. The detail is interesting, as the simile has a father performing a traditionally maternal role.

14 **cum sit**: adversative, although; the subject is *puella*. **viridissimo ... flore**: abl. of description, metaphoric of her youth.

15 **delicatior haedo**: not more delicate, but more frisky than a kid; the idea of her tenderness is in the double diminutive *tenellulo*.

16 **nigerrimis**: very dark, hence ripe, soft, sweet, and juicy (like the young wife).

17 **pili facit uni**: gen. of value; he doesn't care a hair, as in 10.13. **uni** is an adjectival variant of *unius*.

18 **se sublevat**: rouse himself from his lethargy **ex sua parte**, on his own behalf; cf. *excitare* (24).

19 **Liguri ... securi**: abl. of means. Catullus makes the axe Ligurian to give the simile more specific color.

20 **tantundem ... quam si**: just as much as if. **nulla sit**: it didn't exist at all. For *nulla* as an emphatic negative, cf. 8.14, *tu dolebis, cum rogaberis nulla*.

22 **qui sit** = *quis sit*, euphonic to avoid the double *s*.

23 **pronum**: head first and face down, to cure him of his *supinum animum* (25).

24 **si pote** = *si pote est* or *si potest*, if that can arouse his dull senility.

26 **ferream ... soleam**: horses and mules had their shoes strapped on rather than nailed, with the result that such "iron sandals" could be sucked off in the mud. **ut**: sc. *derelinquit*. **mula**: for the emphatic final position of an abusive noun, cf. 37.20 *urina*, 39.21 *loti*, 57.9 *cinaedis*, 112.2 *pathicus*, 113.4 *adulterio*.

18–20

Muretus' 1554 edition of Catullus included three poems at this point that are not in the manuscripts: a four-line fragmentary dedication to Priapus included in Mynors' Oxford text as Catullus Fragment 1, and two poems of twenty-one lines each called *Priapea* traditionally attributed to Virgil. These (Priapea II and III, Bücheler 85 and 86) are part of the *Appendix Vergiliana*. See pp. 131–33 of the Oxford edition edited by Clausen, Goodyear, Kenney, and Richmond. Later editions of Catullus have omitted these poems while retaining Muretus' numbering.

21

Aurelius had been warned in poem 15 to keep his busy hands off Juventius (see appendix A). Once again Catullus states in bluntly explicit terms the dire consequences that await Aurelius if he misbehaves.

Meter: hendecasyllabics.

1 **Aureli**: see appendix B. **pater esuritionum**, father of appetites, is a mock honorific; the point is that like his crony Furius (in poem 23), Aurelius is perpetually out of money for groceries and a lecher to boot. For the grand-sounding three-word line, cf. 37.18 and 49.1 (to Cicero), *disertissime Remi nepotum.*

2–3 **non harum modo**, etc.: ironically fulsome, the same formula as in 24.2–3 and 49.2–3.

4 **pedicare**: a deliberately rude word after three lines of elaborate flattery. What Aurelius has in mind is a sexual invasion of Catullus' young male lover, we assume Juventius.

5 **nec clam**: sc. *cupis*: Aurelius' lust is obvious. **simul es**: sc. *una cum eo.*

6 **haerens ad latus**, etc.: Aurelius has, it seems, been cuddling up to Juventius at dinner parties (where diners reclined) and making blatantly sexual advances. Asyndeton reflects the rapid pace at which this hanky-panky progressed.

7 **mihi**: Catullus views Aurelius' intrigue with Juventius as a plot against himself.

8 **tangam te ... irrumatione**: while you are plotting against me, I'll touch you first with oral rape. For *irrumatio* as a way of humiliating another male, cf. 16.1 and 14, 28.10, 37.8.

9 **id**: i.e. Aurelius' carryings-on with Juventius. **satur**: with your belly full. This wouldn't be so bad if you could provide for yourself and Juventius.

10 **nunc**: as it is. **ipsum id**: emphatic: *this* is what bothers me.

12 **pudico**: sc. *tibi.* Quit while you can with the appearance of propriety, i.e. before I sully your oral virtue.

13 **ne finem facias**, etc.: lest you make an end of your actions, (not intact) but sexually humiliated. The placement of *irrumatus* at the end gives Catullus' threat special emphasis.

22

Suffenus is stylish about everything except the poems he writes, which make him look like a hick. His foolish incongruity is shrugged off with philosophical truisms at the end, but the damage has been done.

Meter: limping iambics (see appendix B).

1 **iste** implies that Catullus is in the middle of a conversation with his friend Varus (see appendix A) in which Suffenus' name has come up: that Suffenus you just mentioned.... **probe** means simply "well" in colloquial usage.

2 **venustus ... dicax ... urbanus** cover Suffenus' stylishness from three different angles, all highly approved by the *poetae novi* and others in the smart set. He has love-ly (*venus-tus*) manners, he speaks well, and he is thoroughly citified.

3 **idemque** is adversative, as in 25.4: but at the same time. **plurimos ... versus**: even the bulk of his writing is gauche.

4 **illi**: dat. of agent with the perf. participle.

5 **sic ut fit**: as it is [usually] done. **palimpsesto**: "scraped again" palimpsest is papyrus recycled by erasure. Paper was expensively handmade, and except for fine copies of carefully finished final drafts, palimpsest was the ordinary medium of preservation.

6 **cartae regiae**: a technical term for large sheets; cf. the modern bookmaker's royal octavo.

7 **umbilici** were the sticks with knobs on which the sheets were wound into *libri.* **lora** were thongs that tied the roll, **membranae** the parchment wrappers protecting the papyrus roll inside, an ancient form of dust jacket.

8 **derecta plumbo**: lined with lead marks to keep the lines of text straight. The papyrus roll was then evened up by rubbing with pumice stone (**pumice aequata**), as in 1.2.

9 **legas**: subjunctive of general statement. **bellus** is another word describing a "nice" person.

10 **unus** works like an indefinite article with **caprimulgus**, goatmilker, and **fossor**, ditchdigger.

11 **rursus**: on the contrary.

12 **scurra**, a wit, without the later buffoonish connotation preserved in our "scurrilous."

13 **aut si quid ... scitius**: for the construction, common in Catullus, see note on 13.10. The comparative **scitius** (from *scio*) = cleverer. **hac re**: i.e., than a *scurra.*

14 **idem** here and in 15 with the long ī is "the same person," its repetition calling attention to the split personality. *infacetus* is boorish, crude, unwitty.

18 **idem** with the short i = similarly.

19 The second foot is a tribrach, composed of three short syllables. The long syllable of the iamb is resolved into two shorts; cf. 37.5 and 59.3. **Suffenum**: predicate noun: as a Suffenus type.

21 **manticae**: partitive gen. with **quod**. we don't see what kind of knapsack is on our own back. The reference is to a fable of Aesop about a man

carrying two satchels, one containing his neighbors' faults in front, and the other containing his own on his back. He complains only of the faults he sees.

23

Catullus, who had no love for Furius (see appendix A), here refuses his request for a loan. Whether such a request was actually made is immaterial, only that it is made the occasion for a comical list of problems that Furius does *not* have. Like Porgy in Gershwin's opera, he's got plenty of nothing and nothing's plenty for him. Catullus turns a Stoic sermon into a big joke at Furius' expense.

Meter: hendecasyllabics.

1 **cui ... est:** dat. of possession. **arca:** a cash box, and by metonymy its contents. The phrase as a whole may be a tag from something Furius himself wrote, quoted here mockingly (as in 24.5, 8, 10). Poverty was a common pose of poets, even the wealthy Catullus (cf. 13.8), but for a prodigal like Furius, it would seem to be more than a pose.

2 **cimex,** etc.: Furius has no bed, and therefore no bedbug; no roof, hence no spider; no hearth, hence no fire.

3 **verum est:** sc. *tibi:* but you *do* have...

4 **dentes,** etc.: their teeth would be an index of their relative youth and good health.

5 **est pulcre tibi cum,** etc.: you are on good terms with your father, so it doesn't matter that you have no slave, cash, or house of your own. But as Catullus goes on to show, there is little to spare in the father's household.

6 **coniuge lignea:** a passing shot at Furius' skinny stepmother.

7 **nec mirum:** posing as Stoic moralist, Catullus reduces well-being to good health and an absence of immediate danger.

8 **pulcre concoquitis:** i.e. you all have good digestion. **nihil timetis:** the Stoics taught that decent poverty was an ideal condition because nobody would be plotting to rob or ruin you; absence of anxiety was tantamount to happiness. The argument is used here in mock seriousness.

12 **atqui:** what's more, ... **sicciora cornu:** cf. our expression "dry as a bone." The cause of this healthy dryness is no doubt a shortage of drink in the house.

16f. **sudor, saliva, mucus, pituita:** bodily humors whose excess would be a symptom of disease.

17 **Hanc ad:** the *ad* is postpositive; understand *Ad*

hanc.

19–23 As crowning evidence of Furius' excellent health, Catullus cites the paucity and condition of his bowel movements, which Furius is invited to examine closely and test manually.

25 **parvi:** gen. of value.

26 **sestertia ... centum:** 100,000 sesterces is a tidy sum, about the annual income of a man of middling wealth. **soles precari:** Catullus represents Furius' appeals as frequent and urgent (*precari* is a strong word).

27 **desine:** (with *sestertia*) lay off, stop talking about.

24

Catullus' boyfriend Juventius has been receiving the advances of Furius, the same person whose poverty Catullus made fun of in the previous poem. Here the poet chides his young friend with a reminder of his suitor's threadbare fortune. The tradition of the money-conscious boy companion comes from Hellenistic epigram.

Meter: hendecasyllabics.

1 **Iuventiorum:** Cicero names the Juventii as an old and distinguished family from Tusculum. For this Juventius, see appendix A.

2–3 **non horum modo,** etc.: for the honorific formula, cf. 21.2–3, 49.2–3.

4 **divitias Midae:** proverbial for endless wealth, like that of Croesus.

5 **isti:** Furius is unnamed in the poem. Catullus mocks him by assuming his poverty is as proverbial as Midas' wealth. The phrase **cui neque servus est neque arca** is in the opening line of poem 23, which names Furius. Here perhaps Catullus alludes to that poem, but it is also possible that the tag was known from a poem of Furius, fobbing off his wastrel's lack of funds as the poet's mantle of poverty.

6 **quam ... amari:** i.e. Catullus would rather Juventius gave Furius money than his love. **sic** indicates he has been giving his love.

7 **homo bellus:** a fine fellow, neat guy, handsome man.

8 **bello huic:** sarcastic: but *this* "neat guy" has nothing.

9 **abice elevaque:** i.e. minimize and dismiss his poverty all you like, he still (*tamen*) has neither slave nor coffer. Catullus closes with a third repetition of the offending phrase. The first syllable of *abice* is long by position, reflecting the suppressed

consonantal *i* of *ab(j)ice.*

25

Before the invention of modern power looms, any fabric was expensive, and some people (such as Asinius in poem 12, Thallus here, and Vibennius *père* in poem 33) could not keep from stealing whatever they could get their hands on. The humor in this poem lies in its colorful abuse of a flabby but rapacious social climber. Thallus' actual offense may have been worse than petty theft; if so, downgrading him to a linen snatcher is Catullus' crowning insult.

Meter: iambic tetrameter catalectic (see appendix B).

1 **Cinaede:** Catullus wastes no time getting into his abuse, starting with a sexual insult. Strictly speaking, a *cinaedus* or catamite takes the passive, submissive role in anal sex between men; generalized, the term refers to a homosexual prostitute willing to perform as required. **mollior** is one side of his character, **rapacior** (line 4) the other. The *cuniculus* was a small Spanish variant of the Italian hare, *lepus.*

2 **anseris medullula:** the diminutive makes this the softest part of the goose's marrow. **imula oricilla:** two diminutives (for *ima auris,* the earlobe) scornfully emphasize its flabbiness.

3 **situ ... araneoso:** cobwebbed decrepitude. *situs* is physical deterioration resulting from disuse.

4 **idemque** has an adversative force, as in 22.3.

5 Putnam describes **Murcia** as the "goddess of sloth and inactivity" who shows that the onlookers (**arbitros,** his fellow diners at a party) are yawning (**oscitantes**). A mock-epic way of saying the same thing as 12.3 *neglegentiorum.*

6 **pallium:** a rectangular Greek cloak, the *himation,* worn as an outer cloak. A diner would lay it aside (where it could be filched) before a meal. **involasti:** swooped down upon, like a bird of prey; see note on *unguibus* (9).

7 **sudarium ... Saetabum** as in 12.14 (see note). **catagraphos ... Thynos** are Bithynian embroideries, no doubt a souvenir of his year there in 57–6 B.C.

8 **palam ... tamquam avita:** Thallus adds insult to injury by flaunting his loot as if it were a collection of heirlooms.

9 **reglutina:** unglue (from your sticky fingers); but **unguibus** invites us to think of them as talons.

10 **laneum** orig. = woolly, here soft as wool, effem-

inate. **mollicellas** is another scornful diminutive.

11 **inusta:** metaphoric. The burned-in lashes will mark you disgracefully (**turpiter**), as if you were a slave.

12 **insolenter aestues:** you will burn in an unaccustomed way, with pain and embarrassment rather than desire. The simile at the end calls on another meaning of *aestuo:* he will toss about like a ship in a storm as he writhes in agony.

13 **vesaniente vento** plays off line 4, *turbida rapacior procella.*

26

A punning epigram at the expense of Furius (see appendix A), whose request for a loan was refused in poem 23.

Meter: hendecasyllabics.

1 **vestra:** Furius and his family, described in poem 23. One manuscript has *nostra* here, making the poem self-mockery at Catullus' own supposed poverty, as in 10.21–23 and 13.7–8.

1 **opposita:** both exposed to the wind, which would make it cold and drafty, and mortgaged for the sum of money in line 3.

3 **milia quindecim et ducentos:** 15,200 sesterces is not an astronomical sum. Cicero says that his client Caelius rented an apartment in Rome for 10,000 (*Pro Caelio* 17). But even this amount is *horribilis atque pestilens* to a man of Furius' weak finances.

27

A drinking epigram of a type later much favored by Horace, but the only one of its kind in Catullus. Originally composed by the sixth-century Greek poet Anacreon, such poems evoke the wine-women-and-song mood of the symposium or Greek stag party. The surprise here is that the master of revels is a woman.

Meter: hendecasyllabics.

1 **puer:** as usual in such contexts, the "boy" is a slave.

2 **inger** = *ingere.* **amariores:** more pungent because undiluted with water. Some readers have seen in *calices amariores* a reference to the theme of invective that is prominent in the polymetric poems which follow, 28–60.

3 **Postumiae magistrae:** it was usual to have a *magister bibendi* who would call the toasts and the strength of the wine, and whose instructions were

the *lex bibendi*. Postumia, otherwise unknown to us, may be put in this role because of her hard drinking, as *ebriosioris* in the next line confirms: she drinks like a man, it is implied.

5 **vos ... lymphae**: apostrophe to the water nymphs, who spoil the wine by diluting it (though it was normal to water the wine).

6 **severos**: as in 5.2.

7 **Hic**: sc. *calix*—as if he is raising his cup. **Thyonianus**: a nonce-word. Bacchus was called Thyoneus after his mother Thyone or Semele. The cup is pure Bacchic because it contains straight wine without the usual admixture of water.

28

A sympathetic verse epistle to Veranius and Fabullus, who are faring no better on Piso's staff in Macedonia than Catullus did under Memmius in Bithynia.

Meter: hendecasyllabics.

1 **Pisonis**: see appendix A. Veranius and Fabullus are a **cohors inanis** because they are empty-handed, but also because they would now feel foolish (inane) for having entered such unrewarding service.

2 **aptis sarcinulis** is abl. absolute; a *sarcina* is a soldier's pack; the diminutive makes it a skimpy one, as does **expeditis**, lightened as if for combat action. They went as administrative staff, but Piso is treating them like foot soldiers.

4 **quid rerum geritis?** is a colloquial greeting as early as Plautus.

5 **vappa**, orig. flat wine, becomes a masc. noun = dud. **-que et** has the same force as *et ... et*.

6 **ecquidnam**: the interrogative pronoun "does anything ...?" with the enclitic particle -**nam** adding emphasis, as in 10.8 *quonam*. It takes the partitive gen. **lucelli**.

6–7 **lucelli / expensum**: enjambment with a surprise. We would expect profit (*lucrum*, dim. *lucellum*) to be *acceptum* (gained) rather than **expensum** (paid out). See appendix C, paraprosdokia.

8 **refero datum lucello** is more bookkeeping language: I chalk up (**refero**) what was paid out (**datum**) by me as incidental expenses in Bithynia to the small-profit (**lucello**) side of my ledger (because I've learned my lesson about unprofitable tours of duty in the provinces).

9–10 Memmius, the governor of Bithynia under whom Catullus served in 57–56 B.C. (see appendix

A), gave him the shaft, as we would say. **irrumasti** is used loosely here with the phallic **tota ista trabe** to denote gross abuse. Cf. 10.12f., where Memmius is the *irrumator praetor*. **diu** (with **supinum**) and **lentus** (adverbial with **irrumasti**) refer to the long, slow months in Bithynia.

11–12 **pari ... casu**: ablative of description or quality; they were of an equal plight with Catullus.

12–13 **verpa farti estis**: sexual abuse again as a metaphor of general mistreatment. The instrument is phallic, the verb is from *farcio*, stuff, cram.

13 **pete nobiles amicos**: the singular verb suggests that this is typical worldly advice—the sort of thing a Polonius type would say to his son—quoted sarcastically.

14 **vobis**: Piso and Memmius.

15 **opprobria**: vocative, referring to Piso and Memmius. For the construction, cf. 3.13 *At vobis male sit, malae tenebrae*. Instead of the genitives *Romuli Remique*, English idiom uses a dative construction: disgraces *to* Romulus and Remus.

29

Roman looting of the provinces for personal profit and the resultant displays of gross private wealth shocked even the cynical Romans. This is the first of several attacks on Caesar's protégé Mamurra (see appendix A), and on Pompey and Caesar for harboring such a corrupt wastrel; written soon after Caesar's invasion of Britain in 55 B.C., and before the death of his daughter Julia (Pompey's wife) in 54. Iambic meter had been used since early Greek times as the medium of abuse. Its rapidity gives Catullus' attack a slashing, insistent ferocity.

Meter: iambic senarius, a pure iambic trimeter (see appendix B).

3 **comata Gallia**: transalpine Gaul, so called because its inhabitants wore their hair long.

4 **ultima Britannia** was naïvely pictured by the Romans as a land of vast silver and gold at the edge of the earth, much as the Spaniards pictured the New World. Unlike the Spaniards, the Romans soon learned otherwise.

5 **Romule**: a sarcastic nickname for Caesar or possibly Pompey, who as consul in 55 would have been in a position to check Mamurra's excesses. Other politicians with sweeping claims to power, such as Sulla and Cicero, had earlier been so labeled by their enemies. The additional epithet **cinaede** vaguely suggests sexual scandal, for which

see poem 57.

8 **columbus**: the pigeon, a traditional pet of Venus because of its strutting courtship displays (*perambulabit* in the previous line).

11–12 **Eone nomine**: was this the reason ...? **imperator unice**: more sarcasm aimed at Caesar, whose grand conquests at the edge of the earth (**ultima occidentis insula**) are wasted on a self-indulgent crony.

14 **ducenties**: a regular abbreviation of *ducenties centena milia sestertium*, 200 hundred thousand or 20 million sesterces' worth.

15 **Quid est alid**, etc.: What else is **sinistra liberalitas** [if this isn't] ? —the Latin equivalent of Eng. "What is this but gauche munificence?" but with a more ethical tint.

16 **parum**, etc.: the sense is: Hasn't he wasted enough?

18 **praeda Pontica**: loot from Pompey's campaign against Mithridates in 64–3 B.C.

19 **Hibera** [*praeda*]: from Caesar's 61 B.C. campaign in Lusitania (mod. Portugal), where Mamurra served as his chief engineer. Spain was Rome's chief source of gold for centuries.

20 **timetur**: impersonal, with dat. of the thing feared for.

21 the plural **fovetis**, coddle, includes Pompey and Caesar.

23 **piissimi**, if correct, is sarcastic overstatement, contrasting the sacrosanct bearing of Caesar and Pompey with the tackiness of their protégé Mamurra. Cicero made fun of Antony for using this fulsome superlative in 43 B.C., saying it wasn't even a Latin word. **urbis**: Rome, partitive gen. with *piissimi*, most dutiful in the city.

24 **soccer**: Caesar married off his daughter Julia to his rival Pompey in 59 B.C., thus pulling his teeth for a time by taking him as a son-in-law (**gener**); but the bond ended with Julia's death in 54. Catullus treats them as one happy family in their indulgence of Mamurra.

30

A poem of personal depression, accusing his friend Alfenus of some betrayal. Like his sexual love, Catullus' personal affection was intense (see for example poems 9 and 50) and no doubt demanding beyond the capacities of those he loved. He is as ready to express its low points as he is its joys.
Meter: greater Asclepiadean (see appendix B).

1 **Alfene**: see appendix A.

2 **miseret** is impersonal, taking the accusative of the person who feels pity and the genitive of the person pitied.

3 **iam ... non dubitas**, etc.: do you no longer hesitate to *prodere* and *fallere*.

5 **quae tu neglegis**: you regard your *facta impia* as having no consequence.

7 **iubebas** [me] **animam** [meam] **tradere**: deliberately strong language for "you asked for my trust."

8 **amorem**, like "love" in Shakespeare, does not necessarily imply sexual love. There is no evidence here, for example, to infer that Alfenus has gotten Catullus embroiled in some love affair with a woman and then refused to intercede for him when it went sour.

9 **Idem** is adversative, to emphasize the inconsistency between the Alfenus who won his confidence and the Alfenus who now draws back. **ac** links the main verbs **retrahis** and **sinis**.

11–12 **Fides, quae ... faciet**: Greek and Latin poets freely personified ideas as divinities. The prose word order here would be *Fides, quae faciet ut postmodo te facti tui paeniteat.*

12 **paeniteat**: another impersonal construction, with the accusative of the person who feels sorry and the genitive of the act regretted.

31

Another outpouring of feeling, like the preceding poem, but this time the emotion is joy on returning home from Bithynia in the summer of 56 B.C.
Meter: limping iambics (see appendix B).

1 **paene insularum**: still two words, but in effect a single noun. The peninsula named Sirmio, the site of Catullus' family villa, runs out into the Lago di Garda about twenty miles west of Verona in northern Italy.

3 **uterque Neptunus**: the god of lakes and the god of the sea.

5 **Thyniam ... Bithynos**: the Thyni and the Bithyni were two originally Thracian tribes who settled in what later became the Roman province in Asia Minor where Catullus served. Catullus plays on the Latin sense of the prefix *bi-*.

9 **fessi venimus**: poetic plural. **larem**: the tutelary god of the hearth, here metonymy for home.

11 **Hoc est quod unum est pro**: a forceful run of emphatic short words: this is the one and only

reward for ....

13 Lydiae ... undae: Etruscans, traditionally believed to be of Lydian origin, had settled in this region; hence the poetic usage, which gives an exotic flavor.

14 quidquid (or *quantum*) **est** + gen. is a favorite idiom with Catullus (cf. 3.2, 9.10, 37.4): whatever (of) laughing sounds you have at home. The traditional metaphor for the cheerful sound of splashing water appears again in 64.273.

32

Catullus the sexual animal fishes for an invitation from a lady friend. Ipsitilla is an independent courtesan, a hetaera with her own house where she entertains male callers as she pleases. Catullus makes no secret of his needs in angling for a postprandial visit.

Meter: hendecasyllabics.

1 amabo: idiomatic "please" with the imperative **iube**, this opener also suggests what Catullus has in mind.

2 deliciae, lepores: plural for singular, buttering her up before the imperative **iube**.

3 meridiatum: the supine in *-um* expresses purpose: properly, *meridiare* (< *meridies* = mid-day) means to take a siesta, but Catullus means to spend siesta time in a more animated way.

4 adiuvato: fut. imperative with acc. of specification **illud**, lit. you will also (*ad-*) help in the following way.

5 obseret tabellam: bar the door; the *liminis tabella* is the leaf of the double house-door usually left unbolted but closed to traffic during the siesta hour.

7 domi: at home, a rare locative form, regular with *domus*.

8 continuas: in a row. On this occasion it is not the quality but the prodigious quantity of sex that appeals to his mind.

9 verum si quid ages: the future: But if you *do* have other plans, **iubeto:** invite me [anyway]; another fut. imperative, picking up **iube** (3) and **iusseris** (4), lest Ipsitilla miss the point of the message.

10 pransus (from *prandeo*) in the active sense, I've lunched.

satur [et] supinus: comic asyndeton, full [and] flat.

11 pertundo: more comic exaggeration. What is pressing on the inside of his tunic and *pallium* will not bore a hole. **tunicamque palliumque** is a mock-

heroic variant of *et tunicam et pallium*.

33

A father and son named Vibennius come under the gun in these lines for crimes unknown. We can if we like take Catullus at his word that the father spent his time stealing apparel from the baths while his son made his way as a homosexual prostitute, but it is possible they had done something more personally offensive to Catullus.

Meter: hendecasyllabics.

1 furum ... balneariorum: the cost of handwoven fabric made theft an attractive opportunity at baths, where garments would be laid aside without close supervision. Cf. the napkin thief Asinius Marrucinus in poem 12 and Thallus in poem 25.

2 Vibenni, fili: vocative.

3 dextra ... inquinatiore: abl. of description with *est*, like *culo voraciore* in the next line; i.e., one can tell them apart because the father is the one with the more corrupt hand, the son the one with the more insatiable *culus*.

5f. exilium ... itis: a compressed construction, where *in* should be understood with *exilium* as well as *malas ... oras*. For such combinations, see appendix C, *apo koinou*.

7 natis pilosas: i.e., the son has outgrown his smooth-skinned boyhood, and his hairy backside is no longer marketable, even at a discount (*asse*).

34

A traditional hymn to Diana sung by unmarried boys and girls, probably intended for reading rather than actual performance.

Meter: six stanzas composed of three glyconics followed by a pherecratean (see appendix B).

1–4 the proem or introduction identifies the performers and the object of their praise. **Dianae:** a blend of the Italian spirit of the wild and the Greek Artemis. **in fide:** under the tutelage of; Artemis was the patron of the young. **integri:** unmarried, as appropriate to this goddess' ritual and their status as her protégés. The repetitions (eight of the stanza's thirteen words) lend a ritual tone.

5–12 invocation: the hymn formula calls for the naming and origin of the divinity and a recital of the places where she rules.

5 **Latonia**: adj., daughter of Latona (or Leto) and Jupiter.

7–8 **Deliam** ... **olivam** is in other versions a palm tree, clutched by Leto as she crouched to give birth: **deposivit**: *dropped* in English applies only to the birth of animals (a mare *drops* a foal); the form of the perfect tense is archaic, suggesting ritual language.

9–12 lists the wild places that are her domain. The succession of *u* and *m* sounds adds a note of solemnity.

9 **fores** = *esses* (see appendix D).

11 **saltuum**: "A *saltus* is wild, rough country with wood or scrub, grazed by hardy beasts and hunted for game" (Fordyce). **reconditorum** is hypermetric, eliding with the next word.

13–20 celebration: the traditional hymnic recital of the god's powers, emphasized by the triple repetition of **tu**. In these stanzas the emphasis is on her benefits to mankind.

13–14 **Lucina** ... **Iuno**: Juno in her capacity as aider of childbirth blends easily with Diana the patron of the young. This syncretism is a distinctive feature of Greek and Roman piety. **dolentibus** ... **puerperis**: women in the pain of childbirth.

15 **Trivia**: in this pre-Christian trinity, Diana/Lucina/Luna is nature goddess, goddess of childbirth, and moon goddess. Images of a triple goddess date back to Mediterranean prehistory.

15–16 **notho** ... **lumine** by your counterfeit light, because it is reflected from the sun.

17–18 **menstrui** / **metiens** plays on the etymological connection of these words: the *monthly* cycles of the moon *measure* the year's course, serving as a calendar for planting and harvesting.

21–24 prayer: beginning with the traditional escape clause that acknowledges any other names by which the goddess may like to be invoked, the hymn concludes with a simple request for her goodwill. The style is marked by strong hyperbaton: **Romuli** ... **gentem** and **bona** ... **ope**, in chiastic order.

22 **Romulique** is hypermetric, the final syllable eliding with the beginning of the next line.

23 **antique ut solita es**: another formula of prayer, reminding the goddess of past blessings.

24 **sospites**: jussive subjunctive, preserve thou, in an archaic and solemn liturgical form.

35

Caecilius has been writing a poem about the goddess Cybele, and Catullus asks him to come from Como to Verona for consultation about the work in progress. His beautiful girlfriend is madly in love with him (and his poem) and will hate to see him go, but she is not invited.

Meter: hendecasyllabics.

1 **poetae tenero**: Catullus has a marked tendency to begin his poems with a noun phrase identifying the person addressed or discussed. This dative phrase (indirect object of *dicas*) uses poets' jargon to identify Caecilius as a love poet: see vocabulary s.v. *tener* and appendix A.

2 **velim** ... **dicas**: optative subjunctives of polite request: I should like you to tell. A common epistolary formula, as in the letters of Cicero.

3 **Veronam**: to Verona; the preposition is regularly omitted with names of cities. **Novi** ... **Comi**: Comum had been refurbished in 59 and renamed Novum Comum when Caesar settled some 5,000 colonists there. Located at the southwestern tip of Lacus Larius (mod. Lago di Como), it lies about 100 miles west of Verona. **relinquens**, etc., is a formula from prayer invocations (see note on 61.27) urbanely pressed into service for a personal invitation.

5 **volo**: for the scansion, see appendix C on iambic shortening. **cogitationes**: thoughts, evidently about the poem Caecilius is working on. The polysyllablic line ending adds a note of mock pomposity.

6 **amici sui meique** probably = Catullus. The poet is slyly mysterious, like a conniving slave in a comedy.

7 **viam vorabit**: comic alliteration.

8: for **candida** as denoting female beauty, see note on 13.4 and cf. 86.1.

9 **euntem revocet**: calls him back as he goes. Catullus' compliment to Caecilius (and half of the poem's lines) concentrate good-humoredly on the passionate love of this *candida puella*, which he and his poem have inspired. He is indeed a *poeta tener*. **revocet** and **roget** are concessive subjunctives with *quamvis*; her supplications are in an imagined scene of departure.

12 **illum deperit**: she is dying (of love) for him: a comic idiom, as in Plautus and Terence. Cf. 45.5 *perire*, 64.119 *deperdita* (of a mother's love), 100.2 *depereunt*. **impotente**: violent (incapable of control), as in 4.18.

14 **Dindymi dominam**: i.e., Cybele, the Asiatic goddess whose worship Catullus himself describes

in poem 63: hence, no doubt, his particular interest. Catullus may be quoting the first words of the Caecilius poem, which would be used as a title. **eo:** sc. *tempore.*

15 **edunt:** we would use a present perfect, have been eating. For the language of this line, cf. 45.16, *ignis mollibus ardet in medullis.*

16–17 **ignosco tibi:** I don't blame you. **Sapphica ... doctior:** interlocked word order. "More learned than the Sapphic muse" is gallant hyperbole for "you have the soul of a poet," with emphasis on the learning (*doctior*) which the *poetae novi* and later the best Augustan writers considered essential to a poet's calling. Sappho (see appendix A) is appropriate because she was a woman and because of her love themes.

18 **Magna ... Mater:** an alternative title for the work in progress. **incohata,** echoing *incohatam* (13), may be taken as a gentle hint to Caecilius: the *"Magna Mater"* has been well begun, but it is not as well finished as his adoring *docta puella* believes.

36

Poem 35 was addressed to a sheet of papyrus; this is to the rolls on which Volusius' inept *Annales* are written. Catullus and Lesbia have quarreled, and she has made a vow to burn a selection of the "worst poet's" writings if she and Catullus can be reconciled and he stops writing nasty poems about her. The poems she has vowed to burn are, of course, by Catullus (attacking her), but Catullus proposes a more appropriate "worst poet" in the hapless Volusius, whose sheets are more fit for sacrifice.

Meter: hendecasyllabics.

1 **Volusi:** see appendix A. **cacata carta:** metaphoric for botched writing; humorous alliteration, as in "shitted sheets."

2 **votum solvite:** fulfill a vow.

5 **desissem:** from *desino.* **truces ... iambos:** the traditional meter of abusive verse, "iambs" came to be used loosely of any poetry of attack. Poem 37 (in limping iambics) is a good example of what Lesbia had in mind.

6 **electissima:** the most select—not, in this case, for their poetic value, but for their potential to damage Lesbia's reputation. **pessimi poetae:** the operative language of Lesbia's vow: she meant Catullus while Catullus himself believes they fit Volusius better.

7 **tardipedi deo:** Vulcan, the lame god of fire.

daturam = *se daturam esse*, indirect statement with *vovit* (4). The periphrasis, the overdone alliteration of *p-* and *d-*sounds, and the compound adjective *tardipedi* parody the trite "high" style of poets like Volusius.

8 **infelicibus ... lignis:** in ritual, the wood of unproductive trees was used to burn evil prodigies; the trees themselves were considered suitable for hanging criminals. **ustulanda:** gerundive expressing purpose after *daturam* (Allen & Greenough §500.4), to be burnt.

9 **pessima ... puella:** Catullus' revenge for *pessimi poetae* (6). **vidit:** she perceived that she was making a witty or clever vow. The verb governs indirect statement *hoc ... se ... lepide vovere*

10 **iocosis divis:** since Homer, Venus had been laughter-loving; Cupid is included here (line 3).

11–17: a mock-formal prayer to Venus, with no fewer than seven haunts listed, from which it was customary to summon the divinity invoked. Cf. 61.27f. and note. The formula, deliberately exaggerated to make fun of Volusius, belongs to the hymn; we are to imagine the poet solemnly preparing the ritual of burning.

11 **caeruleo creata ponto:** follows the myth of Venus' birth from the sea foam.

12 **Idalium,** like Amathus and Golgi, was a town in Cyprus where a sexual goddess identifiable with Venus/Aphrodite/Astarte had been worshipped since prehistory. **Urios** may be the bay of Urias on the "spur" of the Italian boot, or the town of Uria in Calabria between Tarentum and Brundisium. It is called **apertos,** a common geographical term for open terrain.

13 **Ancona** (Gk. *Ancon*), about 140 miles northeast of Rome on the Adriatic coast, was an old Greek colony whose coinage represented the head of its patron goddess Venus. **Cnidum:** situated at the end of a long peninsula on the southwest corner of Asia Minor, Cnidus celebrated its cult of the Asiatic love goddess with a statue of Aphrodite by Praxiteles that was famous throughout the ancient world. Pliny mentions its export of reeds (whence Catullus' *harundinosam*). For the *quaeque ... quaeque* formula in addresses to Venus, cf. 64.96.

15 **Durrachium Hadriae tabernam:** opposite Brundisium on the Illyrian coast (mod. Durrësi, Albania), was an important stopoff for sea traders—hence the inn of the Adriatic, as its boosters would have called it.

16 **face** = the imperative *fac*. The terminology of

acceptum face is close to the jargon of accounting, enter as received.

17 **illepidum neque invenustum**: as in 10.4, and cf. line 10 above. Style in all things was of the essence for Catullus and his circle. Its opposite is represented by the verses of Volusius, *pleni ruris et infacetiarum* (line 19).

20: For the elegant rounding off of a poem by repeating the first line, cf. poems 16, 52, 57.

37

Catullus pillories the lecherous loafers who infest the tavern where Lesbia spends her time, and who take advantage of her promiscuity. Special attention is paid at the end to the Spaniard Egnatius.

Meter: limping iambics (see appendix B).

1 **salax** is vocative: the apostrophe personifies the tavern, which takes on the lascivious character of its denizens; **contubernales**, tentmates, comrades-in-arms, plays on the common origin of *tabernaculum*, tent, and *taberna*, inn or tavern.

2 **pilleatis fratribus**, the capped brothers, are Castor and Pollux, who were often represented in art wearing felt caps. Their temple was near the southeastern end of the Forum. The **nona ... pila** was a pillar, like a barber pole, advertising the tavern, one of many in this part of town.

3 **solis ... vobis**: dative of possession with **esse**. The echoing of **putatis** in *putare* (5), *putatis* (7), and *putate* (10) contrasts what these loafers suppose with what they should consider.

4 **quidquid est puellarum**: for the *quantum* or *quidquid est* + partitive gen. construction, see note on 3.2.

5 **confutuere**: the prefix denotes thoroughness. The second half of the first foot is resolved into two short syllables. See on *resolution* in appendix C. **hircos**: he-goats, distasteful to women. These lechers have a high opinion of their own sexual magnetism.

7 **an ducenti?**: or two hundred, perhaps?

8 **una ducentos irrumare** must of course be understood less literally than as a figure of speech. Line 10 tells what he will really do. **sessores**, sitters or loungers, echoing *sedetis* (6) and anticipating *consedit* (14), tells what barflies really do most of the time. The poem contrasts their conceited indolence with Catullus' angry energy.

10 **sopionibus**, "dicks," is vernacular, a word found elsewhere only in graffiti. Catullus threatens to mark up the wall with graffiti picturing *sopiones*.

11 **mi**: dative of reference or disadvantage.

12: adapted from 8.5 but with an ironic twist, referring now to her promiscuity.

13 **mihi**: dat. of agent, as often with perf. participles.

14 **istic**: in this dive of yours. **boni beatique**, fine and well-to-do, refers to Lesbia's upper-crust lovers.

16 **pusilli et semitarii moechi** are the small-time punks and alleyway sex maniacs who constitute Lesbia's less glamorous partners.

18 **cuniculosae**, etc.: Egnatius' part of Spain was known for its long-haired rabbits; the epithet is fitting because his hair is long, too (17 *une de capillatis*), as was fashionable in certain foppish circles. For the mock-honorific vocative phrasing, cf. 21.1 and 49.1. **Celtiberiae**: Celtiberia, so-called because of its mixture of Celts and native Iberians, lay south of the Hiberus (mod. Ebro) river in northeastern Spain. Its long resistance to Roman rule had been crushed with the sack of Numantia in 133.

19 **bonum**: "good" in the social sense, that is of the monied class. The tone here is ironic.

20 **urina**: positioned for emphasis. Two ancient sources (Diodorus 5.33.5 and Strabo 3.164) confirm that the Celtiberians did in fact keep their smiles white by this bizarre method. See also 39.17–19.

38

An appeal to a friend for a scrap of poetry to alleviate his mental distress. It is possible to read something less than total despair between the lines of this poem.

Meter: hendecasyllabics (see appendix B).

1 **malest** (*male est*) a colloquial way of referring to physical illness, but here probably mental depression. **Cornifici**: a literary friend; see appendix A.

2 **me hercule**: a common mild oath, somewhat colloquial and without strong reference to Hercules. There is hiatus after **hercule**, as often after expletives.

3 **magis magis**: more and more; **in dies**: each day.

4 **quem**: i.e., Catullus. **quod**: relative pronoun, referring to *solatus es allocutione*.

5 **qua ... allocutione**: what word of comfort? The tone of this rhetorical question is perhaps one of mock petulance.

6 **Sic meos amores?** A colloquial omission of the verb suggests vexed impatience: Is this the way you repay my affection?

7–8: Catullus again omits the verb, for which we must understand something like *mitte*, with *paulum allocutionis* as object. **quid lubet** is indefinite: anything you like. **Simonideis**, in the position of emphasis, tells what kind of *allocutio* Catullus is angling for: not a bit of comforting speech, but a bit of comforting sad poetry (for which Simonides was famous). Like Aristotle, who said in the *Poetics* that the pity and fear of tragedy were a remedy for similar anxieties in an audience, Catullus believes that some sad lines from Cornificius will purge his own depression.

19 **russam** is a rare word, used here proleptically: to scour the gum until it is red, suggesting that the process is as harsh as it is disgusting; **defricare** contrasts with *lavit* (14).

20–21 **quo ... expolitior ... hoc ... amplius**: ablatives of degree of difference with comparatives, the usual construction: the more polished that tooth of yours is, the more it proclaims .... The **dens** is collective, because in line 1 Catullus used the plural *candidos dentes*. **bibisse ...loti** maliciously exaggerates, making an already weird custom even more foul. For the emphatic placement of the final word, cf. 37.20, *urina* and note on 17.26.

39

Egnatius, the hairy Spaniard who participates in Lesbia's adventurous sex life and brushes his teeth with urine (37.17–20), gets a second roasting here. *Meter*: limping iambics (see appendix B).

2–7: four repetitions of **renidet**, beams, tell the story. He wears the same foolish grin no matter how inappropriate the situation, because it shows off his shining teeth. The quacking sounds of **usquequaque**, repeated in line 15, also make their point.

2–3 **rei ... subsellium**, the defendant's bench was a scene of dramatic appeals for pity in theatrical Roman trials.

2–5 **ventum est ... lugetur**: impersonal passives: if someone has gone, ... if there is mourning, ...

5 **unicum** is substantive, her only son.

9 **monendum est te mihi**: an uncommon impersonal construction in which the passive periphrastic takes an accusative direct object along with the usual dative of agent, I must warn you.

10 **urbanus** in the strict sense here means a man from the city of Rome. Being a Spaniard, Egnatius is not in this sense *urbanus*.

10–13 **Sabinus ... Tiburs ... Umber**, etc.: provincials from other cities in Italy, like Catullus himself (*Transpadinus*, line 13). The part of Cisalpine Gaul lying north of the Po river was not granted full Roman citizenship until 49, after the death of Catullus.

14 **puriter lavit dentes**: that is, who brushes with clean water.

15 **nollem**: an ironically polite potential subjunctive: I wouldn't want you to ....

17–19: an authentic custom; see note on 37.20.

18 **quod**: obj. of **minxit** (<*meio*). **hoc**: instrumental abl.

40

Somebody named Ravidus has been paying attention to Lesbia (or Juventius), and Catullus brings his iambics to bear on him. These lines are especially reminiscent of a Greek poem by Archilochus (172 West), the seventh-century father of iambic verse. For the meaning of "iambics" as used in this poem, see appendix C. *Meter*: hendecasyllabics.

1 **mala mens**: evil delusion, as in 15.14. **miselle**: contemptuous diminutive (cf. 80.7 *miselli*), with erotic overtones. **Ravide**: pron. *Raude*, with two syllables.

3 **tibi**: dat. of agent with *advocatus*, of reference with *excitare*. **non bene advocatus**: invoked with an incorrect formula, and thereby offended. The ancient belief was that any slight error of ritual could spoil a prayer and bring disfavor.

5 **An ut**, etc.: an incredulous question: Are we to suppose you did this to attract notoriety?

6: a variation of the previous line.

7 **meos amores**: in 15.1 and 21.4, this phrase refers to Juventius; but in 6.16 *tuos amores* is Flavius' girlfriend, and the context of this poem, after the satire on Lesbia's admirer Egnatius, argues that the love is Lesbia.

8 **longa ... poena**: because this lampoon will not be quickly forgotten. There may be a wicked pun here on *pēne*, though that noun is masculine.

41

An attack on Mamurra (the *decoctor Formianus* of line 4) via his alleged girlfriend, a hustler named Ameana who charges an outrageous 10,000 sesterces a trick.

Meter: hendecasyllabics.

1 **puella**: repeated in lines 3, 5, 7.

2 **tota milia ... decem** (sc. *sestertium*): all of 10,000 sesterces. This was a year's rent for a small apartment in Rome (Cicero *Pro Caelio* 17), but small change compared with the fortune of 20 million that Catullus says Mamurra ran through (29.14).

3 **turpiculo ... naso**: a slightly disgusting nose (abl. of description), one of several defects that Catullus lists in poem 43.

4 **decoctoris**, etc.: the same line is repeated in 43.5. Mamurra of Formiae was filthy rich; calling him a bankrupt is a way of highlighting his prodigal spending habits.

5 **Propinqui**, etc.: an apostrophe in mock alarm to Ameana's relatives. **quibus est ... curae**: dat. of reference + dat. of purpose, a double dative construction.

7–8: she is not accustomed to asking her mirror (*aes imaginosum*) what kind of goods she is (*qualis sit*, indirect question). Mirrors were made of polished bronze. Given her looks, she is overpricing herself.

hideous little dog.

11–12 **putida** rotten. **codicillos** = *pugillaria*. The word order is varied in a chiastic pattern.

13 **assis facis**: gen. of value, as in 5.3 and 10.13. She shrugs off their abuse, and Catullus gropes for worse epithets: mud (**lutum**), and no longer just a *moecha* but an entire whorehouse (**lupanar**).

14 **si ... quid**: after *si, nisi, ne*, and *num*, the indefinite pronoun is *quis, quid*. For the construction, cf. 13.10, 22.13, 23.13, 82.2, 4. **perditius**: more depraved.

15 **est ... putandum**: the gerundive, expressing necessity.

16 **quod** acts as a connective particle: so. **potest**: sc. *fieri*. She is unmoved by the demonstration so far.

17 **canis**: the tradition was that dogs are shameless; hence her face is like iron, **ferreo ... ore.**

21 **nihil** is adverbial with **movetur**, whose subject is "she."

22 **vobis**: dat. of agent with the gerundive **mutanda est.**

23 **siquid**: *si quid* is sometimes written as a single word.

42

Catullus marshals a gang of hardy hendecasyllables to harass an unnamed woman until she returns some notebooks of his. The humor of the poem is in personifying the lines of poetry as street toughs hired to conduct a *flagitatio*, in which the victim is publicly embarrassed by noisy abuse until a demand (such as a debt) is satisfied. There is also a surprise at the end.

Meter: hendecasyllabic, of course.

3 **moecha turpis**: abuse is the natural talent of hendecasyllabic lines; Catullus sets the mood for them by calling the offending woman a foul slut, lit. adulteress.

4–5 **vestra .. pugillaria**: the wax-coated wooden tablets, held together by laces, are "yours" because they contain lines of hendecasyllabic verse, fellows of the gang Catullus addresses.

6 **reflagitemus**: hortatory subjunctive, demand them back.

8 **turpe**: neuter acc., used adverbially. **incedere**: simply "walk." Catullus is suggesting they mock her by imitating her disgusting (**turpe**) way of walking. **mimice**: like a *mima* or actress.

9 **catuli Gallicani**: she tries to smile like a celebrity, but succeeds only in looking like a particularly

43

In poem 41 Catullus called attention to the high price Ameana charges for her favors. Here he concentrates on a wider range of defects: besides her colossal nose (adverted to in 41.3), there are ugly feet, washed-out eyes, stubby fingers, a runny mouth, and on top of it all, you should hear her talk. The real butt of all this humor, though, may be the foul Mamurra, whose *amica* she is made out to be.

Meter: hendecasyllabics.

1 **Salve**: a sarcastic greeting. **nec minimo ... naso**: litotes, with abl. of description, a structure continued for all seven of her repulsive features.

2 **nec bello pede**: perhaps as in the 1936 Benson & Fisher song, "Your Feet's Too Big."

3 **longis digitis**: ancient Greek vase paintings exaggerated the length of women's fingers as a mark of beauty.

4 **elegante lingua**: this has been variously understood as the way she shows her tongue (Ellis), her disfigured speech (Merrill), or the things she says (Fordyce). Catullus' vagueness allows us to use our own imagination.

5: the repetition of the fourth line from poem 41 (to which see note) allows him to avoid naming either Ameana or Mamurra.

6 ten = *te* + interrogative *-ne*. **provincia** brings big-city snobbery to bear: are you what they consider *bella* in the backwoods?

7 Lesbia nostra: for the use of Lesbia as a standard of comparison, cf. poem 86.

44

Sestius has sent Catullus a copy of his speech attacking a politician named Antius, along with an invitation to dinner. The idea, it seems, was that Catullus would come to the dinner party with nice things to say about Sestius' forthcoming speech. Not wanting to miss this dinner (at which no expense would be spared), Catullus read the speech, which was so bad that it gave him a cold and he had to go to his country house to recover. The story is put in the form of a letter of thanks to his villa.

Meter: limping iambics (see appendix B).

1 Sabine, Tiburs: vocative adjectives, Sabine or Tiburtine. Tibur (mod. Tivoli) was a fashionable address for summer homes; beyond it lay Sabine country, which was considered outside the pale and lacking in class. Catullus' place was in between, near the edge of town.

2–3 quibus ... cordi: double dative, dat. of reference + dat. of purpose. People who want to put down Catullus say his villa is out in the sticks, while his friends swear it is at Tibur.

4 quovis pignore: i.e., they would bet anything.

6 fui libenter: idiomatic, it was a pleasure to be. **suburbana**: about eighteen miles east of Rome.

8 non inmerenti ... mihi: with *dedit*. He deserved to suffer because his *venter*, hell-bent on *sumptuosas cenas*, overruled his better judgment.

10 Sestianus ... conviva: a dinner guest of Sestius (see appendix A). When it denotes continuous action, **dum** regularly takes the present instead of the imperfect.

11 in Antium: with *oratio*, *in* + acc. = against (as in Cicero's orations *In Catilinam*). **petitorem**: an office seeker, i.e., a candidate for election. Antius is otherwise unknown.

13 frigida: a dull piece of rhetoric was called frigid because it would fail to warm up an audience. Sestius' speech was frigid enough to give Catullus a cold.

15 otioque et urtica: zeugma; the *-que et* combination is poetic. Nettle was a common cough remedy.

16 grates is a solemn, archaic alternative for *gratias*.

17 non es ulta: the subject is *villa* (line 7), having changed from the farm itself (*fundus*, line 1). The villa has forgiven its master's *peccatum* (lines 8–9).

18–19 nec deprecor ... quin, etc.: I have no objection to Sestius (rather than me) getting a cold for his sins. **recepso** is an archaic future in *-so*, regular in Greek and common in Plautus, where it emphasizes the result of an action.

21 tunc ... cum: confirms the innuendo of 10–12, *dum volo esse conviva ... legi*, i.e., he invites me only on condition I have read his stuff (and am prepared to praise it).

45

A scene of mutual love between a Roman man (with an appropriately Roman name, Septimius) and a woman whose name Acme suggests her Greek origin and perfect beauty (Gk. *akmé* = prime, flower, zenith). Much of the poem's interest lies in its portrayal of character. He thinks of love in terms of power, adventure, and empire, she in terms of fidelity, ardor, and pleasure. We are probably meant to think of her as an independent freedwoman, possibly a hetaera, rather than a prospective bride of the same class as Septimius. This is the affinity of opposites. The romantic scene here can be contrasted with the more physical one requested with Ipsitilla in poem 32.

Meter: hendecasyllabics.

1. Acmen: Greek accusative. **amores**: girlfriend, as usual in Catullus (cf. 6.16, 10.1).

3–7 ni...amo...veniam is a type of simple condition in which the protasis (**ni...amo**) is indicative and the apodosis (**veniam**) is an optative subjunctive, expressing a wish. **perdite**: desperately, to perdition.

5 quantum qui pote, etc., is colloquial ellipsis for *quantum is amat qui potest plurimum perire*. **pote** = *potest*, an archaism in informal speech. **perire**: as a figure of speech, to "die" for love, reminding us of **perdite** above. Note the *p* sounds here and earlier (*perdite ... porro ... paratus*), which suggest emphatic statement.

7 caesio: with **leoni**, grey-eyed or more appropriately (given the imprecision of Latin color terms) green-eyed.

8–9 Amor, etc.: this refrain, repeated in lines 17–18, divides the poem into three main sections. Its general sense, that an attendant Cupid sneezes (pf.

sternuit) as an omen of approval, is clear. But the reference to a previous sneeze on the left (**sinistra ut ante**) is confusing. Since the scene represents a Greek woman (for whom an omen on the right was lucky) with a Roman man (who would take an omen on the left to be lucky), Cupid's sneezes can be understood as a green light for both parties. Voss, suspecting that the affair was not always as harmonious as it is now, emended lines 9 and 17 to *Amor, sinister ante*: "previously adverse," making this a reconciliation scene like the lovers' dialogue in Horace (*Odes* 3.9). But it is unlikely the refrain as transmitted in Catullus' poem refers to an earlier falling-out.

10 **reflectens**: raising her head; she has been lying with her head in Septimius' lap (2, *in gremio*).

11 **dulcis** is gen. with **pueri**.

12 **illo** puts special emphasis on those rosy lips; **purpureo** is another imprecise color term, not the bluish red that the cognate suggests to us. Fordyce calls attention to the sensuous, broad vowel sounds of this line.

14 **domino ... serviamus**: as an independent woman she sees love as service not to her lover but to the god of love.

15 **maior acriorque**: she caps his protestation of love with her own of an even fiercer passion. The explosive emphasis of Septimius' *pote plurimum perire* (line 5) has its counterpart here in Acme's liquid sounds, *multo mihi maior acriorque... mollibus ardet in medullis*.

16: cf. 35.15 *ignes interiorem edunt medullam*, also of a woman's love, and 51.9–10, *tenuis sub artus / flamma demanat..*

20 **amant amantur**: for the asyndeton, cf. 32.10, *satur supinus*.

21 **misellus**: dim. of *miser*, of lovesickness as in 35.14.

22 **mavult**: desires more (from *malo*). **Syrias Brittaniasque**: generalizing plural. The places are appropriately remote and fabulous, but they are also appropriate for a young Roman of the time with one eye on the Empire: Caesar campaigned in Britain in 55 and 54 B.C., Crassus set out east against the Parthians late in 55.

24 **facit delicias**: takes her pleasure, as in 74.2. The passions are intense, their satisfaction pleasantly simple.

46

In spring of 56 B.C. Catullus' tour of duty in Bithynia was finished, and he was ready to return home. This poem about spring restlessness soon to be satisfied by travel records the pleasures of anticipation.

Meter: hendecasyllabics.

1 **Iam**, four times at the beginning of a line, provides the note of immediacy; **egelidos ... tepores**, unchilled warmth, is another case of redundancy for emphasis.

2 **aequinoctialis**: the spring equinox (in the third week of March) was notorious for stormy weather in the Mediterranean.

3 **Zephyri**: the warm gentleness of the west wind was axiomatic.

4–5 **linquantur**: hortatory or jussive subjunctive. **Phrygii**: Phrygia included the western part of Bithynia, where Catullus was stationed. Nicaea (line 5), the capital of Bithynia, was an important city in late antiquity. The Christian Nicene Creed is named after the Council of Nicaea in 325 A.D., when it was written. Nicaea became sweltering (**aestuosae**) in the summer months.

6 The **claras Asiae ... urbes** would have included Pergamon, Smyrna, Sardis, and Ephesus, which are once again tourist attractions.

9 The **dulces comitum ... coetus** are the friends who served with him on Memmius' staff, and were also about to leave.

10 **longe ... a domo**: with *longe*, use of the preposition before *domo* is normal.

11 **diversae varie viae** is another redundancy, emphasizing the variety of scenic routes home that Catullus' friends were taking. Tourism was a valued privilege of the well-to-do.

47

Veranius and Fabullus, addressed in poem 28 while on duty under Piso, have been so poorly rewarded that they have to cadge dinner invitations in the street. Two others in his entourage are throwing lavish parties.

Meter: hendecasyllabics.

1 **Porci et Socration**: two nobodies, otherwise unknown. Porcius, notwithstanding its piggish connotations, was an eminently respectable name; "little Socrates" is a mystery. **sinistrae**: Piso's "left hands" would presumably have been up to no good, like Piso himself (see appendix A).

3 **vos**: emphatic by position, as in line 5: are *you* the ones he preferred to Veranius and Fabullus? **Veraniolo**: the diminutive indicates affection, as in 12.17.

4 **verpus ... Priapus ille**: that prick. Figures of the grossly phallic Priapus were used in gardens as a kind of scarecrow; calling the otherwise unnamed Piso by that name suggests his sexual excesses, which were faithfully chronicled by Cicero.

6 **de die**: from daytime on, beginning during working hours. Having helped with Piso's dirty work, they no longer need to work for a living.

7 **vocationes**: invitations; not found elsewhere in this sense, but in the empire slaves specializing in the delivery of invitations were called *vocatores*.

48
A love epigram to Juventius, on the same theme as poems 5 and 7 to Lesbia. The emotional content is delivered in a symmetrical package of two conditional statements: protasis A (lines 1–2), apodosis A (3), apodosis B (4), protasis B (5–6).
Meter: hendecasyllabics.
1 **Mellitos**: cf. 99.1, *mellite Iuventi*. Lesbia's sparrow was her *mellitus*, 3.6. **oculos**: on the kissing of the eyes, cf. 9.9, 45.11–12.
2–3 **sinat ... basiem**: present subjunctives in a future less vivid (should ... would) condition. The second statement (4–6 *videar ... sit*) is the same construction in reverse.
3 **milia ... trecenta**: cf. 9.2 *milibus trecentis*; for 300 as the formula for a large number, cf. also 11.18, 12.10, 29.14.
4 **nec numquam**: a pleonastic negative, = *nec umquam*; cf. 76.3 *nec ... nullo*. **videar ... futurus** = *mihi videar futurus esse*.
5–6: the repetition of *s* sounds suggests whispering, and the swishing of ripe grain in a field.

49
An elaborately fulsome poem of thanks to Cicero for some favor. Five superlatives give the poem a hyperbolic tone. Cicero was always generous with self-praise, and many readers detect a note of irony in Catullus' lines.
Meter: hendecasyllabics.
1: The three-word line is solemn and formal, like the opening of an honorary citation. Cf. 21.1 *Aureli, pater esuritionum*.

2 **fuere**: for this abbreviation of *fuerunt* and similar abbreviated forms, see appendix D. **Marce Tulli**: also formal and ceremonial, not the ordinary style of address. The triple repetition of **quot** adds to the insistent hyperbole of the poem as a whole. The present-past-future formula is used also in 21.2–3 and 24.2–3.
5–6 **pessimus omnium poeta** goes beyond the self-deprecation of poem 1, where he called his poems *nugas*. Its ostensible purpose here is to magnify Cicero by comparison.
7 **optimus omnium patronus**: a possible *double entendre*: taking **omnium** with **patronus** instead of with **optimus** changes the meaning from "best of all patrons" to "excellent patron of everybody," reminding the reader that Cicero was known to change sides in his political maneuvers, defending persons he had previously prosecuted.

50
A verse epistle to Licinius Calvus (see appendix A) on the morning after a day spent writing verses together: "a glimpse of the *poetae novi* at play" (Fordyce). The excitement has left him sleepless, and the resulting poem gives us further insight into a passionate and affectionate personality.
Meter: hendecasyllabics.
2 **lusimus** (cf. line 5 **ludebat**) emphasizes the playful aspect of poetry that the *poetae novi* especially valued. The verb became the regular term for the composition of light verse. **tabellis** are waxed wooden tablets, called *pugillaria* and *codicilli* in poem 42.
3 **convenerat**: impersonal, it had been agreed. **delicatos** covers a range of meanings, including frisky, risqué, elegant, naughty, erotic.
4 **versiculos**: the diminutive makes them short pieces, such as epigrams. **nostrum** is partitive gen. pl. with *uterque*, each of us.
5 **numero**: in meter. **illoc** = *illo* (with **numero**). The deictic -c suffix survived in regular Classical Latin only in *hic, haec, hoc* and adverbs such as *huc, illuc*, etc.
6 **reddens mutua**: "giving and taking" (Fordyce), taking turns with a given subject, trying to outdo each other.
7–8 **lepore ... facetiisque** restates the point of **lusimus** and **delicatos**. Catullus is excited by Licinius' charm and cleverness with words. What the *poetae novi* loved was not grandeur but wit.

9 **miserum** is one of several words describing Catullus' excited condition which could be misread as describing anger or pain. Cf. **incensus** (8), **furore** (11), **dolorem** (17). The words are chosen to denote instead an intense, elevated mood in which pleasure and opposites such as pain and rage are not far apart. There are also erotic undertones, which add intensity to Catullus' confession (see note on *miser*, 8.1).

11 **toto** goes with **lecto** in a chiastic word order, but there is a slight zeugma with **furore**. The confusion is intentional.

12 **versarer** is a passive with middle or reflexive force: I tossed and turned.

14 **labore** is both the physical labor of tossing and turning all night and the mental stress that caused it. See note on **miserum** above. **postquam**, etc.: for a similar emergence into lucidity after a period of frenzy, cf. the awakening of Attis in 63.44–46.

17 **perspiceres** with the intensive prefix = fully appreciate, discern.

18–21 **cave** ... **cave** ... **caveto**: a mock solemn warning lightens the tone at the end. The second syllables scan short due to iambic shortening (see glossary). **sis** and **despuas** are subjunctives of prohibition depending on **cave**; the ellipsis of *ne* is common after *cave*.

20 **Nemesis** is the goddess who enforces fair dealing and reciprocity.

21 **ve(he)mens** has been syncopated. The fut. imperative **caveto** takes **laedere** as object, an alternative form of prohibition.

51

A free translation of an ancient poem in Greek by Sappho (LP 31), perhaps inspired by the poet's first love for the woman he names Lesbia in honor of Sappho of Lesbos, the celebrated woman who wrote love poetry ca. 600 B.C. (see appendix A). It contrasts the happiness of someone sitting close to Lesbia with his own traumatic symptoms, and adds a stanza not in the original poem of Sappho berating his own idleness as the source of this suffering. *Meter*: Sapphic strophe (see appendix B).

2 **si fas est**: a Roman word of caution, as it was not fitting to be superior to the gods.

3 **identidem** (*idem et idem*): again and again, continually (as in 11.19).

7: **super** is the adverb; **est super** = *superest*, remains.

8: **vocis in ore**: Doering's restoration. The original poem of Sappho supports the guess that this line, missing in the manuscript, includes the word *vocis*, gen. with **nihil** in line 7. He is tongue-tied.

9–11 **torpet** ... **demanat** ... **tintinnant** ... **teguntur**: four verbs in asyndeton, emphasizing the multiple symptoms of love's crippling power. They are like the symptoms of fear described by Catullus' contemporary Lucretius, *De Rerum Natura* 3.152ff.

10 **flamma demanat**: a double metaphor of sexual passion, both fire and liquid. In traditional Greek thought, love entered through the eyes and percolated through the body. So here: *simul te ... aspexi* (6–7). **suopte**: the emphatic particle -pte is not necessarily translatable.

11 **gemina**: the meter requires that we take this with the abl. **nocte** rather than the nom. **lumina** (eyes), which we/would have expected.

13–16: this stanza is not inspired by Sappho's original poem. It is rather Catullus' Roman conscience speaking, rebuking him for the idleness (**otium** ... **otio** ... **otium**) that makes him prey to these feelings.

14 **otio**: abl. with **exsultas**

52

An angry epigram aimed at two of Caesar's political hacks, installed in high office by the triumvirs in 55 or 54 B.C. Nonius is not identifiable with certainty; Vatinius, whose prosecution by Calvus is the subject of poem 53, was made praetor and promised the consulship in return for his services to Caesar and Pompey; for some time he had been bragging about his future exploits as consul. See appendix A.

Meter: iambic trimeter (see appendix B).

1 **Quid est?**: an indignant question—What's going on?

2 **sella in curuli**: the curule chair could be used by consuls, praetors, curule aediles, and censors as well as two or three other high officials. No one named Nonius is listed as having held any of the positions named, but Cicero mentions a M. Nonius Sufenas as a supporter of the triumvirs. **struma**: a tumor, appropriate as an epithet of an unsightly parasite on the body politic.

3 **per consulatum peierat** probably refers to Vatinius' exploitation of a consular rank that he had not yet obtained. He is said to have prattled about his *second* consulship years before he attained even his

first (Cicero *In Vatinium* 11).

53

A humorous tribute to Licinius Calvus (see appendix A), whose speech prosecuting Vatinius for bribery became a textbook example of its kind.
Meter: hendecasyllabics.
1 **nescio quem**: the indefinite pronoun; the two words together are translatable as "someone." See notes on 2.6 and 6.4. **corona**: the "crown" of spectators that ringed Roman law courts and was voluble in approval and disapproval of the proceedings.
2–3 **Vatiniana ... crimina**: the charges against Vatinius. See appendix A. **Calvos**: nom. sing. Early Latin orthography regularly used *o* instead on *u* after *v*; hence *servos* instead of *servus*, *voltus* for *vultus*. Cf. 63.92, *tuos*.
5 **salaputium**: the humor of the anecdote rests on this colorful epithet, whose exact meaning is unclear. Calvus was a small man and relatively young at the time, still in his early or mid twenties. Seneca says the epithet refers to his stature, and there is probably some phallic nuance that is funny when combined with **disertum**, learned. The construction is an exclamatory accusative.

54

Nothing is known about the four louts featured in this poem; even their names are uncertain, as the text is badly corrupted. It is plausibly speculated, however, that they are henchmen of Caesar, who is sarcastically addressed as *unice imperator* at the end.
Meter: hendecasyllabics.
1 **oppido**: a frequent asseveration in Terence, = *valde*, absolutely.
2 **crura**: sc. *sunt*; Hirrus was so hurriedly brought in from the farm that he still has mud on his legs.
3–4 **subtile et leve**, etc.: sc. *est*. The point seems to be that the crude Libo is light and delicate only when he farts.
5 **seni recocto**: warmed-over codger.
6 **irascere**: future indicative: you will be angered. If Caesar was indeed annoyed, he seems to have kept it under control. See appendix A s.v. Caesar. **iterum** suggests this is not the first time Catullus believes he has gotten under Caesar's skin.
7 **unice imperator**: cf. 29.11, where Caesar is

imperator unice; that may be the earlier attack implied in *iterum* above.

55

Camerius has dropped out of sight, and is suspected of devoting his attention to some new love affair. The theme is like that of poem 6; it is first found in Hellenistic epigrams, and it is adapted here to the Roman scene with touches of local color.
Meter: hendecasyllabics, with a variation in lines 1, 3, 5, 7–9, 11, 13–14, 16, 18, 20, 22, where three long syllables take the place of the usual choriamb. The tendency is to alternate decasyllables with hendecasyllables.
2 **demonstres**: subjunctive of wish with *oramus*. **tenebrae**: your hideout.
3 **Campo ... minore**: now unknown, some public area in Rome smaller than the Campus Martius.
4 **in Circo**: the Circus Maximus, in the low ground between the Palatine and Aventine hills. **te in**: the triple repetition expresses the long search and constant inquiries; the second repetition is unelided, with the short *tĕ* in hiatus as in comedy and ordinary speech. **libellis**: bookshops.
5 **templo ... sacrato**: the main temple in the city, on the Capitoline hill.
6 **Magni ambulatione**: the poem can be dated after 55 B.C. from this allusion to the colonnade attached to the theater in the Campus Martius, dedicated in that year by Pompey the Great. Shakespeare's Cassius plans a rendezvous with Cinna in "Pompey's Porch" (*Julius Caesar* I iii 147), and Ovid recommends it as a place to pick up women (*AA* 1.67, 3.387).
7 **femellas** (dim. of *feminas*): like our "girlies," referring to ladies of easy virtue.
8 **vultu ... sereno**: abl. of description with *quas*: they looked blank when he questioned them about Camerius.
9 **avelte**: the manuscript gives us these letters which make no sense in Latin and are obelized by editors as corrupt beyond repair. They may represent what Catullus said to the *pessimae puellae*.
10 **Camerium**: trisyllabic, pron. *Ca-mer-yum*. This is the only mention of the name, here the object of an understood verb or the lost verb in the previous line. He represents himself speaking in enough exasperation to elicit the rude reply described in lines 11–12. The language resembles that of the

flagitatio in poem 42.

11 reclusa pectus: made up to supply the missing end of the line, which in the manuscripts stops short with *reduc*.... We learn from the words that follow what action the lost words represent. With this reconstruction, *nudum pectus* is the internal accusative, lit. "uncovered with respect to her bare chest." **reclusa** is a middle passive with reflexive force: uncovering her bare chest. For the construction, cf. 64.65, *non lactentis vincta papillas*.

14 tanto in fastu: with such aloofness; the use here of *in* is unusual.

15f. dic ... ede ... committe, crede: a torrent of impatient commands: Out with it!

17 lacteolae ... puellae: the "milky girls" guard their complexion from the sun; there is also a reference to their breasts: cf. 64.65, *lactentis papillas*.

19 fructus proicies, etc.: i.e., I won't be your friend anymore. But it also implies that it is no fun having a new *amor* if you can't tell your friends. Line 20 emphasizes this second meaning.

20 verbosa ... loquella: abl. with **gaudet**.

21f. Vel, etc.: a private alternative: he can share his find with Catullus and not tell a soul (**obseres palatum** = button your lip). **dum** takes the subj. **sim** in a clause of proviso: provided that I be a *particeps* of your love. There is a play here and in line 19 on *amor*, which can mean both friendship and sexual love. Catullus wants a share of Camerius' friendship, and to participate vicariously in his erotic adventure.

56

A satire on coarse humor, aimed at those who like that sort of thing. The point of the epigram is literary rather than autobiographical. The beginning resembles the opening of an epode by Archilochus (Fr. 168 West), and it overshadows the actual anecdote (lines 5–7), which turns out to have been oversold: it is just a tasteless attempt at sexual humor. Some students of Catullus identify the Cato addressed as the critic Valerius Cato, an important figure in the neoteric movement; others interpret this poem as baiting the moralist Cato Uticensis. A third possibility is a Cato mentioned by Ovid as a writer of licentious verses.

Meter: hendecasyllabics.

1–4: the preface is tied together by the echo of line 1 *rem ridiculam ... et iocosam* in line 4 *res ... ridicula et ... iocosa*. For this technique, a simple form of

ring structure, cf. poem 52 and see note on 36.20.

1 rem: exclamatory accusative. **Cato**: Ovid mentions a Cato in his *Tristia* (II 436) as one of several licentious poets. The coarseness of lines 5–7 may be understood as a parody of the sort of thing this Cato produced.

2 tuo agrees with *cacchino*, but is also to be taken with *auribus*. The adjective is emphatic: this is the sort of thing *you* like.

3 quidquid amas: to the extent that you love Catullus. As this poem is making fun of the person addressed, these words would be ironic.

4 nimis iocosa: more irony, as the feeble anecdote that follows is not really "too funny."

5–6 puellae trusantem: idiomatic for "humping," a sense in which *truso* takes the dative. **si placet Dionae**: ironic again. Dione, in myth the mother of Aphrodite, becomes by metonymy Venus herself.

7 pro telo, etc.: I cut him down with my *rigida*, using it like a spear. Some texts read *protelo*, which could be understood adverbially as "in tandem." Catullus' play on words may be the cause of this textual confusion. **cecidi**: slang for sexual intercourse: I banged him. The verb is used punningly, in two senses.

57

A licentious attack on Julius Caesar and his henchman Mamurra (see appendix A).

Meter: hendecasyllabics.

1 convenit: impersonal with dat. of reference. There is perfect harmony because they are two of a kind. **cinaedis**: passive homosexuals. See notes on 10.24, 16.2, 25.1.

2 pathico: see note on 16.2, where the word is also paired with *cinaedus* as a virtual synonym. The arrangement of the -que ... -que suffixes is unorthodox, but has the effect of distributing the vice to both equally.

3 utrisque: dative plural with **resident (5)**

4 urbana ... Formiana: Caesar's *macula* comes from the city, Mamurra's from Formiae.

7 lecticulo erudituli: contemptuous diminutives; a *lectus* may be a bed (in which sexual vices would take place) or a study couch. Caesar was an author and an authority on style and grammar; Mamurra's literary pretensions are made fun of in poem 105. This line hints that their expertise is of a different kind.

9 et puellularum: even of young girls; the dim.

indicates that Caesar and Mamurra prey upon little girls, not the grown-up "girls" of the demimonde. *Socius*, normally applied to business, war, and politics, is here scornfully extended to their sexual contacts.

58

An angry lament for a wayward Lesbia, clearly relevant to the *Odi et Amo* theme that is prominent in the Lesbia poems. The tone of bitter disillusionment and the poet's reference to himself in the third person invite comparison with poem 11.
Meter: hendecasyllabics.
1 **Caeli**: probably M. Caelius Rufus, Catullus' successor (for a time) in the affections of Lesbia/Clodia (see appendix A).
1–2 **Lesbia ... Lesbia ... Lesbia**: Catullan repetitions effectively arrayed to communicate obsessive grief. **nostra** may be the poetic "we," but if this is the Caelius who also had a bad time with Lesbia/Clodia, she is also "our" Lesbia.
3 **suos ... omnes**: his own family. In 72.4 he compares his love with a father's for his children. Cf. also 8.5, 37.12, and 87.1–2.
5 **glubit**: blunt, profane, and devastating in its context, contrasted as it is with the high-sounding **magnanimi Remi nepotes**. The crude sound of the word contributes to its impact, and we are left to imagine how exactly Lesbia "peels" the descendants of Rome's founder.

58b

A loose fragment on the search for Camerius featured in poem 55, but in a high-flying style full of fancy compounds (*pinnipes, plumipedas*) and mythological allusions. Though attempts have been made to splice it into 55, it is more like an outtake from the cutting room floor. The context that we must supply is a statement to Camerius that he is hard to find. These lines are in the form of a loosely structured conditional sentence: Not even if I were a mythological phenomenon (1–7), even then I would be worn out looking for you (8–10).
Meter: the same hendecasyllabics as 55, with the variant only in lines 1 and 9.
1–4 **non**: the fourfold anaphora marks high rhetorical style. **custos ille Cretum**: King Minos of Crete had Hephaestus build him a mechanical giant of bronze, Talos, to patrol his coast. This one-piece

weapons system walked round the island three times a day. *Cretum* is genitive plural.
2 **Pegaseo ... volatu**: the flight of Pegasus, the winged steed caught by Bellerophon and used to take him around on his exploits. This is another of the oblique allusions favored in Hellenistic poetry, where the mythological name (here Bellerophon, Talos in the previous line) has to be guessed.
3 **Ladas** was a famous Spartan runner who died in the moment of victory at Olympia. In this line and the next we must understand a return to the *si fingar* construction of line 1. **Perseus**, who rescued Andromeda and killed the Gorgon Medusa, received winged sandals from the nymphs to help him find the Gorgons.
4 **Rhesi ... bigae**: the legendary horses of King Rhesus, stolen by Diomedes and Ulysses in the Iliad. An oracle had said that if they cropped the grass of the Trojan plain, Troy would never be taken.
5 **adde huc**, etc.: a highfalutin way of capping off his catalogue with anything plume-footed and flying; the adjectives **plumipedas** and **volatiles** are used substantively, i.e., as nouns.
6 **ventorum ... cursum**: the speed of the winds.
7 **quos ... dicares**: which you could harness and bestow on me. The usual way of translating the participle-verb combination is to make them coordinate English verbs. The subjunctive indicates that this is all hypothetical.
8–10 **defessus ... et ... peresus ... essem**: the apodosis of the condition stated in lines 1–7. The arrangement of elements in 8–9 is chiastic.
10 **mihi**: for myself, dative of advantage with *quaeritando*.

59

A scurrilous epigram against a lady named Rufa, who must have been a particularly obnoxious personality to inspire these lines. Like a political cartoon, this lampoon would be pointless if it did not tell some part of the truth in a particularly funny way. But the details are now lost.
Meter: limping iambics (see appendix B).
1 **Bononiensis**: from Bononia (mod. Bologna). The position of emphasis may be a way of advertising that she is an outsider pushing her way into Roman or Veronese society. **Rufa Rufulum**: both unknown names, perhaps transparent pseudonyms that everybody will be able to figure out. *Rufulum* may

represent a subservient male associate of Rufa, a lickspittle placed here in a position where he receives her humble services.

2 **sepulcretis**: graveyards; a hapax legomenon.

3 **rapere**: three short syllables, of which the first two are a resolved longum in the third foot. Cf. 22.19 and 37.5, and see on resolution in appendix C. **de rogo cenam**: it was the custom to put some food on the funeral pyre for the spirit of the deceased. It was meant to be burned with the corpse—if Rufa didn't steal it first.

4–5 the scenario may have been real enough, where beggars emboldened by hunger had to be kept at bay long enough for the pyre to burn the food offering. The joke is in representing Rufa as such a beggar.

5 **semiraso**: either unkempt, or shaved on one side of the head to mark him as a recaptured runaway slave. The humor of the epigram is increased by the climactic arrangement of squalid details.

60

The last poem of the polymetric section, a reproach addressed probably to Lesbia. Its literary pedigree, going back to Homer and Greek tragedy (*Iliad* 16.31–5, Aeschylus *Ag.* 1232, Euripides *Med.* 1342–3), makes it more effective than if it had been a purely original and spontaneous outburst. Catullus uses the theme again in Ariadne's poignant apostrophe to Theseus (64.154–7); Virgil paid tribute to Catullus in recasting it as Dido's reproach to Aeneas, *Aen.* 4.365–7. G.P. Goold points out that the first and last letters of these lines spell out *NATU CEU AES*, "by birth like bronze."
Meter: limping iambics.

1 **num** pleads for a negative answer: tell me it isn't so.

2 **Scylla**: as described in the Odyssey, she yaps like a puppy; in Lucretius the canine component has grown to a ring of rabid dogs attached to her body. Here and in Virgil, Propertius, and Ovid they comprise the lower part of her body.

3 **mente dura ... ac taetra**: abl. of description, like *fero corde* (line 5).

4 **novissimo casu**: last and final crisis.

5 **contemptam haberes**: hold in contempt; the reference is to *vocem*. **a** is the expletive.

61

The first of a group of longer poems in the collection, this marriage hymn is a medley of traditional wedding themes, combining three types: songs of the wedding feast (such as poem 62), the *hymenaeus* proper (sung during the procession from the bride's former home to her new home with her husband), and the *epithalamium*, sung outside the marriage chamber. Though probably not intended for actual performance at a wedding, it does appear to commemorate a real marriage: that of a Manlius Torquatus with a bride named Junia (line 6) and Aurunculeia (line 82). Composed in the form of a dramatic monologue, the poem combines Greek literary techniques with Roman customs and a hearty enthusiasm for the union of man and wife and the creation of a family.
Meter: Glyconic and Pherecratean stanzas (see appendix B). The tendency in this poem to open each line with a trochee (— ᴗ) rather than a spondee (— —) gives the lines a light, rapid movement.

1–35 Invocation to the marriage god.

1 **Collis Heliconii**: Mt. Helicon, west of Thebes in Boeotia, is a home of the Muses. Hymenaeus is described as a resident, *cultor*, because he is the son of a Muse (*Uraniae genus*).

3 **rapis**: refers to the ancient ritual of marriage by capture, remembered in Roman times by the show of force with which the groom took the bride from her mother (cf. 62.21) and in modern times by the custom of carrying the bride across the threshold.

4 **Hymenaee**: the Greek god of marriage, addressed in refrains similar to this in Euripides, Aristophanes, and Theocritus as well as Plautus.

7 **amarici**: the sweet-smelling marjoram is a fragrant member of the same family as oregano, thyme, and mint.

8 **flammeum**: the bride's veil is so called because of its bright orange color. Hymenaeus is represented as wearing the same floral wreath, veil, and orange slippers (10 *luteum soccum*) as the bride. His epicene character is further suggested by his pale skin (9f. *niveo pede*) and high voice (13 *voce tinnula*).

10 **soccum**: cognate with our *sock*, a loose shoe or slipper worn by women.

12 **concinens**: simply singing, as in 65.13; the prefix does not necessarily mean singing in unison as in line 116.

15 pineam taedam: torches of resinous pine wood were regularly carried in wedding and funeral processions.

16 Iunia Manlio: for the bride's name and the identity of Manlius Torquatus, see appendix A. *Manlio* is dative of reference with *nubet* (20). In the likely original sense of *nubo*, Junia is "putting on the veil" for Manlius.

17–19 qualis ... iudicem: Junia is compared to Venus, inhabitant of Idalium on Cyprus (*Idalium colens*), as she came to the contest of beauty judged by Paris, the Phrygian judge.

19–20 bona ... virgo: inclusive word order: the good virgin marries with a good omen, *cum bona ... alite*. For similar emphasis by repetition, cf. 44 *bonae ... boni*, 179f. *bonae ... bene*, 195–7 *bona ... bonum*. A key word in the poem, *bonus* or *bene* occurs some thirteen times.

21–22: inclusive word order again. In this stanza the bride is compared to a flowering Asian myrtle raised by wood nymphs.

24 ludicrum: in apposition to *quos* above, i.e., the flowering twigs of the myrtle, nurtured as a delight for themselves.

25: an unusually slow pherecratean line, whose double short syllables have been supplanted by the long *u* of *ūmore*. Catullus suits the meter to the action.

26–27 aditum ferens and **perge linquere** are weighty language for coming and leaving respectively, as befits the action of a god and the language of prayer.

27–28: the Thespian rock is Mount Helicon, at whose base lies the town of Thespiae; the Aonian caves (*Aonios specus*, acc. pl. object of *linquere*) are grottoes in the mountain, located in the region called Aonia. It was customary for invocations to call the god from a specific haunt, and to do so in an impressive way: cf. the prayer to Venus in 36.11–17, and note.

29 super = *desuper*, from above.

30 frigerans: cooling the grottoes by pouring water down their walls. Aganippe is both the spring and the resident nymph.

31 Ac, but, breaks off the invocation to Hymenaeus and asks the god to summon the bride, now a *domina*, to her new husband's home. The word music of the line is remarkable for its alliteration (*Ac ... voca, domum dominam*).

32 coniugis ... novi: objective genitive with *cupidam*: she is desirous of her new husband.

36–45. Exhortation to the bridesmaids.

37–38 advenit par dies: i.e., your own wedding day is coming soon. **in modum** is variously interpreted "in measure" (Ellis), "in tune" (Fordyce), "in the right and proper way" (Quinn).

42 citarier: the archaic form of the passive *citari* gives an old-fashioned flavor; cf. *compararier* (65, 70, 75), *nitier* (68).

43 munus: his function as the wedding god. **aditum ferat** recalls line 26, *aditum ferens*. The bridesmaids must do their part in summoning Hymenaeus.

46–75. Praise of Hymenaeus. The bridesmaids' song adopts the formal character of a hymn, cataloguing the virtues of the god through rhetorical questions (*quis* or *quem* 46, 48, 64, 69, 74) and direct address (*te, tibi, tu* 51–2, 56, 61, 64, 66, 69, 74).

46–47 amatis ... amantibus, beloved lovers (those whose love is returned), is like the jingle in 45.20, *amant amantur*. The continuity of lines within the Greek lyric strophe is emphasized by the hyphenation of *ama-tis*. See appendix C, **synapheia.**

51 suis: dat. of reference, for his children. **tremulus:** the parent is imagined in palsied old age, praying for the marriage of his son or daughter.

53 zonula soluunt sinus: free their bosoms of the *zona*, the band or girdle tied beneath the breasts of unmarried girls. Its removal signified loss of virginity at the time of marriage. For the phrase cf. 2.13 *zonam soluit*, 67.28 *zonam solvere virgineam*. The trisyllabic *soluunt* (for *solvunt*) is an archaism, as at 2.13.

54 te: object of *captat*, not of *timens*. The repetition *Te ... tibi ... te ... Tu* (51–56) is typical of the Greek hymnic style. **novos:** archaic for *novus*, like the archaic *thee*'s and *thou*'s still used in prayer.

55 captat aure: the *novus maritus* strains with *cupida aure* to catch the sound of your approach at the head of the bridal procession as he waits anxiously outside his house.

56 fero iuveni may refer to the ancient character of the groom as *captor* (see note on line 3); some see instead a reference to the lover's ardor (cf. 62.23 *iuveni ardenti*). **in manūs ... dedis** suggests the formal act of handing over the bride to the authority of her husband, *manus* being the legal term for the power of the *paterfamilias*. This "giving away" of the bride, traditionally the father's role, is here attributed to the god of marriage.

58f. a gremio ... matris: the bride is represented as moving directly from a child's state to that of a married woman, as in 62.21f., 46f. The extreme youth of brides in the Greco-Roman world lends color to this view.

61–63 **Nil ... commodi capere**: partitive gen. construction. The point is that sex (*Venus*) alone can achieve no reputable benefit outside of marriage.

62 **fama quod bona comprobet** = *quod fama bona comprobet*. The antecedent is *nil*.

65 **compararier**: for the form, see note on line 42. **ausit**: an old subjunctive = *audeat*. Who would dare to be compared (to compare himself) with this god?

66–70 repeats the word patterns of the preceding stanza.

68 **stirpe nitier**: the metaphor of offspring as the stem of the plant by which the parent is supported (*nitier*) inverts our conception of the family tree.

71 **Quae**: the delayed antecedent is *terra*. **careat** is subjunctive because a *terra* without marriage is scarcely conceivable.

72 **praesides**: the sons provided by marriage supply the national defense. The feuding families of the Greek Mani used to refer to their sons as "rifles."

76–113. The bride is urged to come out of her father's house and is praised for her virtues. The scene is outside the house; the guests are waiting to begin the *deductio*, which will take the bride to her new home.

76 **Claustra pandite**: virtually a stage direction, so that we may imagine the bride inside the house, seen through the opened doors.

77 **viden ut**: (*videsne ut*) a colloquial idiom, used earlier by Plautus: do you see how ...? as in 62.8. The shortening of the *e* reflects the usage of everyday speech.

78 **quatiunt comas**: the marriage torches, swung through the air to fan their flames in preparation for the procession, are personified, shaking their fiery locks.

79: The missing lines probably comment on the bride's failure to come forth and begin the procession; **tardet** must be understood as having her as its object.

80 **magis audiens**: heeding the voice of *pudor* rather than that of the crowd urging her to come out.

82 **Aurunculeia**: vocative; lines 82–113 are addressed to the bride. For the hyphenation, see note on *ama-tis*, line 46. For the bride's name, see appendix A.

84–86 **ne**, etc.: i.e., there is no danger in your case (*tibi*) that a prettier woman has seen the light of day. The subjunctive clause expresses a negative wish after *periculum*, which implies fear.

85–86 **clarum**, etc.: the striking way of describing the proverbial "light of day" makes the compliment fresh and memorable.

87 **talis**, etc.: in lines 21–25 she was compared to an Asian myrtle raised by nymphs, here to a hyacinth in a rich man's garden. **vario**: many-colored; with *stare* (89), the thought is that it stands out from the other flowers.

90 **abit dies**: it is now evening and time for the procession to start.

93 **videtur**: seems proper. *Si videtur* = "a rather urgent 'if you please' "—Ellis.

97 **non**, in its prominent position, governs *levis*, *deditus*, and *volet*: your husband is not fickle, he is not devoted to a *mala adultera*, and he won't want to sleep apart from your *teneris papillis*.

102–104 **lenta ... vitis**: grapevines were trellised on trees for shade and support. Here the bride is the pliant vine, twining herself around the tree planted beside her (*adsitus*, from *adsero*).

107 **O cubile**: apostrophe to the marriage bed, suggested by the reference above to the conjugal embrace.

108 **candido pede**: the bed has feet of ivory.

109–11 **quae ... quanta ... quae ... quae**: exclamatory, referring to the *gaudia* the bride will give her husband. See appendix C, anaphora.

110f. **vaga nocte**: in the passing night; the ornamental epithet suggests the passage of night's chariot through the sky.

114–58. The bride appears, and proceeds to her new home. This part of the poem represents the wedding procession or *deductio*, during which guests throw nuts and make coarse jokes.

115 **flammeum**: cf. line 8; the bride's flame-colored veil catches the spectators' eye as the bride emerges.

117 **Io**: monosyllabic "Yo" at the beginning of the line (117f., 137f., *et passim*), disyllabic at the end.

120 **Fescennina iocatio**: ribald extemporaneous joking, common at various Greek and Roman rituals, was associated by the Romans in historical times with the Faliscan town of Fescennium. But the adjective may be cognate with *fascinum*, the evil eye believed to endanger people during times of special happiness (see note on 7.12). It was thought

possible to ward off such malignancy by obscene verbiage.

121–41: the Fescennine raillery centers on the groom's supposed sexual goings-on with a slave boy (123 *concubinus*), a relatively safe topic as it avoids the subject of female rivals to the bride. It was presumed then as now that the groom had sown his wild oats, and homosexual activity, particularly with a boy, was not believed to impugn one's masculinity.

121 **nuces**: Pliny 15.86 identifies *nuces iuglandes* (walnuts) as *nuptialium Fescenninorum comites*. The throwing of nuts at a wedding, probably like our throwing of rice or seeds, originated as a fertility ritual. Greek households observed the rite of *spermobolia*, in which anyone joining a household, whether as slave or bride, would be inducted with a shower of seeds. **nec ... neget**: the joke is that the groom's abandoned *concubinus* should now supply the nuts with which his master's wedding is celebrated.

124 **iners**: the groom's *puer delicatus* is lazy because his sexual favors exempted him from chores; the epithet is ironic because now he is sexually idle.

126 **lusisti nucibus**: refers to playing with nuts as a child's pastime, not as a wedding ritual. The *concubinus* is told to give them up for the latter purpose.

127 **Talasio**: Hymenaeus' Roman name was Talasius.

128 **Sordebant ... vilicae**: suggests the farmer's wife as a type of lusty woman who would make the most of available male companionship while her husband is attending to business. A collection of such "Milesian tales" was found in the baggage of a Roman captured at Carrhae in 53 B.C. A *vilicus* is a farm manager who oversees his employer's slave laborers. The groom's conceited *puer delicatus* formerly considered himself too good for the likes of a *vilica*.

131 **cinerarius**: the hairdresser who once curled the boy's hair now shaves him (*tondet os*). Now he is too old for his former role.

134 **Diceris male**: you will be criticized; takes the indirect statement construction *te ... abstinere*. We are now speaking to the *unguentate marite*, the groom who is oiled and perfumed for his wedding.

135 **glabris**: sleek, effeminate slave boys. For the contemptuous and gross effect of the sound, cf. 58.5, *glubit*.

139–40 **Scimus haec ... sola congita [esse]**: we

know that these peccadilloes (which are permitted you) are the only ones you have known, i.e., we know you have had no female partners. Cf. note on 121–141. **marito**: emphatic: the same license is not granted a married man.

144–73 **Nupta**, etc.: the advice to the bride, though not part of the *Fescennina iocatio*, begins with sexual matters, viz. that she should keep her husband's fidelity by attending to his requests. **tu quoque**: as there are things that *non licent* for the *maritus* (140f.), there are also things that it is unwise for a wife to deny.

146 **ni**: archaic, to avoid repeating the *ne* of the previous line. **petitum**: supine in -*um* showing purpose, like *visum* in 10.2; the implied object is *quae tuus vir petet*. The advice is bluntly practical rather than moralistic.

149 **En ... domus**: the procession has reached the bride's new home; she is urged to make herself mistress of its power and wealth.

151 **sine serviat**: allow it to be of service; verbs of allowing may take an object infinitive or (as here) a subjunctive clause of purpose: see Allen & Greenough §563c.

154–55 **usque ... annuit**: i.e., until advanced old age, personified as a palsied crone whose trembling head (*tremulum tempus*) appears to nod assent to everything. The word groups are emphasized by alliteration (*tremulum tempus, anilitas annuit, omnia omnibus*). For personifications of time in Catullus see 95.6 note.

159–226. Epithalamium. The bride is sung into her new home and wedding chamber; praise of bride and groom, encouragement of the act of love, hope for the offspring to be engendered, and advice to all *boni coniuges* to perform their marital deeds.

159–60 **Transfer ... pedes** = step over (rather than on) the threshold, perhaps to avoid stumbling and incurring bad luck. **aureolos**: gold-colored. We were told in line 10 that her *soccus* was yellow-orange (*luteus*).

161 **rasilem ... forem** refers to the polished wood of the door, or the well-worn threshold, as in 68.71 *trito limine*—the regular epithet of a doorway since Homer.

165 **Tyrio in toro**: a couch draped with precious purple fabric.

166 **totus immineat**: is utterly intent.

169 **illi, tibi**: dat. of reference with *uritur*.

171 **penite** = *penitus*; the groom's love is not as

openly displayed as the bride's, but see lines 196–8.

175 **praetextate**: to one of the three boys who escorted the bride and handed her through the door to the *pronubae* inside, married women who prepared her for the marriage chamber.

179–80 **senibus viris cognitae**: (carnally) known to their aged husbands; periphrasis for *matronae univirae*, goodwives who have lived their life with a single husband; cf. 111.1–2. For the **bonae ... bene** combination, see note on 19–20.

181 **collocate**: the technical term for the formal arraying of the bride on her marriage bed. One presumes the *pronubae* withdrew after performing this final service.

185 **thalamo**: the marriage chamber, which gives its name to the *epithalamium*, [a song] for the marriage chamber.

187–88 **alba parthenicē**, etc.: two more flower similes for the bride (cf. the Asian myrtle in 22 and the hyacinth in 89); here we have the white camomile, chosen perhaps for its name (Gk. *parthenos* = virgin), and the red poppy, whose color matches her veil and slippers.

193 **ne remorare** = *noli remorari*; for the archaism, cf. 62.59 *ne pugna*, 67.18 *ne dubita*. For the theme, cf. W.C. Handy's "Hesitatin' Blues."

194ff.: the apostrophe to the groom continues; now he makes no secret of the passion that he concealed in line 171.

195 **iuverit**: the perfect subjunctive in a wish is archaic.

199–200 **pulveris ... siderum**: for grains of African sand and stars as conventional measures of infinitude, cf. 7.3–7.

201 **subducat**: jussive (let him reckon) or potential (he might reckon) subjunctive.

203 **ludi**: love play, as in 204, *ludite*.

204 **brevi**: abl. of *breve = brevi tempore*.

207–208 **indidem ... ingenerari**: sc. *decet*: a family should regenerate itself from its own stock rather than resort to adoption. The force of the passive is middle or reflexive.

209ff.: the gestures of the **Torquatus parvulus** imply recognition of paternity as well as affection.

214 **suo similis patri**: further proof of paternity, as well as the fidelity of his mother (217f. *pudicitiam suae matris*). The Roman obsession with patriarchal continuity reveals itself in these lines.

219–23 **talis ... qualis**, etc.: may the good reputation (*laus*) derived from his virtuous mother prove the excellence of his *genus*, just like the peerless fame

(that) remains for Penelopean Telemachus from his excellent mother. To balance the paternal bias of the previous stanzas, these lines attribute the prospective child's good character to his mother. Odysseus' son Telemachus was raised by his mother Penelope while his father was away at the Trojan War.

224 **ostia**: the doors of the marriage chamber.

225 **lusimus**: of love poetry, as in 50.2 and 5, 68.17.

227 **munere assiduo**: incessant conjugal activity. *Munus* is both duty and natural function. Its virtuous character is emphasized by *boni* and *bene*.

62

This marriage hymn takes the form of a dramatic dialogue between the marriageable young men and their female counterparts at a wedding feast. It begins with three stanzas of preparation for the *hymenaeus* itself, which starts on line 20. It is called *amoebean* because the boys' lines (26–31, 33–38, 49–58b) respond to the girls' lines (20–25, 32, 39–48) and try to one-up them, as in a contest. The outcome of this poetic debate, particularly the advice to the *virgo* at the end, reflects a traditional Roman patriarchal point of view.

Meter: dactylic hexameters (see appendix B).

1–5. Boys: The evening star has risen: time to leave the tables and sing our wedding song.

1 **Vesper**: the name given the planet Venus when it rose at sunset, the traditional time for weddings. **consurgite**: from the tables where they have been dining, as line 3 makes clear. **Olympo**: in the sky, a generic use of the place-name that goes back at least to Sophocles. Catullus' mixture of Greek and Roman marriage customs indicates that no particular location for this wedding is intended.

2 **vix tandem** emphasizes the youths' impatience, as if the evening star has been so slow coming that it scarcely came at all. Cf. 66.68, *vix sero*.

3 **tempus**: sc. *est*, as completed by *surgere* and *linquere*. **mensas**: the unmarried men recline at their own tables, apart from the unmarried women. The host is the bride's father.

4 **iam veniet virgo**: the bride, who does not attend the pre-wedding banquet, is about to come down from her chamber in her father's house and will be taken in a procession to her new husband's house, accompanied by the singing of marriage songs (such as the *hymenaeus* which is about to begin in this

poem).

5 **Hymen o Hymenaee, etc.:** the refrain of the marriage hymn, which the boys sing as if in practice, is simply an invocation to Hymen or Hymenaeus, the god of marriage.

6–10. Girls: the boys have stood up; we must rise too, and be ready to outsing them.

6 **cernitis ... iuvenes:** the unmarried women see the youths from their separate tables, and take their cue to get up and get ready to perform.

7 **nimirum:** evidently. The boys, sitting near a door or window, have seen the evening star rise; the girls take their cue from the boys' rising to prepare their song. **Oetaeos ignes:** the boys saw the *lumina* of the evening star (which they called *Vesper*) in the sky (which they called *Olympus*); in the symmetrical spirit of amoebean song, the girls call the same star *Noctifer*, whose *ignes* they call Oetaean, associating it with Mt. Oeta, about ninety miles south of Olympus. According to Servius, there was a cult of Hesperus on Mt. Oeta.

8 **sic certest:** yes, that's for sure. The colloquial use of *sic* as an affirmative continues into the late Latin vernacular to become *si* in Italian, French, and Spanish. **viden:** short for *videsne*, as in 61.77. **perniciter:** not perniciously but swiftly; in 2.12, the fast-running Atalanta was described as *pernix*. Throughout this poem, the eagerness of the boys is contrasted with the reluctance of the girls.

9 **canent quod vincere par est:** they will be singing what is up to us to outdo; in this way Catullus anticipates the singing contest that has not (strictly speaking) started yet.

11–19 Boys [aside]: this will not be an easy contest to win. They have been practicing while we were thinking about other things.

11 **palma parata est:** the word order shows that the predication or emphasis is on *non facilis*, but the boys appear confident that the palm of victory has been gotten ready for their benefit.

12 **secum ... meditata requirunt:** they are searching their memory for things they have rehearsed. The boys are worried that the girls have been using their heads, as the next three lines emphasize: *meditantur, memorabile* (13), *mente* (14), *mentes* (15). *Meditor* does not necessarily imply memorization, but thinking out a set of arguments. In Augustan poetry it comes to mean poetic composition.

13 **non frustra:** echoes the girls' *non temere* (9).

The last half of this line similarly echoes the last half of line 9.

14 **nec mirum, etc.:** and no wonder, because they are deep at work (*penitus laborant*) with their entire mind (*tota mente*). The delayed *quae* introduces a relative clause of characteristic expressing cause, using the indicative *laborant* instead of the usual subjunctive (as in 21 *possis* and 27 *firmes*).

15 **nos:** asyndeton suggests the contrast: We, on the other hand, ... **alio ... alio divisimus:** have divided our attention (as we would put it in English), hearing but not attending to business. Catullus' language is too compressed to be translated easily.

17 **saltem** emphasizes *nunc*.

18 **iam ... iam:** reinforcing *nunc* in the previous line, and recalling the four repetitions of *iam* in lines 3–4.

20–30. Girls: Hesperus, you cruelly snatch daughters from their mothers' embrace. Boys: You seal the happy marriage pact.

20 **Hespere:** the girls begin the *hymenaeus* proper with an apostrophe to the evening star, whom they address by his Greek name (Gk. *Hes-* = Lat. *Ves-*). **caelo fertur:** is borne through the sky, because of its nightly course through the heavens. **ignis:** any heavenly body.

21 **Qui possis:** subjunctive in a relative clause of characteristic, explaining *crudelior* above: because you can snatch, etc. See note to line 14 above. **avellere** refers to the Roman custom by which the groom took the bride from her mother with a show of force, an ancient ritual of marriage by capture (cf. 61.3, *rapis*).

22: performers of improvised verse sometimes repeat a line with a slight variation to buy time; here the girls' chorus sings a variation of the preceding verse.

23 **ardenti:** picks up the characterization of Hesperus as an *ignis* in line 20. Cf. *ignis* (26), *flamma* (27), *ardor* (29).

24 **capta urbe:** temporal ablative absolute; the captured city is the classic scene of cruel atrocities, as in Euripides' *Trojan Women* and other plays on the theme.

26 **iucundior:** the boys' amoebean response echoes the girls' opening strophe, but says the opposite.

27 **Qui ... firmes:** same construction as in 21, *qui possis*. **desponsa conubia:** a pledged wedding.

28 **pepigere, pepigerunt:** 3rd pl. perfect of *pango*, arrange or settle. Marriages were traditionally ar-

ranged by the *viri* (the suitor and the bride's father) and the *parentes* of the couple on both sides. The girls have represented marriage as a violation of the bond between mother and daughter; the boys respond that these things are taken care of ahead of time (*ante*) by men, by mutual consent of the *parentes*. The bride is a silent partner.

29 **iunxere:** generalizing perfect; the parents do not join the couple before Hesperus has risen.

30 **felici optatius hora** echoes and contrasts the girls' *capta crudelius urbe*, but here with an ablative of comparison, the happy hour being the time of Hesperus' rising when the wedding takes place. Note the hiatus in the fourth foot, emphasizing *felici*.

32–38 Girls: Hesperus is a thief in the night. Boys: Hesperus catches thieves as the morning star; besides, girls all secretly hope to be stolen away.

32 The second round of stanzas in the marriage hymn has been damaged in transmission. Only the first line of the girls' part survives, and at least one line of the boys' reply is lost. From what remains, it appears that the girls complain of abduction and thievery in the night, for which they hold Hesperus responsible.

33 **tuo adventu:** addressed to Hesperus, probably in his identity as Eous, the morning star. The watchman wakes up when Eous appears, making Hesperus/Eous the enemy of thieves.

34 **quos:** object of *comprendis* in the next line. **idem:** the same star (though by a different name). Greek astronomers had discovered that Hesperus and Eous or Lucifer were the same star (actually the planet Venus), but the boy's argument is somewhat specious, since it is impossible for the same planet to rise twice in the same night, first at evening and again at dawn—as *revertens* implies. In one season it rises in evening, in another at dawn.

36 **ficto ... questu:** the boys accuse the girls of a disingenuous complaint, since (they believe) every unmarried woman secretly wants to be carried off by a man (37 *tacita ... mente requirunt*).

39–58: Girls: a girl is like a flower that nobody wants after her bloom is plucked. Boys: she is like a vine that lies barren on the ground unless married to a tree.

39 **ut flos,** etc.: the third and final round of this poetic debate consists of extended similes. Catullus' poetry reaches its height in the comparison of a virgin girl to a carefully nurtured flower. Four spondees in this line dramatize the slow growth of nature's perfect flower. The power of his poetic description is aided by the effective use of hyperbaton (*secretus* separated from *flos* and hidden in midline between *saeptis* and *nascitur*), asyndeton (line 41), and antithesis (line 42 vs. line 44).

42–44 **multi ... multae, nulli ... nullae:** the antithesis is strengthened by the repetition of the line with only two words changed. **optavere** is the generalizing or gnomic perfect.

43 **tenui ... ungui:** instrumental with *carptus*. The power of this image is attested by its imitation in Propertius I 20.39 *decerpens tenero pueriliter ungui* and Ovid *Heroides* 4.30 *tenui primam deligere ungue rosam*. **defloruit:** intransitive, has lost its bloom. The sexual metaphor survives in modern English *deflower*, *defloration*.

45 **dum ... dum:** as long as ... so long. This co-ordinate usage is repeated in the answering line (56). **suis:** substantive, her people.

47 **pueris ... puellis:** the third repetition in this strophe, emphasizing that the married woman, being no longer a child, is rejected by her former playmates.

49 **vidua ... vitis:** the boys counter with the metaphor of a vine without a tree to support it. In ancient Italy grapevines were trellised on living trees that provided shelter from weather as well as support.

52 **contingit ... radice flagellum:** to emphasize the unnatural condition, they describe the root as if it were reaching up to touch the vine shoot.

53 **iuvenci:** bullocks attached to cultivators, breaking up the soil between the vines to control weeds.

54 **ulmo ... marito:** the metaphor of the vine wed to a husband consisting of a tree was already at least a century old: Cato *De Agri Cultura* 32 *Arbores facito uti bene maritae sint.*

57 **par conubium:** marriage with one of equal rank. **adepta est:** deponent, from *adipiscor*.

59–66: Boys: Bride, do not resist your marriage; respect your parents' rights!

59 **Et** connects the general statement with its specific application: So you too. The symmetry of the amoebean song is now broken, and the boys proceed to their concluding statement, an apostrophe to the bride.

60 **cui:** the antecedent *ei* is omitted.

62 **ex parte:** partly (mostly, as it turns out, leaving

the *virgo* only a *tertia pars* in the choice of her spouse).

63 pātrist (*patri est*): a rare lengthening of the initial vowel.

65 sua iura: their own rights over you.

63

There are eunuchs who have been so from birth, and there are eunuchs who have been made eunuchs by men, and there are eunuchs who have made themselves eunuchs for the sake of the kingdom of heaven.

Matthew 19:12, quoting the words of Christ.

This is the story of how a young Greek, caught up in a religious frenzy, sails to Phrygia and castrates himself the better to serve the goddess Cybele. Though he soon repents and longs for home, the goddess sends her lions to chase him back into the forest, where he must spend the rest of his life as her slave. Though no doubt inspired in some of its details by the wild cults and gloomy forests of Bithynia as seen firsthand by Catullus, this poem represents a specific religion centered in Phrygia, presided over by castrated priests called *Galli*, and imported into Rome itself as early as 204 B.C. Among Catullus' older contemporaries who wrote about this cult, Varro made fun of it in his satirical sketch *Eumenides*, and Lucretius described its noisy processions in *De Rerum Natura* 2.600ff. Catullus' friend Caecilius is working on his own poem about Cybele in poem 35.

In the original myth, Attis was Cybele's consort; in later versions he became her Greek lover, who out of guilt for some infidelity castrates himself so as never to repeat his sin. Catullus brings him a step closer to the life of his own times, making him a religious zealot who realizes too late that his impulsive rejection of sexuality in the name of holiness has permanently removed him from the only civilization he knows.

On another level, many readers today will find a significant resonance between a Catullus whose obsessive devotion to Lesbia unmans him and a religious fanatic who feminizes himself (see notes on lines 8, *citata*, and 63, *ego mulier*).

Perhaps Catullus' best long poem, this is certainly his most remarkable for "a nervous vigor and swing of feeling that are unequalled in Latin literature" (Merrill) as well as for its vivid images and mastery of a rapid and difficult meter.

Meter: Galliambic (see appendix B).

2–3 nemus, silvis the dark, oppressive forest is part of the spiritual landscape of this poem, and we are frequently reminded of its presence (lines 12, 20, 32, 52, 58, 72, 79, 89). This is the sinister opposite of the pastoral *locus amoenus*.

5 ili ... pondera: the weight(s) of his loin = his testicles. ili is a gen. sing. form of the usually plural *ilia, -ium,* n.

6 viro: concrete for abstract, his manhood.

8 citata: Catullus now feminizes the castrated Gallus with feminine adjectives: cf. *adorta* and *tremebunda* (11), *vaga* (31), *comitata* (32), etc. His hands have a feminine whiteness (**niveis manibus**) and slenderness (10, *teneris digitis*). In 27 he is called a counterfeit woman, *notha mulier*.

9 Cybebe: the alternate spelling of the Goddess' name. Cybele's **initia** are her sacred implements.

10 terga tauri ... cava: periphrasis for the hide-covered *tympanum*.

12 Cybeles is a Greek genitive.

13 Dindymenae dominae: the center of the cult was in early times near the foot of Mt. Dindymus in Phrygia.

15 sectam: a *secta* (origin of Eng. *sect*) is a way or plan. **meam ... me mihi** suggest a morbid self-absorption along with his religious obsession. The line repeats the same idea in three ways.

17 Veneris nimio odio: like Euripides' Hippolytus nearly four centuries earlier, Attis and his companions believe sexuality is incompatible with godliness. Eusebius says that Origen castrated himself when he converted to Christianity.

19 sequimini: first person plural imperative.

21 cymbal(or)um is a syncopated gen. pl. **tympana reboant:** the low rattle of the drums is imitated by the meter. Compare line 29.

22 tibicen: a performer on the *tibia* or *calamus*, who makes a deep sound (**canit ... grave**) on his bent reed-pipe (**curvo ... calamo**).

23 Maenades: Attis imagines these forests also have Maenads, who were frenzied female worshippers of Bacchus or Dionysus. **hederigerae,** ivy-wearing, like *properipedem* (34), *sonipedibus* (41), *erifugae* (51), *silvicultrix,* and *nemorivagus* (both in 72) is a Greek type of compound usually avoided by the neoterics. In this poem, Catullus is using a higher and more conventional poetic diction than he employed in the polymetric section of our collection.

24 ululatibus imitates the wild ululations still heard in parts of the Near East at funerals and other occasions of mass excitement.

26 **tripudiis** is an archaic word borrowed from an ancient "three-step" in honor of Mars.

28: A **thiasus** is an orgiastic dance and the group that performs it.

31 **simul**: as soon as, as in 27; here it links *vadit* and *sequuntur*. The two quatrains (27–30 and 31–34) have the same structure. Attis leads, the others follow. **animam agens**, gasping, duplicates the sense of *anhelans*; cf. the redundancy in line 15.

35 **tetigere**: reduplicated perfect of *tango*, as in line 2. Catullus' use of such forms in this poem fits the rattling rhythms of this meter's line endings. Cf. 41 *pepulit* (from *pello*), 47 *tetulit*.

36 **sine Cerere**: without breaking bread (because they are too tired from their orgies to eat). Such mythological metonymy, typical of high poetic language, is generally avoided in the plain style of the polymetric poems (1–60).

39–43: a mythologized account of dawn, featuring the sun god **Sol** driving off the shades of night with his fresh horses (**vegetis sonipedibus**) and the god of sleep **Somnus** leaving Attis to return to the breast of his wife **Pasithea**, who receives him with fluttering breast (**trepidante ... sinu**) because she is eager to make love. The fancy epic diction (e.g., *sonipedibus* for "horses") and the pretty scenario contrast sharply with the tone of what follows.

39 **oris aurei**: gen. of description with *Sol*.

40 **lustravit**, lit up, ranged over, purified, is significant here in all its meanings. Attis wakes up to a different world than the one he fell asleep in. **aethera** is a Greek accusative, like *Attin* in line 42.

42 **excitam**: a proleptic adjective, because Sleep leaves Attis before he is roused.

45 **recoluit**: went over in his mind.

46 **liquida...mente**: with a clear mind, unclouded by last night's frenzy. **quis** is syncopated from *quibus*, as often in poetry. **foret**: an alternative form of *esset*.

47 **rusum** (for *rursum*) **reditum ... tetulit**: he returned back to the beach where he had landed from Greece the previous day. The verb (from *fero*) has the old reduplicated perfect form. For the periphrasis, cf. *tetuli pedem* (52), *reditum ferat* (79).

48: the iterative **visens** intensifies his looking to gazing.

50 **mei**: objective gen., instead of possessive adj. *mea*.

51–52 **erifugae famuli**: runaway slaves, an emphatic redundancy; *erifugae*, a rare compound noun, is used appositively with *famuli*.

53 **nivem, gelida**: the mountainous forests are cold (cf. 70, *algida Idae nive amicta loca*) and dark (3, 32, and 54 *opaca*), contrasting with the warmth of Attis' past (65 *limina tepida*) and the bright luster of the shore and sea from which he will be driven (87–88 *albicantis litoris, marmora pelagi*).

56 **aciem**: his eye's gaze.

60 **foro, palaestra**, etc.: four words in a single line expressing the institutions of the Greek civilization that Attis has cut off and thrown away: the forum where people meet to talk, the palaestra, stadium, and gymnasia where they exercise and compete in games.

62 **figuraest** = *figurae est*. For this and other contractions, see appendix D. **obierim**: deliberative subjunctive, implying the impossibility that he has not taken on every *genus figurae*.

62–71: seventeen repetitions of *ego* and *mihi* in ten lines emphasize his self-recognition, a kind of tragic recognition. Cf. line 15.

63 **Ego mulier, adolescens**, etc.: another set of four significant words, this time recapitulating the stages of his life in reverse order. This is (fittingly) the longest line of the poem. An **ephebus**, properly a Greek youth of 18–20, is used loosely here of a boy.

64 **gymnasi flos** and **decus olei** are two ways of saying the same thing: he was the best-looking young athlete around. *Oleum* is the oil used by athletes after exercise; it imparted a gleam to the body. It is used by metonymy of the wrestling schools.

65 **ianuae frequentes**: the double doors of his house were crowded with suitors who warmed the threshold (**limina tepida**) by camping out on it; his house was encircled (**redimita**, from *redimio*) with flowery garlands that they left for him. These were male suitors. Such courtship of adolescent boys by men in their twenties and thirties, rejected in the Christian era as a perversion, was customary in Greece and tolerated in Classical antiquity generally. It is emblematic here of Hellenism's appreciation of sexuality, as contrasted by the barbarism of Asiatic cults hostile to man's physical nature.

67 **esset**: subjunctive in an indefinite clause, referring to a typical rather than a specific action.

69 **Maenas**: Maenad; again Attis conflates the cults of Cybele and Dionysus.

71 **columinibus** are peaks.

76 **leonibus**: the lions regularly shown drawing the

chariot of Cybele, mistress of animals.

77 laevum pecoris hostem: the left lion of the pair that drew her chariot; Catullus calls the lion a "flock's enemy" in accordance with the Hellenistic taste for poetic periphrasis. Such practices, generally frowned on by the *poetae novi*, mark the diction of Catullan poems that affect an older "high" style.

81 caede terga cauda: it was customary to represent angry lions as lashing their own backs with their tail. **patere** is the imperative.

84 religat: unties, repeating the sense of *resolvens* (76).

85 rapidum: a proleptic adjective, meaning that he rouses himself to speed in his mind.

86 virgulta: the thickets of the forest.

88 marmora pelagi, an epic usage, reflects the marblelike radiance of the sea.

91: in a final prayer like that of a Greek chorus, Catullus prays that such religious **furor** may not come his way.

92 tuos: the archaic form of *tuus*. See note on 53.3, *Calvos*.

64

Although Catullus and the *neoteroi* disliked the old epic style, which by now had been overworked by the hacks of Alexandria, Athens, and Rome, it still remained The Grand Style, and dactylic hexameter was The Meter. By way of compromise, dissenting poets wrote mini-epics that were sometimes subdivided into a story within a story. The *epyllion* (as it is now called) combines the economy of shorter poems with the spaciousness of Homeric epic.

In this, by far his longest poem, Catullus tells about the wedding of Peleus and Thetis, future parents of the mighty Achilles, hero of Homer's Iliad. The story-within-a-story is the embroidered picture of Theseus' abandonment of Ariadne and its disastrous results. This tale of betrayed love is (ironically) woven into the coverlet on the marriage bed of Peleus and Thetis. Although it portends no such betrayal for Peleus and Thetis, this vividly described narrative embroidery dominates the poem (it is more than half of the total) and gives mythic expression to a theme with which Catullus was much concerned. Ariadne's lament (132–201), arguably the centerpiece of the poem, puts into a woman's mouth the grief expressed elsewhere by Catullus at his own abandonment by Lesbia. Theseus' careless forgetfulness, which in the legend

causes his father's mistaken suicide, parallels the fecklessness of Lesbia. Surrounding this, the perfect wedding of Peleus and Thetis represents a kind of high point in the age of heroes. Achilles, destined to be born of this match, will distinguish himself chiefly by his bloodthirstiness (as we learn in the marriage hymn sung by the Fates, 323–381), and the final comment by the poet emphasizes the degenerate state of later generations.

As in poem 63, the style is deliberately higher and more artificial than that of Catullus' short lyrics, which emulate the vigor and economy of the vernacular. Hyperbaton is the norm, with lines featuring chiastic or interlocking word order. Periphrastic and pleonastic expressions, considered elegant in the grand style, are normal in this way of writing, which seems awkward to us and is often very strange if translated too literally. As a builder of elegant lines, Catullus' ideal is the five-word line; the last word in elegance is the so-called "golden line" (see note on line 59). While this does not necessarily fit our taste in language, it fulfills the Classical expectation that poetry should in every way be a separate thing from everyday language.

Meter: dactylic hexameter (see appendix B).

1–21: Departure of the Argonauts

1 Peliaco is adjectival with **vertice**. The first line is oblique in a way favored by the Alexandrians. We are expected to know that the pines begotten on Pelion's peak sail Neptune's clear waves in the form of a ship named the Argo. Legend has it that Jason's expedition with the Argonauts to capture the golden fleece took place a generation before the Trojan War. The poem begins elegantly with a five-word hexameter.

3 Phasidos: Greek gen. of *Phasis*. **Aeëteos**: adjectival with **fines**. As Aeëtes, Medea's father, was king of Phasis, his land is Aeëtean territory. This is Colchis, at the east end of the Black sea, just south of the Caucasus Mountains where Jason met the sorceress Medea. For sorcery and witchcraft, it was the Transylvania of the ancient world.

4 robora: we would call them the flower of Argive youth; Catullus calls them the "oak," meaning the strongest.

5 Colchis is abl. pl. with **avertere**, from Colchis.

7 abiegnis ... palmis: firwood oars. The interlocking word order is a favorite form of poetic hyperbaton. Cf. lines 9 and 10.

8 **quibus**: for them, i.e., the Argonauts, who need a goddess (**Diva** = Athena Polias, protector of cities) to protect their home towns while they are away winning the Golden Fleece.

9 **currum**: their seagoing chariot, the Argo, is built by Athena (Minerva) herself, patron of craftsmen.

11 **Illa** is the Argo, represented as the first ship. She first introduced (**prima imbuit**) the sea, unversed in sailing (**rudem cursu**), [to seafaring]. **Amphitriten** (Gk. acc.) by metonymy = the sea, so-called after the wife of Poseidon (Neptune), queen of the sea.

14 **emersere** is transitive with **vultus**. The Nereids raised their faces from the **candenti** ... **gurgite** of the **freti**.

15 **monstrum** is not a monster but a prodigy, the first ship. The spondaic line (at **admirantes**) dramatizes the Nereids' astonishment.

18 **nutricum tenus**: as far as their breasts, gen. pl. with the preposition **tenus**, is nearly pictorial, and helps explain Peleus' sudden love-at-first-sight.

19–21 **Tum Thetidis ...tum Thetis ... tum Thetidi**: gen., nom., dat., ringing the changes on the name of Peleus' love. **humanos hymenaeos** is plural for sing., marriage to a mortal. As a Nereid, Thetis is one of the immortals. **pater ipse** (Zeus), having been warned by Prometheus that Thetis' son will be greater than his father, decides to give up his own interest in her (line 27 *suos ... amores*) and to marry Peleus to her instead. Homer represents her as marrying against her will (*Iliad* 18.434); Catullus gives us a willing Thetis.

22–30 **Apostrophe to the heroes of old.** The style is that of the hymn.

22 **nimis** = very, not "excessively." **saeclorum tempore** is a grandiose pleonasm in the hymnic style, of a piece with the anaphoras that follow.

23b This line, missing from the early Veronese manuscript on which our line numbering is based, is partially supplied by an ancient commentary on Virgil; the portion in brackets is a restoration suggested by Peerlkamp. **bonarum** goes with **matrum** in the previous line.

24 **saepe** ... **compellabo** is a convention of hymns, not to be taken literally. He does not address them again, though he mourns their passing at the end of the poem.

25 **Teque** is picked up and repeated by *tene* ... *Tene* (28–29). The anaphora is another feature of the high hymnic style. **adeo eximie** ... **aucte**: so especially honored. **taedis**: metonymy again: [marriage] torches, i.e., marriage.

26–30: Randall Skalsky has shown that these lines were ingeniously illustrated a few decades later on the famous Portland Vase now in the British Museum, and that the vase as a whole duplicates this poem's theme and central structure.

27 **divum**: syncopated gen. pl.; for other such forms, see appendix D. **concessit amores**: i.e. Jupiter yielded to Peleus the sexual partner he would have enjoyed himself save for Prometheus' warning (see on line 21 above); for this meaning of *amores*, cf. 10.1.

28 **Nereïne** is a Greek form of the patronymic *Nereïs*, daughter of Nereus. The form is nom. sing., agreeing with **Thetis**.

29 **nep(o)tem**: Thethys is the mother of Doris, whose daughters are the Nereids. By agreeing to Thetis' wedding to Peleus, she and her husband Oceanus become his grandparents by marriage.

31–42 **Arrival of the wedding guests.** This section features two catalogues: the places in Thessaly from which guests arrive (35–36), and the farming tasks that go undone in their absence (38–42).

31 **quae** ... **optatae** ... **luces**: this wished-for day; the poetic plural also reflects the duration of the grandest weddings.

35–37: **Cieros, Pthiotica Tempe** (here neut. acc. pl.), Crannon, Larisa, and Pharsalus are towns in Thessaly, where Achilles was to grow up. In calling Tempe "Phthiotic," the poem conflates Achilles' birthplace Phthia, in southern Thessaly, with a famous valley in the north. **Pharsalia** in 37 is adjectival with **tecta**.

38–42: the deserted-countryside theme, with appropriate hyperbole emphasized by the anaphora of **non** ... **non** ... **non** in a position of emphasis. Alternate lines describe plowing and vineyard work.

39 **curvis** ... **rastris**: this form of *rastrum* is a kind of hoe or rakelike implement used to break up clods of earth.

40 **prono** ... **vomere**: the plow is deep, pressed down by the plowman to break and turn the lumpy soil (**glebam**).

41 **falx** ... **frondatorum**: the pruners' hook, a curved knife, thins the foliage above the grape-vines to let some sunlight in. People who did this work were *frondatores*.

42 **squalida ... rubigo**: scaly rust (from disuse).

43–49: **Description: the royal palace and the marriage bed.**

43 **ipsius** refers to Peleus, at whose palace in Pharsalus the wedding is taking place. **quacumque ... recessit** wherever it extended (giving the sense of a vast, sprawling palace, **regia**).

45 **soliis** and **mensae** are datives of advantage. The ivory and the cups shine literally "for" the high-backed chairs and the table.

47 **pulvinar ... geniale**: because the bride is divine (*divae*), the *lectus genialis* or marriage bed is a *pulvinar*, a couch used for images of the gods. During the traditional Roman wedding, it was customary to display the marriage bed in the atrium of the house before moving it back to its usual place.

48 **Indo ... dente politum**: gleaming with Indian ivory.

49: a purple coverlet (**purpura**), dyed with the rosy dye (**fuco**) of the mollusc (**conchyli**), covers the bed.

50–70 **Ecphrasis: the picture on the quilt.** An ecphrasis is a pictorial digression describing a work of art within the framework of a larger narrative. Here the sad picture of a seduced and abandoned Ariadne contrasts with the wedding story that frames it.

51 **heroum virtutes** is ironic, given that what follows is not exactly a tale of *virtus*. Such ironic views of the heroic age go with a Hellenistic rejection of harsh archaic values and the adoption of a more contemporary, humanistic spirit.

52 **Diae**: the island north of Crete where Theseus abandoned Ariadne was later identified with Naxos, a large, inhabited island in the Cyclades. But Catullus' Dia is described as if it were one of the many desert islands of the Aegean.

54 **indomitos ... furores**: the uncontrolled passions aroused by love are thematic here and in Virgil's story of Dido in the Aeneid. They easily veer into grief, hatred, and revenge.

56 **utpote ... quae**: "no wonder, since she ..." (Fordyce). It governs the subjunctive *cernat* in a relative clause of characteristic explaining cause (Allen & Greenough §535e, note 1).

58 **immemor ... iuvenis**: the theme of young Theseus' forgetfulness leads to the poetic justice of the terrible price he pays for it in the end. Cf. lines 123, 135, 248.

59: the first of several golden lines in this poem (e.g., 129, 163, 172, 235, 351), consisting of five words: adjective a, adjective b, verb, noun A, noun B. Such artful hyperbaton, impossible in English, was a much-admired part of poetic craft.

60 **ex alga**: from the seaweed lining the shore. **Minoïs** (gen. *Minoidis*) is the patronymic, daughter of Minos.

61–62 **prospicit, eheu,⎪ prospicit**: Catullus uses this form of repetition (see appendix C, epanalepsis) more than once to emphasize the pathos of Ariadne's distraught state: 132–33 *perfide, ab aris,*⎪ *perfide*; 186–87 *omnia muta,*⎪ *omnia*;

63–65 **Non ... non ... non** (cf. 39–41): her naked disarray gives pictorial expression to her bewildered grief. **velatum pectus**: internal accusative in an untranslatable construction: not covered (with respect to) her [once] veiled breast. **lactentis papillas** is the same kind of accusative, depending on **vincta**. The **tereti strophio** is the rounded band with a twist between the breasts which served as a brassiere.

67 **ipsius**: Ariadne's. **alludebant**: played with (by washing back and forth, as if mocking her grief). The spondaic line expresses "the flatness of her despair" (Quinn).

69 **vicem curans**: caring for the plight of. The apostrophe **Theseu**, a practice adopted from Homer by Hellenistic poets, gives the story a personal quality.

70 **perdita** is subjective. Ariadne believes herself doomed because, as she later explains, she has burned her bridges and is now stranded on a desert island.

71–75 **Bridge to the background story of Theseus.**

71 **externavit**: maddened.

72 **Erycina**: Venus, so-called from a cult and temple on Mt. Eryx in Sicily. There were many cults to sexual goddesses later generalized under the title "Venus."

73 **tempestate ... quo ex tempore**: poetic periphrasis for "since that time when."

74 **Piraei**: the Piraeus is the seaport of Athens.

75 **Gortynia templa**: the palace of King Minos was at Cnossos, some distance northeast of Gortyn; hence "Cretan," like *Cnosia* in 172. A *templum* was

any enclosure ritually marked out. Using the plural, Catullus refers to the palace and its grounds.

76–115 Flashback I: Theseus kills the Minotaur.

76 perhibent, they say, begins the digression.
77 Androgeoneae: the version of the myth used by Catullus is that the wrestler Androgeon, son of Minos, was killed by Athenian King Aegeus. The resultant pollution caused a plague (**crudeli peste**), to avoid which the Athenians agreed to send a yearly tribute of seven boys and seven girls to be devoured by the Minotaur, a half-man-half-bull kept in the labyrinthine palace at Knossos. Here we have the adjectival form of Androgeon's name with **caedis**, = the killing of Androgeon.
79 Cecropiam: Athens, so-called after Cecrops, the first king. Modified by **coactam** (76), subject of **solitam esse**.
80 Quis: syncopated *quibus*.
82 Cretam: the island name without the prep., to Crete.
83 funera ... nec funera: oxymoron, living corpses, apparently doomed but still alive. **portarentur**: subjunctive in a comparative result clause (*proicere optavit potius quam talia ... portarentur*) omitting *ut*: Allen & Greenough §571a. The same construction recurs in 150 f.
84 nitens with a long ī = pressing onward.
85 maganimum ... Minoa: a stock epic epithet: "great-hearted Minos" is ironic in such a story as this.
86–87 virgo / regia: epic enjambment of noun and epithet: the royal maid is Ariadne.
88 matris: Pasiphaë, wife of Minos and mother of Ariadne.
89–90 on the *suavis odores* (87) of Ariadne's bed: like the [smell of] myrtles that encircle Eurotas' streams, or various flowers that the spring breeze bears. By metonymy, **colores** = *flores*.
91 ff.: Ariadne in love: she is the subject of **declinavit**, while **illo** is Theseus.
94 misere: with unhappy results.
95 sancte puer: Cupid.
96 quae: Venus, queen of Golgi and Idalium, places on Cyprus sacred to the nature goddess identified with Aphrodite/Venus. For the *quaeque ... quaeque* formula, cf. 36.13f.
97 qualibus is exclamatory, with **fluctibus** (98). In 92–93 love was like fire; here the metaphor of a stormy sea is added.

98: in flavo hospite: we would say "over" fair-haired Theseus, ironically called her guest.
100: Ariadne is pale with fear: By how much more than with the color (**fulgore**) of gold did she blanch (**expalluit**)! A similar comparison is made in 81.4, *inaurata pallidior statua*.
103–104 non must be understood with both **ingrata** and **frustra**: yet she did not promise unpleasing gifts to the gods, [nor did she do so] in vain, [as] she undertook her prayers with silent lip. **succepit** is an archaic form of *suscepit*.
105–11: an epic simile comparing the way a whirlwind knocks down a tree to the way Theseus laid out the Minotaur. **in summo ... Tauro** on the top of the Taurus ridge, a massif in southern Asia Minor just north of Cyprus. **brachia** are branches, the tree's arms. **sudanti cortice**, abl. of description, refers to the resin that sweats out through the bark of the Mediterranean pine.
107 robur: the tree's trunk.
108 eruit is emphasized by enjambment. **illa** is the *pinus* (fem.).
109 quaevis cumque obvia: whatever things are in its way.
110 saevum: substantive, the beast.
114–15: the sense of **flexibus**, twists and turns, is repeated by **error**. **frustraretur**, from the dep. *frustror*, assumes Theseus as its object.

116–31 Flashback II: Ariadne's abandonment.

117–21 ut ... ut ... ut, etc.: how ... how, ... how, etc., governing indirect question subjunctives **praeoptarit** (120), **venerit** (122), **liquerit** (123), depending on the deliberative subjunctive **commemorem**.
118 consanguineae: substantive: her sister Phaedra, herself fated later to marry Theseus and to fall in love with her stepson Hippolytus.
119 deperdita + in + the abl.: her mother Pasiphaë "loved her ill-fated daughter to distraction." **misera** is proleptic.
120 Thesei: bisyllabic, objective gen. with **amorem**, love for Theseus. **praeoptarit** (contracted from *praeoptaverit*) is further contracted by synezesis of *-aeo-* to a three-syllable word.
122 lumina: internal acc., lit. bound with respect to her eyes in sleep.
123: Theseus (now her **coniunx**) is the subj. of **liquerit ... discedens**. The descriptive **immemori ... pectore** repeats the theme introduced in 58, *immemor iuvenis*. Cf. 135 *immemor*.

126 praeruptos: steep.

127 unde ... protenderet: rel. clause of purpose: from which to extend her gaze (**aciem**).

128 tremuli salis: the splashing sea; but there is a sense in which this sea reflects her own trembling.

129 nudatae ... surae: her naked calf, like her half-nakedness in 63–66, expresses her helplessness.

130 extremis ... querellis: her final laments as a mortal.

131 the diminutive **frigidulos** elicits pity, like *turgiduli* in 3.18.

132–201 Ariadne's lament. The masterpiece of the poem, written in the tradition of Euripides' *Medea* 165ff., 670ff., and Apollonius' *Argonautica* 4.355ff. (Medea again); the abandoned woman's reproach became a literary topos: cf. *Aeneid* 4.305 ff. (Dido to Aeneas), Ovid *Heroides* 10, *Fasti* 3.459ff. Ariadne's language here is very like that which Catullus used on his own behalf in poem 30.

132 sicine: an indignant form of *sic*: is *this* the way you have abandoned me?

135 devota ... periuria: what Theseus takes home as his "cursed perjuries" is the curse caused by his false vows of love made to the gods, called down upon him by Ariadne in 195–201.

138 nostri: poetic plural, gen. with **miserescere:** to take pity on me.

139 blanda: sweet, with **voce.**

140 miserae: dat. indirect object of **iubebas**, where (at this period) we should expect an acc. direct object.

142 aërii ... venti: the airy winds, insubstantial as they are, scatter Theseus' promises and render them **irrita**, vain and unfulfilled. Catullus himself says something like this about Lesbia's words in 70.4.

143: The redundancy of **nunc iam** conveys a sense of finality.

145 quis (for *quibus*, dat. of reference) refers to men in general. **cupiens ... praegestit:** another emphatic redundancy, with **apisci**, attain. Take **cupiens** as an adj. with **animus.**

147 cupidae mentis ... libido: more emphasis on male lust.

148 metuere is a gnomic perfect, expressing a general truth.

149 te: apostrophe to Theseus. **versantem:** from the iterative *verso*, tossing and turning.

150 germanum, the Minotaur, Ariadne's half-brother, son of Pasiphaë by the white bull sent by Neptune/Poseidon. The story is that when Poseidon sent a perfect white bull for Minos to sacrifice, the king kept the bull instead for breeding. As punishment, Poseidon made Minos' wife Pasiphaë fall in love with this bull, and Daedalus built a model cow within which Ariadne's mother could copulate with it. The result of this union was the Minotaur, half man and half bull. **crevi**, decided, is from *cerno*.

151 tibi fallaci: dat. of reference or disadvantage, depending on **dessem:** impf. subj., from *desum*. For the subjunctive construction, see note on 83, *portarentur.*

154 Quaenam ... leaena... quod mare ... quae Syrtis, etc: a series of indignant questions: what lioness was it? ..., etc. Theseus is too cruel to have a human mother. The theme, used also in poem 60, goes back to Patroclus' rebuke of Achilles in Iliad 16. In Euripides, Jason calls Medea "a lioness more savage than Scylla." The reduplicated present of **genuit** is *gigno*.

158–63: at the depth of her grief, Ariadne in despair wishes she could be with Theseus under any conditions—even those of a servant.

158 tibi ... cordi fuerant: the dative idiom = if it had not been pleasing to your heart.

159: the **saeva ... praecepta** of Theseus' **prisci ... parentis** (Aegeus) forbade him to marry a foreign woman. **prisci** connotes severity, reinforcing **saeva.**

161 quae ... famularer: rel. clause of purpose, to wait on you. There is pathos in this undignified suggestion: she would stoop to anything to be with Theseus, who scarcely deserves such devotion.

162 vestigia: here, your feet.

163: a Golden Line, constructed like line 59.

164 Sed quid ego, etc.: Ariadne recoils from her fantasy of servitude to Theseus and faces the harsh reality of her plight. **ignaris ... auris:** the deaf winds. **conquerar:** deliberative subj. in a question implying indignation and the futility of complaint.

165 externata: crazed, as in line 71. The antecedent of **quae** is **auris.**

167 prope iam: about now. The winds are deaf, and Theseus (**Ille**) is out of earshot.

168 alga: the beach, as on line 60.

169 nimis insultans: cruelly mocking me.

170 invidit, has begrudged, takes the gen. of the thing refused (**auris**, fortune's ear) and the dat. of the object excluded (**nostris ... questibus**); lit., fortune has even been grudging of her ear to my complaints.

172 **Cnosia Cecropiae**: "Cretan" and "Athenian"; see notes on 75 and 79.

173 **dira stipendia**, gruesome payments, are the human sacrifices sent by Athens to the Minotaur.

174–76 Theseus is now the **perfidus** ... **navita** (= *nauta*) and the **malus** ... **hospes**. With **in** + acc., **religasset** ... **funem** (untied the hawser of his ship) = set sail for.

177 **nitor** with long ī = strive.

178 **Idaeos** ... **montes**: Ariadne is probably thinking of Cretan Mt. Ida, a traditional hideout for fugitives. **At** has the force of "No, because ..."

181: "following the youth spattered with my brother's slaughter," another periphrasis for Theseus.

183 **lentos** ... **remos** his pliant oars, bent with the effort to escape.

185 **cingentibus undis**: causal abl. absolute: no exit lies open, because the waves of the sea surround me.

188–90 **non** ... **ante** ... **nec prius** ... **quam**: she will not collapse until she has demanded a just penalty (**iustam** ... **multam**) for her betrayer. The subjunctives after *prius* ... *quam*, stating Ariadne's purpose (**exposcam** and **comprecer**), are sometimes called anticipatory or prospective subjunctives.

192 **virum**: syncopated gen. pl.: Ariadne uses this word instead of the generic *hominum* because she thinks of the Eumenides as fellow women who avenge the sins of males against women; cf. 143–44, *viro* ... *viri*.

193–94: The **Eumenides**, here invoked as the "kindly spirits" who will vindicate her wrong, are also known as Furies or Erinyes, who punish anyone who has violated a taboo or sacred law. In Aeschylus' *Oresteia*, they seek to punish Orestes because he killed his mother Clytemnestra. **quibus** ... **frons**, etc.: whose forehead, bound with snaky lock, displays the breathing angers of their heart.

195 **huc huc adventate**, etc.: Euripides attempted this angry, operatic eloquence; Seneca imitated it; Shakespeare re-created it, e.g. in King Lear's scene on the heath.

197 **inops, ardens**, etc.: asyndeton compresses the emotion of Ariadne's prayer and expresses the urgency of her violent passions.

198 **quae** ... **verae** refers to her *querellas* (195).

199 **nolite pati**: do not let.

200–201 **quali** ... **tali** sets the stage for the poetic justice that befalls Theseus when he returns home. The emphasis is on **mente**, the quality of mind that makes this Theseus such a shabby "hero"—and will

trip him up as he returns home. **funestet**: pollute, also make mournful.

202–14: **Ariadne's curse takes hold.**

202 **voces** = words, as often.

205–206: all three parts of the cosmos are moved by the nod of Jupiter (204, *caelestum rector*): **tellus**, the **horrida aequora**, and the vault of heaven (**mundus**), which in turn shakes the **micantia sidera** that hang from it.

207–208 **mentem** ... **consitus**: a reflexive passive or middle construction; see note on 64–65. In a kind of epic double causation where human action and divine machinery work together, Theseus' forgetfulness is a result both of his own thoughtless character and of Ariadne's curse.

209 **quae mandata**: the commands which..., explained by Aegeus in 232ff.

210: the **dulcia signa** are the *candida vela* of line 235, the white sails signaling that Theseus' mission has succeeded. **nec** should be understood with both **sustollens** here and **ostendit** in the next line.

211 **Erechtheum** ... **portum** is the Piraeus, the port of Athens. For the periphrasis, cf. *moenia divae* for Athens in 212.

212 **ferunt**, they say, serves the same purpose as *perhibent* in lines 76 and 124, to introduce a flashback. **divae** is the goddess Athena, eponymous patron of the city.

215–37: **Flashback: Aegeus' farewell to Theseus.** The old man's speech consists of two long sentences, 215–27 and 228–37.

215: **gnate** ... **unice**: vocative, like *reddite* (217): my only son, ...

217 **reddite** ... **nuper mihi**: Theseus' mother Aethra took him as an infant to Troezen, where her father King Pittheus raised him. When he grew up he went to Athens and was recognized by his father, by then an old man.

218: cf. the wording of 101.5, *quandoquidem fortuna mihi tete abstulit ipsum*, where Catullus grieves for his brother.

219 **cui**: the antecedent is **mihi**; his eyes are **languida**, weak with age.

221 **mittam** is the first of four futures (*sinam* in 222, *expromam* in 223, *suspendam* in 225) followed by an *ut* ... *dicet* purpose clause. The rambling construction imitates an old man's manner of

speaking.

222 **secundae** (from *sequor*) means "favorable" because a following wind was advantageous to sailing.

224 **canitiem ... foedans**: abstract for concrete: fouling my grey hair (in an ancient ritual of grief).

225: the **infecta ... lintea** (dyed sails) which Aegeus hangs from the wandering mast (**vago ... malo**) of his son's ship are the ones Theseus will forget to replace when he returns successful.

227: the sail or **carbasus** will declare (**dicet**) his grief because it is darkened with Spanish *ferrugo*, an iron oxide dye that turns it black.

228 **quod** is adversative, but. The **sancti ... incola Itoni** is Athena because of her sanctuary at Itonus in Boeotia. This is a typically Hellenistic periphrasis, giving a special pleasure to readers who know their Greek geography.

230 **ut ... respergas**: clause of purpose with **concesserit** (228): if she has granted that you spatter, etc.

231 **facito ut**: fut. imperative, taking three *ut*-clauses of result (lines 231, 233, 236) with six present subjunctives: bring it about that...

234 **antennae**: yardarms. The **funestam ... vestem** is the black dyed sail described in 227.

237 **cum te**, etc.: when the happy day (**aetas prospera**) presents you returning.

238–50: **Ariadne's curse fulfilled.**

238 **mandata**, repeated here for the third time (cf. 209, 232), are subject of *liquere* (240).

239 **ceu**, just as, an old epic word, introduces an epic nature simile.

242 **absumens**: wasting away.

244 **scopulorum**: the cliffs of the Acropolis in Athens (cf. 241 *summa ... ex arce*). Another tradition says that he threw himself into the sea from the cliffs at Sunium, thus giving his name to the Aegean Sea.

246 **domus**: gen. sing., depending on **funesta ... tecta**. The abl. **paterna morte** explains **funesta**.

247–48 **qualem ... talem** calls attention to the poetic justice of this tragic legend. **Minoidi** is the dative of the patronymic *Minoïs*, viz. Ariadne.

249–50 brings us back to the scene embroidered on the coverlet: Ariadne (**Quae**) staring in grief (**maesta** and **saucia**) at the fleeing ship of Theseus.

251–66 **Another part of the quilt: Dionysus and his worshipers.** The happy ending of Ariadne's story

was that Dionysus came to her rescue and married her without delay, and that she bore him many children.

251 **Iacchus**: one of Dionysus' cult titles, like *Bacchus*.

252 **thiaso**: as on 63.28. **Nysigenis**: born at Nysa, where legend has it the cult began.

254 **lymphata mente**: with frenzied mind—as regularly shown in paintings of Dionysus, their heads thrown back in ecstasy (255 *capita inflectentes*).

255 **euhoe**: the cry of the Bacchants, exclamatory and not grammatically linked to the context.

256 **tecta ... cuspide**: abl. of material. The thyrsus is a spear topped with a pinecone and wrapped with ivy or vine leaves.

257 **divolso ... iuvenco**: in their wild rituals, Bacchants would tear apart living animals in an act called the *sparagmos*.

258 **tortis serpentibus**: snake handling is common in many orgiastic religions.

259–60 **celebrabant** were honoring. **orgia**: ritual objects, sometimes of a sexual nature, lost their power if not kept secret. For the repetition of *orgia*, see appendix C, apanalepsis. **audire** = hear about. **profani** are the uninitiated.

262: the t- sounds imitate the tinkling (**tinnitus**) of the cymbals: **tereti ... aere**, polished bronze; abl. with **ciebant**, which takes acc. pl. **tenuis tinnitus** as object.

263 **multis**, dat. of reference: some of the women are making deep, noisy booming sounds (**raucisonos ... bombos**) on **cornua**, which must be some kind of bass horns.

264 **barbaraque horribili**, etc: the imagination of the observer takes us so far into the picture that we not only hear the noises produced by this wild band, but we also react unpleasantly to its outlandish racket. Dionysus' rescue of Ariadne is therefore less a happy ending than a distasteful conclusion.

266: clasped the bed and clothed it with its vesture, a triple poetic pleonasm to close the digression.

267–77: **Departure of the mortal wedding guests.**

267 **Quae**, acc. pl., the scenes on the coverlet. **cupide**, eagerly, describes the gerund **spectando**.

268 **decedere divis**: make way for the gods.

269 **Hic**: temporal, at this point. **qualis** begins an epic simile comparing the departing guests to waves

moving before a morning breeze. A variant of similes in the *Iliad* (4.422ff., 7.63f.), it is completed by *sic* (276).

270 **horrificans**, ruffling, takes **mare** in the previous line as its object. **proclivas**: predicate adj.: the west wind sends the waves "tumbling forward."

271 **Aurora exoriente**: abl. absolute. **vagi** here (as in line 277) with no sense of fickleness or uncertainty = moving. **sub** with the acc. **limina** = towards. The morning star **Aurora** rises and moves through the heavens toward the rising sun.

272: the antecedent of **quae** is *undas* (270).

273 **cachinni** may be taken as gen. dependent on **plangore**: the waves, still moving gently, sound with the gentle beat of laughter.

275 **purpurea** ... **ab luce**: the waves glow "with" the rosy light. *Purpureus* may refer to any color in a spectrum of reds to blues.

277 **ad se**: to his own home. **vago, passim**, and the prefix of *discedebant* mutually express the scattering movement of the departing guests.

278–302: The immortal guests arrive.

278 **princeps** is nearly adverbial, "first of all."

279 **Chiron** the Centaur, equine god of Mt. Pelion, was to bring up young Achilles. In Homer, his wedding gift is a spear.

280–81 **Thessala** ... **ora**: the Thessalian region. **fluminis**: we are expected to know that the river in question is the Peneus.

282 **aura parit...fecunda**: the warm west wind was believed capable of generating plant life by itself.

283 **indistinctis** ... **corollis**: swags or festoons of flowers, commonly used to decorate Roman banqueting halls, are imagined here, simply fashioned of every flower in the region. In Catullus' more sophisticated Rome they would have been artfully constructed of one or two color-coordinated varieties.

284 **permulsa** (from *permulceo*) ... **risit**: two metaphors. The nearly personified house is caressed and laughs with delight at the smell of the wild flowers.

285 **Penios**: eponymous god of the river that runs through Tempe between Mts. Olympus and Ossa to the sea. The scenic beauty of the Tempe Valley was proverbial in antiquity. Trees are his appropriate gift.

287 **Minosim** and **doris**: two words in the text which are neither understood nor convincingly emended. **linquens** modifies *Penios* and takes neut.

pl. *Tempe* (both in 285) as its object. The idea is that the river god leaves Tempe to be filled (**celebranda**) with some kind of dancers (**choreis**) in his absence.

288–91: catalogue of trees brought by Peneus. **non vacuos** (archaic form of *vacuus*): litotic. He comes not empty-handed, bearing wedding gifts. **radicitus**: adverb, roots and all. The various trees he brings are for planting. Each is described, in the manner of an epic catalogue, with a particularizing epithet: tall beech-trees (**altas fagos**), lofty laurels with straight trunks, a waving (**nutanti**) plane tree, a supple (**lenta**) poplar, and a towering cypress. Instead of naming the poplar, Catullus gives us a mythological periphrasis. After Phaëthon drove his father's Sun Chariot to a fiery death, his weeping sisters were transformed into poplar trees, which shed "tears" of amber sap.

292 **sedes**: the palace of Peleus. **contexta**: not literally woven together, but planted near to each other to form a natural screen around the *vestibulum*, as the next line explains.

295 **extenuata** ... **vestigia**, faint scars from where the vulture gnawed at his innards. Prometheus was released when he told Zeus that the marriage he should avoid was with Thetis. He is therefore an appropriate guest when she marries somebody besides Zeus.

296 **silici** is dative, to the rock.

298 **pater**, etc. Jupiter and the first family. **-que** is hypermetric, eliding with **advenit** in the next line.

299 **Phoebe** (voc.): Phoebus Apollo, who according to one version of the legend shot the arrow that killed Achilles. He and his sister are represented here as opposed to the union of Achilles' parents.

300 **unigenam**: Apollo's twin sister, Phoebe or Artemis, identified as the inhabitant (**cultrix**) of Idrias in Caria, where a goddess comparable to Hecate/Artemis/Diana was worshiped.

301 **aspernata est**: another ironic ending. The catalogue of divine guests ends with two prominent divinities who (according to this version) boycotted the wedding. The story is otherwise unknown.

302 **taedas** ... **iugalis** = wedding (by metonymy).

303–22 The Fates. Catullus' picture of the Parcae, rich with pictorial features, shows a Hellenistic love of interesting detail in verse descriptions.

303 **Qui**: Jupiter and Juno. **flexerunt artus**: sat. The chairs are **niveis** because they are made of ivory

(line 45).

304 **large** ... **constructae**: piled high.

308–309: **candida purpurea** and **roseae niveo**: a favorite color combination in poetry. Here the Fates wear white robes with purple hem, complemented by a red headband in their white hair.

311 **colum** ... **lana** ... **amictum**: the distaff, wrapped in wool, is in the left hand, while the right pulls out and twists the fibers.

312–15 **supinis** ... **digitis**: with the fingers facing up. **prono in pollice**: with thumb facing down, she would turn her spindle (**versabat fusum**), which is weighted with a round weight (**libratum tereti** ... **turbine**) called a flywheel (*turbo*) because it provided the twisting momentum necessary for spinning. Then (**atque ita**) with her last remaining tooth, she would even up (**aequabat**) the thread by plucking off (**decerpens**) odd strands of fiber. Each of the combined tasks is described with a participle-verb combination: **deducens** ... **formbat, torquens** ... **versabat, decerpens aequabat**.

318 **candentis** describes the white wool (**lanae**).

319 **virgati calathisci** are small wicker baskets made of twigs (a *virga* is a twig). **custodi(e)bant**: were holding.

320 **Haec**: archaic fem. pl., the Fates. **pellentes**: striking the **vellera** of unspun wool, perhaps to fluff them up.

322 **perfidiae**: descriptive gen. with **aetas**: in epic, it is axiomatic that later ages are more wicked than the age of heroes.

323–81 **Marriage Hymn: the song of the Fates.**

323 **decus eximium** is the object of **augens**, which also serves as a substantive referring to Peleus: you who increase....

324 **Emathiae tutamen**: guardian of Emathia, a part of Macedonia that came by convention to stand for Thessaly. **Opis**: Jove's mother was Ops in Roman tradition.

325 **luce**: day; cf. 66.90 *festis luminibus*, holidays.

326 **vos** refers to the *fusi* in the next line. **quae** refers to the *subtegmina* or cross threads on the loom of life that the fates follow.

327 **currite** ... **fusi**: the spindles on which the Fates wound the thread of life (line 314) are now bidden to run through the vertical threads, leading the cross threads (**subtegmina**) in the loom of life. In a modern loom the spindle would fit inside a shuttle; the vertical threads are the warp, the cross

threads are the weft or woof. This line serves as the refrain in the song of the Fates, recurring at irregular intervals of three, four, or five lines at the end of each sentence.

328 **tibi**: the Parcae now speak to Peleus, the groom.

329 **Hesperus**, the evening star, will bring the consummation of the wedding that the bridal couple desire. It is the *faustum sidus* that brings them together, as in the beginning of poem 62.

330 **quae**: the bride, the *coniunx* of the previous line. **flexanimo** ... **amore** is love that moves the heart.

334 **contexit**: sheltered.

335–36 **tali** ... **foedere** ... **qualis concordia**: with such a bond as the harmony which.... **Peleo** is contracted by synizesis into two syllables.

338–71: The central part of the Fates' song is their prophecy about Achilles, whose bloody career in the Trojan War will be an ironic testimony to his glory.

338 **vobis**: Peleus and Thetis.

339 **haud tergo** ... **notus**: the enemy will never see his back turned in flight. **hostibus** is dative with **notus**.

340 **vago victor certamine cursus**: an alliterative way of saying "winner in the far-ranging contest of running." In Homer, he is swift-footed Achilles.

341: the **vestigia** of the **celeris** ... **cervae** are **flammea** because of its speed.

344 **Phrygii** and **Teucro** are both adjectival equivalents of Trojan. Phrygia was just east of the Troad; Teucer was an ancestor of the Trojans.

346 **periuri Pelopis** ... **tertius heres** is a high-sounding periphrasis for Agamemnon, chief of the Greeks besieging Troy. His grandfather Pelops, eager to defeat Oenomaus in a chariot race and win the hand of his daughter Hippodameia, bribed Oenomaus' charioteer Myrtilus to sabotage Oenomaus' chariot. He later murdered Myrtilus to cover up his crime and brought a curse upon his house.

350 **solvent**: the mothers of his defeated adversaries will tear out the unkempt hair from their gray heads.

351: a Golden Line. In their grief, aged mothers will bruise (lit. "mottle," **variabunt**) their breasts, which are **putrida**, withered, with age.

353 **praecerpens**: cutting before him.

354 **sole sub ardenti**: for the word order, see note on 69.6, *valle sub alarum*.

355 **Troiugenum**: gen. pl., an old epic form for

Trojans.

357: **testis** takes the dative, **magnis virtutibus**; the irony is that all his "virtues" are homicidal. **unda Scamandri**, etc.: Homer describes this scene in gory detail in the Iliad, Bk. 21. The Scamander River flows past Troy.

359–60: Achilles is the understood subject of **angustans** and **tepefaciet**.

360 **alta ... flumina**: the river's deep streams. **caede** means blood here and in line 368 below.

362 **morti quoque**: also to his death (as well as his ferocity when alive).

363 **teres ... bustum**: his rounded grave mound, heaped with a high pile of earth, is imitated by the symmetrical word order of this line.

364 **perculsae virginis**: after Troy's fall, Achilles' ghost demanded that Priam's young daughter Polyxena be slaughtered on his grave. She is the second female victim of the *heroum virtutes* mentioned in line 51.

367 **urbis Dardaniae**: Troy, first built by Dardanus. **Neptunia vincla** are Troy's encircling walls, built by Neptune for Laomedon, another early king.

368 explains how Achilles' grave mound (poet. pl. **alta ... sepulcra**) will receive (364 **excipiet**) its victim. **Polyxenia ... caede**: Polyxena's blood.

369 **ancipiti ferro**: the double-headed sacrificial axe.

370 Gruesome elegance: —will fling her trunk onto her bended knee, a corpse. These blunt words end the prophecies of Achilles' illustrious career.

372 **animi**: gen. of source with **amores**, true love.

373 **divam**: the sea nymph Thetis, his bride.

376–80: a mangled and obscure text is rearranged here. Line 378, containing an out-of-place repetition of the refrain, is omitted by most editors. The belief was that if the same thread that fit the bride's neck before the wedding night is too short to go around it the morning after, the bride has been properly deflowered and the marriage will be happy. The bride's nurse (376 **nutrix**) is imagined successfully performing this test when she returns (**revisens**) to her mistress at dawn. Therefore the bride's **anxia ... mater** will have no cause to be **maesta** about the sleeping-apart (**secubitu**) of a quarrelsome daughter (**discordis ... puellae**), and she won't stop (**mittet**) hoping for **nepotes**. In this construction **nec** governs both **maesta** and **mittet**.

382–end: **A final comment on how far we have fallen from the Age of Heroes.** The final 25 lines are reminiscent of a passage in Aratus' *Phainomena*

(96–136), a popular Hellenistic poem on astronomy, describing how Justice (the constellation Virgo) left the earth when humankind became wicked.

384 **praesentes**: in person, as in line 396. **ante**: the adverb, formerly.

386 **nondum spreta pietate**: abl. abs., when righteousness was not yet scorned.

387 **revisens** is intransitive, "paying his regular visit" (Fordyce).

389 **centum ... tauros**: the so-called hecatomb, performed with prodigal frequency in epic poems as a mark of heroic piety (and boundless wealth).

390–91 **vagus Liber**: Dionysus, leading his Bacchants (**Thyadas**) in their annual pilgrimage on Mt. Parnassus. **evantis**: acc. pl., shouting 'Euhoe!'

393 **divum**: acc. sing. = Dionysus.

395 **rapidi Tritonis era**: Athene or Minerva, mistress of the swift Triton River. **Amarunsia virgo** is Artemis, so-called after a place in Euboea where she was worshiped.

396 **est praesens hortata**: urged on in person.

400 **destitit**: from *desisto*.

402 **innuptae ... novercae**: the situation seems to be that a father wants his son to die so that he can then be free to take over the **flore** of his son's intended bride and make her a *noverca*, or stepmother, to the rest of his children.

403 **substernens**: a mother commits incest under cover of a disguise.

405 **fanda nefanda**: asyndeton. **malo ... furore**: abl. of cause; Hellenistic philosophers taught that irrationality was the source of all evil, and that confusion caused by *furor* makes us choose evil behavior. Hence Virgil's emphasis on *furor* in the tragedy of Dido.

406 **iustificam**: a hapax legomenon, justly dealing.

407 **talis coetus**: such as our own weddings.

408 **contingi ... lumine claro**: to be illuminated by the light of day. The gods usually conceal themselves from us in a cloud of mist or are otherwise lost to our mortal vision.

65

This poem, the first of four long elegiac poems, invites the inference that Q. Hortensius Hortalus, the *Ortale* of lines 2 and 15, had suggested translation of some Greek poetry as a way out of a writing slump brought on by the death of Catullus' brother. Whatever the actual facts, a reflection on his brother's death is one of two major digressions in this literary epistle; the other is a remarkable Homeric simile, which closes the poem.

Meter: elegiac couplets (see appendix B): all of the poems from here to the end of the collection are in this same meter.

1 **etsi**: introduces an adversative clause which includes the first fourteen lines, followed by *sed tamen*, the main clause of the poem. Even though *cura* for my dead brother has distracted me, nevertheless I am sending you these lines (probably poem 66).

2 **a doctis virginibus**: from the Muses, viz. the writing of poetry. **Ortale**: for more on Hortalus, see appendix A.

3 **dulcis Musarum ... fetus** = *carmina*.

4 **mens animi**: the thought of my mind. The phrase, which occurs earlier in Plautus and Lucretius, represents the *mens* as part of a larger organ, the *animus*. This and phrases like *doctis virginibus* (line 2) suggest that poetry was conceived as a more rational than intuitive process. **fluctuat**: with *gurgite*, *unda*, and *litore* (5–7), this uses waves and water as a metaphor for grief. Cf. Attis on the beach in 63.47ff., and Ariadne's scene in 64.127ff. For the phrasing, cf. 64.62, *magnis curarum fluctuat undis*.

5 **namque** introduces an explanatory digression (lines 5–14), as often in Catullus.

5–6: complex hyperbaton in elevated poetic style: the running water has recently washed my brother's pale foot in the Lethaean stream. Each noun is modified by an adjective, the verb by an adverb. The word order is inclusive, with emphasis on words for running water. Lethe is the river of forgetfulness in the underworld through which all souls pass.

7–8: highly wrought word order, as in the previous couplet: whom the Trojan earth below the Rhoetean shore crushes, snatched from my eyes. Rhoeteum was the promontory on the Hellespont, near Troy.

10–12: the apostrophe to his brother, whose name he never mentions in his poems, returns to the plain style.

13–14: the simile is as old as Homer (*Od.* 19.518–23) and sets the stage for the more original epic simile at the end of the poem. **qualia** refers to *carmina* in the previous line. **Daulias** [*avis*] is Procne, wife of the Daulian king Tereus, and mother by him of Itylus (or Itys). When he rapes her sister Philomela, Procne kills their son. The

gods take mercy and turn the sisters into a nightingale and a swallow to save them from the wrath of Tereus. Ovid retells the story in *Met.* 6.442ff.

16 **expressa ... carmina**: translated lines. *Exprimo* is the usual term for translation; the plural is collective, referring to the lines of a single poem. **Battiadae**: Callimachus, son of Battus, calls himself this in one of his epigrams (35 Pf.). He was one of the leading poets of the Hellenistic age.

17 **tua dicta**: presumably Hortalus' suggestion that Catullus try his hand at verse translation.

19 **ut**, just as, compares forgetfulness (line 18, *effluxisse ... animo*) to an apple rolling from a girl's lap (*procurrit ... e gremio*) when she is startled by her mother's sudden appearance. The apple is a secret pledge (*furtivo munere*) from the boy who has promised to marry her; she has hidden the love token *molli sub veste* (21), and when she jumps up in confusion, a guilty blush (*conscius ... rubor*) spreads across her face. The simile is significantly irrelevant to the somber tone of the rest of the poem, in the tradition of the long similes that relieve the battle scenes of Homer's Iliad.

66

This is probably the translation of Callimachus introduced in the previous poem (65.16, *expressa ... carmina Battiadae*). The Greek original is lost, but two fragments, republished for the first time since antiquity in 1929 and 1952, show that Catullus took liberties with the text of Callimachus, sometimes glossing over sticky and erudite passages that he could not figure out. Callimachus, a schoolteacher and librarian in third-century Alexandria, was the most popular of the Hellenistic poets during late antiquity, meticulous, learned, and subtle. Catullus and his friends admired his workmanship and economy. Unlike the other poems of Catullus, this may be less an autonomous performance than a technical tour de force in which a not-yet-mature poetic language (Latin) is set head to head with a mature poetic language (Greek) as composed by a superb technician (Callimachus).

The poem as originally written soon after 247 B.C. has to do with a lock of hair vowed as an offering by Queen Berenice of Egypt for the safe return of her new husband, Ptolemy III Euergetes, from a campaign against Syria. Upon his safe return the lock was duly dedicated in a temple, but it soon disappeared mysteriously. The court astronomer, Conon, came to the rescue by claiming to have discovered the lock as a new constellation, and the court poet Callimachus immortalized the face-saving discovery in lighthearted elegiac verses. The theme of a wife's sexually passionate devotion was highly congenial to Catullus, who projects upon Berenice his hopes for a similar devotion from Lesbia. In addition to the personal significance this theme seems to have had for Catullus, Hellenistic and Roman audiences had a strong interest in the idealized sexual love that is the subject of this poem.

1–9: Conon the astronomer saw me gleaming in the heavens.

1 **qui**: i.e., Conon, described first as in an honorific citation before being named in line 7. **lumina mundi**: the bright bodies of the heavens would include the sun, moon, and planets as well as the stars.

3 **ut**: how, as in lines 4 and 5. The reference in this line is to eclipses of the sun. **rapidi**: scorching, devouring. For the spondaic line, cf. lines 41, 57, 61.

4 **cedant ... sidera** refers to the setting of planets or constellations or their disappearance in the sun at regular intervals, *certis ... temporibus*.

5 **Triviam**: the moon (Luna) is a threefold goddess, Diana/Hecate/Proserpina. Cf. 34.15. **Latmia saxa** = Mt. Latmus in Caria, just east of Miletus. The moon-goddess Selene fell in love with the shepherd Endymion, and had trysts with him on the mountain. Cf. the encounter of Venus/Aphrodite with Anchises on Mt. Ida near Troy. Catullus' mythic periphrasis refers to the dark phase of the moon, the single night in each lunar month when it appears to be absent from the sky.

7 **me**: the poem is a monologue spoken by the lock of hair, now a constellation. **caelesti in lumine**: in the bright sky.

8 **caesariem**: a lock of luxuriant hair; appositive with *me* above.

9–14: Queen Berenice vowed me as an offering when her royal husband left to conquer Syria.

10 **protendens brachia**: the traditional attitude of prayer.

11 **novo auctus hymenaeo**: glorified by his new

marriage. Cf. 64.25, *taedis felicibus aucte*. The point of view is appropriately feminine throughout. There is hiatus between *novo* and *auctus*, and the *h* of *hymenaeo* is strong enough to make the previous syllable long by position. The effect is to make the line slow and stately.

12 **vastatum**: supine in -*um* showing purpose, like *visum* in 10.2. **Assyrios** = *Syrios*.

13 **vestigia rixae**: marks of their amatory scuffle on the wedding night; Berenice is no passive lover. For the golden line, see appendix C and note on 64.59.

14 **virgineis ... exuviis**: a play on the metaphor of love as warfare; the spoil or plunder of his victorious encounter was her virginity.

15–20: Are brides unwilling lovers? My mistress Berenice taught me otherwise when her man went off to war.

15–16 **nuptis odio**: double dative: is sex (*Venus*) really hateful to brides? Are the tears false with which the pleasures of her parents [to see her married] are spoiled (*frustrantur*)? **lacrimulis**: a disparaging diminutive, = crocodile tears. According to the lock, brides make a show of grief on leaving their parents, but they are really looking forward to their conjugal pleasures.

18 **divi ... iverint** (=*iuverint*): a bold and unusual hyperbaton.

20 **invisente novo ... viro**: abl. absolute with temporal force: when her new husband went to see fierce battles.

21–26: How you grieved when he left, Berenice! But you were always strong-hearted.

21 **Et tu**, etc.: an apostrophe to Berenice, to line 42. **lux(is)ti**: from *lugeo*.

22 **fratris cari**: though Berenice and Ptolemy III were only cousins, the Egyptian royal couple were officially styled "brother" and "sister." The lock responds here to Berenice's imagined objection that her grief was official mourning for her consort's absence, not lovesickness caused by her *orbum cubile*.

24 **Ut** is exclamatory, like *quam penitus* above, *quae verba* (29), and *ut* (30).

26 **cogno(ve)ram** governs indirect statement, *te [esse] magnanimam*: I knew you were brave since childhood, but this time you have gone to pieces: therefore I know your grief is no official posture.

27–32: Have you forgotten how you won your spouse? Yet now you are broken-hearted: surely this is a lover's longing.

27 bonum ... facinus: a slight oxymoron, referring to an intrigue by which Berenice's mother was trying to arrange a marriage between Berenice and one Demetrius. Demetrius, meanwhile, was having an affair with the mother, and Berenice escaped the tangle by arranging to have Demetrius assassinated. This cleared the way for her marriage to Ptolemy III. The story is cited as evidence that Berenice is no softie.

28 alis = *alius* (male or female); cf. 29.15 *alid*.

30 tri(vi)sti (from *tero*) **lumina**: you rubbed your eyes.

31 mutavit: i.e., changed your mood from joy to grief. **An quod** introduces the lawyerly lock's conclusion from the evidence presented, that Berenice's distress has been caused by sudden withdrawal *a caro corpore*, viz. from sex with her husband.

33–38: That is why you vowed to give me up if he returned, and why I now fulfill her vow up here.

35 tetulisset is a reduplicated form of the regular pluperfect subjunctive *tulisset*.

36 Asiam: the official record claims that Ptolemy carried his conquest beyond Syria to the borders of India.

37 Quīs = quibus. **reddita**: handed over (in fulfillment of her vow).

38 novo munere: a novel thank-offering.

39–50: I left your head unwillingly, O Queen, but who is equal to the power of iron? A curse on those who first brought iron from the earth!

39: Virgil adapted this line for Aeneas' plea to Dido when he sees her in the underworld: *Invitus, regina, tuo de litore cessi* (Aen. 6.460).

41 digna ferat: may he get what he deserves. **adiurarit**: a spondaic ending, syncopated from *adiuraverit*.

42 ferro: i.e., the scissors that severed the unwilling lock. There is a trace of comic overstatement in the lock's self-justification.

43–46: as testimony to the strength of iron *force majeure*, the still lawyerly lock introduces the precedent of the canal dug across the Acte peninsula by

the forces of Xerxes on their way to invade Greece in 483 B.C. **Ille ... mons**: Mt. Athos, neither the largest mountain in Greece nor the site of the canal. The lock is warming to its subject with some rhetorical hyperbole.

44 progenies Thiae: i.e., the sun, offspring of Hyperion and Thia.

45 peperere = *pepererunt*, from *pario*, produce.

47: like a trained orator, the lock concludes this section of her argument by repeating the topic statement (line 42).

48–50: apostrophe to Jupiter. **ut**: would that, with the optative subjunctive **pereat**. **Chalybōn**: Gk. gen. pl. depending on **genus**: the race of the Chalybes (miners and iron-workers from the far end of the Black Sea).

50 institit: began (from *insisto*). **stringere**: work or forge.

51–56: My sister locks grieved when Memnon's brother the west wind appeared and bore me off to the lap of Venus.

51 paulo ante: with **abiunctae comae**, recently detached; appositional gen. with **mea fata**.

52–53 Memnonis Aethiops unigena: Zephyrus, brother of Ethiopian king Memnon, who was killed at Troy. Their mother was the dawn goddess Eos or Aurora. The god of the west wind, he is represented here as a winged horse (54 *ales equos*).

54 obtulit: with *se* (52), presented himself. **Arsinoës Locridos ales equos**: appositive to *unigena*; Arsinoë was Ptolemy II's queen, deified and venerated in a temple on a promontory named Zephyrium; hence the connection with Zephyrus the west wind. She is called Locrian because she was their chief goddess; Epizephyrian Locri in south Italy was also the home of Zephyrus.

57–64: Venus had sent Zephyr on that errand so Ariadne's crown would not be alone in the heavens and we too should have our place. She placed me, still damp, among the stars.

57 Ipsa ... Zephyritis: Venus, who was identified with the deified Arsinoë Zephyritis, "goddess of Zephyrium." **eo ... lega(ve)rat**: had sent him as her envoy for this purpose.

58 an unusual four-word pentameter describing Venus, "the Greek inhabitant of Canopus' shores." Canopus, on one of the Nile's mouths near Alexandria, was also the site of a famous temple of Serapis, a healing deity whose cult was widespread in Catullus' time. See note on 10.26f., *volo ad Serapim deferri.*

59 vario ... in lumine caeli: in the sky's dappled radiance; cf. 7, *caelesti in lumine.*

60–61: ex Ariadneis ... temporibus, etc.: when Dionysus married Ariadne, he turned her wedding wreath *(aurea corona)* into a constellation. See diagram. Venus did not want Ariadne's crown to be the only stellar memento from a royal head.

62 devotae ... exuviae: dedicated memento. The structure of this four-word pentameter closely resembles that of the "golden" hexameter.

63 uvidulam a fluctu: a little damp because it lay at the temple of Aphrodite Zephyritis, near the sea. ad templa deum: to the regions of the gods, i.e., the sky.

64 in antiquis (sc. *sideribus*) is explained by reference to the neighboring constellations Virgo, Leo, Callisto (Ursa Major), and Boötes. diva is Venus.

66 lumina: stars. Callisto ... Lycaoniae: dative with iuncta, close to. Callisto was the daughter of Lycaon, king of Arcadia. A devotee of Diana, she was raped by Jupiter, who approached her disguised as Diana. Juno, in a jealous rage, turned her into a bear, but Jupiter transformed her into the constellation that bears her name. The story is retold by Ovid, *Met.* 2.409ff.

65–68: Near Virgo and Leo and next to Callisto the Bear, I drop beneath the horizon just before Boötes.

67 vertor in occasum, etc.: "I wheel to my setting, leading the way in front of slow Boötes" (Ellis). 68 vix sero: quite late; Cf. *vix tandem,* 62.2.

69–78: But though I inhabit the sky by night and the sea by day (for I must tell the truth though other stars will hate me), I do not enjoy my stardom so much as I miss my mistress, with whom I enjoyed countless perfumes.

69 me ... premunt vestigia divum: variously explained: "I am one of the stars, and keep company with the gods" (Merrill), "she is in the sky, the floor of heaven" (Fordyce), "the gods dwell beyond the stars and in their journeyings to earth and back naturally cross the *limen caeli*" (Quinn). 70 canae Tethyï: Gk. dat. with short *i*. Tethys, wife

of Oceanus, is white-haired with age, and perhaps because of the shining of the morning sea.

71 pace tua: a conciliatory idiom: with no offense to you, by your leave. Ramnusia virgo is Nemesis, because of her shrine in the Attic deme of Ramnus. 73 discerpent: pull me to pieces for my *infestis dictis.*

74 quin ... evoluam: subjunctive result clause after *tegam* (72).

75 non ... tam laetor ... quam ... discrucior: a modest disclaimer: though she appreciates the status of constellation; she chiefly regrets being separated from her mistress.

75–76: afore ... afore = *afuturam esse*, fut. inf. of *absum*. The infinitive construction depends on discrucior: I am tormented that I will be forever absent from my mistress's head. For this type of repetition, cf. 82–83 below and see appendix C on epanalepsis.

77–78: quicum ... una: together with whom. One reason for her regret is that in Berenice's company she was treated with milia multa [*unguentum*]. Berenice was well known for her love of perfumes; her patronage helped make Alexandria one of the great perfumeries of the ancient world.

79–88: Chaste wives, do not make love until you have poured me a libation of perfume. I seek no such offerings from faithless wives; rather let your homes be harmonious and loving.

81 papillas: a typically Catullan touch: cf. 55.12, 61.101, 64.65.

82 onyx: yellow marble, and the perfume jar made from this material which was believed best suited for preserving the scent of perfumes. Note the epanalepsis, as in lines 75–76 above.

85 a: exclamatory. irrita, useless, is proleptic: the dust would drink the libation to no avail because the sacrificer is not pure of heart.

89–94: Queen Berenice, when you sacrifice to Venus do not forget a libation for me. Confound the stars! I'd rather be a royal lock!

90 festis luminibus: on holidays. The noun *lumen* recurs seven times in this poem, with five different meanings.

91 siris: an archaic optative = *sine*: do not allow me to go unperfumed. tuam me: I who am your own. The monosyllabic line ending adds emphasis.

The Coma Berenices and Her Neighbors

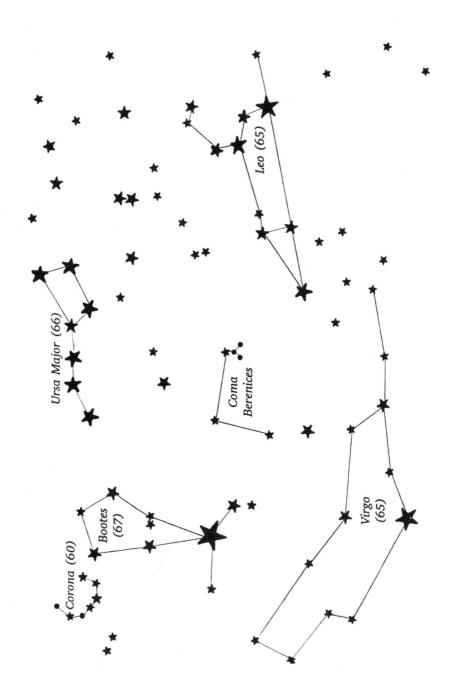

Map 6. Star Map: the Lock of Berenice

93 Sidera corruerint utinam! Repeats the idea of 75f. that being a constellation is far from an improvement over her life as a well-perfumed royal lock and strengthens the implication of 73 that the other stars are saying nasty things about her. **corruerint, fiam,** and **fulgeret** (94) are all optative subjunctives, expressing the lock's preference for her former sublunary existence.

94 proximus ... fulgeret: let Orion shine next to Hydrochoös (Aquarius). A way of wishing confusion on the stars, as these constellations are some 100 degrees separated in the heavens. The lock's irreverence, her defiance of the other stars' jealousy, and h⌐r vicarious delight in conjugal sex are Hellenistic touches of light realism in an elaborate court fantasy.

67

Poem 66 was a monologue spoken by a lock of hair turned constellation; this is an interview with a house door in Verona, behind which there have been scandalous goings-on. Here again, one objective of the poem is to give the inanimate speaker a personality, but the story it tells is of a bad wife rather than a good queen, a negligent door rather than a loyal tress. In this poem Catullus combines the ribald "Milesian tale" (see note on 61.128) with stage comedy, whose garrulous slaves provide the model for the talking door. The door tells of two former masters, the good *senex* Balbus and his son, who married a virgin who was no virgin, but a previously married young woman from Brixia with a well-developed taste for lovers. The door stands accused of having ill served its master and his wife's virtue, and defends itself in this interview.

1 dulci iucunda viro: the interviewer opens with elaborate, ironic courtesy toward a door that has been anything but delightful to the "dear husband" or his deceased father. To the contrary, it has besmirched the family name by admitting a procession of adulterers.

3 ianua comes as something of a surprise, as the opening lines would naturally seem to describe a married woman. See appendix C, paraprosdokia. We are now tipped off that the mood of the poem is to be playful.

5 rursus: on the other hand. The parallel word structures of lines 3 and 5 emphasize the contrast.

6 porrecto ... sene: abl. abs., after the old man was stretched out (in death). **es ... facta marita:** the door became "married" because it now served a married couple.

7–8 mutata feraris ... deseruisse: you are said to have changed and forsaken...

9 Caecilio: the present master, who must be none too pleased to find himself in possession of such a guilty door.

9–10 Non ... culpa mea est: the classic slave's disclaimer whenever disaster strikes.

12 est ius populi, etc.: Munro's repair of a faulty text: it is popular justice to blame the door (as it is a poor workman who blames his tools).

13–14 qui ... omnes: "they all" refers loosely to the *populus*.

15–16 Non istuc satis est, etc. The interviewer objects that such a flat denial (*istuc*, referring to *uno te dicere verbo*) won't do; only a vivid account (**ut quivis sentiat et videat**) will suffice.

19 virgo quod, etc.: as for the story that a *virgo* was entrusted to me, that's a lie. The false element is put first for emphasis.

20 attigerit: concessive subjunctive: granted, her first husband didn't touch her.

21: the impotent first husband's **sicula** is compared unfavorably to a soft beet.

23 sed pater: not Balbus, but the first husband's father, who becomes the first of her many partners.

26 sterili semine: abl. of cause or description; but given what we learned in lines 21–22, the point would be moot.

27 quaerendum: sc. *esset*. **unde unde:** sometimes written as a single word = from somewhere or another. **nervosius illud:** i.e., a *membrum virilius*; subj. of **foret**.

28 zonam solvere: metaphorical, as in 2.13 *zonam soluit diu ligatam*.

29 mira pietate: abl. of description, highly ironical.

30 minxerit: from *meio*.

31 Atqui: strongly disjunctive; you haven't heard the half of it— Brixia (the bride's hometown) says it knows for a fact (**se cognitum habere**) not only this (**non solum hoc**), ...; the construction is resumed in line 35.

32: Brixia Cycneae, etc.: if the text is right, this is Brixia, placed at the foot of Cycnus' look-out, i.e. a high point suitable for use as an observation post. For the construction of the four-word pentameter, cf. line 48 below and 66.62. Nothing is known about the local lore supplied in these lines, except that the river Mella flows about a mile west of the town. The story of Cycnus' metamorphosis is retold in

Ovid *Met.* 2.367–80.

35 Postumio et Corneli: two Lotharios at Brixia; the first is adjectival with **amore**, the second a simple genitive.

37–40: the door anticipates an objection: how can you know all this, since you never leave your post?

37: istaec: i.e., all these things you're telling me.

40: tantum: only.

41–45: answer: she brags about her *flagitia* to her slaves.

43f. utpote quae ... speraret, etc.: naturally anticipating that I have neither tongue nor ear. Relative clause of characteristic expressing the cause of the action expressed in *nomine dicentem*.

46 ne tollat rubra supercilia: lest he raise his red eyebrows (in anger). We learn why in the next two lines. The stereotypical slave being redheaded, *rubra* casts aspersions on this adulterer's rank or ancestry.

47–48: the lady got the best of the unnamed **longus homo** by pretending to be pregnant by him and filing *magnas lites* against him. **falsum puerperium**: subject of **intulit**, which takes *magnas lites* as object.

68

A poem of thanks to a friend who helped Catullus during the early part of his love affair with Lesbia. Although Lesbia is not mentioned by name, she is usually identified as the *domina* referred to in line 68, and the facts alluded to, including grief for his dead brother, are plausibly autobiographical. Its contrived but rambling structure and the identification of Manius (11, 30) or Allius (41, 50, 66, 150) are among many problems that have puzzled students of this poem. One solution has been to break it into two poems, with 68b starting at line 41. Both portions anticipate features of Augustan love elegy in important ways, and they may even be taken as an early example of that genre. The structure, "highly finished and intricate," is at the same time criticized as "heavy and awkward" (Fordyce). Quinn describes it as "an early experiment in stream of consciousness technique," but agrees that the poem as a whole "reads clumsily." None of its perceived flaws, however, make the poem (or two poems) less interesting to read.

1–2 Quod ... mittis: the fact that you send me a letter. The thought is completed in line 9, *id gratum est mihi*. The lines that follow describe the depression of Manius, who is not addressed by name until

line 11. Manius has written a letter to Catullus something like Catullus' to Cornificius (poem 38), asking for some poems to relieve his pain.

3 ut: with *sublevem* and *restituam*, expressing the purpose of the letter.

5–6 quem ... desertum, etc.: Manius has been abandoned by the woman he loves and cannot sleep. Typically in Catullus and later love elegy, it is the woman who is in control and the man who suffers.

7 veterum ... scriptorum: the old (Greek) poets have nothing to solace this Roman lover. If we read this as a general statement, Catullus seems to imply that a new kind of love poetry is needed.

10 muneraque et ... et: and because you seek the gifts of both the Muses and Venus, i.e., both general poetry and love verses. **hinc**: from me. The writer of Latin love elegy welcomes his role as aid and comforter of fellow lovers.

11 incommoda: misfortunes. **Mani**: the manuscripts here read *Mali* or *Manli*, adding to the confusion of characters; Lachmann proposed the reading adopted here, and that his name was Manius Allius. This reconciles the names in the poem as referring to a single friend.

12 hospitis officium: the obligation of a [former] guest; refers to the time when Manius made his house available to Catullus, as told in line 68.

13 quīs [*quibus*] ... fluctibus: a favorite metaphor for mental distress in the long poems: cf. line 3 above and 64.62 and 97, 65.4.

15 vestis ... pura: the unbordered *toga virilis*, put on in exchange for the *toga praetexta* when a boy reached 15 or 16.

17 multa lusi: I had plenty of playful affairs; but the verb is also used of poetry, as we see in 50.2 and 5, 61.225. **dea** would therefore be Venus, but a secondary meaning might be the Muse.

19 luctu: instrumental, because of grief.

20–24: apostrophe to his dead brother. It is echoed like a refrain in lines 92–96, with the words slightly changed. Cf. also 101.6.

21 commoda, advantages, plays off *incommoda* (11).

22–23 tecum una: together with you, repeated for emphasis.

24 dulcis amor: the theme that binds together the two topics of this poem, sexual and fraternal love.

25–26 mente, animi: see note on 65.4, *mens animi*.

27 Veronae: locative, with an understood *esse*: to be in Verona, where Catullus is writing in reply to

Manius' letter from Rome.

28–29: Manius' reason for thinking it a shame (27 *turpe*) for Catullus to be in Verona: provincials sleep alone. **quisquis de meliore nota**: anyone who *is* anyone, i.e., of the upper crust. 29 is a golden line.

30 **non est turpe, magis miserum**: it is not just a shame, but a source of real grief in addition to what he suffers for his brother (because he cannot be in Rome with Lesbia).

31 **quae**: the *munera* (32) of a poem that his grief prevents him from writing.

33 **quod**: as for the fact that. **scriptorum**: writings, probably his own. Catullus is not ready to write anything new (line 19), and he does not have access to poems he has already written or drafted. **apud me**: i.e., at my family home in Verona, which he contrasts emphatically (*illa ... illa ... illic*) with his personal home in Rome.

36 **capsula**: a small *capsa*, a cylindrical case for the rolled books of the time.

38 **non satis ingenuo**: i.e., not in the frank and generous way appropriate for one of my freeborn position.

39 **utriusque**: i.e., of both poems in general and of love poems, as mentioned in line 10, *et Musarum ... et Veneris*. **tibi non ... pos(i)ta est**: has not been provided to you.

41 **deae**: vocative, in an invocation to the Muses. **Allius**: for the poem as it stands to make sense, this must be the same person as the Manius addressed in lines 11 and 30. Manius could be the *praenomen*, Allius the *nomen*.

45 **dicam vobis**, etc.: the usual relation of the epic poet to the Muses is reversed here: instead of the Muses speaking to the poet who is then their mouthpiece, he tells the Muses, and they do the talking.

46 **carta loquatur anus**: personification—the *carta* is to tell the story when she is old. Cf. 78b.4, *fama loquetur anus*. **loquatur** is subj. of purpose with *facite*.

47: the masculine subject of **notescat**, probably the poet's benefactor Allius, is in the missing hexameter. Catullus will tell his tale to the Muses so that Allius may become known; **mortuus** is adverbial, when he is dead.

50 **opus faciat**: do her work. The poet imagines a tombstone on which his friend's name is covered with cobwebs; but his fame will have people clearing them away. By this oblique method Catullus

predicts the immortality of his own poetry and its power to confer fame.

51 **Amathusia**: i.e., Venus, worshiped at Amathus on Cyprus. She is **duplex** because love is bittersweet; cf. line 18, *dulcem amaritiem*.

52 **in quo ... genere**: in what manner.

53 **Trinacria rupes**: the Sicilian crag is the volcanic Mt. Aetna.

54 **lympha ... Malia**: the seething spring water of Thermopylae, whose hot springs gave the passage between Mt. Oeta and the Malian Gulf its name (Hot Gates).

55 **lumina**: eyes, as in 66.30.

56 **imbre**: the rain of tears.

57–62 **qualis**, etc.: the first of several epic similes compares the relief (61 *levamen*) provided by a cool stream to a thirsty traveler with the help (66 *auxilium*) provided by Allius to Catullus The **rivus** starts high on a mountain (**in aërii ... vertice montis**) and runs quickly down a steep valley (**de prona ... valle**) before crossing a populous area (**per medium densi ... populi**) where it does its good work.

61 **lasso in sudore**: transferred epithet. The adjective, which logically goes with *viatori*, is linked by phrasing with his sweat.

63–65 **ac velut**, etc.: a second epic simile, comparing Allius' aid to a helpful breeze (**aura secunda**) at sea.

65 **Pollucis, Castoris**: subjective genitive. Like the Christian saints of a later age, these deified heroes, patrons of mariners, intercede on behalf of the storm-tossed sailors. Others read these genitives as objective, prayer *to* Pollux and Castor. The line is spondaic, like 87, 89, 109.

67 **lato ... limite**: a wide path, abl. of means. This is nearly a golden line, but with chiastic word order.

68 **dominae**: probably Lesbia. The term implies a submissiveness to the woman one loves, which became conventional in Latin love elegy.

69 **ad quam exerceremus**: rel. clause of purpose, to which we could come to ply our mutual love. Particularly for those with servants, privacy was hard to get.

70 **quo**: to which, i.e., Allius' home. **mea ... candida diva**: Lesbia again, put on a divine pedestal as often in Latin elegy.

71 **plantam**: the sole of her foot.

72 **arguta ... solea**: with a squeaky sandal. This detail may be added as a bad omen, to avoid which (some believed) a bride was carried across the

threshold. Cf. 61. 160, *Transfer omine cum bono limen aureolos pedes*. **constituit**: the poet stops her motion here while he takes time out for a long series of similes and digressions. When we return to her in line 131, the moment of entrance is past.
73 **ut quondam**: like the elegists of a later generation, Catullus goes to myth to illustrate his love. The story is that Laodamia first crossed the threshold of her new husband, Protesilaus, without making due sacrifice. He left soon after their wedding to become the first Greek to land at Troy and the first to die in the Trojan war. The relevant points of the simile, which emerge slowly, are deep love and rash haste. Catullus was separated from Lesbia by his brother's death near Troy, Protesilaus from Laodamia by his own death in the Trojan War.
74: for the three-word pentameter, cf. line 112.
75 **inceptam frustra**: begun in vain, because Protesilaus would not live long enough to finish building it.
76 **pacificasset**: made peace with the gods. The contractual *modus vivendi* of Roman religion called for sacrificial payoffs to purchase a *pax deorum*.
77 **Ramnusia virgo**: the goddess Nemesis, as in 66.71. She punishes rash actions taken *invitis eris*, without divine approval.
79 **Quam desideret**: how much (the empty altar) lacked.
81–83 **ante ... quam ... satura(vi)sset**: Laodamia was forced to let her husband leave her embrace before the passage of winters had satisfied her *avidum amorem*.
84 **posset ut** = *ut posset*, the result of *saturasset*.
85 **quod**: the *abruptum coniugium*. The Fates knew the marriage would be broken off by Protesilaus' death *si miles ... i(vi)sset* if he went as a soldier to Troy.
87f. **primores Argivorum ... viros**: the Greek heroes destined to fight in the Trojan war. **Troia**, subject of *coeperat ... ciere*, is nearly personified as a malign force bent on human destruction.
90 **cinis**: here = funeral pyre, and (by metaphor) ruin. In this transitional line Catullus associates the deaths in the legendary Trojan war with the recent death near Troy of his own brother.
91–96: Cf. lines 20–24, and note. The anaphora of *ei misero* and *tecum una* add to the tone of a tragic refrain.
97 **Quem**: his brother, object of *detinet* (100).
98 **cognatos ... cineres**: i.e., the ashes of his relatives.

99 **Troia obscena, Troia**: the idea that Troy was a place not of great exploits but of the atrocities of war had been a persistent theme of Euripides. It was the dominant image of Troy in Hellenistic poetry, and Catullus uses it to heighten the pathos of his brother's death.
103–104 **ne Paris**, etc.: so that Paris would not delight in his stolen adulteress and while away his idleness with impunity in his peaceful bedroom. For the complex hyperbaton where each of a series of nouns is modified by an adjective (*abducta ... moecha, libera ... otia, pacato ... thalamo*), cf. 65.5–6 and note. For the meaning of **libera**, cf. 64.402.
105 **Quo ... casu**: that was the plight by which. After a digression on his brother's death, Catullus returns to Laodamia.
107–108 **tanto ... vertice, amoris aestus**: her love was like a swirling flood which bore her into a sheer pit (**in abruptum ... barathrum**) of catastrophe.
109–16 **quale ferunt**, etc.: an epic simile comparing Laodamia's pit of catastrophe with the deep tunnel dug (supposedly) by Hercules to drain the swamp near Pheneus in Arcadia. The digression contrasts Hercules' achievement of immortality with the mutability and death reflected elsewhere in the poem.
111–12 **fodisse ... audit**: is said to have dug. The use of *audit* = *dicitur* is borrowed from Greek idiom.
112 **falsiparens Amphitryoniades**: a playful departure from the usual plain style of Catullus. Hercules is the falsely fathered son of Amphitryon because Jupiter came to his mother Alcmene disguised as her husband. Plautus dramatized the story in a rare mythological travesty, the *Amphitruo*.
113 **certa ... sagitta**: the unerring arrow; Hercules was aided in his Labors by a magical bow that never missed. **Stymphalia ... monstra**: Hercules' fifth Labor was to kill the man-eating birds of Stymphalus, also in NW Arcadia.
114 **deterioris eri**: as punishment for killing his sons in a fit of madness, Hercules undertook to serve Eurystheus, king of Mycenae, the "lesser master" who devised the twelve Labors.
115f.: the purpose (or result) of the Labors was the apotheosis of Hercules and his marriage in heaven to Hebe, goddess of youth.
117 **Sed tuus**, etc.: back to Laodamia, whom the poet has been addressing in an apostrophe that began in line 105 and continues to 130.

119-24 **nec tam carum**, etc.: the first of two epic similes describing the love of Laodamia, this compares it to an aged parent's love for a newborn grandson who will inherit his wealth.

120 **caput seri nepotis**: high diction for *serum nepotem*.

121 **qui**: the *nepos*. **vix tandem**: as in 62.2.

122 **nomen ... intulit**: has had his name entered in the *testatas tabulas* that officially record his status as heir.

123 **derisi gentilis**: the distant relative who will be made ridiculous (because he had been counting on a fat legacy, which according to law must stay in the *gens*). The epithet is proleptic.

125-28 **nec tantum**, etc.: the second simile, on the devotion of a dove to its mate. **gavisa est**: from the semi-deponent *gaudeo*.

131 **cui**: to Laodamia; there is a certain irony in the comparison of Lesbia to the devoted Laodamia. Catullus concedes that Lesbia is good enough to concede nothing **aut paulo** (=*paulum*) to Laodamia's fidelity, a qualification that he explains in line 135.

133 **circumcursans ... Cupido**: on the presence of Cupid as appreciative witness at a love scene, cf. 45.8f., 17f.

136 **furta feremus erae**: the submissive tolerance of the elegiac lover. In other poems, such as 11 and 58, Lesbia is far from *verecunda* and her *furta* are anything but *rara*.

138-39 **Iuno ... concoquit iram**: Even Juno swallows her anger against her spouse's philanderings. There is another irony in comparing Catullus' tolerance of infidelity with Juno's, since her persecution of Jove's sexual partners was proverbial; cf., for example, 66.66 note. Like Juno, Catullus made some of his most savage attacks on sexual rivals (e.g., Ravidus in poem 40, Gellius in 91 and other poems).

141 **componier**: archaic, = *componi*. Most editors mark a lacuna of at least two lines between 141 and 142, as the thought of the pentameter does not follow naturally that of its predecessor in the manuscripts.

142 the number and arrangement of words closely resembles that of a golden line in hexameter verse.

143-44 **Nec tamen**, etc.: another reason for Catullus to tolerate Lesbia's infidelities: she's not my wife, anyway.

145 **mira ... nocte**: continues the story of their tryst in Allius' home from line 72.

146 **viri gremio**: Lesbia was married at the time to Q. Metellus Celer (see appendix A). For the phrasing, cf. 132, *se nostrum contulit in gremium*.

147-48 **is ... dies**: if the text is correct, the hyperbaton is violent and confusing; **illa** is a pronoun (for Lesbia), not an adjective with *dies* (as it is in line 152). It is enough if the day that she marks with a whiter stone is given to me alone. Special days (our "red letter days") were proverbially marked with a white stone.

149-60 an *envoi* to Allius, for whose benefit this account was written.

149 **quod potui**: parenthetic, as well as I could. **confectum carmine munus**: a gift wrought in verse (Fordyce).

151-52: returns to the immortality theme introduced in lines 41-50.

154 **antiquis piis**: worthy men of old. **munera ferre**: to confer as rewards. Themis is the goddess of justice.

156 **domina**: Lesbia, as in line 68.

157 †**terram dedit aufert**†: obelized as hopelessly corrupt; it is also unclear who **qui** is, unless Catullus means Allius himself.

158: for the hiatus at the diaeresis, cf. 101.4.

159 **me carior ipso**: cf. 14.1, *Ni te plus oculis meis amarem*. The predicate to be supplied from line 155 is *sis felix*.

69

Even the ancient Romans, it seems, had limits on their tolerance of body odor. Here Catullus tells one Rufus that his failure to attract women is the work of a goat that has taken up residence in his armpits.

2 **Rufe**: perhaps M. Caelius Rufus (see appendix A). If so, he was not as unattractive to women as this poem indicates. **tenerum ... femur**: her dainty thigh. **supposuisse**: an archaic and metrically convenient equivalent to *supponere*.

3 **si illam ... labefactes**: if you should undermine her resistance. **rarae ... vestis**: a fine garment such as the *palla* with which Menaechmus bribes Erotium in Plautus, or a gauzy negligee. Catullus probably has in mind the sexy, diaphanous silk outfits for which the Aegean island of Cos was famous.

4 **perluciduli**: *hapax legomenon*, a sensuous diminutive, setting up a play with *l*'s, *d*'s, and *i*'s that continues through the line.

5 fabula: a rumor.

6 valle sub alarum: a preposition of one syllable which normally precedes its noun may be placed between the noun and an adjective or limiting genitive (Allen & Greenough 599d). Cf. 64.354, *sole sub ardenti*.

8 quicum: either a rare feminine (with *bestia*), or masculine (= *cum quo*, referring to *caper*).

9 crudelem nasorum ... pestem: comic periphrasis for the *trux caper*.

10 fugiunt: to emphasize the hard fact, Catullus uses the indicative where we would regularly expect the subjunctive: cf., for example, 1–2 *velit* after *admirari*. For comic emphasis on the last word of a poem, see note on 17.26, *mula*.

70

On Lesbia's evasiveness, possibly after the death of her husband Metellus early in 59 B.C. when she could have made a permanent commitment to Catullus. The theme and its presentation are traditional.

1: nulli: the dative in *-i* is regular in all genders of this adjective.

1–3: the repetitions of **dicit**, like that of **mulier**, are thematic for this epigram.

2 non si: emphatic, not even if. **Iuppiter ipse** is notorious for his collection of "marriages," and was the hardest to refuse. **petat** is the potential subjunctive.

4 in vento et...aqua: proverbial for impermanence. The metaphor of writing in wind and water goes back to Sophocles and Plato. Cf. the metaphor in 30.10.

71

The Rufus of poem 69 who suffers from goat in the armpit is also tormented by gout in the foot. Both turn out in this epigram to be venerially transmitted diseases: with unique poetic justice, Rufus' unfaithful girlfriend has contracted body odor, and she has passed on the gout to his rival.

1–2 iure bono, merito: justly. **sacer**: accursed. **tarda** has factitive force: slowing. Gout (*podagra*) affects the joints of the foot, making it painful to walk. **secat**: torments.

4 est ... nactus: from *nanciscor*, has contracted. This is the apodosis of the condition in lines 1–2, somewhat abbreviated. More clearly stated, if anyone

deserves to suffer odor and gout, your rival does: he has contracted both from you by sexual contact with your girlfriend.

5 ulciscitur ambos: he punishes both himself and her.

6 illam affligit is confusing, because we were told in line 4 that the unnamed rival has picked up Rufus' two ailments from his girlfriend. Here, though, the girl is punished by contracting the rival's body odor. The poet's desire to distribute poetic justice evenly exceeds the logical coherence of his language.

72

A disillusioned but rational Catullus explains his love before and during the breakup with Lesbia.

1–2 te is evidently to be understood as the subject of both **nosse** (syncopated *no(vi)sse*, from *nosco*) and **velle**. Lesbia has said that she alone knew Catullus, and preferred him even to Jove.

4 gnatos: children, a generic masculine. Catullus here compares his love to a father's; in a similar context in 76.2–3 he considers himself *pius* and speaks of *sancta fides* and the bond or *foedus* that he kept in his relation with Lesbia.

5 cognovi contrasts with Lesbia's *nosse* in the first line: Now *I* have gotten to know *you*. **uror**: with love, not anger.

7 Qui: the adverb: how? **iniuria talis**, called a *culpa* in 75.1, can be deduced from such poems as 58.

8: the paradox is developed further in poems 75 and 85.

73

A bitter epigram about personal betrayal, a theme to which the poet returns in poem 77 (cf. also poem 30). In this poem the ungrateful friend is unnamed.

1–2 Desine governs both *velle* and *putare*, each of which in turn is completed by another infinitive, *mereri* and *posse* respectively. **quicquam**: in any respect.

4 immo etiam: no—in fact, ... The combination introduces qualifications that make a prior statement more extreme.

5 ut mihi (sc. *obest*): as (kindliness) is a hindrance to me. The specific example in the third couplet proves the general statement in the second.

5–6 quem nemo gravius ... quam ... qui me, etc.:

whom no one oppresses worse ... than the one who just now held me to be his one and only friend.
6: for five elisions in a single line, cf. 22.4. This is one of eighteen pentameters in Catullus where diaeresis is prevented by elision, and the elisions make it his longest pentameter. The effect is to heighten the effect of bitterness and frustration: "a harsh, slurred rush of words" (Quinn).

74

The first of seven epigrams to an enemy named Gellius, usually identified as L. Gellius Poplicola (see appendix A). Gossip had it that this Gellius was having an illicit relationship with his stepmother. Here, Gellius is represented as keeping his stern uncle quiet by threatening to make public a similar relation with the uncle's wife.
1 **patruum obiurgare solere**: the proverbial Dutch uncle was preceded in sternness by the Roman uncle.
2 **delicias**: hanky-panky of any sort, particularly voluptuary.
3 **perdepsuit**: lit. kneaded, here *sensu obsceno*.
4 **Arpocratem**: The young Egyptian sun god *Horpa-khred*, Horus the child, was a popular figure in classical art. Represented as a little boy with a finger to his lips as if enjoining silence, his name was Hellenized as (H)arpocrates. See also 102.4.
5 **quamvis irrumet**, etc.: i.e., even if Gellius should sexually abuse the uncle himself, there would be no trouble because the latter would prefer to keep things quiet.

75

A variation on the theme of 72. Here Catullus dwells on the external and internal sources of his misery, comparing the effects of Lesbia's wrongdoing and the action of his own mind.
1 **tua mea**: interlocked word order; the meter shows that **tua** is abl. with **culpa**, **mea** nom. with **mens** (she is no longer *mea Lesbia*).
2 **se ... perdidit ipsa**: his mind compounds the mischief done by Lesbia's *culpa* through its own unreasoning devotion (**officio ... suo**). Here *officio* combines the sense of moral duty and natural function.
3 **bene velle**: feel kindly, as in 72.8, cognate with our noun *benevolence*.
4 **omnia**: everything bad, that is.

76

In this meditation on his shattered love for Lesbia, Catullus reasons that he must free himself from his *longum amorem* and asks the gods to help him put away "this sickness" (25 *morbum*). It contrasts with the subtle self-mockery of poem 8, "Miser Catulle." In mood, subject, and meter this anticipates the love elegies of Propertius, Tibullus, and Ovid. The language is plain and logical, reasoning that if (1 *siqua*, 17–19 *si ... si ... si*) a person has acted ethically, he will be rewarded.
1–8: good deeds (**benefacta**) and good faith (**esse pium, sanctam ... fidem**) should be rewarded with **voluptas** (1) and **gaudia** (6). The repetition **homini** (2), **homines** (4), **homines** (7) emphasizes that he is generalizing about human life.
1 **siqua**: cf. 42.23 *siquid*.
3 **nec foedere nullo**: nor in any contract; a pleonastic negative, not litotes.
4 **ad fallendos ... homines**: accusative with the gerundive to express purpose.
9–16: the second set of eight lines moves from the logical statement of what should be (1–8) to the assertion of what must be done.
9 **quae**: the relative pronoun in Latin is used here as English would use the demonstrative: all these things.
11–12 **atque...teque...et**: the polysyndeton (see appendix C) seems awkward to many readers. **atque** links **offirmas** to the actions that follow; **teque** and **et** are a "both ... and" combination: make up your mind and both take yourself out of there and stop being unhappy because the gods are unwilling [to help you]. **dis invitis** is abl. absolute, or dat. of ref. (in front of unwilling gods).
13 **Difficile est**, etc.: a concessive statement, sometimes punctuated as a question, as if he were having a dialogue with himself.
14 **efficias**, jussive subjunctive (like **facias** in 16), answers the objection raised in line 13.
15 **haec** varies the anaphora of 14–16 **hoc ... hoc ... hoc**: your only **salus** is **haec** [salus]. The dat. of agent **tibi** is normal with the gerundive expressing necessity.
16 **pote** = *pote est*; cf. 24 *potis est*, where Catullus uses the other form of this indeclinable adjective.
17–22: the formula of prayer is to remind the gods: *if* A, B, and C are true (as we know they are), *then* grant my prayer. Hence si ... si ... si express not doubt but the protasis of a logical statement. The appeal to prayer seems to contradict line 12 **dis**

invitis.
23 **contra**, in return, is the adverb.

77

These lines are probably addressed to M. Caelius Rufus (see appendix A), who succeeded Catullus in the affections of Clodia/Lesbia but eventually ran afoul of her vindictive temper. If so, what we have here appear to be *vers d'occasion* expressing the poet's reaction to Rufus' success with Lesbia.

1 **mihi ... credite amice**: believed friendly to me.
3 **sicine**: is this the way ...? Compare Ariadne's apostrophe to Theseus, 64.132. **subreps(is)ti**: you insinuated yourself; the verb is used in the previous poem (76.21) of a *pestis*, which is what Catullus calls Rufus in the end of this poem.
4 **misero** (sc. *me*): abl. with *eripuisti*. The words recall the colloquial expletive *ei misero mihi!*—but the construction is different.
4–5 **eripuisti ... ? Eripuisti**: the rhetoric of anguish in this poem features anaphora; cf. *frustra ... frustra* (1–2), *heu heu nostrae ... heu heu nostrae* (5–6).

78

Someone named Gallus is arranging sexual liaisons within his own family; Catullus predicts that this pretty business will backfire. Poems like this, with their playful arrangement of words and a sting at the end, anticipate the satirical epigrams of Martial (later first century A.D.).

1–2 **quorum ... alterius**, etc.: one brother has a most delightful wife, the other a delightful son; a more prosaic word order would be *quorum alterius coniunx est lepidissima, alterius filius (est) lepidus*. **lepidissima** and **lepidus** refer here to physical appearance.
4 **bella puella**: the boy's aunt, in fact. The matching of words, both diminutives, stresses the irony of the mismatched pair.
6 **patruus**: on the traditional severity of the Roman uncle, see poem 74. **patrui ... adulterium**: objective genitive. Though he is an uncle, he teaches adultery against an uncle.

78b

Though joined in the manuscript with 78, this clearly belongs to another poem and represents a different situation. At least one couplet seems to be

missing from the beginning. The lecher addressed in this fragment has been slobbering on a *pura puella* who has done nothing to deserve his foul attentions.

1–2 **purae pura puella** contrasts phonetically and ethically with **spurca saliva**. Cf. 99.10; the meaning of **comminxit** is vividly metaphorical: your vile spit has pissed upon the pure lips (*suavia*) of a pure girl. For a similar use of *meio*, cf. 67.30 *gnati minxerit in gremium*.
3 **non impune feres**: you won't get away with it; cf. 99.3, *Verum id non impune tuli*.
4 **fama loquetur anus**: fame will tell *qui sis* when she is old. For the personification and phrasing, cf. 68.46, *carta loquatur anus* and note on 95.6.

79

Cicero often hinted publicly that P. Clodius Pulcer was incestuously involved with his sister Clodia. When Lesbia dropped or abused her affair with Catullus, Clodius was a credible target for the poet's wrath. This epigram is our best internal evidence for identifying Lesbia with Clodia.

1 **Lesbius**: the poetic pseudonym, given in honor of Sappho of Lesbos (see appendix A), is here treated as a *nomen gentile* and given to Lesbia's brother. **pulcer** plays on his cognomen.
1–2 **malit quam**: likes better than.
3 **vendat**: pres. subjunctive, the apodosis of the condition stated in line 4: either he would sell, if he found (perf. subj.), or let him sell if he finds (fut. perf. ind.).
4 **tria notorum suavia**: three kisses of friends. This kind of kiss, like a handshake, was a friendly greeting. The point is that while Clodius may be handsome enough to seduce his own sister, he has no friends willing to get close enough to exchange greetings.

80

The alleged sex maniac of poem 74 is back, this time as an oral sex artist. For more reliable information about this Gellius, see appendix A.

1 **Quid dicam quare**: How shall I explain why. **rosea ista labella** is sometimes taken as an indication of Gellius' youth; cf. 45.12, *illo purpureo ore*.
2 **fiant** = *sint*.
3–4 **te**: object of *suscitat*. **octava ... hora**: the period

of daylight was divided into twelve *horae* that would be longer or shorter depending on the time of year. The eighth hour is two-thirds of the way through the day, just after siesta time. **quiete e molli**: from a gentle nap. **longo die**: lit. when the day is long. This has been variously interpreted to mean "in the long hours of the day" (Ellis), "well along in the day" (Merrill), or "in summer, when the daylight hours are longer" (Quinn).

6 **grandia ... tenta**: full-grown erections.

7 **clamant** has two subjects, Victor's **ilia** and Gellius' **labra**. Cf. the eloquent bed in 6.7, *cubile clamat*. **Victoris ... miselli**: an unknown sexual athlete. Cf. *misellus* in 45.21 and 35.14; here it is heavily ironic, as in 40.1.

8 Victor's **ilia** have been **rupta**, drained by the efforts of Gellius. For the diction, cf. 11.20, *ilia rumpens*, where Lesbia is the subject.

81

A stranger from Pisaurum has caught the eye of Catullus' boyfriend Juventius (see appendix A). Catullus professes to be concerned not that Juventius is involved with another man but that he made such a bad choice.

1 **in tanto populo**: i.e., Rome.

3 **moribunda ab sede Pisauri**: from the dying town of Pisaurum. On the Adriatic coast in northern Italy, this town has been said even in modern times to have an unhealthy climate. The placement of new settlers there in 43 B.C. suggests it was not thriving.

4 **hospes**: stranger. **pallidior**: paleness in the Mediterranean is not so much the lack of color as a sickly yellowish, sallow complexion, compared here to the hue of a gilded bronze statue. Sappho compared it to the color of dead grass. Cf. 64.100, where Ariadne blanches to the color of gold.

6 **facinus facias**: an etymological figure like "do a deed," as in 110.4 *facis facinus*.

82

This Quintius, who appears also in poem 100, is a Veronese. It is usually understood that he has put himself in rivalry for Lesbia's love. The pleading tone is built up with frequent anaphora of *oculos, -is* and *carius*.

2 **carius ... oculis**: repeated three times in as many lines; cf. 104.2 (of Lesbia), *ambobus mihi quae*

carior est oculis.

3 **ei**: monosyllabic here. **illi**: i.e., Catullus.

83

Catullus wishfully speculates that if Lesbia speaks angrily to him in front of her husband, she must be infatuated with him. If the identification of Lesbia with Clodia is correct, the husband would be Q. Metellus Celer, and the dramatic date (if not the date of composition) would be prior to his death in 59 B.C.

1 **praesente viro** (abl. abs.) implies that the scene is for her husband's benefit, to avert suspicion of an affair—or that she is deliberately embarrassing Catullus. **dicit**, with *taceret* (3), *obloquitur* (4), and *loquitur* (6), all at the ends of lines, puts the poem's emphasis on acts of speech.

2–3 **illi fatuo**, to that idiot, and the apostrophe **Mule**, You mule, puts Lesbia's husband in the comic role of the cuckold.

4 **gannit et obloquitur**: snarls and interrupts me, further evidence (if only to Catullus) of Lesbia's infatuation.

5 **acrior** combines "more intense" (anger is sharper than simple remembrance) with "shrewder" and perhaps "more to the point."

6 **uritur** can mean both erotic and angry passion; *et* implies a logical consequence: she's on fire, and so she talks. Catullus draws a similar inference in poem 92, which begins with the same words *Lesbia mi*.

84

A satire on an ambitious hick who doesn't know where to put his aitches, and to everyone's relief is dispatched to Syria.

1–2 **Chommoda ... hinsidias**: his talk of advantages ("hadvantages") and ambuscades ("hambuscades") is worldly, and his attempt to use *h*- sounds mimics the fashion of the day (*pulcher* for *pulcer*, *sepulchrum* for *sepulcrum*, etc.), but he overdoes it and gets most of the words wrong. It had become fashionable to show off one's higher education in Greek by sounding the Greek chi (χ) in certain words. But Arrius has no such education, and is faking it. **Arrius**: see appendix A.

3 **mirifice sperabat**, etc. suggests a certain conceit in his foolish excess, like that of the poetaster Suffenus in 22.17.

5–6 mater ... avunculus ... avus ... avia: the tone of *credo* is sarcastic because Arrius' family (who are just plain folks) would not in fact have taught him his highfalutin phony phonemes. Unlike Greek, traditional Latin has few aspirates. Like us, the Latins would not have sounded the *h* in *Achilles*. In scansion, the weak Latin *h* does not count as a consonant: for example, the third syllable of *nuntius* in line 10 scans short because of the weakness of the subsequent *h* sound in *horribilis*. **liber avunculus**: his free uncle (as opposed to the ones who were still only slaves). Such innuendo was not uncommon in a society that depended on slavery but despised slaves and people of servile origin. Cf. note on *rubra*, 67.46.

7 Hoc misso (abl. abs.): Arrius' ambition paid off, and he was sent off on some mission of empire to Syria.

8 audi(e)bant eadem haec [verba]: viz., *commoda* and *insidias*, correctly pronounced.

9–10 metuebant ... horribilis: comic overstatement, as usual in satire.

11 Ionios fluctus: the Ionian Sea just beneath the boot of Italy, which Arrius crossed on his way to Syria (**illuc**).

85

Conflicting passions towards Lesbia, as shown by a series of poems on this theme (72, 75, 92). This is Catullus' best-known couplet, remarkable for its compression and power, due in part to its composition from eight verbs and no adjectives. The hexameter's four active verbs contrast with the four of the pentameter, which describe a passive state. Cf. especially *faciam* vs. *fieri*.

1 Quare id faciam, fortasse requiris: chiastic sound.

2 nescio scans as a dactyl, as normally in poetry. **fieri sentio**: I feel it happen.

86

Lesbia's beauty is more than meets the eye, as is shown by this comparison with Quintia. The key word is *formosa*, repeated three times in three couplets. There is also a play on the relation between *venustas* (3) and *Veneres* (6).

2 haec ... singula: used substantively as object of **confiteor**, individual points of beauty as opposed to its totality.

3 Totum illud formosa: that "beautiful" as a whole,

consisting of more than looks, needs **venustas** and a **mica salis**. In the middle couplet of his epigram, Catullus stretches the meaning of his key word to include more than the *forma* that one can see.

4 tam magno corpore does not imply obesity but a statuesque figure (cf. lines 1–2 *longa, recta*), prized in an area where women come short. There is a contrast between her impressive stature and the lack of so much as a grain of wit's salt.

5 pulcerrima may contain a pun on Lesbia's family name; see note on 79.1, *Lesbius est pulcer*.

5–6 cum ... tum is the not only ... but also combination. In addition to being physically *pulcerrima*, Lesbia has stolen her rivals' sexy charms or **Veneres** because she has a **venustas** (line 3) that women such as Quintia lack. The emphatic position of the last word calls attention to the point.

87

Another Lesbia poem, implicitly protesting her violation of the bond created by his love. Catullus is unable to accept Lesbia's rejection of the obligation that he believes his love imposes on her.

1 amatam: sc. *esse*. For the theme, cf. 8.5 and 37.12, *amata ... quantum amabitur nulla*.

3 ullo ... foedere: in any bond.

4 in amore tuo = in my love for you, in effect an objective genitive, as **ex parte ... mea**, on my part, makes clear. The grouping of words makes the diaeresis unusually weak.

88

Gellius, the sexual overachiever introduced in poem 74, is here pilloried as a specialist in incest of every type and color.

1 cum matre: an exaggeration, as often in Catullus; Gellius was accused before the senate of *stuprum* with his stepmother. See appendix A.

2 prurit: normally of the sexual itch, here apparently of its actual satisfaction.

3 patruum, etc.: more details in poem 74.

4 Ecquid scis: do you have any idea.

5 ultima Tethys: the wife of Oceanus, so-called because she lives at the edge of the world.

7 quo prodeat ultra: to which he can proceed further.

8 demisso ... capite: with his head lowered. **se ipse voret**: for this meaning of *vorare*, cf. 80.6, *grandia te medii tenta vorare viri*. Permissible sex finds external objects; incest is sex that does not go far enough afield.

89

The first of three poems in a row in the continuing campaign against Gellius, the most frequently attacked of Catullus' enemies (see appendix A). The chief objective of the campaign is to label Gellius as a sexual pervert specializing in incest.

1 **quid ni**: why shouldn't he be? For the opening, cf. 79.1, *Lesbius est pulcer: quid ni?*

1–2 **Cui ... vivat** = *cui sit*, subj. in a rel. clause of characteristic expressing cause: Gellius is thin because he has so many female relatives to occupy him.

3 **bonus patruus**: because he supplies Gellius with another incestuous partner; see poem 74.

3–4 **omnia plena**: an abundance of, with the abl. **puellis cognatis**, young female relatives.

5 **ut ... attingat**: ironically concessive, though he has no contact except with forbidden partners.

90

A touch of fantasy in the defamation of Gellius, taking its inspiration from the notion that a Persian magus must be born of an incestuous union.

1 **nascatur**: hortatory, let a magus be born.

3 **gnato gignatur**: a nearly etymological figure for comic effect; the tradition that Persian magi (and Persians generally) practiced incest with their mothers is reported by Strabo and other sources, and the priestly office was hereditary. Catullus conflates the two ideas. The Greeks and Romans were ready to believe the worst about easterners.

4 **si vera est ... religio**: i.e., if the report of it is true. **impia religio**: oxymoron.

5 **gratus ... accepto ... carmine**: for the redundancy, cf. 67.26, *iners sterili semine*.

6 **omentum ... pingue**: the fatty tissue around the intestines. Strabo reports that the Persians did not sacrifice the actual flesh to the gods. **liquefaciens**: the first *e* is normally short. The compound gives the ending a mock-solemn effect.

91

Catullus exploits the image he has built of Gellius as a specialist in incest. I didn't expect you would make a pass at Lesbia, he says, since she is neither your mother nor your sister. Furthermore, I didn't think your association with me was close enough to justify your taking my Lesbia to bed as if she were related to you. This poem explains why Catullus attacked Gellius so doggedly, in a total of seven poems.

1–3 **Non ideo ... quod ... cogno(vi)ssem**: not because I knew; the subjunctive indicates a hypothetical situation; Catullus knew he was untrustworthy.

5 **neque quod** = quod neque. The construction is *Non ideo sperabam quod cognossem ..., sed quod videbam.*

6 **hanc**: Lesbia.

7 **multo coniungerer usu**: I was joined with you in a bond of association; the underlying Roman belief is that *usus* creates a presumptive *coniunctio* that forbids associates from taking advantage of each other.

9 **Tu satis id dux(is)ti**: disjunctive asyndeton, with emphasis on the first word: But *you* thought this *coniunctio* was sufficient reason to make your move—not only because of your taste for *culpa* and *scelus*, but (implicitly and specifically) because you prefer women who are connected to you.

92

As in poem 83, Catullus takes comfort from Lesbia's frequent abuse as a sign that she loves him.

1–2 **Lesbia mi ... Lesbia me**: a typical repetition for emphasis on the main concern of the poem. Cf. the beginning of poem 83. The diaeresis after **me** is strong.

2–4 **dispeream nisi amat ... dispeream nisi amo**: the second significant repetition, emphasizing both the supposed mutuality of feeling and the perilous condition of the speaker. The diction is colloquial, using optative subj. *dispeream*: damned if she doesn't love me!

3 **sunt totidem mea**, perhaps another colloquialism, refers loosely to the bad things Lesbia says about Catullus: I say as many bad things about *her*. **deprecor** means both "I pray to be rid of her" (as in poems 8 and 76) and "I deprecate her," i.e., he merely expresses disapproval. The poem is full of ambiguity, contradiction, and wishful thinking.

93

Perhaps a reply to some attempt to bring Catullus and Caesar together. For the relations between the two, see Gaius Julius Caesar in appendix A. The indifference expressed in this epigram is more cutting than hatred.

1 **nil nimium studeo:** like our colloquial "I'm not too eager...." **velle placere,** slightly pleonastic after *studeo,* is idiomatic: "make an effort to please" (Fordyce).

2 **albus an ater** is purely metaphoric; though the Greeks and Romans were not particularly sensitive to skin color, white suggested something good and black something bad.

94

The Mentula made fun of here and in poems 105, 114, and 115 is probably a nickname of Caesar's protégé Mamurra (see appendix A). This couplet explores the obvious connotation of the name.

1 **Mentula ... mentula:** the nickname and the generic noun, respectively.

2 **Hoc est quod dicunt:** i.e., that's the proverb; cf. 100.3, *hoc est quod dicitur.* **olera olla legit:** i.e., the pot takes vegetables as naturally (and mindlessly) as a *mentula* takes to fornication. Mentula is doing what comes naturally.

95

Catullus' friend C. Helvius Cinna has finished his short historical epic about Smyrna after nine years of careful work. This epigram compares the result to the hasty outpourings of Hortensius, Volusius, and Antimachus.

1 **Zmyrna:** title of the poem and subject of a verb lost in line 4 (unless *edita (est)* in line three is the verb).

1–2 **nonam post ... messem quam coepta est:** after the ninth harvest after it was begun. In this compressed construction, *post* is used as both preposition (with acc. *messem*) and adverb (with *quam* and *coepta est*). **edita:** published.

4: Froelich made up *versiculorum anno quolibet ediderit* to fill the gap. For more about Q. Hortensius Hortalus, see appendix A.

5 **Satrachi:** the river in Cyprus where Adonis, son of the eponymous princess Myrrha or Smyrna, spent time with his lover Aphrodite.

6 **cana ... saecula pervoluent:** the personified ages will leaf through the pages of Cinna's poem—but as books were on rolls instead of pages, they will roll through it. The vocalic *u* of the verb gives it four

syllables. For similar personifications, cf. *cana anilitas* (61.155), *cana senectus* (108.1), *carta anus* (68.46), *fama anus* (78b.4).

7 **Volusi annales:** the *cacata carta* that Catullus wanted to have burned in poem 36. For more about this poet and his connection with the Padua (a mouth of the Po river), see appendix A.

8 **laxas scombris ... tunicas:** either as fishmongers' wrappings for mackerel (loose because there was so much paper to use up), or as loose-fitting jackets in which they were cooked.

9 **mei ... sodalis:** i.e., Cinna. **mihi sint cordi:** double dative, they can be *my* favorite.

10 **populus:** one theme of Callimachus and other Hellenistic *cognoscenti* was that popularity is the kiss of death in matters poetic. They preferred small, discriminating audiences and short, polished poems. This was also the view of Catullus and the *poetae novi.* **tumido Antimacho:** a prolific writer of the 5–4 centuries B.C., Antimachus of Colophon became identified with the swollen torrents of verbiage that the best Hellenistic and Roman writers preferred to avoid.

96

Propertius wrote that Licinius Calvus composed an elegy on the death of his wife or mistress Quintilia (2.34.89–90). Catullus' lines may have as much to do with that elegy as they do with the death itself and Calvus' personal grief. For example, the *missas amicitias* mentioned in line 4 may refer to Calvus' neglect of Quintilia as a result of various *furta* that he is said to have admitted in his elegies (Ovid, *Tristia* 2.431–2). One theory is that Calvus' elegy was an imaginary dialogue with the dead Quintilia (like Propertius' with Cynthia's ghost in 4.7.13ff) in which they discuss their past troubles. Whatever the case, this epigram has to do with a bereaved person's strong desire to communicate with a loved one who has recently died.

1 **mutis ... sepulcris:** cf. 101.4, *mutam ... cinerem.*

2 **accidere:** reach, get through to (with *sepulcris* above). **Calve:** see appendix A.

3 **quo desiderio,** etc.: by the longing with which we renew old loves; *desiderio* specifies the meaning of *dolore.*

4 **olim missas amicitias** suggests love discarded at some time in the past through some wrongdoing.

5–6 **tanto ... quantum:** coordinate (so much ... as), though syntactically not parallel. **dolori est Quin-**

Notes

tiliae: double dative, a cause of pain to Quintilia. Your love matters more to her than her untimely death.

97

Understandably condemned by Merrill as "exceedingly coarse," this tirade against a lecher who suffers from advanced gum disease is appropriately foul-mouthed.

1 **non ... referre putavi**: I didn't expect I would have to decide: *refero* here = assign to a category. **ita me di ament**: a common form of asseveration in comedy: cf. 61.189–90, 66.18. The *i* of *di* is shortened in hiatus. The indefinite **quicquam**, obj. of *referre*, is explained by line 2.

2 **utrum ... olfacerem**: whether it was his *os* or his *culus* that I was getting a whiff of. **Aemilio**: dat. of reference; nothing is known of this person.

3 **Nilo** = *nihilo*, abl. of degree of difference. **hoc ... illud**: reverses the usual terms of reference: *hoc* (his *os*) is no cleaner, *illud* (his *culus*, made neuter for the occasion) is no dirtier.

5 **sine dentibus est**: *culus* in the understood subj., the point being that because it has no teeth, it is free of gum disease. **Hoc** is Aemilius' mouth, *os*. **dentis sesquipedalis**: another Catullan exaggeration. A conspicuous symptom of gingivitis is the shrinking of gum tissue, making the teeth appear longer. Because it is a common disease of middle life, people who are getting on in years are said to be "long in the tooth."

6 **ploxeni ... veteris**: an old carriage body. Ellis explains: his gums are "receding from the teeth and forming fissures or gaps like those in the body or frame of a gig, when the leather or other soft material with which it is covered gives way and falls into a number of uneven notches or slits all round."

7 **praeterea**, etc.: unable to leave bad enough alone, Catullus goes on to describe his victim's slack mouth, the result of the shrinkage of gums and underlying bone tissue. The imagery is disgusting but clinically vivid.

9 **se facit esse**: makes himself out to be.

10 **pistrino**: in comedy, misbehaving slaves worried about being sent out to work in the mill. **asino**: the ass that turns the mill wheel.

98

The manuscripts give this babbler's name as Vic-

tius, Viccius, or Vittius. He may be a notorious perjurer of the time named L. Vettius. Nothing is too dirty for his vile tongue.

1 **In te**: against you. **putide**: both literal and figurative: you rotter. We are invited to imagine (esp. in lines 5–6) that Victius has some festering disease of the tongue.

2 **verbosis, fatuis**: dat. of reference.

3 **cum**: the archaic instrumental preposition. **usus**: the opportunity.

4 **crepidas carpatinas**: thick-soled leather sandals such as peasants might wear in mud and manure. *C-* sounds and other mutes (*p, d, t*) are at work in this line.

6 **hiscas**: open your mouth to speak; jussive subjunctive.

99

Catullus has received a stinging rebuke from Juventius after making an unsuccessful advance. This short elegy, thematically related to the preceding two poems, is his artful but tender apology.

1 **tibi**: dat. with *surripui*, = *a te*; cf. 86.6, *omnibus surripuit Veneres*. **ludis**: historical present with **dum**, like *purgo* and *possum* (line 5).

1–2 **Surripui ... suaviolum ... ambrosia**: the beginning of a chiastic ring structure that connects the beginning of the elegy to the end; cf. lines 13–16, *ambrosia ... suaviolum ... surripiam*.

3 **Verum id non impune tuli**: but I didn't get away with it. Cf. 78b.3, *Verum id non impune feres*. The use here and in line 10 of language from a poem attacking another person for his lechery is a special form of self-abasement, perhaps comparable to the placement of this elegy right after the scorn of poems 97 and 98. **horam**: acc. of duration of time instead of the usual abl. of comparison.

6 **vestrae** = *tuae*.

7–8: Juventius washes his lips with tears and wipes them clean with his fingers. We are not meant to believe that the boy has been genuinely traumatized by Catullus' impulsive action.

10 **comminctae ... lupae**: a dirty whore; the line is probably meant to recall 78b.2, *suavia comminxit spurca saliva tua*.

11 **infesto amori**: oxymoron; cf. line 15, *misero ... amori*, and 91.2 (of his love with Lesbia), *in misero hoc nostro, hoc perdito amore*.

12 **non cessa(vi)sti**: Juventius has not let Catullus forget his offense. It became conventional in elegy

159

for the lover to cherish his lady's cruel temper.
14: the words echo line 2, but now the kiss is bitter medicine.

100

Two Veronese friends of Catullus are in love, one with Aufillenus and the other with his sister Aufillena. The prettiness of what at first appears to be a love-idyll half covers a sexual insult to Caelius. This Caelius, a Veronese, is probably not the Caelius Rufus described in appendix A. A Quintius was addressed in poem 82, apparently as a rival for Lesbia's love.

1 **Aufillenam**: a professional *amica*, to judge from her role in poem 110; she is worse yet in poem 111.

2 **flos Veronensum ... iuvenum**: Caelius and Quintius collectively; cf. 63.64, *gymnasi fui flos*.

3 **hic** and **ille** refer to the former and the latter respectively (as in 97.3), contrary to the usual practice. The effect is to emphasize Caelius, who turns out to be the target of Catullus' ironic compliments. **Hoc est quod dicitur**: this is what people call; cf. 94.2, *hoc est quod dicunt*.

5 **Cui faveam ...? Caeli, tibi**: cf. 1.1–3, *Cui dono ...? Corneli, tibi*.

6 **igni**: instrumental abl.; the fire of sexual need, as the next line explains. **unica amicitia**, as Philip Levine has argued, is special because it consisted in Caelius' passive homosexual service to Catullus. Others have seen in it a reference to some assistance rendered in Catullus' affair with Lesbia.

7 For the *medullae* as the seat of sexual passion, cf. 35.15, 45.16, 64.93.

101

Catullus' brother died somewhere near Troy, and it is likely that on his way to Bithynia in 57 the poet stopped to make an offering at the grave. This memorial of his visit is written in the manner of a Hellenistic grave epigram.

2 **advenio** in the present perfect sense (I have come) makes the poem more dramatic monologue than grave inscription. **inferias**: rites for the dead, including offerings of wine, milk, honey, and flowers. Such offerings to the *dis manibus* were a family duty (or *munus*, as in line 8).

3 **donarem**: to honor, with the ablative of thing given and the accusative of recipient.

4 **nequiquam**, to be understood with *alloquerer*,

emphasizes the sense of futility; Catullus can address the ashes in the tomb, but they will not answer.

5 **quandoquidem**: since, with iambic shortening of the o. See note on 64.218; Catullus' grief for his brother is like Aegeus' for his son. **abstulit**: from *aufero*.

6 **indigne**: adverb with **adempte**, undeservedly taken from me. For the phrasing of the line as a whole, cf. 68.20 and 92.

7 **interea** strengthens the adversative force of **tamen**: not meanwhile but in the present situation, under these circumstances. He cannot speak to his brother, but he can make a ritual offering.

7–9 **haec ... quae ... tradita sunt ... manantia**: these [rituals] that are offered (or handed down by tradition) are metaphorically dripping with tears. **tristi munere** is a modal abl., as a sad gift and duty; **ad** indicates purpose rather than movement as in line 2.

10 **ave atque vale**, hail and farewell, may be words of the ritual itself. Aeneas' farewell to the dead Pallas in *Aeneid* 11.97–8 uses a similar formula.

102

Catullus reassures Cornelius that he can keep a secret. This is probably not the Cornelius of poem 1, or the man from Brixia in 67.35.

1 **tacito**: substantive, to a discreet person.

2 **penitus nota**: known without reservation; **fides animi** is pleonastic, like *mens animi* (65.4) *animi curas* (2.10), and *furor animi* (63.38).

3 **illorum iure sacratum**: bound by the code of those whose *fides* is *penitus nota*.

4 **Arpocratem**: i.e., a veritable Harpocrates, proverbial for silence. See note on 74.4.

103

Silo, whose business it is to supply men with willing dates, has delivered faulty goods (or none at all). Catullus has protested, and has received an uncivil answer.

1 **sodes**: < *si audes*, = if you please. **decem sestertia** = *decem milia sestertium*: 10,000 sesterces, a tidy sum for an evening's pleasure. Ameana had her nerve charging that much in poem 41.

4 **leno ... atque idem saevus**: a pimp, and at the same time foul-tempered. For *idem* emphasizing an inconsistency, cf. 22.14. It was necessary for the

leno in comedy (as no doubt also in real life) to be cheerful and accommodating and to take abuse philosophically.

104

Addressed to someone (perhaps imaginary) who has criticized Catullus' submissive attitude toward Lesbia. Showing anger to her is impossible, he replies; if he could speak harshly, he would not be in love. Only a clown (he implies) could do something so unnatural. The attitude of the lover anticipates Augustan love elegy. Catullus says angry things *about* Lesbia (e.g., in poems 11—where a bitter message is sent via intermediaries—and 58), but nothing harsher than poems 60, 72, and 75 is addressed to her directly.

1 **meae maledicere vitae**: Catullus cannot, but Lesbia can in 83.1 and 92.1 (*Lesbia mi dicit semper male*), where it is taken as proof of her love. The woman benefits from this double standard. For Lesbia as *mea vita*, cf. 109.1. Acme calls Septimius *mea vita* in 45.13.

2 **carior ... oculis**: cf. poem 82, where *carius ... oculis* is repeated three times, probably also with reference to the love of Lesbia.

3 **potui, possem**: with *potuisse* in line 1, the key word of the poem. For Catullus, power is negatively related to love: the more love, the less power. **nec ... amarem**: nor, if I could (say bad things to her), would I be so helplessly in love with her.

4 **tu cum Tappone**: Tappo appears to have been a stock figure from south Italian farce; if so, the meaning is that anyone who believes a lover can say angry things to his beloved joins Tappo in doing all kinds of outrageous things.

105

The "Renaissance man" was a revival of a Roman tradition, where public figures such as Cicero, Caesar, C. Cinna, Q. Hortalus, and Licinius Calvus tried their hand at poetry as well as oratory. Mentula (see appendix A: Mamurra) has aped the efforts of his betters with poor results; in this verbal cartoon, the Muses eject him.

1 **Pi**(m)**pleium montem**: Pimpleia is a place in Pieria just north of Mt. Olympus, sacred to the Muses and associated with the cult of Orpheus.

2 **furcullis**: with pitchforks, a humorously realistic touch for Muses who live in the country.

106

Catullus suspects his young friend Juventius of promiscuity; in poem 24, there was the bankrupt Furius; in 81, it was an unhealthy man from Pisaurum. Now, he has been seen with an auctioneer; Catullus taunts him with readiness to auction off his favors to the highest bidder. Tradition allowed a boy to receive the sexual attentions of older men, but if he sold himself, he permanently lost his claim to respectability.

1 **Cum**: the preposition, with *puero bello* (i.e., Juventius).

2 **discupere**: is intent upon; *dis-* is an intensifying prefix, as in 92.2 *dispeream*.

107

A happy poem on the unexpected return of Lesbia after a breakup in their relationship. Repetitions of *cupido*, *optanti*/*optandam*, *insperanti*, *gratum*, *nobis*, *restituis*, and *vivit*/*vita* tell the story in a way that is almost an exaggeration of Catullan style.

1 **cupido optanti**: note the hiatus at the principal caesura.

2 **gratum ... proprie**: truly pleasing.

3 **nobisque**: the dative goes with both *gratum* and *carius auro*. The plural is understood in the singular sense, as in line 6.

5 **ipsa**: of your own accord.

6 **lucem**: exclamatory acc., day (cf. *festis luminibus*, holidays, in 66.90). **candidiore nota**: abl. of description. Special days were proverbially marked with a white stone. Cf. 68.148, *lapide candidiore*.

7 **vivit** = est; cf. 89.1–2, *cui tam bona mater ... vivat*.

7–8 **magis hac rem optandam in**: Postgate's emendation of an unreadable ms: who will have been able to tell of a thing in life more to be wished for than this?

108

Lines describing the undignified fate of a hated person's corpse became a minor topos of abuse, going back perhaps to Callimachus' lost *Ibis*; cf. Horace *Epodes* 5.96–100, Ovid *Ibis* 165–172. This wishful account of the end of an old scoundrel named Cominius starts slowly and ends quickly.

1 **populi arbitrio**: by popular demand.

3 **inimica bonorum**: the enemy of upstanding citizens. *Bonus* in contexts such as this was commonly applied to citizens of the "better" (i.e.,

wealthier) class. Applied to **lingua**, the phrase suggests that this Cominius spent his time bringing accusations against wealthy persons in hopes of getting out-of-court settlements.

4 **sit data**: not the perfect subjunctive, but a periphrastic alternate for *detur*; cf. *voret* in the next line. Both subjunctives complete the *non dubito quin* construction and represent a fulfillment of the hypothetical (future less vivid) *si ... intereat* condition.

6: *vorent* is to be understood as the verb.

109

Catullus wishes the *amor* that Lesbia says will be both pleasant and permanent could only become a bond of *sanctae amicitiae*. The epigram consists of two apostrophes, first to Lesbia and then to the gods. The content is similar to that of poem 70: he doesn't really trust Lesbia's assurances, knowing as he does that he wants a commitment which Lesbia is not prepared to make.

1–2 **iucundum** and **perpetuum** are predicative with **fore**; **proponis** implies a declaration of willingness or intent; it governs the infinitive **fore** in indirect statement.

5 **tota ... vita**: ablative for duration of time instead of the usual accusative.

6: the interlocked phrases imply marriage. Lesbia wants a pleasant affair (line 1: **iucundum ... amorem**); Catullus wants something more serious, as his collection of solemn words (**aeternum ... sanctae foedus**) indicates. The poem thus hangs on the contrast between the language of the first couplet and that of the last, between the *amor* that Lesbia proposes and the bonding of a sacred *amicitia* that Catullus prays for, upgrading what she says to what he desires. This reveals a central problem in the relationship: Catullus hopes for more than Lesbia wants.

110

Aufillena and her brother were ironically romantic figures in poem 100; here she is just a tart, and a dishonest one at that.

1 **bonae ... amicae**: disapproval of prostitution has deprived the English language of neutral terms for women who sell sexual services. "Courtesan" evokes a world of kings and courtiers; "prostitute" suggests furtive depravity and exploitation; "whore"

evokes something even worse. Here, *bona amica* is a friendly woman who keeps a deal.

2 **pretium,** [*eorum*] **quae**: a specific one of the prices they establish for various services. *quae* is neut. accus. pl.

3–4 **quod**: three conjunctions, leading up to *facis facinus*. Because you promised, because you lied, because you often take without giving, you are a crook. The second verb is **mentita ... es**, but with *inimica* there is a calculated ambiguity: having lied, you are my enemy (or no *amica* of mine; cf. *amicae* in line 1).

4 **nec das et fers saepe**: i.e., you do not deliver the services agreed though you often take the money.

5 **ingenuae, pudicae**: substantives, gen. of quality. The words are ironic, since these words would not normally be applied to a woman who performs sexual acts for money. A freeborn woman would have performed as agreed; a chaste (or decent) one wouldn't have made the deal in the first place.

7 **fraudando officiis**: by cheating someone of the service undertaken as an obligation. Once she has taken the money, her *officium* is to perform as promised. More irony, as *officium* (moral obligation, duty) is not usually applied to sex for money. **meretricis avarae**: gen. of quality. The greedy *meretrix* is a character type from New Comedy (e.g., Erotium in Plautus' *Menaechmi*), but what Aufillena has done is more than (*plus quam*) even such as that type would do.

111

More abuse of Aufillena, accusing her of incest with an uncle. As in the previous poem, Catullus seems to be playing off her aspiration to respectability; the first couplet and *matrem* in line 4 suggest that at the time of this epigram she may in fact have been the married mother of legitimate children.

1 **viro solo**: women who spent their lives married to a single man were *univirae*; for their special function as attendants to the bride in her wedding chamber, see 61. 179–81 and note.

2 **nuptarum laus** [*est*], etc.: i.e., it is the cardinal glory of married women.

3–4 **cuivis**: dat. with *succumbere*. **quamvis**: acc. subject of *succumbere*. **potius ... par est ... quam**, etc.: i.e., it is better to be promiscuous than to conceive cousins by an uncle.

4 **fratres** [*patrueles*]: cousins, specifically sons of a

maternal uncle (*patruus*). **concipere**: added by Rossbach to fill out the meaning and meter of a defective ms. text.

112

A brief sally at an unknown Naso, who is large and sexually active with other men. The couplet plays on two meanings of *multus*.

1 **multus homo**: a large man or a lot of man; in its second appearance, many a man or many men.
2 **te scindat**: splits you, subjunctive with *quin*: i.e., there are not many men who do not use you for anal sex. **pathicus**: it is to Naso's discredit not that he has sex with men, but that he plays the passive role.

113

The number of Maecilia's lovers has grown from two to two thousand in the last fifteen years.

1 **Consule Pompeio primum**: i.e., in Pompey's first consulship, 70 B.C.; dates were normally reckoned in this way. **Cinna**: see appendix A. **solebant**: a euphemistic ellipse for habitual sexual contact: sc. *futuere* or the like. In this idiom *solebant* becomes a transitive verb, with *Maeciliam* as its object.
2 **facto consule nunc iterum**: Pompey's second consulship was in 55 B.C., fifteen years after his first, and evidently the date of this poem.
3–4 **creverunt**: from *cresco*. **milia in unum singula**: a thousand (rivals) against each; *unum = utrumque*. **adulterio**: dat. of possession (sc. *est*).

114

Caesar's stooge Mentula (a.k.a. Mamurra) is land-poor: he has a magnificent estate, but its expenses outrun the income it produces.

1 **saltu**: abl. of cause with *dives fertur*; strictly speaking a *saltus* is rough woodland broken with glades, here the country estate as a whole.
2 **in se**: in his possession.
3 **aucupium**: gen. pl., wildfowl. With the other assets catalogued in this line (cf. 115.5), it appears that Mamurra's place near Firmum on the Adriatic coast is essentially a game farm, whose *prata* and *arva* are more for forage than cash crops.
4 **fructus** (acc. pl.) **sumptibus exsuperat**: he exceeds the land's yield with his expenses. Instead of producing income, Mamurra's land is another of the

many luxuries upon which he fritters away his vast wealth. For more about Mamurra, see appendix A.
5 **modo ipse**: a very unusual hiatus in the second half of the pentameter; some editors believe the text is corrupt. **egeat**: a joke, as Mentula was one of the richest men in Italy.

115

More about Mentula/Mamurra, whose lands seem to go on forever but are not much better than he is.

1 **habĕt**: the *e* is normally short. **instar**, about, is used adverbially and with contempt; cf. the US colloquialism, "Mentula has like thirty *iugera*." **triginta iugera**: about twenty acres, not a large amount of grazing land (*prati*), even by ancient standards. Except for a bit of farmland, Mamurra has mostly wilderness.
2 **maria**: humorous exaggeration for swamps; cf. line 5, *paludes*.
4 **saltu**: country estate, as in 114.1 and 6.
5 **prata arva**, etc.: asyndeton for humorous effect; the list is anticlimactic, going from good land to useless swamp. **saltus**: broken woodland, good only for light grazing and hunting. **paludesque**: the last syllable is hypermetric, eliding with *usque* in the next line. This occurs nowhere else in elegiac poetry and puts special emphasis on the vast extent of Mamurra's underwater holdings.
7 **ipse ... ultro**: he himself.
8 **homo**: iambic shortening of the second syllable. **mentula magna minax**: comic alliteration; like his land that is mostly swamp, Mamurra is mostly a big *mentula*.

116

The last poem in the collection records Catullus' vain attempt to make peace with the infamous Gellius (see appendix A) and his decision to make war instead.

1 **tibi**: ind. object of *vertere*. **studioso animo venante**: abl. abs., as my eager mind was hunting (for peace).
2 **uti possem vertere**: ind. question with *requirens*, how I might translate. **Battiadae**: Callimachus, as in 65.15.
3 **qui**: the relative adverb, = *quibus*, whereby, referring to *carmina*. **conarere** = *conareris*. This is the only entirely spondaic hexameter after Ennius

(239–169 B.C.).5 **mihi**: dative of agent.
6 **hic**: in this matter.
7 **contra nos ... acta**: hurled against us.

8 **nostris**: sc. *telis*, viz. lines such as those in poems 74, 80, 88, 89–91.

Appendix A

PEOPLE

A note about Roman names: In the time of Catullus, Cicero, and Caesar, freeborn Roman men regularly had three names: a *praenomen* or personal name, a *nomen gentile* (the name of his clan or *gens*), and *cognomen* or family name. Gaius Valerius Catullus (*praenomen* + *nomen gentile* + *cognomen*), like other Romans of his time, refers to himself in his poems by his *cognomen*—Catullus. We generally follow the same usage in identifying Marcus Tullius Cicero as "Cicero" rather than "Tully" (as he was sometimes called in the Renaissance and afterwards). Publius Vergilius Maro is known to us as Virgil, however, rather than Maro.

The most common *praenomina* were usually abbreviated: C. for Gaius, L. for Lucius, M. for Marcus, P. for Publius, and so on. The regular form of the *nomen gentile* is adjectival (Valerius, -a, -um), because the *gens* is a category to which many people, male and female, belonged. There was no regular system for the naming of women. Caesar's wife, for example, whom he divorced during the Bona Dea scandal of 62 because she must be above suspicion, is known to history only as Pompeia, her *nomen gentile*.

For a complete account of who's who in Catullus, see C. L. Neudling, *A Prosopography to Catullus* (Iowa Studies in Classical Philology #12), Oxford, 1955.

Acme, the Greek girl in love with **Septimius** in poem 45, seems to have stepped out of a romantic comedy. Her Greek name means "zenith, peak, prime." Probably a freedwoman, she could well be one of the many hetaeras common in Rome since at least 160 B.C. If so, she would be a colleague of **Ipsitilla**, though more romantically viewed. Such women were often more intriguing to men of Catullus' station than the less sophisticated and mature girls they were expected to marry.

Alfenus, the friend whose perceived disloyalty Catullus complains of in poem 30, cannot be positively identified. He may be the Varus of poems 10 and 22 (see **Varus** below).

Ameana is a lady of delight who spends her time with the swinish millionaire **Mamurra** and charges 10,000 sesterces for her services when not otherwise occupied. Her nose is several sizes too big. Catullus attends to her immortality in poems 41 and 43.

Arrius, the social climber in poem 84 who mimics the accents of the intelligentsia, may be the self-made orator Q. Arrius mentioned by Cicero (*Brutus* 242). He was a follower of the triumvir M. Licinius Crassus, who may have arranged the transfer to Syria mentioned in 84.7.

Aufillena is a woman of Verona who first appears with her brother Aufillenus in poem 100 as the object of a double romance. Apparently a figure of scandal (or Catullan character assassination), in poem 110 she is accused of taking money for sex and then welshing on the deal. Worse yet, in 111 she conceives children by her own uncle.

Aurelius in poems 11, 15, 16, and 21 is an otherwise unidentified acquaintance of Catullus, and is paired with **Furius** in 11 and 16. In 15 and 21 he is a sexual rival, probably for the favors of **Juventius**.

Aurunculeia: the bride in poem 61. See Junia Aurunculeia.

Caecilius is the love poet from Como whom Catullus invites to visit him in poem 35. Otherwise unknown, he is working on a poem about the Asiatic goddess Cybele (perhaps like Catullus' own poem 63) and has a passionately devoted girlfriend. He may be an ancestor of the younger Pliny (Gaius Plinius Caecilius Secundus, ca. 61–112 A.D.), who was also a native of Como.

Caelius: see M. Caelius **Rufus**.

Gaius Julius **Caesar** (100–44 B.C.), the last great

general and politician of the Republican era, was a friend of Catullus' family and a frequent guest at his family home in Verona. In spite of attacks of varying intensity (see poems 29, 54, 57, and 93), Caesar remained well-disposed. According to Suetonius (*Div. Jul.* 73), Catullus eventually apologized for his scurrilous but damaging attacks and was invited to dine with Caesar the same day.

C. Licinius Macer **Calvus** (82–47 B.C.) was Catullus' closest friend, the fellow poet with whom he spends an exciting day in poem 50, and whose famous oratory he praises in 53. His personal cognomen Calvus ("Baldy") suggests something of his appearance. In 14 he sends Catullus an anthology of the worst new poems he can find. Small and lively, his speech against **Vatinius** mentioned in poems 14 and 53 (**Cicero** spoke for the defense) was used over a century later in textbooks of oratory as an example of the plain Attic style. Only a few scraps of his speeches and poetry survive, one of them a scurrilous poem about Caesar's sex life quoted by Suetonius, *Div. Iul.* 49.

Marcus Tullius **Cicero** (106–43 B.C.), the leading orator of his time and one of the leading politicians, moved in the same social circles as Catullus. He provided the Latin names by which Catullus' poetic circle is known: *neoteroi, novi poetae,* and (with a note of scorn) *cantores Euphorionis.* Westphal goes so far as to suggest that Cicero actually introduced Catullus to the circle of Clodia/Lesbia. Clodia's brother P. Clodius **Pulcher** was in fact a political enemy who got Cicero banished in 58 B.C. and had his gang wreck Cicero's house on the Palatine and his villa in Tusculum. Catullus addresses Cicero with elaborate (and perhaps ironic) flattery in poem 49.

Gaius Cinna, referred to in poem 10 as Catullus' *sodalis*, is praised in poem 95 for his small epic *Zmyrna* and is addressed in poem 113. Usually identified as C. Helvius Cinna, he was a poet of Catullus' neoteric group and apparently was with Catullus in Bithynia. A political ally of Caesar, he was tribune in the fateful year of 44 B.C. when an angry mob, mistaking him for the anti-Caesarian L. Cornelius Cinna, tore him to pieces (Plutarch, *Caesar* 68.2). When he protests in Shakespeare's *Julius Caesar* (III iii 30) that he is not Cinna the conspirator but Cinna the poet, the crowd shouts

"Tear him for his bad verses!"

Clodia Metelli, often identified with Catullus' lover **Lesbia**, was one of three daughters of Appius Claudius Pulcher (consul 79 B.C.) and the sister or half sister of Cicero's enemy P. Clodius **Pulcher**. Of patrician ancestry on both sides, she married Q. Metellus **Celer**, but her reputation (partly as a result of character assassination in Cicero's *Pro Caelio*) was not that of a respectable Roman matron. Though Catullus is not mentioned as one of her lovers, she allegedly took up with M. Caelius **Rufus** after her husband's death. Cicero charged that when Caelius broke with her she attempted to have him convicted on a poisoning charge.

Cornificius, the friend from whom Catullus asks a sad poem in poem 38, is probably Quintus Cornificius, the friend and correspondent of Cicero, who was a successful orator, military commander, and colonial administrator. After Caesar's death he cast his lot with the senate against the second triumvirate and was killed in North Africa when his troops deserted him (42 B.C.). As a poet, he is mentioned by Ovid with Catullus, **Calvus**, and **Cinna**.

Egnatius is the bearded, long-haired dandy from Spain who brushes his teeth (in the manner of his region) with urine. In poem 37 Catullus singles him out as a habitué of the tavern where Lesbia's lovers hang out. In poem 39 he is mocked for his all-purpose toothy grin. It is likely that he was (or aspired to be) one of Lesbia's lovers.

Fabullus, colleague of **Veranius** in Spain, sent Catullus napkins of fine Spanish linen as a souvenir in poem 12; in 13 he is invited to dinner. He later served under **Piso** in Macedonia with his friend **Veranius**, but was ill-rewarded for it, as we read in 28 and 47.

Flavius, otherwise unknown, is involved in poem 6 in a torrid new love affair.

Furius in poems 11, 16, 23, and 26 may be the poet Furius Bibaculus, a northerner like Catullus and one of the *novi poetae*. He is paired with **Aurelius** in 11 and 16; both were Catullus' successful rivals for the love of **Juventius**. Catullus' picture of him is unflattering: a fool and a spendthrift, suitable only to carry the disdainful message to Lesbia in poem 11.

Gellius: see L. Gellius **Poplicola.**

Quintus Hortensius **Hortalus** (114–50 B.C.) is probably the *Ortale* addressed in poem 65 and the fast-working Hortensius mentioned (unfavorably, perhaps after a quarrel) in 95.3. Some thirty years older than Catullus, he was **Cicero's** chief rival in the law courts, a master of the flowery and theatrical style of oratory that came to be known as Asianism. In addition to *risqué* light poetry, for which Ovid and Pliny associate him with the circle of Catullus, he wrote some historical prose.

Ipsitilla is the courtesan to whose house Catullus seeks an invitation for an amorous afternoon in poem 32. She belongs to a class comparable to that of the Greek *hetaera*, common in Rome in the last two centuries of the Republican era. Many such women moved freely in high society and were much sought after. Cf. **Acme.**

Junia Aurunculeia, the bride of **Manlius Torquatus** in poem 61, has two family names. Possibly Aurunculeia was her mother's family name, though the use of such metronymics was not common until the period of the Empire. She may be the woman from Asculum mentioned by **Cicero** (*pro Sulla* 25) as the bride of a Manlius.

Juventius is the name of a boy with whom Catullus was sexually involved. He is usually assumed to have been a native of Verona living in Rome under the guardianship of Catullus. The so-called "Juventius Cycle" (poems 15, 21, 23, 24, 48, 81, 99, and perhaps 16 and 40) records various aspects of that relationship, including the rivalry of the hated **Furius** and **Aurelius.** The name, if not fictitious, belongs to an old and distinguished family from Tusculum, according to Cicero *pro Plancio* 19.

Lesbia, the woman mentioned in some twenty-five of Catullus' love poems, is usually identified with **Clodia** Metelli, elder sister of the politician P. Clodius **Pulcher.** She has also been identified with Clodia Metelli's younger sister, named Clodia Luculli because of her marriage to L. Licinius Lucullus. See Introduction and entry for **Clodia** above. The pseudonym Lesbia is metrically equivalent to the real Clodia (as was the custom), no

doubt as a tribute to the sixth century Greek love poet **Sappho** of Lesbos.

Licinius: see C. Licinius Macer **Calvus.**

Mamurra of Formiae became wealthy as a protégé of Caesar in Spain and Gaul, and was a notorious big spender. Catullus attacks Mamurra's girlfriend **Ameana** in 41 and 43, his association with **Caesar** and other vices in 29 and 57, and his literary pretentions in 105. He is referred to as Mentula "the Prick" in 94, 105, 114, and 115.

Asinius Marrucinus, the napkin thief warned in poem 12, gets his cognomen from the Marrucini, an Italian tribe whose capital Teate was the home of his family, the Asinii. His brother Pollio is listed here as **C. Asinius Pollio.**

Gaius Memmius, praetor who governed the province of Bithynia in 57–56 B.C., when Catullus served on his staff or *cohors.* Catullus speaks harshly of him in 10.9–13 and 28.7–10 for not having provided his staff with adequate opportunities to profiteer. He was also a man of letters, friendly to the neoteric group of Catullus. Lucretius dedicated *De Rerum Natura* to him; **Cicero** mentions his literary connoisseurship, Ovid his love poetry.

Mentula: see **Mamurra.**

Q. **Metellus** Celer, husband of **Clodia,** is probably the husband mentioned in 68.146 and poem 83. Ill-matched to his scandalous wife, he served as praetor in 63, governor of Cisalpine Gaul in 62, and consul in 60. He died in 59, allegedly poisoned by his wife.

Cornelius Nepos (c. 99 – c. 24 B.C.), dedicatee of Catullus' little book referred to in poem 1. Pliny says he came from a town in Cisalpine Gaul, making him a countryman of Catullus. A friend and correspondent of **Cicero,** he wrote light verse besides his serious prose work. The three-roll history (*Chronica*) mentioned by Catullus is lost, but some of his biographical work (*De Viris Illustribus*) survives.

A **Piso** is scornfully mentioned as *iste vappa* (that dud) in poem 28 (and worse things in 47) out of sympathy for **Veranius** and **Fabullus,** who served on his staff in Spain and were ill-rewarded for it. Traditionally identified as Caesar's father-in-law L. Calpurnius Piso Caesonius, consul in 58 B.C., whom **Cicero** maliciously caricatured in two extant speeches (*De Provinciis Consularibus* and *In Pisonem*), he may in fact have been L. Piso Frugi.

C. Asinius **Pollio** (76 B.C. – 4 A.D.), brother of the napkin thief **Asinius Marrucinus** in poem 12, came from a distinguished family and went on to earn distinction of his own as an orator, critic, and historian of the civil wars between 60 and 42 B.C. A close associate of Julius Caesar, he was also an esteemed friend of Horace (*Odes* 2.1) and Virgil (*Ecl.* 4), and he founded the first public library in Rome some time between 39 and 28 B.C.

L. Gellius **Poplicola** is usually identified as the Gellius of poems 74, 80, 88, 89, 90, 91, 116. Reportedly uninhibited in his choice of sexual partners, he appears from the virulent attack in poem 91 to have been a rival for **Clodia/Lesbia**. There is evidence elsewhere that he belonged to the political circle of **Clodius**. Valerius Maximus says he was accused before the senate of having an affair with his stepmother and plotting his father's murder. The son of a consul, he later held the consulship himself (36 B.C.) and commanded the left wing of Antony's doomed fleet at the Battle of Actium in 31 B.C.

Postumia is the hard-drinking lady imagined as the master of revels in poem 27. The name suggests she is not a hired party girl but a woman of rank. She is otherwise unknown.

P. Clodius **Pulcher,** younger brother of **Clodia,** political opportunist and antagonist of **Cicero,** was not always on the best of terms with Catullus, as we see in poem 79. A member of the blue-blooded Claudian *gens,* he changed the spelling of his name to appeal to the plebeians whose political support he sought. His street gangs were a notorious instrument of his power.

Quintia, the good-looking woman compared to Lesbia in poem 86, may be related to the **Quintius** of poems 82 and 100, but the name is common enough.

Ravidus is the cognomen of a rival against whom Catullus directs his iambics in poem 40.

Romulus and **Remus,** legendary founders of Rome, mentioned as heroic ancestors to whose memory various scoundrels of Catullus' own time (Piso and Memmius in 28.15, Mamurra in 29.5, Lesbia's lovers in 58.5) are a disgrace. **Cicero** is praised in 49.1 as *disertissime Romuli nepotum.*

M. Caelius **Rufus** is probably the Caelius addressed in poem 58; he may also be the Rufus of 69 and 77, but probably not the Caelius of 100, whom Catullus calls a Veronese (Caelius Rufus is believed to come from Picenum). **Cicero's** successful defense of him (*Pro Caelio*) alleges that he had an affair with Clodia Metelli after her husband's death, and that when he finally disentangled himself in 57 or 56 she had him arraigned on the charge that he tried to poison her. An ambitious politician, orator, and big-spending *bon vivant,* he was a correspondent of Cicero and a political ally of Caesar. He is said to have called Clodia a "two-bit Clytemnestra," *quadrantaria Clytemnestra.*

Sappho of Lesbos, the most celebrated woman poet of early Greece (b. ca. 612 B.C.), was best known by Catullus' time for her love poetry. **Lesbia** was almost certainly so called in honor of Sappho. Catullus' poem 51 is based upon a poem of hers, and he calls Caecilius' literary girlfriend "more learned than the Sapphic muse" (35.16) as a gallant compliment. Only a few fragments of her nine books of poetry have survived. The Sapphic strophe, used twice by Catullus, is named after her. Catullus was attracted to her emphasis on the pathos of love, her use of the vernacular, and her marriage hymns, which may have influenced poems 61 and 62.

Septimius is the young Roman in love with **Acme** in poem 45. Attracted by her exotic nature, he compares his love for her with the romance of faraway adventure and empire-building.

Publius **Sestius** is probably the Sestius made fun of in poem 44 for his *In Antium,* which was so boring it gave Catullus a cold. A stooge of the senatorial party, he was defended in 56 by Cicero for organizing a mob of goons to attack the gang of Clodius. Cicero himself (*Ad Fam.* 7.32.1) confirms that he was a well-known dullard.

Suffenus is the conceited poetaster who gets up his feeble verses in exquisite editions in poem 22. He is mentioned along with a couple of other dilettantes in 14.19.

Sulla, the *litterator* mentioned in poem 14 as a *cliens* of **Licinius Calvus**, allegedly gave him a collection of bad poems, which Calvus then passed on to Catullus as a mischievous gift on the Saturnalia. He is not otherwise identifiable.

Thallus is the otherwise unknown thief of woven goods who is verbally lacerated in poem 25.

Manlius **Torquatus**, whose wedding to **Junia Aurunculeia** is celebrated in poem 61, may be L. Manlius Torquatus, a slightly older contemporary of Catullus' who served as praetor in 49 B.C. Cicero dramatizes him as the exponent of Epicureanism in *De Finibus* and mentions his distinction as a scholar and orator in *Brutus* 265.

Varus, who has a new lady friend in poem 10, is probably the same as the Varus addressed in poem 22. He could be either of two men from Cremona in northern Italy: a) Alfenus Varus, the jurist who became consul suffect in 39 B.C. and served under Octavian, or b) Quintilius Varus, the critic whose death in 24 B.C. is mourned in Horace's Ode I 24, addressed to Virgil.

Publius **Vatinius**, a political ally of Caesar attacked in poem 52 for bragging about his future consulship, was the beneficiary of a phony election to the praetorship in 55 B.C. He was prosecuted in 54 B.C. by **Calvus**, whose speech became famous as one of the best of its kind; it is praised by Catullus in poem 53 (in 14.3 Vatinius' name is proverbial for odium). He was successfully defended on that occasion by **Cicero**, who had previously spoken out against him. The earlier speech, *In Vatinium* (56 B.C.), survives.

Veranius, friend of Catullus, welcomed home from Spain in poem 9, appears with **Fabullus** in poems 12, 28, and 47. In 28 they are on provincial duty, probably in Macedonia, under **Piso** during Catullus' own service under **Memmius** in Bithynia (57–56 B.C.). Poem 47 commiserates further with their ill luck in Macedonia.

Vibennius steals clothing from the baths while his aging son tries to peddle his sexual favors to men, according to poem 33. Nothing more is known of this infamous pair.

Volusius is the author of some verse *Annales* that Catullus proposes to burn in poem 36, or use to wrap fish in poem 95. Judging from 95.7, he came from northern Italy, near a branch of the Po River named the Padua. The reasons for Catullus' dislike are unknown; Livy, who came from the same area (Patavium, mod. Padova or Padua), was criticized for his *patavinitas*, a quality in his Latin style that marked him as a provincial.

Appendix B

METERS

Poetry is rhythmic sound married to meaning. Without sound, poetry ceases to exist as such. In written form it is like sheet music, waiting to come to life in performance. This means, of course, that Catullus should be read out loud (the ancient Romans did not read silently), and the sound should be naturally rhythmic.

Meter is the "measure" or rhythm of poetry. It is as old as language itself; the actual meters used by Catullus are believed to be prehistoric Indo-European rhythms developed and handed down by the Greek poets. For our purposes, lines of poetry are best understood as a sequence of metrical *feet*. Each foot is a series of two, three, or four syllables that combine to form a metrical building block.

The commonest such building blocks in Catullus are:

—the dactyl, as in dáctylŏs, moeniă, Lesbiă.

—the spondee, as in optŏ, aeque, Acme.

—the iamb, as in cănŏ, sŭis, mĕaĕ.

—the trochee, as in quaeris, essĕ, unŭs.

—the choriamb, as in prŏgeniĕs, essĕ dĕŏ, et puĕri.

As the last example shows, a foot does not necessarily begin or end with a single word. In fact, word divisions and foot divisions are more or less independent of each other, as in this line made up of six iambs:

Phaselus ille, quem videtis, hospites

When a meter does call for word ending at the end of a foot, that pause in the line is a *diaeresis*. There is a strongly felt diaeresis in the middle of the elegiac pentameter:

cogit amare magis, ‖ sed bene velle minus

In scansion, feet may be marked by single vertical lines; a regular pause (diaeresis or caesura) is indicated by double lines (‖).

The rhythm of poetic language is also independent of its regular prose accent. *Cano*, for example, is accented on the penult, but its natural rhythm is iambic. Syllables have *quantity* or length as well as accent. Because a long syllable takes more time to pronounce than a short one, every word has a built-in *quantitative* rhythm as well as a stress accent. Quantity is the basis of meter in Latin poetry. In poetry, the regular stress accent of words is subordinated to the metrical rhythm set up by the patterns of long and short syllables.

Latin poetry is thus different from English because our poetic rhythms are felt in the beat of word-accent. Hence in the meter of Longfellow's *Evangeline*

This is the fórest primévꞏal, the múrmuring píne and the hémlock

the natural accent of the words falls into a rhythmic beat of six dactyls that we recognize as a dactylic hexameter. A corresponding line of Homeric, Catullan, or Virgilian hexameter carries its rhythms more musically, in a sequence of long and short syllables that strike the ear like half notes and quarter notes:

Vesper adest, iuvenes, consurgite: Vesper Olympo

To sense the difference between long "half-note" syllables (marked $-$) and short "quarter-note" syllables (marked $\smile$), it is necessary to keep in mind two basic rules of quantity.

I. A syllable is long if it contains a vowel that is long by *nature*, like the ablative singular ending in the first declension *puellā*, or the dative and ablative plurals of the first and second declensions (e.g., *puerīs*). The lexicon in this book indicates naturally long vowels with a macron (e.g., *prōgeniēs*). Such vowels are long because they take longer to pronounce. Diphthongs, because they contain two vowels, also take longer to pronounce and are therefore long by nature: *aequor, coepi, aurum, deinde* (*ei* as in *deign*), and *Eumenides* all begin with a long syllable containing a diphthong.

II. A syllable is long if it contains a vowel that is long by *position*, that is, if it is followed by two consonants. These consonants have the effect of slowing down pronunciation of the syllable, whether or not they are technically part of that syllable. For example, in the phrase *lepidum novum libellum*, the otherwise short last syllable of *lepidum* becomes long because it is followed by the consonant beginning *novum*. It takes longer to pronounce *um-n* than to say *um*. By the same token, the end of *novum* becomes long by position because of the duration of the *um-l* sound. Finally, the *e* of *libellum* is phonetically short, but the foot is metrically long because it precedes two *l*'s that are pronounced individually: *libel-lum*. Exceptions: $x = cs$ and counts as a double consonant: a preceding vowel therefore "makes position." The combination of a mute (*b, c, d, f, g, p*, and *t*) with a following liquid (*l, m, n*, and *r*) makes a blended consonant before which a vowel may or may not "make position." This is the "*muta cum liquida*" rule.

Reading Latin meter, like riding a bicycle, is more complicated to explain than to do. The commonest Catullan meters, such as the hendecasyllabic verse and the elegiac couplet, can be read instinctively after a little practice because the rhythm will come naturally.

Dactylic hexameter, the traditional meter of epic since Homer, is used in poems 62 and 64. It also forms the first line of every elegiac couplet. Rapid and flexible, it avoids monotony by permitting the substitution of a spondee for a dactyl in any of the first four feet. "Spondaic lines" (with a spondee in the fifth foot) are exceptional, though they appear more often in Catullus than in Virgil or Ovid, some 30 times in poem 64 alone. The final syllable, marked with the ×, is *syllaba anceps*, either long or short. The metrical schema is written as follows:

$$- \overset{\smile\smile}{} \quad - \overset{\smile\smile}{} \quad - \parallel \overset{\smile\smile}{} \quad - \overset{\smile\smile}{} \quad - \smile\smile \quad - \times$$

Allowable substitutions or resolutions are indicated by superscripted long or short marks in the schema. The fifth foot of the hexameter is regularly a dactyl; the exceptional line, where a spondee is substituted in the fifth foot, is called a *spondaic line*, even if there are no other spondees in the line. Catullus admits more spondaic lines than Virgil in his hexameters. This meter usually has a *caesura* near the middle, so called because it cuts the third foot in two. When a word ends immediately after the first syllable of the third foot, it makes a *masculine caesura*, also called the *principal caesura* because most hexameter lines pause at this point:

$$- \;\; - - \smile \smile \; -, \parallel \; - \; - - \; - \smile \smile \; - \times$$
cum lectī iuvenēs, ‖ Argivae robora pubis,

Sometimes, as in this and the next example, the caesura is reinforced by a break in the phrasing, marked by a comma. When the pause comes between the short syllables of a dactylic third foot, it is a *feminine caesura*:

$$- \;\; - - \smile\smile \; - \smile, \parallel \; \smile \; - - - \; \smile \; \smile \; - \times$$
sed conubia laeta, ‖ sed optatos hymenaeos

More often than not, the caesura in dactylic hexameter is neither strongly felt nor marked by a pause in phrasing; in this respect it is quite different from the diaeresis in the pentameter of elegiac verse.

Hexameter tends to observe line end with a break in the phrasing. When that break is strong enough to be punctuated by a semicolon, colon, period, or question mark, the line is *end stopped*. At the other extreme, when the absence of a break is conspicuous, the resulting run-on is called *enjambment*:

$$\text{Certe ego te in medio versantem turbine leti}$$
$$\text{eripui, et potius germanum amittere crevi,}$$

Here Catullus has held back the verb *eripui*, forcing us to hurry on to the next line to complete the sense. This gives dramatic force to the verb in a speech filled with emotion (the words are Ariadne's, seduced and abandoned by Theseus on a desert island). The passionate rush of the first line in this pair is enhanced by *elision*, which makes the words stream together: *cert-ego tein medio*. In Latin verse, a word ending in a vowel elides with the next word if it begins with a vowel. In scansion, elision is marked by a connecting symbol beneath the line: *certe ego, te in*. A final *m* in Latin is so weak that it is ignored as a phonetic element and elided: note the elision of *germanum* above and the resultant pronunciation: *german-amittere*. Likewise, an initial *h* is weak enough to be elided:

$$\text{Atqui non solum hoc dicit se cognitum habere}$$

In the above line both final *m*'s and initial *h*'s are lost in elision: *soloc dicit se cognitabere*. These rules of elision apply in all Latin meters. Actual practice in pronouncing elided words varies. Some readers prefer to pronounce all elided sounds, reducing one of the two to a kind of grace note: *te in* would thus become *tein*. Elisions in Dante and Italian opera are usually treated in this way. The other method is to omit the first of the elided syllables, for example reading *solum hoc* above as *soloc*. There is no hard and fast rule.

Elegiac couplets, named after the meter used in Archaic Greek elegy and Hellenistic epigram, are Catullus' favorite meter, used in poems 65–116. In this meter, the rapid **dactylic hexameter** (see above) alternates with a rather slower pentameter, so called because of its two and a half dactyls on either side of a strongly felt diaeresis. Diaeresis is cancelled by elision only eighteen times in a total of 323 pentameters, almost always for pictorial or emotional effect. No substitution is permitted in the last half of the pentameter, imposing a predictability and restraint on the line as well as a sense of closure on the couplet as a whole. The alternation of lines and the divided pentameter give poems in this meter an ebb and flow that is adaptable to many moods.

$$- \overset{\smile}{\smile} \ - \overset{\smile}{\smile} \ - \ \| \ \overset{\smile}{\smile} \ - \overset{\smile}{\smile} \ - \smile \smile \ - \times$$
$$- \overset{\smile}{\smile} \ - \overset{\smile}{\smile} \ - \ \| - \smile \smile \ - \smile \smile \ \times$$

Galliambic, a one-purpose meter invented for poems about Cybele and her *Galli* or castrated priests, is better suited to the more frequent short syllables of Greek. Catullus uses it only in poem 63, where its usual pattern is

$$\smile \smile \ - \smile \ - \smile \ - \ - \ \| \ \smile \smile \ - \ \smile \smile \smile \smile \ \times$$

Pairs of short syllables are fairly interchangeable with long syllables; resolutions of long syllables make line

63 the longest line in the poem:

$$\overset{\smile\;\smile}{E}\text{go } m\overset{\smile\smile}{u}l\overset{\smile}{i}er, \text{ ego } \overset{\smile\smile}{a}d\overset{\smile}{u}l\overset{\smile\smile}{e}sc\overset{--}{e}ns, \parallel \text{ ego } \overset{\smile}{e}ph\overset{--\smile}{e}bus, \text{ ego } p\overset{\smile\smile}{u}\overset{\smile\;\times}{e}r;$$

At the other extreme, substitutions make line 73 the shortest and heaviest:

$$\overset{-}{I}am \overset{-}{i}am \overset{\smile}{d}\overset{-}{o}let qu\overset{\smile}{o}d \overset{--}{e}gi, \parallel \overset{-}{i}am \overset{-}{i}am\overset{\smile}{q}ue p\overset{\smile\;\times}{a}enitet.$$

The caesura is always clear, and the line is heavily end-stopped.

Glyconic and Pherecratean stanzas in poems 34 and 61 combine three or four glyconic lines

with a pherecratean:

The system is as old as the Greek lyric poet Anacreon (sixth century B.C.). Each stanza observes *synaphaea*, a fastening together of lines into a single metrical unit. Hiatus between lines is avoided, and each glyconic ends with a syllable that is long by nature or position (the next line beginning with a consonant).

Greater Asclepiadean goes as far back as Sappho and Alcaeus but is named after the third century B.C. Greek epigrammatist Asclepiades of Samos. It is a sixteen-syllable line built around three choriambs, with a tendency to pause between each. There are no substitutions or resolutions. Catullus uses this meter only in poem 30.

Hendecasyllabic, also called Phalaecian after the fourth-century B.C. Greek poet Phalaecus, is a lyric meter like the glyconic and the sapphic. Its name derives from its eleven syllables. All but seventeen of the first sixty poems in our collection are in this meter. Its insistent iambic second half gives it a colloquial, vernacular quality that evokes the comic stage and the rhythms of street language.

$$\overset{\smile}{\underset{=}{}}\overset{-}{\underset{\smile}{}} - \smile\smile - \smile - \smile - \times$$

Iambic senarius, a pure iambic trimeter composed of six iambs, appears only in Catullus 4 and 29.

$$\smile - \smile - \smile - \smile - \smile - \smile \times$$

Iambic tetrameter catalectic is four (*tetra-*) pairs of iambs with the final syllable lopped off (hence catalectic, "stopping" or "leaving off" before the end). There is a caesura in the middle, after the second iambic pair. Appears only in poem 25.

Iambic trimeter, used in poem 52, is the meter of Archilochus and other writers of Greek iambic poetry. Its three pairs of iambs are broken by a caesura in the middle of the third foot. A spondee may be substituted for an iamb in the first and third feet.

Limping iambics, also called **choliambics** and **scazons**, have five iambs (˘ —) and a trochee (— ˘) or spondee (— —). Spondees may be substituted in the first and third feet. Invented by the Greek poet Hipponax (sixth cent. B.C.), it is associated with satirical themes. Catullus uses this meter seven times, once in self-mockery (8), typically in mocking others (22, 39, 44, 59, 60), once in an expression of joy (31). Because Latin words are always accented on a long penult, the prose accent corresponds with the metrical emphasis in the last word of each line, giving the meter a conversational quality.

Priapean is named after the phallic god Priapus because hymns to him were written in this meter in Hellenistic times. It combines in a single line the glyconic and pherecratean measures used in poems 34 and 61, with a caesura in between. It is used in poem 17 only.

$$\_ \ \smile\!\!\!- \ \_ \ \smile\smile \ \_ \ \smile \ \_ \ \| \ \_ \ \smile\!\!\!- \ \_ \ \smile\smile \ \_ \times$$

Sapphic strophe, named after Sappho of Lesbos (seventh-sixth cent. B.C.), is used in poems 11 and 51, perhaps his last and first poems to Lesbia respectively. A lyric meter, it consists of three identical lines followed by an adonic, which gives the stanza a sense of closure because it is the normal rhythm at the end of a hexameter. The caesura marked in this schema is observed in about two-thirds of Catullus' Sapphics.

$$\_ \ \smile \ \_ \ \overset{\smile}{\_} \ \_ \ \| \ \smile\smile \ \_ \ \smile \ \_ \ \overset{\smile}{\_} \quad \text{(3 times)}$$

$$\_ \ \smile\smile \ \_ \times$$

175

Appendix C

GLOSSARY OF TERMS

The following terms are essential vocabulary for the description of Catullus's poetic craft and its tradition. For a fuller account, see *The New Princeton Encyclopedia of Poetry and Poetics* (Princeton, 1993) and *The Concise Oxford Dictionary of Literary Terms* (Oxford, 1990).

amoebean (Greek *amoebaios*, "giving like for like") describes poems where one person or group exchanges remarks with another, as in poem 62, where a chorus of girls sing lines that are answered point for point by a chorus of boys. Amoebean technique is also employed in the love duet between Septimius and Acme in poem 45.

anaphora is the rhetorical repetition of a word or phrase for greater emphasis. It tends to heighten the emotional intensity and the rhetorical level. Catullan style is distinctive for its repetitions, some of which are classic oratorical anaphora; but more commonly they are not typical of "high" rhetorical anaphora, as in these lines from poem 5 where *mille*, *dein(de)*, and *centum* are repeated:

Da mi basia **mille, deinde centum**;
dein mille altera, **dein** secunda **centum**;
diende usque altera **mille, deinde centum**.

antithesis is a striking contrast of ideas brought face to face, as in the famous beginning of poem 85, *Odi et amo*. One type is **oxymoron**; a less compressed variety is the description of the flower in 62.42–44 before and after it has been plucked:

multi illam pueri, multae optavere puellae:
idem cum tenui carptus defloruit ungui,
nulli illum pueri, nullae optavere puellae.

apodosis: the main clause of an "if ... then" conditional sentence, stating what should (or will) follow if the condition stated in the **protasis** is met. In poem 45, Septimius tells Acme "If I don't love you madly, then may I run afoul of a lion." In formulas of prayer, the supplicant says "If I have been your faithful worshipper [protasis], then grant my prayer [apodosis]. See note on 76.17–22.

apo koinou (ἀπὸ κοινοῦ): two constructions depending "on a common [word]" in a compressed phrase where a single word has a double syntactic function. See for example 33.5, where *in* must be understood with *exilium* as well as *malas oras*.

apostrophe: a "turning away" from one audience to another that is dead, absent, or inanimate, to raise the emotional tone, sometimes, as in this example from poem 3, for mock-tragic effect:

O factum male! O miselle passer!

archaism: the use of an old-fashioned word or expression ("Our Father who *art* in heaven") to give a traditional feeling. Though some archaisms linger in colloquial speech (like Septimius' *pote* in 45.5), Catullus tends to avoid archaic language in his polymetrics. The longer poems and the elegiacs, where Catullus uses a higher, more traditionally literary diction, admit more archaisms: in poem 61, a marriage hymn, see notes on 53 *soluunt*, 54 *novos*, 193 *ne*, 195 *iuverit*.

asyndeton: the omission of conjunctions for rhetorical effect, as in Caesar's laconic report of his victory over Pharnaces: *veni, vidi, vici*. See poem 32.10 *satur supinus*, 45.20 *amant amantur*, 64.405 *fanda nefanda*. Sometimes it introduces a contrast, taking the place of an adversative adverb such as *tamen*, as in 62.15. Its speed and economy can achieve effects of striking beauty, as in the description in 62.41 of the virgin flower

quem mulcent aurae, firmat sol, educat imber.

Its opposite is **polysyndeton** (see below).

caesura is the regular pause or "cutting" of a metrical foot, particularly near the midpoint of a poetic line, by the end of a word. It is marked ‖ and functions in the same way as the **diaeresis**, inserting a pause in the line. It is felt more strongly when reinforced by word grouping, punctuation, and the

177

like.

catalogue: any poetic list. This is a common **topos**, the most famous of which is the Catalogue of Ships near the beginning of Homer's Iliad. Especially common in the grand style, it may be a short list of place names (64.35–6) or a longer list of activities such as farming tasks (64.38–42).

chiasmus, named after the Greek letter *chi* (X), is the concentric ordering of words or other elements in a poem: A, B, B, A. In 50.11, *toto indomitus furore lecto*, the first and last words *toto* and *lecto* belong together, and *furore* depends upon *indomitus*. Chiastic arrangements typically distinguish poetic word order from regular prose word order. See also **hyperbaton**.

conceit: an elaborate or far-fetched idea, sometimes dreamed up for humor, as when in poem 42 Catullus invokes hendecasyllables as if they were a gang of street people. From Italian *concetto*, "conception."

deictic (<Gk. δείκνυμι, "point out"): having the purpose of pointing out or showing. "This" and "that" are deictic words, as is *illoc* in 50.3 (but not the *illius* in 3.8).

diaeresis is a slight pause in mid-line, a regular "drawing-apart" where the end of a word matches the end of a metrical foot. In the elegiac couplet, there is a strongly felt diaeresis in the exact center of the pentameter. It functions the same way as a *caesura*, and is similarly marked (‖).

diminutive: any word, usually a noun or adjective, modified by the addition of a -lus suffix. Especially frequent in common speech and hence in the language of Catullus, where it usually expresses affection and heightens the sense of informal intimacy, e.g., in 12.17 *Veraniolum* (for *Veranium*). It may also be used in contempt (as in 57.7 *erudituli*) or to elicit pity (as in 64.131 *frigidulos singultus*).

double dative: a combination of a dative of personal reference with a dative of purpose or result, as in the idiom *mihi sunt cordi*, they are for a delight to me, i.e., dear to my heart (95.9). See notes on 41.5, 44.2–3, 66.15, 95.9, 96.5–6.

ecphrasis (<Gk. "digression"): Broadly defined as a vividly descriptive passage in a larger story, ecphrasis typically describes a picture on some artifact (e.g., the engravings on Achilles' shield in *Iliad* 18). This originally epic device may have a symbolic meaning relevant to the larger story that frames it. The ecphrasis in poem 64 is an embroidery on the quilt covering the marriage bed of Peleus and Thetis (a happy union), representing the abandonment of Ariadne by Theseus (an unhappy union).

ellipsis: omission of a word that can be understood from context. Colloquial usage is full of elliptical phrases, as is Catullus. See note on 45.5 *quantum qui pote plurimum perire*.

enjambment (<Fr. *enjamber*, skip over, run on) is the running on of phrasing from one line of verse to the next, particularly where the words separated by line ending are closely connected. The opposite of end stopping, it puts emphasis on the word at the beginning of the next line, which may be a surprise. See for example the dinner invitation in 13.3–4, where Fabullus will dine well

si tecum attuleris bonam atque magnam
cenam, ...

As a rule, only a single word is enjambed, usually a noun, verb, or adjective that the poet wishes to stress. It is followed by a pause in phrasing which editors usually mark with a comma or stronger punctuation.

epanalepsis (<Gk. "resumption, repetition"): a form of dramatic emphasis in which a word is repeated after an intervening word and a line break. Catullus uses it three times to stress the pathos of Ariadne in poem 64: see note on 61–62 *prospicit, eheu, ‖ prospicit*, and cf. 132–33, 186–87. Other examples: 259–60, 321–22, 403–04. In other dactylic verse of Catullus it occurs only at 62.63–64, 66.75–76. Perhaps a characteristic of neoteric epyllion, it appears only occasionally in Virgil (see Thomas on *Geo.* 4.339–40).

epic simile: an extended comparison, also called a Homeric simile, typically comparing an event in combat to something in nature or some contrasting domestic action. It is slightly digressive because of its length, and it often contains a subordinate or

178

parenthetical clause with a change of subject. See 64.105–111, where Theseus' killing of the Minotaur is compared to a whirlwind's uprooting of a mountain tree.

epigram: originally meaning "inscription," an epigram came to mean any short poem. In the hellenistic era, such poems were usually written in elegiac couplets. After Catullus, the great master of Latin epigram was Martial (ca. 50–104 AD), whose short poems combined wit, extreme condensation, and satiric bite. Today the word is used of any concise, clever statement in prose or verse.

epyllion: a short epic in the Hellenistic style (see introductory note on poem 64). The word did not have this technical sense until modern times, but the genre was well established by poems such as Callimachus' *Hecale* (ca. 250 B.C.), which elaborates a minor episode in the life of Theseus.

gnomic perfect: a generalizing use of the perfect tense, developed from the Greek gnomic aorist. The assumption is that what has been true in the past is always so: "Faint heart ne'er won fair lady." As in this example, it is usually used in negative statements. It can usually be translated as a present or present perfect. See notes on 62.44, 64.148.

golden line: a dactylic hexameter line "of two substantives and two adjectives with a verb betwixt to keep the peace" (Dryden, preface to *Sylvae*). The term usually applies to the five-word line arranged adjective a, adjective b, verb, noun A, noun B. See note on 64.59 and L. P. Wilkinson, *Golden Latin Artistry* pp. 215f.

hapax legomenon, Gk. "once said," is a word attested only once in the extant literature. Such rarities are usually a coinage by the poet or a usage rare even in his own time and are used for special effect.

Hellenistic: as distinguished from Helladic (prehistoric) and Hellenic (generically Greek of any period), Hellenistic refers to the period of Mediterranean civilization beginning with the death of Alexander the Great in 323 B.C. and running down to the end of Rome's republican period (ca. 31 B.C.). Though not a time of literary greatness for the Greeks, it witnessed the development of hu-

manistic philosophy and significant advances in science and mathematics. Its achievements in the arts, architecture, and city planning were considerable. Even in literature there were important developments in comedy, epigram, the literary epistle, biography, history, and other forms. For Catullus and the Roman poets of the first century B.C., Hellenistic emphasis on literary economy and discipline had a salubrious effect. Although the *novi poetae* of Catullus' circle insisted on a native idiom that went beyond mere imitation of Greek models, Hellenistic poets like Callimachus set a standard of workmanship without which the achievements of Roman poetry would have been poorer.

hendiadys, Gk. "one through two," expresses a single thought through two independent words joined by a copulative conjunction, as in "nice and warm." In 14.8, "newly discovered" is *novum ac repertum*.

hetaera or **hetaira**, Gk. "companion," a highly cultivated courtesan of a type originally trained in Asia Minor but made famous in Greece. Roughly comparable to Japanese Geishas, these independent demimondaines had become a prominent part of Roman society a century before the time of Catullus. Ipsitilla in poem 33 and Acme in 45 probably belong to this class, as does the unnamed mistress of Varus in 10.

hiatus is a metrical "yawning" between words that would normally be elided but are not. In the middle of 3.16 the enforced pause has a mock-tragic effect:

o factum male! ¦ o miselle passer!

hyperbaton (Gk. "stepping over"): the tactical separation of words that naturally go together, as often in Catullus 13, e.g., line 14:

totum ut te faciant, Fabulle, *nasum*.

Hyperbaton is also an essential feature that distinguishes the elevated language of poetry from the mundane style of prose. It is therefore especially common in the more formal modes of poetry, such as the epic diction of poem 64 and the lyric style of poem 61. It is the technique of verbal leapfrogging that makes possible the artful ordering of words in

chiasmus, the **golden line**, and interlocked word order.

hypermetry is the hyphenation or elision of a syllable at the end of a line with the syllable at the beginning of the next. In Catullus, 11.19 and 22, 34.11 and 22, 64.298, and 115.5 are hypermetric. So is the hyphenation of *ultimosque* in 11.11. See **synapheia** below.

iambic shortening is the colloquial shortening of an iambic disyllable such as the imperative *căvē* to two short syllables, a pyrrhic: *căvĕ* (in 50. 18 and 19). Cf. *pŭtă* (102.4), *mănĕ* (10.27), *vŏlŏ* (17. 18 and 23, 35.5), *dăbŏ* (13.11), *hŏmŏ* (24.7, 115.8).

iambics are poems or verses of abuse, so called because they were traditionally written in the iambic meter. The tradition goes back to the seventh-century Greek poet Archilochus, whose verses were so devastating that one of his victims is said to have hanged himself. Catullus used his hendecasyllables for "iambics," as well as the limping iambic or choliambic (poems 8, 22, 39, 44, 59, 60), iambic tetrameter catalectic (poem 25), and the iambic senarius in poem 29 (see appendix B).

litotes (<Gk. λιτότης, "plainness"): understatement, usually by way of a double negative. The effect is normally to intensify or affirm: having a glossary of literary terms is "not a bad idea." See Catullus' appraisal of Varus' mistress in 10.4, *non sane illepidum neque invenustum*. 13.4 *non sine candida puella* is also litotic. See also **meiosis**, of which litotes is a form. It should not be confused with pleonastic expressions such as *nec numquam* (48.4) or *nec foedere nullo* (76.3), where the negatives reinforce each other.

lyric: the type of poetry associated originally with song and the lyre, it is linked to the poetry of praise at special public occasions such as weddings (e.g., poem 61) and victories. This is choral lyric. Another type is monody, personal poetry such as the love poems of Sappho that Catullus admired and sometimes emulated (e.g., poem 51). Lyric poetry is distinct in its meters and uses from epic poetry (narrative of legendary exploits) dramatic poetry (verse for stage dialogue), elegiac poetry (associated with Hellenistic epigram), and iambic poetry (mockery, comedy, humor). These poetic

genres are not always distinct even as practiced by the Greeks, but they exerted a powerful influence on Catullus at a time when Roman literature had few developed traditions of its own.

meiosis: the opposite of hyperbole, meiosis is rhetorical understatement calculated to make a thing seem greater than it is by making light of it. When Catullus calls his poems *meas ... nugas* in 1.4 he is being disingenuous. In 45.24, *facit delicias libidinesque* is a meiotic description of Acme's satisfaction with Septimius. Coyness ("little me") is a social form of meiosis.

metonymy: any change of name by which one thing is substituted for something associated with it: "The White House has denied knowledge of the scandal," or "I am reading Catullus," where the White House stands for someone in the White House and Catullus stands for his poetry. In poem 64.11 Amphitrite stands for the sea over which she rules.

obelus: a dagger-shaped editorial symbol (†) marking a corruption in the transmitted text where the manuscripts have given us nonsense and no convincing repair has been suggested. See note on 55.9, †*avelte*†, which has been obelized.

oxymoron: paradox arrestingly expressed by the juxtaposition of opposite words: "loveless love." Phrases like "military intelligence" are sometimes jokingly characterized as oxymoron. See note on 5.3.

paraprosdokia (<Gk. παρά προσδοκίαν) is impressive-sounding jargon for a "surprise" where we expect a different word than we get. Often it is used with **enjambment**, where the first word of the new line is the surprise. In poem 28, Catullus asks his friends if their accounts show a little profit / "paid out" instead of gained:

> Ecquidnam in tabulis patet lucelli
> *expensum, ...*

The effect of such surprises is usually humorous. See note on 67.3.

parataxis is the simple juxtaposition of words without logical conjunctions. **Asyndeton** (veni vidi vici) is a type of parataxis, rhetorically effective because its logic is implicit. The strung-together style of paratactic composition is typical of oral poetry such as that of Homer. Its opposite is hypotaxis, where each part of a sentence is related to the whole by a conjunction that states its logical relation or subordination to the main idea. "I overslept. I missed my flight." is paratactic. "I overslept; therefore I missed my flight" is hypotactic.

periphrasis is the longer, indirect rather than the shorter, direct way of saying something. In English prose, it is usually bad practice (e.g., "effect a finalization" for "finish"). In the high diction of Latin poetry, such flourishes as *pecoris hostem* (63.77) for *leonem* were considered elegant. Athena is called *sancti incola Itoni* in 64.227 in a typically Hellenistic display of obscure learning. We are expected to know of her temple at Itonus in Boeotia and to get pleasure from recognizing "the inhabitant of sacred Itonus" as Athena.

persona: the "mask" that an orator, politician, or poet assumes in order to project a suitable image of himself. Part of the poet's usual persona is poverty, as we see in 10.22 where Catullus claims to have no more than a cot with a broken foot to sleep on and in 13.8 where he describes his purse as full of cobwebs.

personification: in Greek, the tendency to treat any thing as if it were in some way a person is so strong that inanimate objects and abstractions readily take on human features. This habit found its way into Latin poetry, as when the marriage torches of 61.78 "shake their shining locks" and when Ariadne grieves that a personified fortune "has denied her ear to my complaints" (64.170).

pleonasm is redundancy for emphasis. Usually considered awkward in written prose, it reflects usages of common speech and is thus used by poetic license. Pleonastic negatives reinforce each other: *nec foedere nullo* in 76.3 means "nor in any contract." Cf. 48.4 *nec numquam* "not ever" and contrast the effect of double negatives in **litotes**, where the negatives cancel each other out.

polysyndeton is the multiplication of connectives such as *-que* or *et* for rhetorical effect. In 76.11, *offirmas atque istinc teque reducis / et ... desinis* puts added emphasis on the three verbs, which are

things Catullus must do for himself. Its opposite is **asyndeton** (see above).

proleptic words anticipate something that will happen later in a story. So in 64.119 *miseram* anticipates the future misery of Ariadne, whom we see in her mother's embrace.

protasis: the part of a conditional sentence that states the conditions under which a logical result (the **apodosis**) will follow. In poem 76, Catullus states that if a virtuous person is rewarded with pleasure, he can anticipate pleasure in the aftermath of his unhappy love (because he behaved virtuously). In conditional sentences, the protasis is a dependent clause and the apodosis is the main clause.

resolution in meter is the use of two short syllables where the meter regularly calls for a long. See notes on 22.19, 37.5, and 59.3, and the description of the Galliambic meter in appendix B.

strophe: so called because of its association with a dance movement (Gk. στροφή = "turn"), it represents a stanza of **lyric** poetry. In Latin lyric, a strophe is a set of two or three repeated lines and a closing shorter line. Examples: poems 34 and 61 (Glyconic + Pherecratean), 11 and 51 (Sapphic).

substitution in meter replaces two short syllables with a long. In dactylic hexameter, it turns a dactyl into a spondee. Its reverse is **resolution**.

synapheia: Gk. "fastening together" of the lines that make up a **strophe**.
Some Greek lyric meters treat a strophe as a set of continuous lines combined into a single unit or *period*, for example the glyconic-pherecratean stanza of poems 34 and 61 (see appendix B). The resulting metrical continuity from one line to the next minimizes the pause between lines within a stanza, resulting in elision from one line to another (see **hypermetry**), as in 34.11 and 22. Further examples of such elision occur in 61.115, 135, 140, 184, and 227. Hyphenation (61.46 and 82) is another feature of synapheia.

syncope: the abbreviation of a word, usually a verb, for the sake of metrical economy. See the syncopated forms *dona(ve)runt* (13.12), *puta(vi)stis* (16.3), *ve(he)mens* (50.21). Syncopation, which always occurs within a word, should not be confused with the elision of a final syllable before an initial vowel.

synizesis is the "collapsing" of two vowels into one for metrical purposes. It is like elision, but within a single word. In 64.336, for example, the last two vowels of *Peleo* are squeezed into a diphthong, reducing the name to a two-syllable word, *Pel-yo*.

topos: lit. a "place," a traditional poetic theme or type of passage such as a catalogue, a battle scene, or an epic simile. Because it is a kind of set piece, it is generically familiar to a knowing audience.

zeugma is the "yoking" of dissimilar words in a single construction, e.g., 12.2 *in ioco atque vino* (cf. 50.6). It usually links a literal with a metaphorical meaning: "She removed her inhibitions along with her hat."

Appendix D

POETIC USAGE

The forms and usages learned in basic Latin courses reflect a standardization imposed on Latin prose during and soon after the Augustan age. In order to feel comfortable with the Latin Catullus wrote, it will help to know some of the common variants in use a generation before other standards were adopted. Many of these usages continued in later poetry because of the flexibility and euphony they provided.

-ere is often used instead of **-erunt** for the 3rd person plural perfect indicative active; *fuēre* = *fuērunt* in 4.25 and 49.2; cf. *fulsēre* in 8.3 and 8, *incidēre* (10.5), *exsiluēre* (62.8 and 9), *pepigēre* (62.28), *iunxēre* (62.29), *optavēre* (62.42 and 44), *coluēre* (62.53 and 55), *tetigēre* (63.35), *emersēre* (64.14), *advenēre* (64.32), *metuēre* (64.148), *liquēre* (64.240), *perfudēre* (64.399), *avertēre* (64.406), *peperēre* (66.45).

-īs = -ēs (accusative plural of third declension adjectives and i- stem nouns): *acrīs* (2.4) *tristīs* (2.10), *natīs* (33.7), *omnīs* (51.5 and 86.6), *pinguīs* (62.3), *lactentīs* (64.65), *suavīs* (64.87), *iugalīs* (64.302), *euantīs* (64.391), *dulcīs* (65.3), *finīs* (66.12), *caelestīs* (68.76), *penetralīs* (68.102), *omnīs* (86.6), *dentīs* and *sesquipedalīs* (97.5), *piscīs* (114.3). Scansion often makes it easy to distinguish these forms from the nominative and genitive in *-is*.

mi = mihi, the dative singular. See 5.7, 10.21, 14.10, 27.2, 30.8, 31.5, 37.11, 44.20, 51.1, and 7, 67.43, 72.6, 77.3, 76.26, 83.1, 92.1, 99.13, 107.4. This is not to be confused with the vocative *mi*, 10.25, 13.1, 28.3.

nil = nihil: see 6.12, 17.21, 30.2, 42.21, 61.61, 64.146, 68.77, 93.1; cf. 97.3, *nilo* for *nihilo*.

quīs = quibus: see 63.46, 64.80, 64.145, 66.37, 68.13.

sese = se: see 3.8, 63.85, 64.55, 244, 258, and 385, 68.88, 110.8.

Syncopation (shortening) of a perfect or pluperfect active verb for meter or euphony, usually resulting in the deletion of a syllable containing *-ve-* or *-vi-*:

norat for *noverat* (3.6)	*adiurarit* for *adiuraverit* (66.41)
comparasti for *comparavisti* (10.15)	*legarat* for *legaverat* (66.57)
pararim for *paraverim* (10.32)	*siris* for *siveris* (66.91)
misti for *misisti* (14.14)	*servisse* for *servivisse* (67.3, 5)
cupisti for *cupivisti* (15.3)	*violasse* for *violavisse* (67.23, 76.3)
putastis for *putavistis* (16.3)	*conscelerasse* for *consceleravisse* (67.24)
nosti for *novisti* (22.1, 67.37)	*pacificasset* for *pacificavisset* (68.76)
involasti for *involavisti* (25.6)	*saturasset* for *saturavisset* (68.83)
irrumasti for *irrumavisti* (28.10)	*nosse* for *novisse* (72.1)
explicasset for *explicavisset* (53.3)	*audierat* for *audiverat* (74.1)
evirastis for *eviravistis* (63.17)	*violasse* for *violavisse* (76.3)
nasse for *navisse* (64.2)	*subrepsti* for *subrepsisti* (77.3)
iactastis for *iactavistis* (64.97)	*requierant* for *requieverant* (84.7)
praeoptarit for *praeoptaverit* (64.120)	*cognossem* for *cognovissem* (91.3)
religasset for *religavisset* (64.174)	*duxti* for *duxisti* (91.9)
fugarunt for *fugavērunt* (64.398)	*cessasti* for *cessavisti* (99.12)
luxti for *luxisti* (66.21)	*promisti* for *promisisti* (110.3)
cognoram for *cognoveram* (66.26)	*promisse* for *promisisse* (110.5)

Other contractions: *nequisse* (4.4), *desissem* (36.5), forms of *eo* such as *dessem* (for impf. subj. *deessem* in 64.151), fourth conjugation imperfects *custodibant* (64.319), *scibant* (68.85), *audibant* (84.8). See also *vemens* for *vehemens* in 50.21, *comprendis* for *comprehendis* in 62.35, *saeclum* for *saeculum* in 43.8.

Contractions with *est*: *malest* (38.1–2), *certest* (62.8), *patrist* (62.63), *figuraest* (63.62).

Syncopated genitive plural in *-um* instead of *-orum* or *-arum*:
caelicolum for *caelicolorum* (68.138)
cymbalum for *cymbalorum* (63.21)
deum for *deorum* (63.68, 64.23, 66.63)
divum for *divorum* (64.27, 134, 298, 387; 66.69, 76.4)
Troiugenum for *Troiugenarum* (64.355)
virum for *virorum* (64.192, 68.90)

Fore is sometimes used for the future infinitive of *sum*, and *forem, fores, foret* for the imperfect subjunctives *essem, esses, esset*, etc. See for example *afore* (66.75–6), *fore* (for *futurum esse* in 91.2 and 109.2), *forem* (for *essem* in 63.53), *fores* (for *esses* in 34.9), *foret* (for *esset* in 4.5, 63.46, 66.61, 67.27, 68.40, 68.116, 99.13), *forent* (for *essent* in 30.8).

Second person singular passives in *-re* instead of *-ris*: *irascēre* = *irascēris* in 54.6, *conarēre* = *conarēris* in 116.3.

Archaic passive infinitives: *citarier* (61.42), *compararier* (61.65, 70, 75), *nitier* (61.68), *componier* (68.141).

Nominative singular in *-os*: *Calvos* for *Calvus* (53.3), *novos* for *novus* (61.54), *tuos* for *tuus* (63.92); cf. *aequom* for *aequum* in 62.60.

Greek case-endings: these are normal with Greek proper nouns and loan words.

Vocatives: *Amastri* (4.13), *Peleu* (64.26), *Theseu* (64.69, 133).

Genitive singulars: *Cybelēs* (63.12, 68), *Cybebēs* (63.20, 35), *Phasidos* (64.3), *Aethiopis* (66.52), *Arsinoēs* and *Locridos* (66.54).

Dative singulars: *Callisto* (66.66), *Tethyï* (66.70), *Hydrochoï* (66.94).

Accusative singulars: (in *-a*) *Propontida* (4.9), *Ancona* (36.13), *Amathunta* (36.14), *aethera* (63.40), *Pelea* (64.21 and 301), *Thesea* (64.53, 239, 245), *Minoa* (64.85), *aëra* (66.53).
(in *-n*) *Acmen* (45.1 and 21), *Attin* (63.42 and 88), *Amphitriten* (64.11), *Athon* (66.46), Boöten (66.67).

Accusative plurals: (in *-as*) *Cycladas* (4.7), *Arabas* (11.5), *Thyiadas* (64.391)
(in *-ē*, neuter plural) *Tempē* (64.35 and 285).

THE CATULLAN VOCABULARY

NOTA BENE: *Any lexicon definition is an approximate equivalent, not an exact meaning. A translation which mechanically substitutes English "meanings" for Latin words is courting disaster. Avoid "translationese" by interpreting units of meaning rather than isolated words. The English words provided here are based on Catullan usage and the Oxford Latin Dictionary (abbr. OLD). Basic and root meanings precede secondary, derived, or metaphoric meanings.*

ABBREVIATIONS

abbr. = abbreviated	indecl. = indeclinable	pl. = plural
adj. = adjective	indef. = indefinite	postpos. = postpositive
adv. = adverb	infin. = infinitive	pple. = participle
cf. = *confer*, compare	intr. = intransitive	prep. = preposition
comp. = comparative	iterat. = iterative	pron. = pronoun
conj. = conjunction	metaph. = metaphoric	sg. = singular
dep. = deponent	mod. = modern	spec. = specifically
dim. = diminutive	OLD = Oxford Latin Dictionary	sts. = sometimes
encl. = enclitic	orig. = originally	subst. = substantive
Eng. = English	part. = particle *or* partitive	superl. = superlative
esp. = especially	pass. = passive	w/ = with
freq. = frequentative	perh. = perhaps	w/abl., w/dat., etc. = syntactically
Gk. = Greek	pers. = person	linked with nouns in ablative,
impers. = impersonal	pf. = perfect	dative, etc.
		< = derived from

ā: expletive of distress, pity, or entreaty.

ā, ab: prep. w/abl., from

abdūcō, -dūcere, -dūxī, -ductum: lead off, entice away

abeō, -īre, -īvī, -itum: go away or out; come off, turn out; escape criticism or other consequences

abhorreō, ēre, -uī: shrink back from; be inconsistent

abiciō, -icere, -iēcī, -iectum: throw away, cast off; dismiss, belittle, minimize

abiegnus, -a, -um: made of silver fir; poet., wooden

abitus, -ūs, m.: departure, exit

abiungō, -iungere, -iunxī, -iunctum: separate, detach

abluō, -luere, -luī, -lūtum: wash away, wash clean

abrumpō, -rumpere, -rūpī, -ruptum: break; break off, separate

abruptus, -a, -um: steep, sheer

abscondō, -ere, -ī, -itum: conceal

absorbeo, -sorbēre, -sorbuī, -sorptum: devour, engulf

abstergeō, -tergēre, -tersī, -tersum: wipe clean

abstineō, -ēre, -uī, -stentum: keep away

absum, -esse, āfuī, fut. infin. **āfore:** be absent

absūmō, -sumere, -sumpsī, -sumptum: use up, consume, exhaust; do away with, remove by death

abūtor, -ūtī, -ūsus: use up; squander, exploit, abuse

ac, atque: and; with comparisons, than

acceptus, -a, -um: welcome, acceptable, pleasing

accidō, -cidere, -cidī: reach, get through to, impinge upon; fall; befall; happen

accipiō, -cipere, -cēpī, -ceptum: receive, accept; hear

accubō, -āre: lie, recline

ācer, ācris, ācre, comp. **ācrior, -ius:** sharp, bitter, vehement, intense

acerbus, -a, -um, comp. adv. **acerbius:** bitter; cruel, harsh, painful

acervus, -ī, m.: heap, pile, mass

Achillēs, -is, m.: son of Peleus and Thetis, greatest of the Greek warriors in the Trojan War, tragic hero of Homer's Iliad

Achīvus, -ī, m.: an Achaean, a Greek man

aciēs, -ēī, f.: a sharp edge; the sight of one's eyes, vision

acinus, -ī, m.: grape

Acmē, -ēs, f.: (Gk. = flower, prime) woman's name in poem 46

acquiescō, -quiescere -quiēvī: rest, relax, subside

acūtus, -a, -um: sharp

ad: prep. w/acc., to, at

addō, addere, addidī, additum: add

adeō, -īre, -īvī, -itum: approach, go to, visit

adeō: adv., to a point (where); to such a degree, so

adhortor, -ārī: urge on

adimō, -imere, -ēmī, -emptum: remove, take

adipiscor, -ipiscī, -eptus: catch up with, attain, win

aditus, -ūs, m.: approach

adiūrō, -āre: affirm with an oath; swear by (w/acc.)

adiuvō, -iuvāre, -iūvī, -iūtum: help; make things easy

admīror, -mīrārī, -mīrātus: marvel or wonder at, admire

admoveō, -movēre, -mōvī, -mōtum: move near, stretch out toward

adolescens, -entis, m. or f.: youth

Adōneus, -ī, m.: archaic Lat. form of Adonis, handsome youth loved by Venus

adorior, -orīrī, -ortus: attack; begin

adserō, -serere, -sēvī, -situm: plant near

adservō, -āre: keep safe, guard

adsum, -esse, afuī: be present

adulter, -erī, m.: an illicit lover, adulterer

adultera, -ae, f.: an unchaste woman; a mistress

adulterium, -ī, n.: an adulterous act; adultery

adveniō, -īre, -vēnī, -ventum: arrive at, come to

adventō, -āre: (freq. of *advenio*) approach, draw near

adventus, -ūs, m.: approach, arrival

adversus, -a, -um: opposite, facing

advocō, -āre: call upon, summon

Aeētēus, -a, -um: of Aeëtes, king of Colchis and father of Medea

Aegeus, -eī, m.: king of Athens, father of Theseus

aegrōtus, -a, -um: diseased

Aegyptus, -ī, f.: Egypt

Aemilius, -a, -um: Roman *nomen gentile* in poem 97

aemulus, -ī, m.: rival

aequālis, -is, m. or f.: peer; companion of one's own age, contemporary

aequē: adv. to the same degree, as

aequinoctiālis, -e: adv., associated with the vernal or autumnal equinox

aequō, -āre: make level, even, or smooth

aequor, -oris, n.: a smooth expanse; hence water, the sea

aequoreus, -a, -um: of the sea, maritime

aequus, -a, -um: level, equal; fair, just

āēr, āeris, m., acc. āera: air

āērius or āëreus, -a, -um: of the air, airy

aes, aeris, n.: copper, bronze, or brass; coin, money

aestimātiō, -ōnis, f.: price, monetary value

aestimō, -āre: appraise, value, esteem

aestuō, -āre: blaze; swelter; burn with pain or desire; toss about, seethe, writhe

aestuōsus, -a, -um: hot, sweltering

aestus, -ūs, m.: heat, hot weather; swell (of the sea), flood; tumult

aetās, aetātis, f.: age, lifetime

aeternus, -a, -um: eternal, everlasting

aethēr, -eris, m.: the upper regions of space; upper air

aetherius, -a, -um: of the sky or heavens

Aethiops, -opis, m.: an Ethiopean

aevum, -ī, n: time; a very long period of time, an age

afferō, -ferre, attulī, allātum: bring along, come with

afficiō, -ficere, -fēcī, -fectum: produce an effect on; treat, visit

afflīgo, -flīgere, -flīxī, -flīctum: hit; afflict

afore: see *absum*

Africus, -a, -um: of Africa

Aganippē, -ēs, f.: a spring in Boeotia sacred to the Muses, and the nymph who lived there

ager, agrī, m.: a piece of land; territory

agger, -eris, m.: fill, rubble; a mound

agitō, -āre: freq. of *ago*, shake

agnoscō, -noscere, -nōvī, -nitum: recognize

agō, agere, ēgī, actum: drive, do, conduct, throw; draw (breath); be engaged in; colloq. imper. **age! agedum! agite!**, come!

agricola, -ae, m.: farmer

āiō (but 3rd sing. **āit** regularly in Catullus): say

āla, -ae, f.: wing; upper arm

alacer, -cris: moving nimbly, lively; eager

albicō, -āre: have a whitish tinge

albus, -a, -um, dim. **albulus**: white; transparent, clear, colorless

āleō, -ōnis, m.: a habitual gambler

āles, -itis: winged

āles, alitis, m. or f.: a large bird, bird of prey; an omen or augury, such as might be obtained from the observation of birds

Alfenus, -i, m.: *nomen gentile* of P. Alfenus Varus and others; see appendix A

alga, -ae, f.: seaweed

algidus, -a, -um: cold

alid: see *alius*

aliēnus, -a, -um: belonging to another person or people; foreign

aliō: adv., to another place; *alio ... alio*, in one direction ... in another

aliquis, aliquid: indef. pron., someone, something; indef. adj., some

aliunde: adv. from elsewhere

alius or alis, alia, aliud or alid: other, another

Allius, -i, m.: friend of Catullus addressed in poem 68

allocūtiō, -ōnis, f.: encouraging talk

alloquor, -loquī, -locūtus: speak to, address

allūdō, -lūdere, -lūsī, -lūsum: play with

alluō, -uere, -uī: flow past, wash, lap

alnus, -ī, f.: an alder tree

alō, -ere, aluī, altum: nurse, feed, foster; cherish

Alpēs, -ium, fem. pl.: the Alps, high mountains bordering Italy on the north

alter, -era, -erum: a second, one or the other (of two); alter ... alter: one ... the other

altus, -a, -um: high, deep; loud

amābilis, -e, comp. amābilior: lovable

amans, -ntis, m. or f.: sweetheart, lover

amāracus, -ī, m.: marjoram, an aromatic plant related to thyme and mint

amāritiēs, -ēī, f.: bitterness

Amarunsius, -a, -um: belonging to a place in Boeotia sacred to Artemis/Diana; Amarunsia virgo: Diana

amarus, -a, -um, comp. amarior: bitter; (of wine) dry, tart

Amastris, -idis, f.: the capital of Paphlagonia, on the southern shore of the Black Sea

Amathus, -untis, f., Gk. acc. Amathunta: a town in Cyprus

Amathusia, -ae, f.: Venus, so-called because of her worship at Amathus

ambō, -ae, -ō, dat./abl. ambobus, -abus: pl. adj. & pron., both

ambrosia, -ae, f.: the food of the gods, ambrosia

ambulātiō, -ōnis, f.: the act of walking; a place for walking, covered walk, portico

Ameana, -ae, f.: prostitute associated with Mamurra in poem 41; see appendix A

āmens, -ntis: demented, mad, insane

amīca, -ae, f.: any female friend; girlfriend, mistress; (euphemistic) courtesan, prostitute

amiciō, -cīre, -cuī, -ctum: cover, cloak

amīcitia, -ae, f.: friendship

amictus, -ūs, m.: a mantle or cloak

amīcus, -ī, m. dim. amiculus: friend

āmittō, -ere, āmīsī, āmissum: dismiss, give up, forfeit; lose

amnis, -is, m. & f.: river

amō, -āre: love

amor, -ōris, m.: love; personified, the god of love; amores: loves; affection; the object of one's *amor*, a boyfriend or girlfriend

Amphitrītē, -ēs, f.: wife of Neptune; by meton., the sea

Amphitryōniadēs, -ae, m.: Hercules, male descendant of Amphitryon

amplector, -plectī, -plexus: embrace

amplificē: magnificently, splendidly

amplius: adv., more, further; longer

an: particle introducing questions with note of surprise or indignation: can it be that ...?; (after *utrum*) or

anceps, -cipitis: double-edged

ancilla, -ae, f.: slave girl, female slave

Ancōn, -ōnis, f., Gk. acc. Ancona: a town on the Adriatic coast in Picenum

Androgeōnēus, -a, -um: of Androgeos, son of Minos and Pasiphaë

angiportum, -ī, n.: alley, lane

anguīnus, -a, -um: snaky, made of snakes

angustō, -āre: to make narrow, confine

angustus, -a, -um: narrow

anhēlō, -āre: breathe hard, gasp, pant

anīlitās, -ātis, f.: old womanhood

anima, -ae, f.: breath

animus, -ī, m.: the mind; ex animo, from the heart

annālis, -is, m.: a book of annals or chronicles; (pl.) a chronicle in several books

anne (*an* + *ne*): = *an*; introducing questions with note of surprise or indignation: can it be that ...?

annuō, -uere, annuī, annūtum: nod assent; consent

annus, -ī, m.: year

annuus, -a, -um: yearly

anser, -eris, m.: goose

ante: adv., before, previously

ante: prep. w/acc., in front of, before

anteā: adv. (*ante* + *ea*), previously

antenna, -ae, f.: the horizontal yardarm of a sailing ship

Antimachus, -ī, m.: Greek name, e.g., of Antimachus of Colophon, poet of 5/4 cent. B.C. famed for his prolixity

antīquē: adv., in the ancient way

antīquus, -a, -um: lying in front; ancient

antistō, -stāre, -stitī: (w/dat.) surpass

Antius, -a, -um: Roman *nomen gentile*; see appendix A

anus, -us, f.: old woman; as fem. adj., old, aged

anxius, -a, -um: anxious

Āonius, -a, -um: of Aonia, the part of Boeotia which includes Mt. Helicon

aper, aprī, m. or f.: wild boar

aperiō, -īre, aperuī, apertum: open

apertus, -a, -um: open

Aphēliōtēs, -ae, m.: the east wind

apiscor, apisci: seize, grasp; obtain

appāreō, -ēre, -pāruī, -pāritum: be visible

appetō, -ere, -īvī, -ītum: try to reach; seek; attack

applicō, -āre: press, lean against

approbātiō, -ōnis, f.: approval, assent

approbō, -āre: express approval of, commend; prove the excellence of

aptus, -a, -um: tied, prepared, ready

apud, aput: prep. w/acc., at, near, by; at the house of

aqua, -ae, f.: water

Aquīnus, -ī, m.: name of a Roman poet

āra, -ae, f.: altar

Arabs, -is, m., Gk. acc. pl. **Arabas**: an Arabian

arānea, -ae, f.: spiderweb, cobweb; spider

arāneōsus, -a, -um: cobwebby

arāneus, -ī, m.: spider

arātrum, -ī, n.: plow

arbiter, -trī, m.: spectator, onlooker

arbitrium, -ī, n.: arbitration; authority; will

arbitror, -ārī: observe, consider, judge, reckon

arbor, -oris, f.: tree

arca, -ae, f.: chest, coffer; money

ardens, -ntis: passionate, ardent

ardeō, ardēre, arsī: burn, blaze

ardor, -ōris, m.: conflagration; passion

argentum, -ī, n.: silver

Argīvus, -a, -um: Argive; by meton., Greek

arguō, -uere, -uī, -ūtum: show, reveal; prove wrong

argūtātiō, -ōnis, f.: a creaking, squeaking, chattering noise

argūtus, -a, -um: clear-sounding, squeaking, creaking

Ariadna, -ae, f.: Ariadne, daughter of Minos and Pasiphaë, half-sister of the Minotaur

Ariadneus, -a, -um: of Ariadne

āridus, -a, -um, dim. **aridulus**: dry

arista, -ae, f.: an ear of grain

armō, -āre: arm, equip with arms

Arpocratēs, -is, m.: Harpocrates or Horus, Egyptian god represented with finger to mouth as if enjoining silence; hence, a person who keeps a secret

Arrius, -i, m.: Roman *nomen gentile* (see appendix A)

ars, artis, f.: craftsmanship (cf. Gk. *technē*)

Arsinoē, -ēs, f.: wife of Ptolemy II, deified and identified with Aphrodite

articulus, -i, m.: joint; finger

artus, -ūs, m.: joint; limb; part of the body, member

aruspicium, -iī, n.: divination, interpretation of omens

arvum, -ī, n.: tilled field; field; tillable land

arx, arcis, f.: the fortified eminence of a city, citadel

as, assis, m.: a copper coin of negligible value, like a penny

Asia, -ae, f.: Asia, esp. Asia Minor; the East

Asinius, -a, -um: belonging to the Roman *gens Asinia*; see appendix A, Asinius Marrucinus

asinus, -ī, m.: ass, donkey

Āsius, -a, -um: belonging to the Lydian coast in the area of Ephesus, near the mouth of the Cayster River

aspernor, -ārī: push away, reject, scorn, spurn

aspiciō, -spicere, -spexī, -spectum: look upon; look

aspīrō, -āre: breathe; blow

assiduē: adv., continually, constantly

assiduus, -a, -um: settled; constantly present, persistent, unremitting

Assyrius, -a, -um: Assyrian; (by extension) Asiatic, oriental

at: disjunctive conj., but, nevertheless, yet, however, yes but

āter, ātra, ātrum: black, dark-complexioned

Athēnae, -ārum, f.: Athens

Athos, -ōnis, m.: mountain on the peninsula of Acte in the Chalcidice.

atque, ac: and

atquī: conj., but; moreover

attamen: nevertheless

attenuō, -āre: make thin, reduce, thin out

attingō, -tingere, -tigī, -tactum: touch; touch upon (in speaking), mention

Attis, -idis, m. & f.: in myth, a eunuch consort of the goddess Cybele

attrahō, -trahere, -traxī, -tractum: draw with force; draw up

attribuō, -tribuere, -tribuō, -tribūtum: assign, allot

attrītus, -a, -um (pple. of *attero*): worn away

auctō, -āre: cause to grow or prosper; bless (w/abl.)

auctus, -a, -um: increased in size, power, wealth, or importance; enriched, enhanced

aucupium, -iī, n.: the sport of fowling; game birds, wild fowl

audac(i)ter: adv., boldly

audax, audācis: bold; audacious, reckless, rash

audeō, -ēre, ausī or **ausus:** semi-dep., dare

audiō, -īre, -īvī, -ītum: hear, pay attention to

auferō, -rre, abstulī, ablātum: carry away

Aufillēnus, -a: name of brother and sister in poem 100 (see appendix A)

augeō, augēre, auxī, auctum: augment, increase; glorify; enhance, equip, furnish

aura, -ae, f.: breeze, wind

aurātus, -a, -um: gilded; golden

Aurēlius, -a, -um: belonging to the Roman *gens Aurelia*; see appendix A

aureus, -a, -um, dim. **aureolus:** golden

auricula, -ae, f.: dim. of *auris*, ear

aurifer, -era, -erum: gold-bearing

auris, -is, f., dim. **auricula:** ear

Aurōra, -ae, f.: the goddess of Dawn

aurum, -ī, n.: gold

Arunc[u]leia, -ae, f.: the bride in poem 61 (also named *Iunia* in line 16—see appendix A)

auscultō, -āre: listen, overhear, eavesdrop on

auspicātus, -a, -um, comp. **auspicātior, -ius:** approved by augury; auspicious, fortunate, lucky

auspicium, -ī, n.: augury or omen taken from birds; any portent or omen

Auster, Austri, m.: the south wind

aut: or

autem: postpos. part., on the other hand, while, furthermore, also

autumō, -āre: say

auxilium, -ī, n.: aid, assistance, help

avārus, -a, -um: greedy, avaricious

avē: interj., a formal expression of greeting, hail! greetings!

āvehō, -vehere, -vexī, -vectum: carry off

āvellō, -vellere, -vellī, -volsum: tear away

aveō, -ēre: desire, yearn

āvertō, -vertere, -vertī, -versum: divert; remove, steal

avia, -ae, f.: grandmother

avidus, -a, -um: greedy; ardently desirous, passionate

avītus, -a, -um: of a grandfather; ancestral

āvolō, -āre: fly away

avunculus, -ī, m.: maternal uncle

avus, -ī, m.: grandfather

axis, -is, m. dim. **axulus:** board, plank

Bacchans, -antis, f.: a Bacchant or Maenad, female worshiper of Bacchus/Dionysus

bacchor, -ārī: celebrate rites of Bacchus; act like a Bacchant, rave

Balbus, -ī, m.: Roman cognomen in poem 67

balneārius, -a, -um: of the baths

barathrum, -ī, n.: pit, chasm, abyss

barba, -ae, f.: beard

barbarus, -a, -um: outlandish; "barbarian," spec. non-Greek, e.g., Persian

bāsiātiō, -ōnis, f.: a kissing, kissification

bāsiō, -āre: kiss

bāsium, -ī, n.: a kiss

Battiadēs, -ae, m.: an inhabitant of Cyrene (founded by Battus), esp. the poet Callimachus

Battus, -ī, m.: legendary founder of Cyrene

beātus, -a, -um, adv. **beātē,** comp. **beātior, -ius:** happy, blessed; rich, well-to-do

bellē: nicely, becomingly

bellum, -ī, n.: war

bellus, -a, -um: pretty, nice, fine, charming

bene: adv., well

benefactum, -ī, n.: benefit, good deed

benignē: adv., benevolently, kindly

Beronīcēus, -a, -um: belonging to Berenice

bestia, -ae, f.: beast, creature

bēta, -ae, f.: beet

bibō, bibere, bibī: drink

bīgae, -ārum, f. pl.: a pair of horses (or the chariot drawn by them)

bīmus, -a, -um, dim. **bīmulus:** two years old

Bīthȳnia, -ae, f.: Roman province on the northwest coast of Asia Minor, where Catullus served on the administrative staff of Memmius in 57-56 B.C.

Bīthȳnus, -a, -um: Bithynian

blandus, -a, -um: charming, ingratiating, seductive, sweet

bombus, -ī, m.: a low, booming sound

boni, -orum, m. pl.: men of substance and social standing

Bonōniensis, -e: from Bononia (mod. Bologna)

bonum, -ī, n.: any good thing or circumstance, boon, blessing, benefit; pl., "goods" as property, one's estate

bonus, -a, -um: good; of "good" social standing

bonus, -ī, m.: a solid citizen; a citizen of the better class

Boōtēs, -ae, m.: the constellation Bootes

Boreās, -ae, m.: the north wind

brāchium, -ī, n. dim. **brachiolum:** arm

breve, -is, n.: a short space of time; abl. **brevi,** within a short time

brevis, -e: short, brief, scant

Britannia, -ae, f.: Britain

Britannus, -ī, m.: a native of Britain, a Briton

Brixia, ae, f.: mod. Brescia, a town in Cisalpine Gaul

bustum, -ī, n.: funeral pyre; grave mound

buxifer, -era, -erum: producing box-trees (the *Buxus* yields boxwood, a close-grained, heavy, tough hardwood)

cachinnus, -ī, m.: laugh, guffaw; metaph. of rippling waves

cacō, -āre: defecate

cacūmen, -inis, n.: peak, tip

cadō, -ere, cecidī, casum: fall

Caecilius, -a, -um: Roman *nomen gentile*; see appendix A

caecus, -a, -um: blind; dark

caedēs, -is, f.: killing, murder; gore

caedō, caedere, cecīdī, caesum: strike, strike dead; to "beat" with sexual intercourse; cut through, hew

caelebs, -libis: without a spouse; unpartnered, celibate

caeles, -itis: heavenly; as subst., god or goddess

caelestis, -e: of the heavens, celestial

caelestis, -is, m. or f.: a god or goddess

caelicola, -ae, gen. pl. **-um, m. or f.:** an inhabitant of heaven, god or goddess

Caelius, -ī, m.: Roman *nomen gentile*, e.g., of M. Caelius Rufus; see appendix A

caelum, -ī, n.: the sky or heavens

caenum, -ī, n.: mud, filth, slime

caerulus or **caeruleus, -a, -um:** sea-blue

Caesar, Caesaris, m.: Gaius Julius Caesar; see appendix A

caesariēs, -ēī, f.: long hair

caesius, -a, -um: having gray or gray-blue eyes; gray-eyed

Caesius, -a, -um: a Roman *nomen gentile*

calamus, -ī, m.: a reed; reed pipe

calathiscus, -ī, m.: a small basket

calīgō, cālīginis, f.: darkness, murk

calix, -icis, m.: dish; drinking cup

Callistō, f., Gk. dat. Callistō: daughter of Lycaon, changed into a she-bear and then into the constellation Ursa Major

Calvus or **Calvos, -ī, m.:** cognomen of C. Licinius Calvus; see appendix A

Camerius, -a, -um: *nomen gentile* of Catullus' friend sought in poem 55 and 58b

campus, -ī, m.: plain, field

candeō, -ēre, canduī: shine, gleam, glisten, sparkle

candidus, -a, -um, comp. **candidior:** bright; white; fair-skinned (implying beauty); gorgeous (of a woman)

canis, -is, m. or f.: dog; (f.) bitch

canitiēs, -ēī, f.: white or gray coloring; whiteness of hair; gray hair

canō, -ere, cecinī, cantum: sing

Canōpītae, -ārum, f.: adj., Canopic; of Canopus, a suburb of Alexandria on the Nile delta

cantus, -ūs, m.: song; sound of instruments

cānus, -a, -um: white, whitened

caper, caprī, m.: he goat, billy goat

capillātus, -a, -um: long-haired

capillus, -ī, m.: hair

capiō, capere, cēpī, captum: catch, snatch

caprimulgus, -ī, m.: goat milker

capsula, -ae, f.: a small cylindrical case for holding book rolls

captō, -āre: try to catch; w/*aure*, try to hear

caput, capitis, n.: head

carbasus, -ī, f.: sail, canvas

careō, -ēre, -uī, -itum: lack, be free of

carīna, -ae, f.: keel, hull; by meton., ship

carmen, carminis, n.: song, poem; incantation

carnifex, -ficis, m.: executioner; scoundrel

carpatinus, -a, -um: made of hide

carpō, -ere, carpsī, carptum: pluck, pull at; press on along (a way, journey, period of time, etc.); carp at, criticize

carta, -ae, f.: a sheet or roll of papyrus

cārus, -a, -um, comp. **carior,** superl. **cārissimus:** dear

Castor, -oris, m.: son of Leda and Tyndareus, twin brother of Pollux; one of a twin constellation used in navigation; patron (with his brother Pollux) of seafarers and ships

castus, -a, -um: free from vice, pure, chaste

cāsus, -ūs, m.: fall; accident, chance, fortune,

situation, plight

catagraphus, -ī, m.: a piece of embroidery, an embroidered cloth

catēna, -ae, f.: chain, fetter

caterva, -ae, f.: company, squadron, mass

Catō, -ōnis, m.: Roman cognomen in poem 56

Catullus, -ī, m.: *cognomen* of Gaius Valerius Catullus

catulus, -ī, m.: puppy, whelp

cauda, -ae, f.: tail

caveō, -ēre, cāvī, catum: beware

cavus, -a, -um: hollow; deep

Cecropia, -ae, f.: Athens, the city of Cecrops, first king of Attica

Cecropius, -a, -um: Athenian

cēdō, -ere, cessī, cessum: go; go away, depart

celebrō, -āre: throng, fill, crowd; perform, celebrate

celer, celeris, celere, superl. **celerrimus, -a, -um**: swift

celerō, -āre: hurry

celō, -āre: conceal

Celtibēr, -era, -erum: of or from Celtiberia

Celtibēria, -ae, f.: district in the northeastern part of central Spain, so-called because its natives were a mixture of Celts and Iberians

cēna, -ae, f.: dinner (the principal Roman meal, normally eaten in the evening)

cēnō, -āre: dine

centum: indecl. adj., a hundred

Cerēs, Cereris, f.: Demeter, goddess of grain; by meton., food

cernō, -ere, crēvī, crētum: sift; distinguish; decide, determine; make out, perceive

certāmen, -inis, n.: contest

certātim: adv., with eager rivalry

certē: certainly, surely

certest: abbr. form of *certum est* (see appendix D)

certus, -a, -um: fixed, definite, sure, unerring

cerva, ae, f.: hind, doe

cervix, -īcis, f.: the neck

cessō, -āre: hold back, desist

cēterī, -ae, -a: the rest of, the other; (as pron.) the rest

ceu: part. introducing similes: in the same way as, as, like

Chalybes, -ōn, m. pl.: a tribe of miners and ironworkers on the SE shore of the Black Sea

Charybdis, -is, f.: a whirlpool on the Sicilian side of the Strait of Messina opposite Scylla that devours men and ships

Chīrōn, -ōnis, m.: Chiron, centaur of Mt. Pelion,

tutor of Achilles, famous for his medical skill

chommodus, -a, -um: see **commodus**

chorēa, -ae, f.: a circle dance; choral dancers

chorus, -ī, m.: a singing and dancing performance; a singing and dancing group, chorus, troupe

cibus, -ī, m.: food

cieō, ciēre, cīvī, citum: move, set in motion; rouse, raise, produce

Cieros: an old town in Thessaliotis, southwestern Thessaly

cīmex, -icis, m.: bedbug

cinaedus, -ī, m.: a catamite or passive homosexual, one who submits to anal intercourse; an effeminate male

cinaedus, -a, -um, comp. **cinaedior, -ius**: resembling or typical of a *cinaedus*; loosely used of a lewdly contemptible person, (fem.) slut

cinerārius, -ī, m.: hairdresser

cingō, cingere, cinxī, cinctum: surround; crown

cinis, cineris, m. or **f.**: ash; burned-out funeral pyre

Cinna, -ae, m.: a family name, e.g., C. Helvius Cinna, Catullus' friend. See appendix A

circum: pre. w/acc., around

circumcursō, -āre: run around

circumdō, -dare, -dedī, -datum: ring, circle, enclose

circumsiliō, -īre: spring or leap around

circumsistō, -sistere: gather or crowd around, surround

circumstō, -stāre: stand around

circus, -ī, m.: a circle; a circular or oval arena where public games are held, esp. the Circus Maximus in Rome

cista, -ae, f.: wicker box for sacred objects in mystery cults

citātus, -a, -um: hurried, rapid

citō, -āre: set in motion, rouse; call, summon

citus, -a, -um: moving quickly, rapid, swift

clam: adv., secretly, on the sly

clamō, -āre: shout, cry out

clārisonus, -a, -um: clear-sounding, loud, shrill

clārus, -a, -um, adv. **clārē**: loud; bright; clear; famous

classis, -is, f.: any designated group or class; fleet

claudō, claudere, clausī, clausum: close, shut

claustrum, -ī, n.: the bolt or bar that secures a door

clēmens, -ntis: gentle, mild, lenient

clēmentia, -ae, f.: mercy, pity, clemency

cliens, -entis, m.: a person attached to a *patronus* for legal and other protection in a semi-feudal relationship

Cnidus, -ī, f.: town on the coast of Caria, in SW

Asia Minor, where Venus/Aphrodite was worshiped

Cnōsius, -a, -um: of Cnossos; Cretan

coacervō, -āre: pile up

cōdicillus, -ī, m.: pl., a set of writing tablets

coeō, -īre, -iī, -itum: come together, meet

coepī, coepisse, coeptum: begin

coetus, -ūs, m.: meeting; band, company, group, crowd

cōgitātiō, -ōnis, f.: a thought

cōgitō, -āre: think

cognātus, -a, -um: related; as m. or f. subst., a relative

cognitus, -a, -um, superl. **cognitissimus, -a, -um:** known; sexually intimate

cognōscō, -noscere, -nōvī, -nitum: get to know; know

cōgō, cogere, coēgī, coactum: round up, collect; compel

cohors, -hortis, f.: retinue, staff, entourage

Colchī, -ōrum, m. pl.: Colchis, the country of King Aeëtes, his daughter Medea, and the Golden Fleece, located at the eastern end of the Black Sea south of the Caucasus Mts.

colligō, -ligere, -lēgī, -lectum: gather

collis, -is, m.: hill, mountain

collocō, -āre: set, place; set out, arrange on a marriage bed

collūceō, -lucēre, -luxī: shine

collum, -ī, n.: neck

colō, colere, coluī, cultum: inhabit; till; look after

colōnia, -ae, f.: a colony; name of town in poem 17

color, -ōris, m.: color

colōrō, -āre: to color or stain

columbus, -ī, m.: a male or cock pigeon

columen, -inis, n.: roof, summit, peak; a key person, top man

colus, -ī, m.: distaff, a short staff for holding wool that is being spun into thread

coma, -ae, f.: hair, lock of hair; foliage

comātus, -a, -um: covered with hair or foliage; **comata Gallia:** Gaul north of the Alps, where the natives wore their hair long, as opp. to *togata Gallia* or Cisalpine Gaul.

comedō, comesse, comēdī, comēssum: eat up; squander

comes, -itis, m.: companion, friend, comrade (often in an inferior capacity or of humbler rank)

Cominius, -a, -um: Roman *nomen gentile* in poem 108

comitātus, -a, -um: attended, accompanied

commēiō, -mēire, -minxī, -mictum: defile with urine; soil, pollute

commemorō, -āre: recall, recount

commendō, -āre: commit, entrust

commictus, -a, -um: (*commeio*) filthy

committō, -mittere, -mīsī, -missum: bring into contact with; entrust, give up, hand over

commodō, -āre: lend

commodum, -ī, n.: advantage, benefit

commodus, -a, -um: of full size or weight, standard; convenient, opportune, timely; beneficial; (neut. pl. substantive) advantages, beneficial courses of action

commūnis, -e: shared, common, mutual

compar, comparis, f.: wife, mate

comparō¹, -āre: prepare; acquire, obtain

comparō², -āre: place side by side; compare

compellō, -āre: address, invoke

comperiō, -perīre, -perī, -pertum: find out, ascertain

complector, -plectī, -plexus: embrace, surround

complexus, -ūs, m.: embrace

compōnō, -pōnere, -posuī, -positum: place beside, match, compare

compositus, -a, -um: composed; well arranged; orderly, calm

comprecor, -ārī: pray to, invoke, supplicate

compr(eh)endō, -endere, -endī, -ensum: seize, catch

comprobō, -āre: demonstrate the goodness of

Cōmum, -ī, n.: mod. Como, town in Cisalpine Gaul

concēdō, -cēdere, -cessī, cessum: withdraw; grant, hand over

conchȳlium, -ī, n.: mollusk, a shellfish that yields a costly purple dye; purple dye from the mollusk

conciliō, -āre: unite, join; attract, endear, win over, obtain

concinō, -ere, -uī: sing together; celebrate in song

concipiō, -ere, -cēpī, -ceptum: take in, catch, conceive, contract (a disease); conceive (a child), produce, be the mother of

conclāmō, -āre: shout out, shout in unison

concoquō, -coquere, -coxī, -coctum: cook down; digest; tolerate, stomach

concordia, -ae, f.: harmony

concrēdō, -credere, -credidī, -creditum: entrust

concubīnus, -ī, m.: catamite, male homosexual partner

concutiō, -cutere, -cussī, -cussum: cause to vibrate; shake

conditus, -a, -um: put away, preserved

confectus, -a, -um: worn out, exhausted

conferō, -ferre, -tulī, -latum: compare

confestim: adv., immediately

confiteor, -fitērī, -fessus sum: admit

confutuō, -futuere, -futuī, -futūtum: have sexual intercourse with

cōniger, -era, -erum: coniferous, e.g., a pine tree

coniugātor, -ōris, m.: conjoiner, one who joins

coniugium, -ī, n.: marriage, union; spouse

coniungō, -iungere, -iunxī, -iunctum: join together; associate

coniunx, -iugis, m. or f.: spouse, consort, mate, wife, husband

Conōn, -ōnis, m.: royal astronomer of Ptolemy III Euergetes (III cent. B.C.)

cōnōr, -ārī: attempt, try

conqueror, -querī, -questus: complain, lament

consanguinea, -ae, f.: sister, female relative

conscelerō, -āre: stain with crime, pollute

conscendō, -ere, -scendī, -scensum: climb up

conscius, -a, -um: sharing knowledge; self-conscious; conscious of guilt, guilty

conscribillō, -āre: scrawl over, cover with scribbling

conscrībō, -scrībere, -scripsī, -scriptum: enroll; write down

consequor, -sequī, -secūtus: come after, follow

conserō, -serere, -sēuī, -situm: sow, plant; beset

conservō, -āre: save or keep from danger, preserve

consīdō, -sīdere, -sēdī: take a seat, sit, settle; take up a position

consilium, -ī, n.: deliberation; advice; resolution, purpose

consōlor, -ārī: comfort, console, solace

conspiciō, -ere, -spexī, -spectum: catch sight of, lay eyes on

constans, -ntis: steady, resolute, steadfast

consternō, -ere, -strāvī, -strātum: cover, spread

constituō, -stituere, -stituī, -stitūtum: place in position; set down

construō, -uere, -struxī, -structum: pile up

consul, consulis, m.: one of two top magistrates in the Roman republic

consulātus, -ūs, m.: the office of consul, consulship

consurgō, -surgere, -surrexī, -surrectum: stand up, rise

contegō, -tegere, -texī, -tectum: cover up; shelter

contemptus, -a, -um: despicable, contemptible

contendō, -ere, -tendī, -tentum: stretch, strain; contend

contentus, -a, -um: satisfied

contexō, -ere, -texuī, -textum: weave together; arrange, combine

continenter: adv., in an unbroken line

contingō, -tingere, -tigī, -tactum: come in contact with; touch, reach

continuō: adv., immediately, without delay

continuus, -a, -um: uninterrupted, in a row, continuous

contorqueō, -torquēre, -torsī, -tortum: twist, agitate

contrā: adv., in front, opposite; in return; on the other hand

contrā: prep. w/acc., against

contrahō, -trahere, -traxī, -tractum: draw in; catch, contract (as a disease)

contremō, -ere, -uī: tremble violently

contubernālis, -is, m.: tentmate, comrade-in-arms

conturbō, -āre: mix up, confuse

cōnūbium, -ī, n.: marriage; pl., a wedding

convellō, -vellere, -vellī, -volsum: tug at; plow up, dislodge, uproot

conveniō, -īre, -vēnī, -ventum: meet together; agree

conventus, -ūs, m.: a coming together, assembly, meeting

convertō, -vertere, -vertī, -versum: turn around; direct

convīva, -ae, m.: table companion, guest

convīvium, -ī, n.: banquet, dinner party

convocō, -āre: call together

cōpia, -ae, f.: abundance; supply; opportunity

cor, cordis, n.: heart; abl. cordi esse + dat. = be dear or pleasing to

Cornēlius, -a, -um: Roman nomen gentile (see appendix A)

Cornificius, -a, -um.: Roman nomen gentile (see appendix A)

cornū, -ūs, n.: horn

corolla, ae, f.: dim of corona; garland, small wreath

corōna, -ae, f.: wreath, crown; a circle of bystanders, esp. at a legal proceeding

corpus, -oris, n.: body

corripiō, -ripere, -ripuī, -reptum: seize hold of

corruō, -ruere, -ruī: fall down, collapse

cortex, -icis, m.: bark, cortex

corvus, -ī, m.: raven

Crannon, Crannonis: a chief town in central Thessaly

creātrix, -īcis, f.: mother, creatress

crēdō, -ere, credidī, creditum: entrust; believe

creō, -āre: beget, give birth to, produce

crepida, -ae, f.: a thick-soled sandal of a Greek type

crescō, crescere, crēvī, crētum: come into existence; grow

Crēta, -ae, f.: Crete, large island south of the Aegean Sea, home of King Minos and Ariadne

Crētēs, -um, m. pl.: the Cretans

crīmen, -inis, n.: indictment, charge, accusation

crīnis, -is, m.: a lock or braid of hair; hair

crocinus, -a, -um: made of saffron; saffron yellow

Croesus, -ī, m.: sixth century B.C. king of Lydia, famous for his wealth

crūdēlis, -e, comp. crudelior, -ius: savage, cruel

cruor, -ōris, m.: blood (usually that of a wound)

crūs, crūris, n.: leg

crux, crucis, f.: a cross; a stake for impalement

cubiculum, -ī, n.: bedroom

cubīle, -is, n.: bed, couch

cubō, -āre: lie down; go to bed

culpa, -ae, f.: fault, wrongdoing

cultor, -ōris, m.: inhabitant

cultrix, -īcis, f.: a female inhabitant; local goddess

cūlus, -i, m. or n.: anus

cum: prep. w/abl., with; (archaic) by means of

cum: rel. adv., when; cum ... tum: not only ... but also

cumque: postpos. adv., giving preceding pron. or adv. indefinite force: -ever, -soever

cunctus, -a, -um: the whole of, all

cunīculōsus, -a, -um: abounding in rabbits

cunīculus, -ī, m.: rabbit

cunnus, -i, m.: vulva, the female pudenda (cf. Eng. cunt)

cupidē: eagerly

cupīdō, -inis, m.: desire; object of desire (as term of affection); Cupid or Eros, companion of Venus/Aphrodite, personification of sexual desire

cupidus, -a, -um: desirous, eager

cupiō, -ere, -īvī, cupītum: want, desire

cupressus, -ī, f., abl. cupressu: the cypress tree

cūr: interr. & rel. adv., why

cūra, -ae, f.: care, concern, anxiety

cūriōsus, -a, -um: excessively careful, meddlesome; as subst., a busybody

cūrō, -āre: watch over, care for, care about

currō, currere, cucurrī, cursum: run

currus, -ūs, m.: chariot; poet., ship

cursus, ūs, m.: the action of running; a race; travel; course

curūlis, -e: of high state office; sella curulis = the chair of state used by consuls, praetors, and other high officeholders

curvus, -a, -um: bent, curving

cuspis, -idis, f.: sharp point or tip; spear; pointed stick

custōdia, -ae, f.: protection, safekeeping, watch

custōdiō, -īre, -īvī, -ītum: keep safe; hold

custōs, -ōdis, m.: guardian, watchman

Cybēbē or Cybelē, -ēs, f.: Phrygian goddess of nature, known also in Rome as the Magna Mater

Cyclas, -adis, f.: an island of the Cyclades; pl. the Cyclades, islands in the Aegean surrounding Delos

Cycnēus, -a, -um: of Cycnus, mythical king of Liguria who was changed into a swan

Cyllēnaeus, -a, -um: of or near Mt. Cyllene, in Arcadia; epithet of Pheneus

cymbalum, -ī, n., gen. pl. cymbalum: cymbal

Cȳrēnae, -ārum, f. pl.: Cyrene, a town in northwest Libya; the province of Cyrene

Cytōrius, -a, -um: of Mt. Cytorus, in Asia Minor

Cytōrus, -ī, m.: a mountain in Paphlagonia east of Amastris, part of the coastal ridge along the southern shore of the Black Sea

daps, dapis, f.: a sacrificial meal; any feast or meal; food

Dardanius, -a, -um: of Dardanus, an ancestor of Priam; Trojan

Daulias, -ados, f.: the Daulian [bird], i.e., Philomela, from Daulis in Phocis, a few miles east of Delphi

dē: prep. with abl., away from, down from, off; of, out of, from; immediately after; [diem] de die: day after day; about, concerning

dea, -ae, f.: goddess

dēbeō, dēbēre, dēbuī, dēbitum: owe

dēcēdō, -cēdere, -cessī, -ceptum: go away, leave; make way for

decem: indecl. adj., ten

dēcerpō, -cerpere, -cerpsī, -cerptum: pluck off, snatch

decet, -ēre, decuit: 3rd. pers. only, be suitable or fitting

deciēs: adv., ten times

dēclārō, -āre: make known, declare, tell

dēclīnō, -āre: lower, decline

dēcoctor, -ōris, m.: a bankrupt person, insolvent debtor

decorō, -āre: embellish, adorn

dēcurrō, -currere, -currī, -cursum: run down; travel over

dēcursus, -ūs, m.: descent, downward fall

decus, -oris, n.: glory; the best of anything

dēdicō, -āre: dedicate, consecrate

dēdō, dēdere, -didī, -ditum: give up, deliver, hand over; reflexive, devote oneself to

dēdūcō, -dūcere, -dūxī, -ductum: lead or bring

down
defendō, -fendere, -fendī, -fensum: ward off; defend
dēferō, -ferre, -tulī, -lātum: carry, bring, fetch; carry off or away, take
dēfessus, -a, -um: exhausted, tired out
dēflectō, -flectere, -flexī, -flexum: bend downwards
dēflōrescō, -escere, -uī: shed petals
dēfricō, -āre: rub thoroughly; scour
dēfutūtus, -a, -um: exhausted by sexual intercourse
dēgō, dēgere: spend (one's time, leisure, etc.)
deinde, dein: adv., afterwards, then, next
dēlābor, -lābī, -lāpsus: fall, slip down
dēlectō, -āre: lure, entice; delight, amuse
dēlicātus, -a, -um, comp. delicatior: given to luxury or pleasure; pampered; frisky, wanton, frivolous; elegant
dēlicia, -ae, f.: pleasure; pl. pet, darling; **dēlicias facere**: to find pleasure, enjoy oneself; put on foppish airs, act in an affected manner
Dēlius, -a, -um: Delian; of the island of Delos, birthplace of Apollo and Artemis/Diana
Delphī, -ōrum, m. pl.: place in Phocis, Greece, sacred to Apollo and Dionysus; meton., the people of Delphi
dēmānō, -āre: run or drip down
dēmens, -ntis: out of one's mind, maddened, crazy
dēmetō, -metere, -messī, -messum: mow, reap, harvest
dēmittō, -mittere, -mīsī, -missum: drop; lower
dēmō, dēmere, dempsī, demptum: remove, take away
dēmonstrō, -āre: show
dēnique: adv., finally
dens, dentis, m.: tooth
densus, -a, -um, comp. densior: dense, closely packed
dentātus, -a, -um: well provided with teeth, toothy
dēperditus, -a, -um: lost, ruined
dēpereō, -īre, -iī: perish; (hyperbolic) love to death, love to distraction
dēpōnō, -ere, -posuī or -posīvī, -positum: put down, lay down (in birth), put away
dēprecor, -ārī: try to avert by prayer, beg off, entreat relief from; execrate
dēpre(he)ndō, -ndere, -ndī, -nsum: seize, catch
dērelinquō, -linquere, -līquī, -lictum: leave behind
dērigō, -rigere, -rexī, -rectum: align, make straight, aim
dērīsus, -a, -um: laughable, ridiculous
dēserō, -serere, -seruī, -sertum: forsake, leave
dēsertus, -a, -um: deserted, solitary, lonely

dēsīderium, -ī, n.: desire (esp. for someone absent), longing; an object of desire, darling
dēsīderō, -āre: long for, desire; need
dēsinō, -ere, -iī, -itum: cease, leave off, stop
dēsistō, -sistere, -stitī: cease, desist
despiciō, -spicere, -spexī, -spectum: look down on, scorn
despondeō, -spondēre, -spondī, -sponsum: promise, betroth, pledge
despuō, -ere: spit down on the ground (to avert some evil); avert by spitting, spurn, reject
dēstinātus, -a, -um: stubborn, obstinate
dēsum, desse, defuī: be wanting or lacking; fail
dēterior, -ius: worse
dētineō, -tinēre, -tinuī, -tentum: detain, hold
deus, -ī, m. or f., nom. pl. di: god
dēvellō, -vellere, -velli or -volsi, -volsum: pluck out
dēvinciō, -vincīre, -vixī, -vinctum: tie fast, bind
dēvocō, -vocāre: call down, summon
dēvolvō, -volvere, -volvī, -volūtum: roll something down from
dēvorō, -āre: eat up, devour
dēvōtus, -a, -um: accursed; vowed as an offering
dexter, -era, -erum: right; the right hand; on the right side
dextrā: adv., on the right
dextra, -ae, f.: the right hand
Dīa, -ae, f.: an Aegean island, usu. identified with Naxos
Diāna, -ae, f.: Roman goddess identified with Artemis, nature, and the moon.
dicax, -ācis: well-spoken, quick with repartee
dicō[1], -āre: indicate, show; assign, bestow
dīco[2], -ere, dixī, dictum: talk; say, declare; sing, recite; name, call
dictum, -ī, n.: anything said; word, saying
diēs, diēī, m. or f.: day
differtus, -a, -um: filled, stuffed
difficilis, -e: not easy
diffindō, -findere, -findī, -fissum: split
diffundō, -fundere, -fūdī, -fūsum: diffuse, spread out
diffutūtus, -a, -um: subjected to widespread sexual demands; dissipated by sex; sexually overworked
digitus, -ī, m.: finger
dignor, -ārī: consider worthy; deign, see fit
dignus, -a, -um: appropriate, worthy
dīgredior, -gredī, -gressus: go off; digress
dīlacerō, -āre: tear to pieces
diligentius: comp. adv., more carefully
dīligō, -igere, -lexī, -lectum: love, be fond of

dīluō, -luere, -luī, -lūtum: dissolve away; moisten, wash, bathe

dīmittō, -mittere, -mīsī, -missum: let go

Dindymēnē, -ēs or -ae, f.: of or belonging to Mt. Dindymon in Phrygia; Cybele

Dindymon, Dindymī, n.: mountain in Phrygia sacred to the goddess Cybele

Diōna, -ae, f.: the goddess Dione, mother of Aphrodite/Venus

dīrus, -a, -um: awful, dread, dire, frightful

discēdō, -cēdere, -cessī, -cessum: scatter; depart, desert, run away

discernō, -cernere, -crēvī, -crētum: separate, divide off

discerpō, -ere, -cerpsī, -cerptum: tear to pieces

discidium, -ī, n.: splitting; separation

discō, discere, didicī: learn

discors, -cordis: in conflict, at odds, quarreling

discruciō, -āre: torment, vex

discupiō, -cupere: desire passionately

disertus, -a, -um: skilled in speaking, articulate

dispereō, -perīre, -periī: perish; go for nothing, be wasted

dispiciō, -spicere, -spexī, -spectum: look around; investigate

displiceō, -ēre, -uī, -itum: be displeasing or offensive (+ dat.)

dissolvō, -solvere, -solvī, -solūtum: break up; pay, discharge

distinctus, -a, -um: separate, different, distinct,

diū: adv., for a long time

dīva, -ae, f.: goddess; any female immortal, e.g., the sea nymph Thetis

dīvellō, -vellere, -vulsī, -volsum: tear apart

dīversus, -a, -um: turned or headed in different directions

dīves, dīvitis: wealthy, rich

dīvidō, -ere, -vīsī, -vīsum: separate, divide

dīvīnus, -a, -um: divine

dīvitiae, -ārum, f. pl.: riches

dīvus, -ī, m., dīva, -ae, f.: a god, goddess

dīvus, -a, -um: divine, holy

dō, dare, dedī, datum: give, pay

doceō, docere, docuī, doctum: tell, inform; teach

doctus, -a, -um: learned

doleō, -ēre, -uī, -itum: suffer pain, grieve, hurt; impers., cause pain, rankle

dolor, -ōris, m.: pain, distress

dolus, -ī, m.: a guilty act or intention; trickery; plot

domina, -ae, f.: mistress

dominus, -ī, m.: master

domō, -āre, -uī, -itum: subdue

domus, -ūs, f., loc. domī: home; house, family

dōnō, -āre: give, dedicate

dōnum -ī, n.: gift

dormiō, -īre, -īvī or -iī, -ītum: sleep

dōs, dōtis, f.: a dowry, property brought by a bride to her husband as her portion of the new family's endowment

dubitō, -āre: be in doubt; hesitate, scruple

dubius, -a, -um: uncertain, doubtful; perilous

ducentī, -ae, -a: two hundred

ducentiēs: adv., two hundred times

dūcō, ducere, duxī, ductum: lead, take; take as one's wife; consider, reckon

dūdum: adv., some time ago; w/*iam*, now after all this time

dulce: adv., sweetly

dulcis, -e: sweet

dum: conj., as long as; (w/historical pres.) while; (w/subjunctive) provided that; (w/ind. or subj.) until

duo, -ae, -o: two

duplex, -icis: folded double; double, two-sided

dūritiēs, -ēī, f.: hardness

Durrachium, -i, n.: town on the coast of Illyria, mod. Durazzo

dūrus, -a, -um, comp. dūrior: hard; harsh, pitiless; dull; wooden, heavy, solid

dux, ducis, m.: leader

ē, ex: out of, from, in accordance with

ēbriōsus, -a, -um, comp. ebriosior: addicted to drink

ēbrius, -a, -um: intoxicated; metaph., drunk with love

ebur, eboris, n.: ivory

ec- prefixed to interrogatives with intensive or indefinite force (OLD)

ecfutuō, -uere, -uī, -ūtum: wear out with sexual intercourse

ecquis, -quid: interr. pron., is there anyone (anything) that? anyone, anything, something

edō[1], esse, ēdī, ēsum: eat, eat away, consume

ēdō[2], ēdere, ēdidī, editum: emit, bring forth, yield; publish

ēdūcō[1], -ducere, -duxī, -ductum: bring out

ēducō[2], -āre: bring up, nurture, rear

efferō, efferre, extulī, ēlātum: carry away

efficiō, -ficere, -fēcī, -fectum: make, cause to occur

effigiēs, -ēī, f.: statue, effigy

efflō, -āre: breathe out, emit, blast out

effluō, -fluere, -fluxī: flow out, slip away

effodiō -**fodere**, -**fōdī**, -**fossum**: dig or gouge out

effūsus, -**a**, -**um**: loose; disorderly, in disarray

ēgelidus, -**a**, -**um**: thawed, unchilled, tepid, warm

egeō, **egēre**, **eguī**: need; be in need, lack the necessities of life

Egnātius, -**ī**, **m.**: Roman *nomen gentile*; see appendix A

ego, gen. **meī**: first personal pron., I

ēgredior, -**gredī**, -**gressus**: come out, depart

ēgregius, -**ia**, -**ium**: outstanding, preeminent, illustrious

ēgressus, -**ūs**, **m.**: escape, egress, exit

ēheu: interj., Alas!

ei: interj., monosyllabic expression of anguish

ēiciō, **ēicere**, **ēiēcī**, **ēiectum**: throw out, expel, eject

ēlectus, -**a**, -**um**, superl. **electissimus**: select, choice

ēlegans, -**ntis**, comp. **ēlegantior**, -**ius**: discriminating, refined, elegant

ēlevō, -**āre**: raise; diminish, make light of

ēligō, -**ere**, **ēlēgī**, **ēlectum**: pull out; select

elleborum, -**ī**, **n.**: hellebore, any of a number of acrid and poisonous plants used medicinally, esp. as a cure for insanity

elluor, -**ārī**: overspend on food and luxury

ēluō, **ēluere**, -**luī**, -**lūtum**: wash clean, wash out

Ēmathia, -**ae**, **f.**: district of Macedonia; in poetry, Thessaly

ēmergō, **emergere**, **emersī**, **emersum**: come out of the water, emerge

ēmorior, **ēmorī**, **ēmortuus**: perish, die

ēmulgeō, -**mulgēre**, -**mulsī**, -**mulsum**: milk; draw off

ēn: interjection, see! behold!

enim: postpos. part., emphasizing prec. word: for

ēniteō, -**ēre**: shine forth; be outstanding

eō[1], **īre**, **īvī**, **itum**: go

eō[2]: adv., to that place, thither

Eōus[1], -**i**, **m.**: the dawn god

Eōus[2], -**a**, -**um**: of or connected with *Eōs*, the dawn; eastern, oriental

ephēbus, -**ī**, **m.**: ephebe, a Greek youth (in Athenian law, between 18 and 20)

epistolium, -**iī**, **n.**: short letter

equidem: part., I for my part

equus or **equos**, -**ī**, **m.**: horse

era, -**ae**, **f.**: a woman in relation to her servants; mistress, i.e., the woman or goddess one serves (as opp. to a kept woman)

Erechtheus or **Erectheus**, -**eī**, **m.**: legendary king of Athens

Erechthēus, -**a**, -**um**: of or associated with Erechtheus, legendary king of Athens; (poet.) Athens

erifuga, -**ae**, **m.**: fugitive slave; one who runs away from his master

ēripiō, -**ripere**, -**ripuī**, -**reptum**: snatch away, remove

errābundus, -**a**, -**um**: prone to err or make a wrong turning; wandering

errō, -**āre**: wander

error, -**ōris**, **m.**: a wandering; deviation, mistake

ērudītulus, -**a**, -**um**, dim. of **ērudītus**: well-instructed, learned

ēruō, -**uere**, -**eruī**, **erutum**: remove, uproot

erus, -**ī**, **m.**: master

Erycīna, -**ae**, **f.**: Venus, goddess of Mt. Eryx in NW Sicily

estō: fut. imperative sing. of *sum*

ēsuriō, -**īre**, -**ītum**: feel hunger; (metaph.) feel desire

ēsurītiō, -**ōnis**, **f.**: hunger, appetite

et: and, too, also; *et ... et*, not only ... but also

etiam: adv., still, yet, even now; (introducing a more extreme case) even, actually; **etiam atque etiam**, ever more urgently, more and more

Etruscus, -**a**, -**um**: from Etruria (mod. Tuscany), the region of western Italy north of Rome.

etsī: conj., although

euans, **euantis**: uttering the Bacchic cry *euan!*

euhoe!: interj., the ritual cry of Bacchants

Eumenides, -**um**, **f. pl.**: Kindly Spirits, Furies, Erinyes, punishers of outrage

Eurōpa, -**ae**, **f.**: daughter of Phoenician king Agenor, carried off by Zeus in the form of a bull; Europe

Eurōtās, -**ae**, **m.**: the river that runs through Sparta

ēvertō, -**vertere**, -**vertī**, -**versum**: turn upside down; bring down

ēvirō, -**āre**: unman, emasculate

ēvītō, -**ēre**: avoid, dodge

ēvolvō, -**volvere**, -**voluī**, -**volūtum**: unwrap; make known, take the wraps off

ex, **ē**: prep. out of, from, in accordance with

exagitō, -**āre**: stir up

exardescō, -**ardescere**, -**arsī**: catch fire, blaze up

excelsus, -**a**, -**um**: lofty

excidō, -**cidere**, -**cidī**: fall off, drop out; lapse, fail

exciō, -**cīre**, -**cīvī**, -**cītum**: rouse (from sleep)

excipiō, -**ere**, -**cēpī**, -**ceptum**: take out, exclude, except; receive

excitō, -**āre**: rouse, wake; stir up, arouse, excite

excruciō, -**āre**: torture, torment

excutiō, -**cutere**, -**cussī**, -**cussum**: shake out

exedō, -**esse**, -**ēdī**, -**ēsum**: eat up, eat away

exeō, -īre, -īvī, -itum: go out, leave

exerceō, -ēre, -uī, -itum: exercise, keep busy, ply

exilium, -ī, n.: exile

eximiē: exceptionally, especially

eximius, -a, -um: excepted; exceptional, choice

exorior, -orīrī, -ortus: rise up from

expallescō, -escere, -palluī: turn pale

expatrō, -āre: waste, squander

expedītus, -a, -um: unencumbered; lightened, as for action or travel

expellō, -pellere, -pulī, -pulsum: drive out

expendō, -pendere, -pendī, -pensum: weigh; pay out

experior, -perīrī, -peritus: try out

expers, -ertis: having no share of; immune to

expetō, -petere, -petīvī, -petītum: request, desire

expleō, -plēre, -plēvī, -plētum: fill up, satisfy

explicō, -āre: explain, explicate

expoliō, -īre, -īvī, -ītum: smooth down, polish

expolītior, -ius: more polished

exposcō, -poscere, -poposcī: ask for, demand, beg

exprimō, -primere, -pressī, -pressum: squeeze out, extort; translate

exprōmō, -promere, -prompsī, -promptum: bring out, express

exsecō, -āre: cut out

exsequor, -sequī, -secūtus: follow, pursue

exsiliō, -silīre, -siluī: spring forth

exsolvō, -ere, -soluī, -solūtum: unfasten; discharge, pay

exspectō, -āre: anticipate, expect, look out for

exspīrō, -āre: exhale, pant, emit (a fragrance); be exhaled

exspuō, -spuere, -spuī, -spūtum: spit out

exstō, -stāre, -stitī: stand out

exsultō, -āre: spring up; let oneself go, run riot; show unrestrained pleasure, exult

exsuperō, -āre: surmount, exceed

extenuō, -āre: make thin, reduce, diminish

externō, -āre: drive out of one's wits, madden, panic

extinctus, -a, -um: dead, deceased

extollō, -ere: lift up, raise

extrēmus, -a, -um: farthest, the farthest part of; final

exturbō, -āre: drive out, remove by force

exul, -ulis, m. or f.: an exile

exustus, -a, -um: burnt; parched

exuviae, -ārum, f. pl.: spoils of a defeated enemy

faba, -ae, f.: bean

fābula, -ae, f.: talk, gossip; report

Fabullus, -ī, m: dim. of Fabius, a *nomen gentile* of the Roman *gens Fabius*; see appendix A

facētiae, -ārum, f. pl.: cleverness, wit

facile: adv., easily

facilis, -e, superl. facillimus, -a, -um: easy

facinus, -oris, n.: deed; evil deed, wrong, crime

faciō, -ere, fēcī, factum: do, make; achieve, attain, reach

factum, -ī, n.: deed, something done

fāgus, -ī, f.: beech-tree

Falernum, -i, n.: Falernian wine, from a northern district of Campania

fallax, -ācis: treacherous, deceptive

fallō, fallere, fefellī, falsum: trick, deceive, mislead; pass., err

falsiparens, -entis: having a pretended father; falsely fathered

falsō: adv., wrongly, falsely

falsus, -a, -um: untrue; deceitful, faithless

falx, falcis, f.: a curved knife for pruning trees and vines

fāma, -ae, f.: fame; rumor

famēs, -is, f.: hunger; famine

famula, -ae, f. or famulus, -i, m.: servant, slave

famulor, -ārī: be a servant

fandus, -a, -um: speakable; proper, lawful

farciō, farcīre, farsī, fartum: stuff

fās: indecl. n., that which is right or permissible by divine law; meet and right, fitting, proper

fascinō, -āre: to cast a *fascinum* or spell upon; bewitch

fastus, -ūs, m.: conceit, arrogance

fateor, -ērī, fassus: concede, admit, confess

fātum, -ī, n.: a prophetic utterance; fate

fatuus, -a, -um: feeble minded, silly, foolish, asinine

faustus, -a, -um: fortunate, lucky

faveō, -ēre, fāvī, fatum: be well-disposed, show favor

Favōnius, -ī, m.: the west wind, zephyr

fax, facis, f.: torch

febrīculōsus, -a, -um: feverish, fever-ridden

fēcundus, -a, -um: productive of offspring; fertile, fruitful

fēlix, -īcis: fruitful; lucky, prosperous; happy

fellō, -āre: suck milk; perform oral sex on a man

fēmella, -ae, f.: dim. of *femina*; woman, girl

fēmina, -ae, f.: woman

femur, -inis, n.: thigh

fera, -ae, f.: wild animal

ferō, ferre, tulī or tetulī, lātum: bear, carry; endure, withstand; say; take, accept; **impune ferre**: get away with something

The Catullan Vocabulary

ferox, -ōcis: fierce
ferreus, -a, -um: made of iron; hard, harsh; shameless, brazen
ferrūgō, -inis, f.: rust; any color from reddish purple to nearly black.
ferrum, -ī, n.: iron, steel; sword
ferus, -a, -um: fierce, wild, savage; inhuman, cruel
ferus, -ī, m.: a wild animal
fervidus, -a, -um: hot; fervent, passionate, lusty
Fescennīnus, -a, -um: of Fescennia, a town in Etruria famous for its ribald verses; ribald, obscene
fessus, -a, -um: tired, exhausted
festus, -a, -um: festal, holiday
fētus, -ūs, m.: parturition, birth; offspring, fruit
fictus, -a, -um: made up, sham, false, lying
fidēlis, -e: faithful, worthy of trust
fidēs, fidēi, f.: tutelage, faith, trust; trustworthiness; promise (personified in 30.11)
fīdus, -a, -um: faithful, loyal, devoted
fīgō, fīgere, fīxī, fīxum: drive in; pierce
figūra, -ae, f.: form, shape, aspect, appearance
fīlia, -ae, f.: daughter
fīlius, -ī, m.: son
fīlum, -ī, n.: thread, string, filament
fingō, fingere, finxī, fictum: shape, mold, make
fīniō, -īre, -īvī, -ītum: mark out the boundaries; finish
fīnis, -is, m.: boundary; end; (pl.) territory
fīō, fierī, factum: to take place, happen; to be made or done, become
Firmānus, -a, -um: of Firmum, the home town of Mentula
firmō, -āre: strengthen
fixus, -a, -um: set
flagellum, -ī, n.: whip, lash; the whiplike shoot of a vine
flāgitium, -i, n.: disgrace, dishonor; shameful act, outrage
flāgitō, -āre: beset with demands, importune
flagrans, -ntis: flaming, burning, intense
flagrō, -āre: burn
flāmen, flāminis, n.: a blast or gust of wind; wind, breeze
flamma, -ae, f.: flame, fire
flammātus, -a, -um: burning
flammeum, -ī, n.: the flame-colored veil worn by a Roman bride at her wedding
flammeus, -a, -um: fiery; swift as fire
flātus, -ūs, m.: blowing, breath, breeze
flāvens, -entis: yellow

Flāvius, -ī, m.: a Roman nomen gentile, applicable to a member of the Flavian gens
flāvus, -a, -um: yellow, gold-colored, blonde
flēbilis, -e: worthy of tears, lamentable
flectō, -ere, flexī, flexum: bend; turn, avert
fleō, -ēre, -ēvī, -ētum: weep, cry; weep for, mourn
flētus, -ūs, m.: weeping; tears
flexanimus, -a, -um: persuasive
flexus, -ūs, m.: a bending, turning, curve
flōrens, -entis: flowering; in the flower of one's youth; fresh, vigorous
flōridus, -a, -um, dim. flōridulus: full of flowers, flowery
flōs, flōris, m., dim. flosculus: flower; youthful beauty; the finest specimen of a type or class
fluctuō, -āre: surge like a wave; be in turmoil
fluctus, -ūs, m.: wave
fluentisonus, -a, -um: resounding with the noise of the sea
fluitō, -āre: flow; float, drift
flūmen, -inis, n.: river
focus, -ī, m.: hearth
fodiō, fodere, fōdī, fossum: pierce; dig
foedō, -āre: make foul, soil
foedus, -eris, n.: any formal agreement or bond, incl. marriage and (sometimes) other sexual unions
for, fārī, fātus: speak, say, tell
forās: adv. w/vbs. of motion, to the outside, out
fore: fut. infin. of sum (see appendix D)
forem, fores, foret, etc.: impf. subj. of sum (see appendix D)
foris, -is, f.: the door of a building
forīs: adv., outdoors, outside, away from home
forma, -ae, f.: appearance; beauty, good looks
Formiānus, -a, -um: of Formiae (e.g., Mamurra)
formō, -āre: shape, form
formōsus, -a, -um: full of looks; handsome, beautiful
fors, fortis, f.: chance, luck
fortasse: adv., perhaps
forte: (abl. of fors) adv., by chance
fortis, forte: strong; brave
fortūna, -ae, f.: fortune
forum, -ī, n.: a public square, piazza; Forum, -ī n.: the Roman Forum, the main public place in Rome
fossa, -ae, f.: ditch
fossor, -ōris, m.: a digger, agricultural laborer, ditchdigger
foveō, fovēre, fōvī, fōtum: keep warm; cherish,

199

coddle

fractus, -a, -um: broken

frāgrans, -ntis: fragrant, redolent, sweet-smelling

frangō, -ere, frēgī, fractum: break

frāter, -tris, m.: brother

frāternus, -a, -um: of or from a brother, fraternal

fraudō, -āre: cheat, defraud, swindle; w/abl., cheat out of

fremitus, -ūs, m.: a low roar, rumble, growl

fremō, -ere, -uī, fremitum: roar, rumble, growl

frequens, -entis: occurring at close intervals; crowded, thronged

frequentō, -āre: fill with people; occupy, crowd, throng

fretum, -ī, n.: any place where the sea boils up; sea

fricō, -āre: rub, chafe

frīgerō, -āre: make cool, chill

frīgidus, -a, -um, dim. **frīgidulus**: chilly, cold; (of language, rhetoric, etc.) feeble, tedious, frigid

frīgus, -oris, n.: cold

frondātor, -ōris, m.: a foliage tender, pruner

frondōsus, -a, -um: leafy

frons¹, frondis, f.: foliage

frons², frontis, f.: forehead; front, facade

fructus, -ūs, m.: the enjoyment of something; satisfaction; crops, produce; yield, profit, revenue

frustrā: adv., in vain

frustror, -ārī: deceive, baffle; disappoint, frustrate

frux, frūgis, f.: fruit, crop

fūcus, -ī, m.: seaweed; dye (orig. that derived from a seaweed)

Fūfidius, -a, -um: Roman *nomen gentile* in 54.5

fuga, -ae, f.: flight, escape

fugiō, fugere, fūgī: run away, flee, escape, slip off

fugō, -āre: put to flight, drive off, expel

fulgeō, -gēre, fulsī: shine brightly, gleam

fulgor, -ōris, m.: brightness, luster

fūmō, -āre: emit smoke, smoke

funditus: adv., from the bottom up; utterly

fundō, -ere, fūdī, fūsum: pour, pour forth, emit, utter

fundus, -ī, m.: bottom, base; country estate, farm

fūnestō, -āre: pollute with death

fūnestus, -a, -um: associated with mourning; funereal

fūnis, -is, m.: rope; a ship's hawser, mooring rope

fūnus, -eris, n.: funeral rites; a corpse; death

fūr, fūris, m.: thief, robber

furcilla, -ae, f.: a two-tined wooden pitchfork

furibundus, -a, -um: frantic, excited

Fūrius, -i, m.: Roman *nomen gentile*; see appendix A

furō, furere: be mad or crazed; rage with passion, rave

furor, -ōris, m.: passion, rage, frenzy

furtim: adv., secretly, stealthily

furtīvus, -a, -um: secret, furtive

furtum, -ī, n.: theft; any sneaky act

fūsus, -ī, m.: a weighted spindle on which yarn is wound and twisted

futuō, futuere, futuī, futūtum: have sex with, fuck; copulate

futūtiō, -ōnis, f.: an act of copulation

Gāïus, -iī, m.: a Roman *praenomen*, regularly abbr. to C.

Galla, -ae, f.: an emasculated priest of Cybele

Gallia, -ae, f.: Gaul, in Catullus' time a Roman province only in the north Italian portion south of the Alps (Cisalpine); Transalpine Gaul (*comata Gallia*) included what is now France and Belgium

Gallicānus, -a, -um: of Gaul (partic. *Gallia Cisalpina* or *Narbonensis*)

Gallicus, -a, -um: of or belonging to Gaul

Gallus, -ī, m.: cognomen of an uncle in poems 78-78b

ganniō, -īre: snarl; speak in a hostile manner

gaudeō, -ēre, gāvīsus: rejoice, take pleasure

gaudium, -ī, n.: joy, delight, gladness

gāza, -ae, f.: treasure

gelidus, -a, -um: frozen

Gellius, -a, -um: Roman *nomen gentile*, identified with L. Gellius Poplicola (see appendix A)

gemellus, -a, -um: twin (adj. or subst.)

geminus, -a, -um: double, twin

gemō, -ere, gemuī, gemitum: groan, moan, lament

gena, -ae, f.: cheek

gener, generī, m.: son-in-law

genetrix, -īcis, f.: mother, creator

geniālis, -e: of or pertaining to a person's *genius*; of or pertaining to marriage

genitor, -ōris, m.: father; pl., parents

gens, gentis, f.: race, people, nation; clan; class, set, kind

gentīlis, -is, m.: a member of the same *gens*, i.e., a distant relative

genus, generis, n.: stock, family; offspring; kind, type; way, method, mode

germāna, -ae, f: sister

germānus, -ī, m.: brother

gerō, gerere, gessī, gestum: bear, conduct, carry on,

do; wear

gestiō, -īre, -īvī: desire eagerly; act without restraint, exult

gignō, gignere, genuī, genitum: create, beget, give birth to

gingīva, -ae. f.: the gums

glaber, -bris, m.: a hairless, effeminate type of slave

glēba, -ae, f.: a lump of earth, clod

glūbō, -ere: peel

gnāta, -ae, f.: (<*nascor, gigno*) daughter

gnātus, -ī, m.: son

Golgī, -ōrum, m. pl.: a town in Cyprus noted for the worship of Aphrodite/Venus

Gortȳnius, -a, -um: of Gortyn; poet., Cretan

grabātus, -ī, m.: a low, cheap bed, pallet, cot

gradior, -ī, gressus: step, walk

Graecus, -a, -um: Greek

Grāius, -a, -um: Greek

grandis, -e: grown up; big

grātēs, -ium, f. pl.: thanks

grātia, iae, f.: good will, favor; pl., gratitude, thanks

grātus, -a, -um: pleasing

gravēdō, -dinis, f.: a cold in the head

gravis, -e: heavy, grevious, severe; low-pitched

gravius: adv., comp. of *graviter*: more heavily or harshly; more grievously

gremium, -iī, n.: lap

gurges, gurgitis, m.: a swirling mass of water; sea

gutta, -ae, f.: a drop; teardrop

guttur, -uris, m.: throat

gymnasium, -ī, n.: an athletic center

gȳrus, -ī, m.: circular course, orbit

habeō, -ēre, -uī, -itum: have, hold

habitō, -āre: live in; dwell

Hadria, -ae, f.: the Adriatic sea

Hadriāticus, -a, -um: Adriatic; as neut, subst., the Adriatic Sea

haedus, -ī, m.: a young goat, kid

haereō, haerēre, haesī, haesum: stick, cling

Hamadryas, -ados, f.: a wood nymph

harēna, -ae, f.: sand, beach

harundinōsus, -a, -um: reedy

haud or **haut:** part., not

Hēbē, -ēs, f.: daughter of Zeus and Hera, goddess of youth, married to Hercules after his apotheosis

hedera, -ae, f.: ivy

hederiger, -era, -erum: ivy-carrying, wearing ivy

Helena, ae, f.: daughter of Zeus and Leda, wife of Menelaus, cause of Trojan War when Paris took her to Troy

Helicōnius, -a, -um: of Helicon, the mountain in Boeotia that was sacred to Apollo and the Muses

Hellespontus, -ī, m.: the Hellespont or Dardanelles, the channel near Troy linking the Propontis with the Aegean

hendecasyllabus, -i, m.: an eleven-syllable verse of poetry, esp. a line of poetry in the Phalaecian meter; a cutting or sarcastic verse

hercule: interj. in the form of an appeal to Hercules, used to express strong feeling

Herculēs, -ī, m.: Greek hero who performed the Twelve Labors

hērēs, -ēdis, m.: heir

heri: yesterday

hērōs, hērōös, m.: a hero

Hesperus, -ī, m.: the evening star

hesternus, -a, -um: of or belonging to yesterday

heu: interj., alas

Hibēr, -ēris, m.: an Iberian or Spaniard

Hibēri, -ōrum, m. pl.: the Iberians or Spaniards (properly, the inhabitants of the valley of the Hiberus River); **ex Hibērīs** = from the country of the Spaniards

hībernus, -a, -um: of winter

Hibērus, -a, -um: Iberian, Spanish

hīc: adv., here, in this place; in the present case or circumstances

hic, haec, hoc: demon. pron., this

hiems, hiemis, f.: winter

hilaris, -e: cheerful

hilarō, -āre: cheer, gladden

hinc: adv., from this place or point

hinsidiae, -ārum, f. pl: see **indisiae**

Hīonius, -a, -um: see **Ionius**

hircus, -ī, m.: he goat

Hirrus or **Hirrius, -ī, m.:** Roman cognomen in 54.2

hiscō, hiscere: begin to open; open the mouth to speak

hiulcō, -āre: cause to crack open

hodiē: (*hoc die*) adv., today

homō, -inis, m.: generic word for human; person, plur. people

hōra, -ae, f.: hour

horreō, -ēre, -uī: bristle; shudder or tremble at, fear; regard with awe or dread

horribilis, -e: fearful, dreadful; rough, uncouth

horridus, -a, -um: rough, rugged, wild, uncouth, harsh

horrificō, -āre: roughen, ruffle

Hortensius, -a, -um: Roman *nomen gentile*, e.g., of

Q. Hortensius Hortalus (see appendix A)
hortor, -ārī: exhort, urge on
hortus, -ī, m., dim. **hortulus:** garden
hospes, hospitis, m.: guest, visitor; stranger
hostia, -ae, f.: a sacrificial animal
hostis, -is, m.: enemy
hūc: adv., to this place or point; to this total or amount; **huc et huc:** this way and that
hūmānus, -a, -um: human; of or with a mortal human being
humilis, -is: low
humus, -ī, f.: earth, ground
hyacinthinus, -a, -um: of the hyacinth; hyacinth-colored
Hydrochoos, -ī, m.: Gk. water pourer, the constellation Aquarius
Hymēn, m.: refrain chanted at Greek weddings; personified as god of marriage
Hymenaeus, -ī, m.: the Greek wedding refrain; pl. marriage; personified as god of marriage
Hyperboreī, -ōrum, m. pl.: a legendary people of the far north
Hyrcānus, -ī, m.: a native of Hyrcania, a country at the southeast side of the Caspian Sea
Iacchus, -ī, m.: Bacchus
iaceō, -ēre, -uī, iacitum: lie, recline
iaciō, iacere, iēcī, iactum: throw
iactō, -āre (freq. of *iacio*): throw; toss about, torment
iam: adv., now
iambus, -ī, m.: an iamb or iambic verse; (pl.) invective verse, esp. that written in iambic meter
iamque: strengthened form of *iam*
iānua, -ae, f.: door to a house, other building, or heaven
ibi (final vowel long or short): adv., there, in that place; then, there and then
ictus, -ūs, m.: stroke, blow, impact
Īda, -ae, f.: Mount Ida, a range in the Troad (western Phrygia), a center of Cybele worship
Īdaeus, -a, -um: of Mt. Ida
Īdalium, -ī, n.: town in Cyprus sacred to Aphrodite/Venus
īdem, eadem, idem: pron. & adj., the same, the same person; w/adverbial & sts. adversative force, likewise, at the same time
identidem: adv. = *idem et idem*, repeatedly, continually
ideō: adv., (w/*quod*): for the reason (that)
Idrus, -i, m.: unkn., perh. the eponymous founder of Idrias in Caria (see n. to 64.300)

iēiūnus, -a, -um: fasting, hungry, starved
igitur: conj., therefore
ignārus, -a, -um: ignorant, uncomprehending
ignis, -is, m.: fire; funeral pyre; any luminous object in the sky, such as a star; love's fire
ignoscō, -noscere, -nōvī, -nōtum: forgive (w/dat.)
ignotus, -a, -um: unknown
īlia, -ium, n. pl.: groin, genitals
Īliacus, -a, -um: of Ilium, Trojan
ille, illa, illud, gen. sing. **illīus** or **illĭus:** demonst. adj. & pron., that; he, she, it
illepidus, -a, -um: unbecoming, ungraceful, awkward
illic[1], illaec, illuc: pron., that person or thing
illīc[2]: adv., there, at that place
illinc: adv., from there
illūc: adv., thither, to that place
imāginōsus, -a, -um: full of images; **aes imaginosum:** mirror
imber, -bris, m.: rain; (metaph.) a shower of tears
imbuō, -uere, -uī, -ūtum: drench, steep; dip or wet for the first time; inaugurate, give first experience
immātūrus, -a, -um: unripe, immature; premature, untimely
immemor, -oris: forgetful, heedless, feckless
immineō, -ēre: be intent on
immītis, -e: ungentle, pitiless, violent
immō: particle, correcting a previous statement
immundior, -ius: more unclean
impellō, -pellere, -pulī, -pulsum: beat against, drive, compel
impendeō, -pendēre, -pensum: hang above
impensius: adv., more immoderately, more excessively
imperātor, -ōris, m.: ruler, commander
imperium, -ī, n.: command
impetus, -ūs, m.: forceful or rapid movement; attack
impius, -a, -um: wicked, irreligious, without *pietas*
implicō, -āre: entwine, entangle
implorō, -āre: ask for something with entreaty
impotens, -entis: powerless; lacking in self-control, hence headstrong, wild, violent, intemperate
imprimō, -primere, -pressī, -pressum: press on, imprint
improbus, -a, -um, comp. adv. **improbius:** morally unsound, wicked, flagrant, shameless; wanton
impudīcus, -a, -um: sexually immoral, licentious
impūne: adv., without punishment, with impunity
impūrus, -a, -um: dirty; morally foul, impure

īmus, -a, -um, dim. īmulus: lowest, deepest

in: prep. w/abl., in, on; w/acc., into, onto, against

inambulātiō, -ōnis, f.: a walking or similar movement

inānis, -e, adv. inaniter: empty, empty-handed; foolish; vain, futile, unprofitable

inaurātus, -a, -um: gilded, gold plated

incānescō, -canescere, -canuī: become white or hoary

incedō, -cedere, -cessī: arrive, step up; step or walk (esp. in a slow or stately manner), strut

incendium, -ī, n.: conflagration; inflammation, agony

incendō, -ere, -cendī, -censum: set on fire; inflame

incidō, -ere, incidī, incāsum: fall or impinge upon, occur

incingō, -cingere, -cinxī, -cinctum: wrap

incipio, -cipere, -cēpi, -ceptum: begin

incitō, -āre: incite, provoke, stir

incohātus, -a, -um: unfinished, only begun, incomplete (cf. Eng. inchoate)

incohō, -āre: start work on, begin

incola, -ae, m. or f.: inhabitant

incolō, -colere, -coluī: inhabit, dwell in

incolumis, -is, -e: safe and sound

incommodum, -ī, n.: detriment, harm; pl., misfortune

incrēbescō, -ere, -crebuī: intensify, increase in frequency

incultus, -a, -um: unkempt

incurvō, -āre: bend

inde: adv., thence, from that point

India, -ae, f.: "An ill-defined region of Asia, extending from the present subcontinent of India to the borders of China; popularly confused with Ethiopia, Arabia, etc." (OLD)

indicō, -āre: reveal, declare, disclose, show

indidem: adv., from the same place

indignē: undeservedly

indignus, -a, -um: unworthy; undeserved

indistinctus, -a, -um: indiscriminate, disordered, not arranged by type

indomitus, -a, -um: untamed; indomitable; violent

indūcō, -dūcere, -dūxī, -dūctum: lead or bring in, admit

Indus, -a, -um: Indian

Indus, -ī, m.: a native of India

inēlegans, -ntis: inelegant, clumsy, infelicitous

ineptiae, -ārum, f.: instances of folly; frivolities

ineptiō, -īre: play the fool, be silly

ineptus, -a, -um, comp. ineptior, -ius: foolish,

gauche, awkward

iners, -ertis: clumsy; lazy, idle, useless

infacētiae, -ārum, f. pl.: clumsiness, gaucheries, blunders

infacētus, -a, -um, comp. infacetior, -ius: boorish, gauche

infectus, -a, -um (from *inficio*): dyed

infēlix, -fēlīcis, adv. infēlīce: infertile; disastrous, unlucky

inferiae, -ārum, f. pl.: offerings made to a dead person's *manes*; rites in honor of the dead

inferō, inferre, intulī, illātum: bring in; bring on; incur; enter (as in a document, will, etc.)

infestus, -a, -um: hostile, warlike; troublesome

infimus, -a, -um: lowest

infirmus, -a, -um: feeble, weak

inflectō, -ere, -flexī, -flexum: bend

inflexus, -a, -um: curved

infundō, -fundere, -fūdī, -fūsum: pour in or on

ingenerō, -āre: engender, produce children

ingens, -gentis: huge, vast

ingenuus, -a, -um: native, natural; befitting a freeborn person, generous, frank; (m. or f. subst.) a freeborn person

ingerō, -gerere, -gessī, -gestum: bring in, pour

ingrātus, -a, -um: thankless, unwelcome, disagreeable

ingredior, -gredī, -gressus: enter

inguen, -inis, n.: groin, (pl.) loins

inhibeō, -hibēre, -hibuī, -hibitum: restrain

iniciō, -icere, -iēcī, -iectum or -iactum: throw in or on

inimīcus, -a, -um: unfriendly; as m. or f. subst. w/gen., enemy, opponent

inīquus, -a, -um: uneven; unfair, ill-disposed

initium, -ī, n.: beginning; pl. rites, mysteries, and objects used in such rites

iniūria, -ae, f.: unlawful conduct; injurious treatment

iniustus, -a, -um: unjust

inmerens, -merentis: undeserving, unoffending

innītor, -nītī, -nīxus: lean on, put one's weight on, press

innupta, -ae, f.: an unmarried girl

innuptus, -a, -um: unwed

inobservābilis, -e: undetectable to the eye; difficult to trace or observe

inops, inopis: destitute; defenseless; powerless

inquam, 2nd pers. sing. inquis, 3rd pers. sg. inquit, pl. inquiunt: say

inquinātus, -a, -um, comp. inquinātior: dirty, de-

based, corrupt
inquinō, -āre: make dirty, soil, stain
insapiens, -entis: unwise, foolish
inscius, -a, -um: unknowing
insidiae, -ārum, f. pl.: ambush, plot
insistō, -sistere, institī: stand on; set about, set to work on
insolenter: adv., contrary to custom; immoderately; arrogantly
inspērans, -antis: not hoping or expecting
instar, n. (indecl.): the equivalent or equal; adverbial w/gen., to the extent (of)
instituō, -stituere, -stituī, -stitūtum: establish; begin, set out
instruō, -struere, -struxī, -strictum: construct, arrange
insula, -ae, f.: island
insulsus, -a, -um, superl. **insulsissimus:** witless, stupid
insultō, -āre: leap or trample on; behave insultingly, scoff
intactus, -a, -um: untouched, unscathed
integellus, -a, -um: dim. of *integer*, untouched, uninjured, safe
integer, -gra, -grum: untouched, unimpaired by age, unblemished; virgin, unmarried
inter: prep. w/acc., between, among
intereā: adv., in the meantime; with adversative force, in these circumstances
intereō, -īre, -iī, -itum: die
interficiō, -ficere, -fēcī, -fectum: kill
interior, -ius: inner
interitus, -ūs, m.: violent or untimely death
intestīnum, -ī, n.: (pl.) intestines, guts
intestīnus, -a, -um: internal; personal
intimus, -a, -um: inmost
intortus, -a, -um: twisted or twined
intrā: prep. w/acc., within, inside
intus: adv., inside, within
inūrō, -ūrere, -ussī, -ustum: burn, burn in, brand
inveniō, -venīre, -vēnī, -ventum: meet, find; acquire, get
invenustus, -a, -um: not *venustus*, unlovely, unattractive
invictus, -a, -um: unvanquished
invideō, -ēre, -īdī, -isum: to look at with ill will or envy; begrudge
invīsō, -vīsere, -visī, -visum: go to see; look upon
invītus, -a, -um: unwilling
invocō, -āre: call upon, invoke
involō, -āre: fly at, swoop down upon (to steal)

iō: interj., a ritual exclamation, Yo!
iocātio, -ōnis, f.: jesting
iocor, -ārī, -ātus: joke
iocōsus, -a, -um: full of laughs, jolly, happy
iocus, -ī, m.: joke, jest
Īonius, -a, -um: Ionian, spec. of the Ionian sea, west of Greece and south of Italy
Iovis: see *Iuppiter*
ipse, ipsa, ipsum: pron., adj., himself, herself, itself; acting of his/her/its own accord; as subst., master or mistress
Ipsitilla, -ae, f.: see appendix A
īra, -ae, f.: wrath
īrascor, īrascī, īrātus: feel resentment, be angry
īrātus, -a, -um: angry, furious, wrathful
irrigō, -āre: make wet, flood, drench
irritus, -a, -um: not ratified, null and void; empty, unfulfilled, vain
irrumātiō, -ōnis, f.: the act of forcing another person to give oral sex
irrumātor, -ōris, m.: a man who compels others to perform *fellatio* (oral sex); hence, one who treats others with contempt
irrumō, -āre: to force someone to give oral sex (*fellatio*), as a means of humiliating him
is, ea, id: this, that
iste, ista, istud: pron. & pron. adj., this (which you have or see); this
istic, istaec, istuc: that which you have, mention, or refer to
istīc: adv., there by you; over where you are
istinc: from the place you are in, from this situation of yours
ita: adv., so
Italus, -ī, m.: an Italian
itaque: adv., accordingly, in consequence, so
item: adv., similarly, likewise
iter, itineris, n.: journey, path, road, course
iterum: adv., again; for the second time
Itōnus, -ī, f.: Boeotian town famous for its cult of Athena
Itylus, -ī, m.: Itys, son of Tereus and Procne, killed by Procne
iuba, -ae, f.: mane
iubeō, -ēre, iussī, iussum: order, bid; w/dat. of person bidden in 64.140
iūcundus, -a, -um, comp. **iūcundior, -ius,** superl. **iūcundissimus:** pleasant, delightful
iūdex, -icis, m. or **f.:** judge
iugālis, -e: yoke-bearing; matrimonial
iūgerum, -ī, n.: a measure of land, about two-thirds

of an acre
iugō, -āre: join, hitch, yoke
iugum, -ī, n.: yoke; ridge
iunctus, -a, -um: connected
iungō, iungere, iunxī, iunctum: yoke, join, unite
Iunia, -ae, f.: a woman of the *gens Iulia*, the bride in poem 61 (also named Aurunculeia in line 86—see appendix A)
Iūnō, -ōnis, f.: Juno, consort of Jupiter, identified with Gk. Hera
Iuppiter, Iovis, m.: Jupiter or Zeus, chief of the Olympian gods; by meton., the weather, wind, sky
iūre: adv., rightly
iūrō, -āre: swear an oath
iūs, iūris, n.: law; right; legal standing, authority, jurisdiction; (sing. or pl.) code
iustificus, -a, -um: acting justly, righteous
iustitia, -ae, f.: justice
iustus, -a, -um: just
iuvenca, -ae, f.: a young cow, heifer
iuvencus, -ī, m.: young bull or ox, bullock
iuvenis, -is, m.: youth, young man
iuventa, -ae, f.: youth
Iuventius, -iī, m.: Roman *nomen gentile*: see appendix A
iuventūs, -tūtis, f.: the youth; men of military age, the soldiery
iuvō, -āre, iūvī, iūtum: help; please, gratify
labefactō, -āre: make unsteady; undermine, cause to weaken in resolve
labellum, -ī, n.: (dim. of *labrum*) lip
labō, -āre: stand unsteadily, totter
labor or labōs, -ōris, m.: labor, effort, toil
labōriōsē: adv., painfully
labōriōsus, -a, -um: laborious, much worked-upon
labōrō, -āre: work, labor
labrum, -ī, n.: lip
labyrinthēus, -a, -um: of or like a labyrinth, labyrinthine
lacessō, -ere, -īvī, -ītum: challenge, provoke, harass
lacrima, -ae, f., dim. **lacrimula**: tear
lacrimō, -āre: weep
lactens, -entis: milky; milk-white
lacteolus, -a, -um: dim. of *lacteus*, milk-white
lacus, -ūs, m.: lake
Lādās, -ae, m.: Spartan runner, proverbial for speed
laedō, -ere, laesī, laesum: injure, offend; handicap
laetitia, -ae, f.: happiness
laetor, -ārī: rejoice, be glad

laetus, -a, -um: glad, happy
laevus, -a, -um: left; the left hand
lāna, -ae, f.: wool
lancinō, -āre: tear to pieces, mangle
lāneus, -a, -um: woolly
langueō, -ēre: be faint, droop, be sick
languescō, -escere, -escī: weaken, grow feeble
languidus, -a, -um, dim. **languidulus**, comp. **languidior**: weary, drooping, flaccid
languor, -ōris, m.: faintness, exhaustion, lassitude
Lānuvīnus, -a, -um: from Lanuvium, a town in the Alban hills south of Rome.
lapillus, -ī, m.: (dim. of *lapis*) pebble
lapis, -idis, m.: stone
lar, laris, m.: household god
largē: adv., abundantly
Lārīsaeus, -a, -um: of or at Larisa, capital of central Thessaly
Lārius, -a, -um: belonging to the *Larius Lacus*, mod. Lago di Como, lake in Cisalpine Gaul
lāsarpīcifer, -era, -erum: (<*laserpicium, lac sirpicium*) silphium-bearing; producing silphium, used as a contraceptive (see n. on 7.4)
lassus, -a, -um, dim. **lassulus, -a, -um**: tired, weary
lātē: adv., far, at a distance, far and wide
lateō, latēre, latuī: hide, skulk, lurk
latibulum, -ī, n.: hiding place, lair, den, hole
Latmius, -a, -um: of Mt. Latmus in Caria (SW Asia Minor)
Lātōnia, -ae, f.: daughter of Latona or Leto; epithet of Diana
latrō, -āre: bark
lātus, -a, -um: wide, broad
latus, lateris, n., dim. **latusculum, -ī, n.**: side, flank
Lāudamia, -ae, f.: Laodamia, wife of Protesilaus
laudō, -āre: praise
laurus, -ī, f., acc. pl. **laurūs**: laurel or bay tree
laus, laudis, f.: praise; cause of praise, virtue, glory
lautus, -a, -um: washed clean; sumptuous, luxurious
lavō, lavere, lāvī, lautum: wash
laxus, -a, -um: spacious; loose
leaena, -ae, f.: lioness
lectīca, -ae, f.: litter, a covered and curtained couch used for carrying a person
lector, -ōris, m.: reader
lectus, -a, -um: chosen, choice, picked
lectus, -ī, m., dim. **lectulus** or **lecticulus, -ī, m.**: bed, couch
legō, -āre: send as an envoy
legō, -ere, lēgī, lectum: gather; remove; pick out; read, read about

lēniō, -īre, -īvī, -ītum: make less violent, assuage; appease; mollify

lēnis, -e: easy, gentle

lēniter, comp. lenius: adv., gently; without drastic effect

lēnō, -ōnis, m.: brothel keeper, pimp, procurer

lentus, -a, -um: supple, pliant; slow, taking one's time, unconcerned, at ease

leō, leōnis, m.: lion

lepidus, -a, -um, adv. lepidē, superl. lepidissimus: charming, witty

lepos, -ōris, m.: charm, grace, wit; term of endearment

Lesbia, -ae, f.: poetic name given the woman loved by Catullus. See appendix A

Lesbius, -a, -um: *nomen gentile*, probably satirical and fictitious, in poem 79

Lēthaeus, -a, -um: of the Lethe, river of forgetfulness in the underworld; meton., of death

lētifer, -era, -erum: bringing death, deadly

lētum, -ī, n.: death

levāmen, -inis, n.: relief, solace, comfort

levis¹, -e, comp. levior, -ius: light in weight; light, gentle; trivial, shallow, insignificant

lēvis², -e: smooth

leviter: adv., lightly

levō, -āre: lighten

lex, lēgis, f.: law

libellus, -ī, m (dim. of *liber*): little book; bookshop

libenter: adv., with pleasure; willingly, gladly

līber¹, -era, -erum: free

liber², -beri, m. or -berae, f.: child

Līber³, -erī, m.: the wine god, Bacchus/Dionysus

liber⁴, -brī, m.: the inner bark of a tree; book, volume, roll

līberālitās, -itātis, f.: generosity, munificence

līberē: adv., freely

libīdō, -inis, f.: desire; sexual craving

lībō¹, -āre: pour as a libation

Libō², -ōnis, m.: Roman cognomen in 54.3

librārius, -ī, m.: scribe; book dealer

lībrō, -āre: make level; hold suspended; balance, poise

Libya, -ae. f.: North Africa

Libyssa, -ae, f. adj.: of or belonging to North Africa; African

Libystīnus, -a, -um: African

licet, -ēre, licuit: impers., it is permitted

Licinius, -ī, m.: *nomen gentile* of C. Licinius Macer Calvus; see appendix A

ligneus, -a, -um: wooden; tough, stringy

lignum, -ī, n.: wood, firewood

ligō, -āre: tie, bind

Ligus, -uris: Ligurian; from Liguria, in NW Italy

līmen, līminis, n.: threshold, doorway

līmes, līmitis, m.: boundary; lane, path

limpidus, -a, -um: clear, transparent

lingō, lingere, linxī, linctum: lick

lingua, -ae, f.: tongue

linquō, linquere, līquī: leave, quit

linteum, -i, n.: linen cloth; napkin; sail

liquefaciō, -facere, -fēcī, -factum: melt

līquens, -entis: liquid, flowing; clear, transparent

liquidus, -a, -um: liquid, fluid; clear, unclouded

līs, lītis, f.: lawsuit

lītorālis, -e: of the shore

litterātor, -ōris, m.: schoolteacher

lītus, -oris, n.: shore

līvidus, -a, -um: a dull, grayish-blue color

locō, locāre: place

Locris, -idos, f.: Locrian (epithet of Arsinoë)

locus, -ī, m. & locum, -ī, n.: place, region, part

longē: far, for a great distance or time; by far, to a considerable degree

longinquus, -a, -um: far-off; drawn-out, long

longus, -a, -um: long; tall, svelte

loquella, -ae, f.: speech

loquor, loquī, locūtus: speak; tell

lōrum, -ī, n.: a leather strap for tying

lōtium, -ī, n.: urine

lubentius: adv., more gladly

lubeō or libeō, -ēre, intr. w/dat. of person pleased: to be pleasing; **quid lubet**: anything you like, anything at all

lucellum, -ī, n.: dim. of *lucrum*, a small profit

lūceō, -ēre, luxī: shine; dawn

Lūcīna, -ae, f.: goddess of childbirth, identified with Juno or Diana

luctus, -ūs, m.: the expression of grief; lamentation, grief, sorrow

lūdicrum, -ī, n.: an amusement; plaything

lūdō, -ere, lusī, lusum: play

lūdus, -ī, m.: sport, play; love-play

lūgeō, -ēre, luxī, luctum: mourn

lumbus, -ī, m.: groin, pl. loins

lūmen, -inis, n.: radiance, light; day; the light of life; by meton., eye; a light-giving body in the heavens

Lūna, -ae, f.: title of Diana, the moon goddess

lupa, -ae, f.: she wolf; prostitute

lupānar, -āris, n.: brothel, whorehouse

lupus, -ī, m.: wolf

lustrō, -āre: purify ceremonially; move through
luteus, -a, -um: reddish yellow
lutum, -ī, n.: mud
lux, lūcis, f.: light, ray; by meton., day; sweetheart
Lycāonius, -a, -um: of or descended from Lycaon, e.g., Callisto
Lȳdius, -ia, -ium: Lydian, of Lydia (see note to 31.13)
lympha, -ae, f.: a water nymph; (poet.) water
lymphātus, -a, -um: frenzied, frantic
macer, -cra, -crum: thin, scrawny, emaciated
macula, -ae, f.: stain, blemish
maculō, -āre: spot, spatter, stain
madefīō, -fīerī, -factus: become wet, be soaked
madeō, -ēre: be wet, e.g., with tears
Maecilius, -a, -um: Roman *nomen gentile*, e.g., of the woman in poem 113
Maenas, -adis, f.: a "raver" or Maenad, female votary of Bacchus, Bacchante
maeror, -ōris, m.: grief
maestus, -a, -um, comp. **maestior, -ius**: sad
magis: adv., more
magistra, -ae, f.: mistress, i.e., woman in charge
magnanimus, -a, -um: noble-spirited, brave, bold
Magnus, -ī, m.: cognomen of Pompey the Great, Cn. Pompeius Magnus
magnus, -a, -um, superl. **maximus**: large, great
magus, -ī, m.: a Persian priest, diviner, magus
male: adv., badly, improperly; **male esse** + dat. (impers.): be distressed, feel ill, suffer
maledīcō, -dīcere, -dīxī, -dīctum: speak ill of, abuse, insult
malignus, -a, um, adv. **malignē**: ungenerous, spiteful; grudging, poor, mean, scanty
Mālius, -a, -um: of Malis in southern Thessaly, near Thermopylae
mālō, malle, maluī: prefer, desire more
malum¹, -ī, n.: trouble, misfortune, woe, ailment
mālum², -ī, n.: apple
malus¹, -a, -um: bad, evil, malicious
mālus², -ī, m.: pole; mast of a ship
Māmurra, -ae, m.: name of a family at Formiae; see appendix A
mandātum, -ī, n.: command
māne: adv., in the morning
maneō, -ēre, mansī, mansum: remain, stay, wait
Mānius, -ī, m.: Roman praenomen in poem 68
Manlius, -ī, m.: *nomen gentile* of the groom in poem 61, Manlius Torquatus (see appendix A)
mānō, mānāre: flow, run, drip
mantica, -ae, f.: knapsack

manus, -ūs, f.: hand
Marcus, -ī, m.: Roman *praenomen*, e.g., of M. Tullius Cicero
mare, -is, n.: sea
marīnus, -a, -um: of the sea, marine
marītus¹, -a, -um: married
marītus², -ī, m.: husband
marmor, -oris, n.: marble; the marblelike surface of the sea
Marrūcīnus, -a, -um: of or belonging to a people living on the east coast of central Italy; see appendix A
mās, maris, m.: a male
māter, -tris, f.: mother
māternus, -a, -um: of a mother; on the mother's side of the family
mātūrus, -a, -um: ripe
mātūtīnus, -a, -um: of the morning, matutinal
Māvors, Māvortis, m.: Mars, god of war
maximus, -a, -um, adv. **maximē**: greatest (superl. of *magnus*)
medicus, -ī, m.: physician, doctor
meditor, -ārī, -ātus: contemplate, think out, rehearse
medius, -a, -um: middle; the middle of
medulla, -ae, f., dim. **medullula**: the marrow of the bones; the interior, inside
Mēdus, -ī, m.: a Mede or Persian
meī, gen. of *ego*: of me, of mine
meiō, meiere, minxī, minctum: urinate
melior, -ius: (comp. of *bonus*) better
Mella, -ae, m.: river near Brixia in Cisalpine Gaul
mellītus, -a, -um: honey-sweet
membrāna, -ae, f.: sheepskin or goatskin used as parchment or as a cover for manuscripts
membrum, -ī, n.: any part of the body; limb
memet: my own self (*me* + emphatic enclitic *-met*)
meminī, -isse: (pf. used with pres. force) remember
Memmius, -ī, m.: Roman *nomen gentile*: see appendix A
Memnōn, -onis, m.: legendary king of Aethiopia, son of Eos/Aurora, brother of Zephyrus
memor, -oris: remembering, mindful
memorābilis, -e: worth remembering
mendax, -acis: mendacious, lying, false
Menēnius, -a, -um: name of a plebeian *gens*; see poem 59
mens, mentis, f.: mind
mensa, -ae, f.: table
menstruus, -a, -um: monthly
mentior, mentīrī, mentītus: lie; make a false prom-

ise

mentula, -ae, f.: penis; pseudonym given Mamurra of Formiae (see appendix A)

mereor, merērī, meritus: win, earn, deserve

meretrix, -īcis, f.: courtesan, hetaera; a woman who makes money from lovers

mergō, mergere, mersī, mersum: dip, plunge, immerse

merīdiō, -āre: take a siesta

meritō: adv., deservedly, with good cause

mersō, -āre: submerge, plunge, overwhelm

merus, -a, -um: pure, undiluted (esp. of wine)

messis, -is, f.: harvest

messor, -ōris, m.: reaper, harvester

-met: encl. part., attached for emphasis to certain pronouns

mētior, -īrī, mensus: measure, mark off

metuō, -ere, metuī, metūtum: fear; w/*a, ab*, fear danger (from)

meus, -a, -um: my, mine

mī: abbr. form of dat. *mihi*, to me; vocative masc. sg. of *meus*

mīca, -ae, f.: particle, grain

micō, -āre: quiver, dart, flicker; flash, glitter, gleam

Midās, -ae, m.: legendary king of Phrygia, possessor of the golden touch

migrō, -āre: move, migrate

mīles, mīlitis, m.: soldier

mīliēs: adv., a thousand times

mille, pl. mīlia: a thousand

mīmicē: in the manner of a *mīma*, an actress in a licentious kind of farce

minax, -ācis: menacing, threatening

minimus, -a, -um: superl. of *minor*, least

minister, -trī, m.: servant, attendant, acolyte

ministra, -ae, f.: handmaid, temple attendant

Mīnōïs, -idis, f.: Ariadne, daughter of K. Minos

minor, minus: smaller

Mīnōs, Mīnōïs, acc. Mīnōa, m.: Minos, legendary king of Crete, husband of Pasiphaë, father of Ariadne and Phaedra

Mīnōtaurus, -i, m.: the Minotaur, son of Pasiphaë

minus: adv. less

minūtus, -a, -um: small

mīrificē: adv., amazingly, remarkably

mīror, -ārī: be amazed, wonder, marvel

mīrus, -a, -um: extraordinary, remarkable

misceō, -ēre, miscuī, mixtum: mix, combine

misellus, -a, -um: dim. of *miser*, poor little; wretchedly in love

miser, -era, -erum: wretched, unhappy (see note on 8.1)

miserābilis, -e: pitiable, pathetic

miserē: adv., wretchedly; with piteous result, unhappily

misereō, -ēre, -uī and misereor, -ērī, -itus: impers., feel sorry for; dep., have pity

miserescō, -ere: w/gen., have compassion on

miseriter: adv., pitifully, in a manner that incites pity

mītis, -e: sweet and juicy; succulent; soft

mitra, -ae, f.: an oriental headdress fastened with ribbons under the chin.

mittō, -ere, mīsī, missum: send, send forth; (of weapons) throw, cast, hurl; emit, utter; cease, desist, omit; let go, release, abandon, discard; give

mnēmosynum, -ī, n.: keepsake, souvenir

modo: adv., just, only; **dum modo,** provided only; just now; **modo ... modo:** at one time ... at another; **non modo ... sed:** not only ... but...

modus, -ī, m.: measure, quantity; manner, way; **in modum:** rhythmically, in time

moecha, -ae, f.: adulteress; slut

moechor, -ārī: commit adultery

moechus, -ī, m.: adulterer, sexual aggressor; fornicator

moenia, -ium, n. pl.: town walls

molestus, -a, -um, adv. **molestē:** troublesome, annoying

mollescō, -escere: become soft

molliculus, -a, -um: dim. of *mollis*, somewhat voluptuous, unmanly, or erotic

mollis, -e, dim. **mollicellus, -a, -um:** soft, mild, languid, voluptuous

moneō, -ēre, monuī, monitum: warn

monimentum, -ī, n.: anything that serves as a commemoration, reminder, or memorial

mons, montis, m.: mountain

monstrō, -āre: show; teach

monstrum, -ī, n.: portent, prodigy, apparition; monster; a monstrous act, atrocity

mora, -ae, f.: delay

morbōsus, -a, -um: unhealthy, disease-ridden; morbidly lustful

morbus, -ī, m.: disease

mordeō, -ēre, momordī, morsum: bite

moribundus, -a, -um: dying, moribund: decaying

morior, morī, mortuus: die

moror, -ārī: delay, stay, wait

mors, mortis, f.: death

morsum, -ī, n.: a piece bitten off (cf. Eng. morsel)

morsus, -ūs, m.: bite
mortālis, -is, m.: a mortal, human being
mortuus, -a, -um: dead
mōs, mōris, m.: custom; manner, (pl.) morals
mōtus, -ūs, m.: motion, movement
moveō, -ēre, mōvī, mōtum: move
mūcus, -ī, m.: mucus, snot
mūgilis, -is, m.: a sea fish, the gray mullet (used in punishing adulterers)
mūgiō, -īre, -īvī, -ītum: low, moo, bellow, roar
mūla, -ae, f.: a she mule
mulceō, mulcēre, mulsī, mulsum: caress
mulier, -is, f.: woman
multa, -ae, f.: penalty
multiplex, -plicis: having many twists and turns; varied
multivolus, -a, -um: promiscuous, lusting after many, amorous
multō, -āre: penalize
multum: adv., much
multus, -a, -um: much; a lot of, many a; (pl.) many
mūlus, -ī, m.: mule; metaph., a stupid person
munditiēs, ēī, f.: cleanliness
mundus¹, -a, -um, comp. **mundior**: clean
mundus², -ī, m.: heavens, sky, firmament; world, earth
mūniceps, -ipis, m.: citizen of a *municipium*; townsman
mūnus, -eris, n.: function, duty, task; gift; favor
mūnusculum, -ī, n.: a small gift or favor
Murcia, -ae, f.: a goddess, app. assoc. with sloth
mūrus, -ī, m.: city wall
musa, -ae, f.: a muse, divine patroness of poetry
muscōsus, -a, -um: mossy
mūtō, -āre: change; in pass., w/acc. of thing received in exchange & abl. of price paid, buy; exchange, take in exchange
mūtus, -a, -um: inarticulate, mute, dumb, silent
mūtuus, -a, -um: felt or shared by each of two in relation to each other, mutual, reciprocal; neut. pl. with adv. force, reciprocally, in equal measure
myrtus, -ī, f., nom. pl. **myrtūs**: the myrtle tree, a bushy shrub with oval leaves and fragrant white or rosy flowers, common to southern Europe
nam: explanatory particle, for; as encl., for lively or impatient emphasis, indicating the point of a line of questioning
namque: explanatory conj., for
nanciscor, -ciscī, nactus: acquire, get; contract (a disease)

narrō, -āre: give an account, tell; say
nascor, nascī, nātus: to be born; originate
Nāsō, -ōnis, m.: Roman cognomen in poem 112
nāsus, -ī, m.: nose
nāta, -ae, f.: daughter
nātiō, -ōnis, f.: people, race, nation
natis, -is, f.: buttock
natō, -āre: swim; float
nātus, -ī, m.: son; **nātī**: children, offspring, sons and daughters
naufragus, -ī, m.: a shipwrecked person
nauta, -ae, m.: sailor
nāvis, -is, f.: ship
nāvita, -ae, m.: = *nauta*, sailor
nē: neg. adv. & conj., introducing prohibitions, clauses of purpose, etc.: do not, let not, lest, in order that not, etc.
-ne: interr. particle suffix, introducing a question and attached to the emphatic word
nebula, -ae, f.: mist, cloud
nec: = *neque*, and not
necdum: conj., and not yet, but not yet
necesse: adv., essential, necessary
nefandus, -a, -um: unspeakable; wicked, unlawful, impious
nefārius, -a, -um: wicked, horrible
nefās, n. indecl.: sacrilege; wicked act, crime, horror
neglegens, -ntis, comp. **neglegentior, -ius**: careless
neglegō, -ere, -exī, -ectum: regard as of no consequence, be indifferent to, disregard, ignore, fail to respect
negō, -āre: deny, refuse, say that ... not
Nemesis, -eōs, f.: Greek goddess of retribution
nēmō, neminis, m.: nobody, no one
nemorivagus, -a, -um: forest wandering
nemus, -oris, n.: a wood, forest
nepōs, nepōtis, m.: grandson, descendant
Neptūnius, -a, -um: of or belonging to Neptune
Neptūnus, -ī, m.: Neptune or Poseidon, god of the sea; the sea
neque: conj., adv. and not; **neque ... neque**: neither ... nor
nequeō, -īre, -īvī or -iī: to be unable (to)
nēquīquam: adv., to no purpose, in vain
Nērēīnē, ēs, f.: a Nereid
Nērēïs, -idis: a Nereid, sea nymph born of Nereus and Doris
nervōsus, -a, -um: full of muscles, sinewy; vigorous
nesciō, -īre, -īvī or -iī, -ītum: not to know; **nescio quis, quid**: indef. pron. or adj., someone, some-

thing (N.B.: The personal ending of *nescio* scans as a short syllable.) **nescio quid** + part. gen.: some sort of.

neu: conj., and that ... not

nī, nisi: unless; **quid ni**: why not? of course

Nīcaea, -ae, f.: a city in Bithynia, mod. Iznik

niger, -gra, -grum, superl. **nigerrimus**: dark, black

nihil, nīl: indecl. n., nothing; w/adv. force, an emphatic form of *non*: not at all

nihilum, -ī, n.: nothing; abl., w/comparisons, by no degree, no

Nīlus, -ī, m.: the Nile River in Egypt

nīmīrum: part., no wonder, doubtless

nimis: adv., too much; very much

nimium: adv., too much, excessively

nimius, -a, -um: excessive

nisi: conj., unless, except if

nitens, -ntis, ppl. of *niteo*: shining, radiant

nītor¹, nītī, nīxus: lean; press onward; rely, depend

nitor², -ōris, m.: brightness, brilliance

niveus, -a, -um: snowy, white

nix, nivis, f.: snow

nō, nāre: swim; float, sail

nōbilis, -e: well-known, famous, illustrious

Noctifer, -erī, m.: the night bringer or evening star

nocturnus, -a, -um: of the night, night time

nōlō, nolle, noluī: be unwilling, not to wish; imp. **noli** + infin. = do not

nōmen, -inis, n.: name; a reason, pretext, or purpose

nōn: adv., not

nōndum: adv., not yet

Nōnius, -ī, m.: Roman official attacked in poem 52

nōnus, -a, -um: ninth

nōs: 1st pers. pron., we, us

noscitō, -āre: (freq. of *nosco*) recognize

noscō, -noscere, nōvī, nōtum (pf. forms with pres. force): know

noster, -tra, -trum, gen. pl. **nostrum**: poss. adj., our, (poet.) my

nota, -ae, f.: mark; quality, character

nōtescō, -escere, -uī: become known or famous

nothus, -a, -um: illegitimate; spurious, counterfeit

notō, -āre: mark, stain

nōtus, -a, -um: known, familiar; famous

notus, -ī, m.: friend, acquaintance

novem: indecl. num. adj., nine

noverca, -ae, f.: stepmother

novus, -a, -um: new; superl. **novissimus, -a, -um**: latest, last

nox, noctis, f.: night

nūbēs, -is, f.: cloud

nūbō, nūbere, nūpsi, nūptum: get married

nūdō, -āre: make naked, denude, bare

nūdus, -a, -um: bare, naked

nūgae, -ārum, f. pl.: trifles, things of no consequence

nullus, -a, -um: adj. & subst., not one, no, none; with adverbial force, not at all

num: interrogative particle, introducing questions where a negative answer is expected

nūmen, nūminis, n.: a nod; divine power

numerō, -āre: count

numerus, -ī, m.: number; verse, meter

nummus, -ī, m.: a coin; (pl.) cash

numquam: adv., never

nunc: adv., now

nuntiō, -āre: announce, communicate, tell

nuntium, -ī, n.: message, communication

nuntius, -ī, m.: messenger; message, pl. news

nūper: adv., recently

nupta, -ae, f.: wife; **nova nupta**: bride

nuptiālis, -e: of or pertaining to marriage or a wedding

nūtō, -āre: nod, sway; beat rhythmically

nūtriō, -īre, -īvī, -ītum: feed, nourish, nurture

nūtrix, -icis, f.: nurse; breast

nux, nucis, f.: nut

nympha, -ae, f.: a semidivine female nature spirit

Nȳsigena, -ae m. adj.: born on Mt. Nysa, birthplace of Bacchus/Dionysus

Ō: interjection, expressing grief, pleasure, indignation, or adjuration

Ōarion, -ōnis, m.: the constellation Orion

obdūrō, -āre: be persistent or obdurate

obeō, -īre, -īvī, -itum: meet, go into, take on

obēsus, -a, -um: fat

obitus, -ūs, m.: approach; death; setting (of a heavenly body)

obiurgō, -āre: rebuke, scold

oblectō, -āre: delight

oblītterō, -āre: cause to be forgotten, wipe out

oblīviscor, -viscī, oblītus: forget, w/gen. or acc. of object forgotten

obloquor, -loquī, -locūtus: interrupt

obscēnus, -a, -um: unpropitious, ill-omened; loathsome; indecent

obscūrō, -āre: darken

obscūrus, -a, -um: dark; unknown, secret

obserō, -āre: place a bar across (a door), bolt

obsideō, -sidēre, -sēdi, -sessum: occupy; besiege, beset obstinātus, -a, -um: stubborn, obstinate, resolute

obstō, -āre, -stitī, -stātum: (w/dat.) face; obstruct, hinder, impede

obsum, -esse, -fuī: be a hindrance, nuisance, disadvantage

obterō, -terere, -trīvī, -trītum: crush

obvius, -a, -um: in the way or path of something

occāsus, -ūs, m.: opportunity; setting (of a heavenly body)

occidens, -entis, m.: the region where the sun sets, the west

occīdō, -ere, occidī, occāsum: fall; (of heavenly bodies) set

occupō, -are: grasp; occupy; engross, preoccupy

Ōceanus, -ī, m.: Ocean, god of the sea, husband of Tethys

ocellus, -ī, m.: dim. of oculus, eye; as term of endearment, darling

octāvus, -a, -um: eighth

octo: indecl. adj., eight

oculus, -ī, m.: eye

ōdī, ōdisse, ōsum: hate; repudiate, have no patience for

odium, -ī, n.: hatred

odor, -ōris, m.: smell, odor, fragrance

Oetaeus, -a, -um: of Mt. Oeta in southern Thessaly, traditionally associated with the evening star and the hot springs of Thermopylae

offerō, offerre, obtulī, oblatum: put in one's path; provide, offer; cause

officium, -ī, n.: fulfillment of an obligation; service, duty; function, action

offirmō, -āre: make firm; get tough

olens, -ntis: having a smell; aromatic

oleum, -ī, n.: olive oil; by meton., wrestling, wrestling place

olfaciō, -facere, -fēcī, -factum: smell

ōlim: adv., formerly, once, once upon a time

olīva, -ae, f.: olive; olive tree

olīvum, -ī, n.: olive oil

olla, -ae, f.: pot, jar

olus, oleris, n.: vegetable

Olympus, -ī, m.: Greek mountain on borders of Thessaly and Macedonia, legendary home of the gods; by meton., the sky, the heavens

ōmen, -inis, n.: something that foreshadows an outcome or event

ōmentum, -ī, n.: the fatty membrane covering the intestines; peritoneum

omnīnō: adv., absolutely, altogether

omnipotens, -ntis: all-powerful

omnis, -e: adj., all, whole, entire

omnivolus, -a, -um: that desires all, all-desiring

onus, -eris, n.: burden, load

onyx, onychis, m.: a perfume jar of onyx

opācus, -a, -um: dark

opera, -ae, f.: activity, work, effort

operiō, -īre, -uī, opertum: shut, close; cover

oportet, -ēre, -uit: it is proper, right; it ought, should

oppidō: adv., utterly, altogether

oppleō, -plēre, -plēvī, -plētum: fill up

oppositus, -a, -um: situated in front of; opposite, facing; pledged, pawned, mortgaged

opprimō, -primere, -pressī, -pressus: press against; overwhelm

opprobrium, -ī, n.: shame, disgrace

ops, opis, f.: power; wealth; help

Ops, Opis, f.: a Roman goddess, wife of Saturn, mother of Jove

optātus, -a, -um, comp. optatior, -ius: (opto) wished for

optimus, -a, -um: (superl. of bonus) extremely good, the best

optingō, -tingere, -tigī: occur, fall to one's lot

optō, -āre: wish, choose, desire

opulentus, -a, -um: wealthy, opulent

opus, -eris, n.: that which needs to be done; work. opus est: there is need

ōra, -ae, f.: edge, border; region, district, land

ōrāc(u)lum, -ī, n.: oracle

ōrātiō, -onis, f.: speech

ōrātor, -ōris, m.: public speaker, courtroom advocate

orbis, orbis, m.: disk; sphere

orbus, -a, -um: bereaved, destitute

Orcus, -i, m.: Dis, god of the underworld; the underworld

orgia, -ōrum, n. pl.: secret rites, mysteries

ōricilla, -ae, f.: dim. of auris, a little ear

orīgō, -inis, f.: origin, beginning

orior, oriri, ortus: rise

ōrō, -āre: pray, beseech, supplicate

Ortalus, -ī, m.: cognomen of person addressed in poem 65, probably Q. Hortensius Hortalus.

ortus, -ūs, m.: rising (of a heavenly body)

ōs, ōris, n.: mouth; face, countenance

oscitō, -āre: yawn

osculātiō, -ōnis, f.: the action of kissing

osculum, -ī, n.: kiss

ostendō, -tendere, -tendī, -tensum: show, display; reveal

ostentō, -āre: freq. of °*ostendo*, exhibit, display conspicuously

ostium, -i, n.: door

Othō, -ōnis, m.: Roman cognomen in 54.1

ōtiōsus, -a, -um: full of *otium*, at leisure, idle

ōtium, -ī, n.: unoccupied spare time, leisure, rest, idleness

pācātus, -a, -um: peaceful, calm, tranquil

pācificō, -āre: placate, appease

Padua, -ae, f.: one of the mouths of the Padus (Po) River

paene: adv., almost; adj. w/*insula*, peninsula

paeniteō, -ēre, -uī: cause dissatisfaction or regret (impers. const. w/acc. of person affected & gen. of cause)

palaestra, -ae, f.: a wrestling place, usu. a wrestling floor with adjacent changing rooms, etc.

palam: adv., openly

palātum, -ī, n.: roof of the mouth, palate; by meton., the mouth (as the organ of speech)

palimpsestum. -ī, n.: a palimpsest, papyrus recycled by erasure to make a low-cost writing material

pallidus, -a, -um, comp. **pallidior**, dim. **pallidulus**: pale

pallium, -iī, n.: a rectangular cloth worn as an outer garment, Gk. *himation*

palma, -ae, f.: the front of the hand; the palm or palm leaf; the palm of victory; an oar

palmula, -ae, f.: the palm of the hand; oar; palm tree or leaf

palūs, -ūdis, f.: swamp

pandō, -ere, pansum: spread out, disclose, reveal; open

pangō, pangere, pepigī, pactum: fix in place, settle, arrange

pānis, -is, m.: bread

papāver, -ris, n.: poppy

papilla, -ae, f.: nipple; breast

papȳrus, -ī, f.: an Egyptian reed used in making paper; paper made from the papyris reed

pār, paris: equal, comparable; fitting

parātus, -a, -um: ready, prepared

Parca, -ae, f.: a Roman goddess of birth; one of the Fates or Moirai

parcō, parcere, pepercī: act sparingly, refrain from, show restraint

parcus, -a, -um: thrifty, frugal; skinny, lean

parens, -entis, m. or f.: parent

pāreō, -ēre, -uī, -itum: submit, be obedient

pariō, parere, peperī, partum: give birth to; produce

Paris, -idis, m.: Paris, son of Priam, seducer of Helen

pariter: adv., equally

Parnāsus, -ī, m.: Parnassus, the mountain near Delphi

parō, -āre: furnish, supply; obtain; **paratum habere** + infin.: to be ready to

pars, partis, f.: part; some; standpoint, side

parthenicē, -ēs, f.: a flower, perh. the white camomile

Parthī, -ōrum, m. pl.: Parthians, members of an Iranian tribe south of the Caspian Sea

particeps, -cipis, m.: participant, sharer

parum: adv., too little

parvus, -a, -um dim. **parvulus**: little

Pāsithea, -ae, f.: one of the three Graces, wife of Somnus

passer, -eris, m.: sparrow or blue rock-thrush, a common domestic pet in Italy

passim: adv., dispersedly, all over the place

patefaciō, -facere, -fēcī, -factum: make open, open up

pateō, -ēre, patuī: be open; show as entered (in accounts)

pater, -tris, m.: father

paternus, -a, -um: of a father; paternal

pathicus, -ī, m.: a pathic or catamite, one who submits to anal sex

patior, patī, passus: undergo, suffer, be subjected to; bear, put up with, tolerate, let, allow

patria, ae, f.: fatherland

patrimōnium, -ī, n.: estate, fortune

patrist: abbr. for *patri est*

patrius, -a, -um: of one's father or fathers; paternal, ancestral

patrōnus, -ī, m. or patrōna, -ae, f.: patron or patroness, guardian, protector, supporter, sponsor

patruus, -ī, m.: paternal uncle

paucī, -ae, -a: a few

paulum[1], -ī, n.: a little bit

paulum[2]: adv., for a little while

pax, pācis, f.: peace; *pace tua*: by your leave

peccātum, -ī, n.: error, mistake, offense

peccō, -āre: err; do wrong

pectus, pectoris, n.: breast, chest; soul, heart, mind

pecus, -oris, n.: livestock, cattle

pēdīcō, -āre: sodomize, bugger, or inflict anal sex upon a person (sts. as a way of humiliating him)

pēditum, -ī, n.: a fart

Pēgaseus, -a, -um: of the winged horse Pegasus

pēierō, -āre: swear falsely, perjure oneself

pelagus, -ī, n.: the sea
Pēleus¹ (disyllabic), **-eī,** acc. **Pēlea,** voc. **Pēleu:** son of Aeacus, mortal spouse of Thetis, father of Achilles
Pēlēus², -a, -um: of Peleus; of Mt. Pelion
Pēliacus, -a, -um: of Mt. Pelion, in Thessaly
pellis, -is, f.: pelt, skin, hide, fleece
pellō, pellere, pepulī, pulsum: push; strike, beat; drive, drive off
Pelops, -opis, m.: son of Tantalus, father of Atreus and Thyestes
penātēs, -ium, m.: household gods, the tutelary gods of the Roman pantry
pendeō, -ēre, pependī: hang; depend, rely
Pēnelopēus, -a, -um: descended from Penelope
penetrālis, -e: situated at the inside of a house; innermost
penetrō, -āre: w/*in* + acc., make one's way into, penetrate
Pēnīos, -īī, m.: river that flows through the vale of Tempe in Thessaly, and its eponymous river-god
pēnis, -is, m.: tail; penis
penitē: (*=penitus*) adv., deep down inside, secretly
penitus: adv., from within; far away; deeply
penna, -ae, f.: wing
per: prep., through, along
peraequē: adv., uniformly, equally
perambulō, -āre: walk around in; make a tour of
percellō, -cellere, -culī, -culsum: strike down, kill
percurrō, -currere, -cucurrī, -cursum: run through quickly
perdepsō, -depsere, -depsuī, -deptum: knead thoroughly; (metaph.) screw, have sex with
perditē: adv., to distraction, to a ruinously excessive degree
perditus, -a, -um, comp. **perditior, -ius:** ruined; depraved
perdō, -ere, -didī, -ditum: ruin, spoil
perdūcō, -ducere, -duxī, -ductum: conduct
peregrīnus, -a, -um: foreign
perennis, -e: constant, enduring
pereō, -īre, -iī, -itum: vanish; be done in, perish, die; (hyperb.) suffer, be in big trouble
perēsus, -a, -um (*peredo*): eaten up, worn away, wasted
perferō, -ferre, -tulī, -latum: carry on, endure
perfidia, -ae, f.: treachery, lying, perfidy
perfidus, -a, -um: treacherous, perfidious
perfundō, -fundere, -fūdī, -fūsum: pour through, drench, suffuse, imbue
pergō, pergere, perrexī, perrectum: proceed

perhibeō, -ēre, -hibuī, -hibitum: present, bestow; say, hold, maintain, give out
perīculum, -i, n.: a test; danger, peril
periūrium, -ī, n.: a breach of oath, false oath, perjury
periūrus, -a, -um: oath breaking, perjured, treacherous
perlūceō, -ēre: transmit or emit light; shine
perlūcidulus, -a, -um: transparent, translucent
permisceō, -miscēre, -miscuī, -mixtum: blend thoroughly, mix up
permulceō, -mulcēre, -mulsī, -mulsum: caress, soothe, refresh
perniciēs, -ēī, f.: ruin, bane
perniciter: nimbly, with quick motion of the legs
pernix, -īcis: leggy, long-legged
pernumerō, -āre: fully enumerate, count out
perpetior, -petī, -pessus: undergo; allow
perpetuus, -a, -um: continual, everlasting, perpetual; **in perpetuum,** in perpetuity, forever
Persa, -ae, m.: a Persian or Parthian
persaepe: adv., very often
perscrībō, -ere, -scripsī, -scriptum: write out in full, finish writing
persequor, -sequī, -secūtus: follow persistently, catch up with, pursue, harass, seek requital or restitution
Perseus, -eī, m.: son of Zeus and Danaë, hero who killed the Gorgon and rescued Andromeda
Persicus, -a, -um: Persian
persolvō, -ere, -solvī, -solūtum: pay
perspectus, -a, -um: known from experience, proven
perspiciō, -spicere, -spexī, -spectum: inspect thoroughly; discern, recognize
pertundō, -tundere, -tudī, -tūsum: beat or bore a hole through, perforate
perūrō, -ūrere, -ussī, -ustum: burn up
perveniō, -venīre, -vēnī, -ventum: come
pervigilō, -āre: stay awake all night
pervincō, -vincere, -vīcī, -victum: prevail over, overcome
pervolvō, -volvere: go on unwinding (a book scroll)
pēs, pedis, m.: foot; (poet.) a metrical foot; (naut.) the line or sheet by which each of the two lower corners of a square sail is made fast to the ship
pessimus, -a, -um: superl. of *malus,* extremely bad, worst
pestilens, -entis: unhealthy, noxious, pernicious
pestilentia, -ae, f.: plague, pestilence
pestis, -is, f.: physical destruction; plague, affliction,

bane

petītor, -ōris, m.: one who tries to obtain something; a candidate for office

petō, petere, petīvī, petītum: seek

Phaëthōn, -ontis, m.: son of the sun-god Helios, who lost control of his father's chariot

Pharsālius, -a, -um: of or at Pharsalus

Pharsālus, -ī, f.: town in south central Thessaly, near which Caesar defeated Pompey in 48 B.C.

phasēlus, -ī, m.: a light ship, so-called because of its resemblance to a green bean

Phāsis, -idos, m.: a river in Colchis, flowing into the eastern end of the Black Sea; city at the mouth of the Phasis R.; by meton., Colchis

Pheneus, -ī, m.: town in northern Arcadia with underground channels

Phoebus, -ī, m.: Phoebus Apollo, twin brother of Diana

Phrygius, -a, -um: of Phrygia, Phrygian

Phryx, Phrygis: Phrygian

pietās, -tātis, f.: dutiful respect

piger, -gra, -grum: sluggish, torpid, lazy

pignus, -oris, n.: anything given as security or risked in a bet: pledge, stake

pīla, -ae, f.: pillar, column

pilleātus, -a, -um: wearing a felt cap (*pilleus*)

pilōsus, -a, -um: hairy, shaggy

pilus, -ī, m.: a hair; something of no value or significance

pīneus, -a, -um: of pinewood

pinguis, -e: fat, rich

pinnipēs, -pedis: wing-footed, with winged feet

pīnus, ūs, f.: pine tree

pīpiō, -āre: chirp

Piplēius, -a, -um: of Pi(m)pla, a place or spring in Pieria associated with the muses

Pīraeus, -ī, m.: the Piraeus, port of Athens

Pisaurum, -ī, n.: an Umbrian town on the Adriatic coast, mod. Pesaro

piscis, -is, m.: fish

Pīsō, -ōnis, m.: cognomen of the Gens Calpurnia. See appendix A

pistrīnum, -ī, n.: mill

pītuīta, -ae, f.: mucus, phlegm

pius, -a, -um, superl. **piissimus**: dutiful, conscientious, upright

placeō, -ēre, -uī or **-itus**: be pleasing to

placidus, -a, -um: quiet, peaceful

plācō, -āre: cause to be favorably disposed, conciliate, appease

plangō, -ere, -xī, -ctum: beat, strike

plangor, -ōris, m.: a beating or slapping action

planta, -ae, f.: sole of the foot

platanus, -ī, f.: plane tree

platea, -ae, f.: street

plectō, plectere, plexī, plexum: plait, twine

plēnus, -a, -um: full

ploxenum, -ī, n.: the body of a carriage

plumbum, -ī, n.: lead, used for drawing lines

plūmipēs, -pedis: having feathers on the feet

plūrimī, -ae, -a: superl. of *plus*, the greatest number of, a very great number of

plūrimum: adv., superl. of **plus**

plūs, plūris, n.: more

plūs, plūris: adj. & adv., more

pōculum, -ī, n.: cup

podagra, -ae, f.: gout, a painful inflammation of the joints of the foot

poēma, -atis, n.: poem

poena, -ae, f.: penalty

poēta, -ae, m.: poet

poliō, -īre, -īvī, -ītum: polish

pollex, -icis, m.: thumb

polliceor, -ērī, -pollicitus: offer, promise

Polliō, -ōnis, m.: a Roman cognomen, e.g., of C. Asinius Pollio; see appendix A

polluō, -uere, -uī, -ūtum: stain, soil, make ritually impure

Pollux, -ūcis, m.: son of Tyndarus and Leda, brother of Castor and fellow-patron of sailors

Polyxenius, -a, -um: of Polyxena, Priam's daughter, sacrificed at Troy to appease the shade of Achilles

Pompēius, -a, -um: Roman *nomen gentile*, e.g., of Cn. Pompeius Magnus, Caesar's chief rival for power until his death in 48 B.C.

pondus, -eris, n.: weight

pōnō, pōnere, posuī, positum: put, place; provide

pons, pontis, m., dim. **ponticulus**: bridge

Ponticus, -a, -um: of or on the Black Sea

pontus, -ī, m.: sea

poples, poplitis, m.: the knee

populus, -ī, m.: the people; the public, people in general; populace

Porcius, -a, -um: name of a Roman *gens*; see appendix A

porrigō, -rigere, -rexī, -rectum: stretch out

porrō: adv., straight on; hereafter

porta, -ae, f.: city gate; place of entry or exit

portō, -āre: carry

portus, -ūs, m.: harbor, port

poscō, poscere, poposcī: demand (esp. money)

possideō, -sidēre, -sēdī, -sessum: have (land) in one's control; hold as property

possum, posse, potuī: to be able

post: prep. w/acc, adv. behind; later, afterward

posthāc: hereafter

postillā: adv., afterwards, after that time

postmodo: adv., later

postquam: conj., after

postrēmus, -a, -um: final

postulō, -āre: demand; claim, assert

Postumius, -a, -um: name of a Roman *gens*

pote: see *potis*

potens, -entis: powerful

potior, potīrī, potitus: get possession of

potis or pote: indecl. adj., having the power, able; possible. Catullus uses *potis* with *est* or *sit*; with *pote* the verb must be supplied.

potius: adv., more, more than, rather

prae: prep. w/ abl., before, in front of; in comparison with

praeceps, -cipitis: plunging headfirst; headlong; sudden

praeceptum, -ī, n.: advice, precept; instruction, order

praecerpō, -ere, -cerpsī, -cerptum: cull or reap ahead

praecingō, -ere, -cinxī, -cinctum: encircle, stand around

praecipuē: adv., peculiarly, especially

praecō, -ōnis, m.: crier; auctioneer

praecurrō, -currere, -currī, -cursum: run ahead of or past

praeda, -ae, f.: booty, prey

praedicō, -āre: proclaim, declare, announce

praefor, -fārī, -fātus: say by way of preface

praegestiō, -īre: have an overpowering desire, be especially eager for

praemium, -ī, n.: payment, offering, prize, reward

praeoptō, -āre: prefer, choose in preference

praepōnō, -pōnere, -posuī, -positum: place if front; give preference to

praeportō, -āre: carry before one, carry in front

praeruptus, -a, -um: broken off into a cliff, steep

praesens, -ntis: face to face, in person, present

praesertim: especially, particularly

praeses, -idis, m.: guardian

praestō: adv., available, ready

praeter: prep., adv., conj., beyond

praintereā: adv., besides, moreover

praetereō, -īre, -īvī, -itum, pres. pple. *-iens, -euntis*: go beyond, pass

praeterquam: conj., except as; beyond, except

praetextātus, -i, m.: a boy wearing the child's bordered toga

praetor, -ōris, m.: commander; magistrate, governor

praetrepidō, -āre: tremble in anticipation

praevertō, -vertere, -vertī, -versum: outstrip, outrun

prandeo, prandēre, prandī, pransum: (pf. pple. in active sense) eat one's morning or midday meal, to lunch

prātum, -ī, n.: meadow

precor, -ārī: ask for, beg; implore

premō, premere, pressī, pressum: press, weigh down

prendō, prendere, prendī, prensum (prehendo): take hold of; accost

pretium, -ī, n.: price; cost

prex, precis, f.: prayer, entreaty

Priāpus, -ī, m.: phallic fertility god, used in gardens to keep off birds and thieves

prīmaevus, -a, -um: youthful

prīmōres, -ium, m. pl.: chiefs, captains, leading men

prīmum: adv., first, for the first time; quam prīmum: as soon as possible

prīmus, -a, -um: first; the tip of

princeps, -cipis: first, earliest

principiō: adv., first of all

prior, -ius: former

priscus, -a, -um: ancient, olden, old-fashioned, archaic

pristinus, -a, -um: ancient; previous

prius: adv., before, earlier

prō: prep. w/ abl., in front of; on behalf of; in return for; in the capacity of

probē: well

probrum, -ī, n.: disgrace, scandal

probus, -a, -um: good, virtuous

procax, -ācis: importunate, impudent, licentious

prōcēdō, -cēdere, -cessī, -cessum: move forward

procella, -ae, f.: storm, gale

prōcērus, -a, -um: tall, long

prōclīvus, -a, -um: downward sloping, (of whitecaps at sea) tumbling forward or down

prōcreō, -āre: procreate, engender, beget

procul: adv., far off; to a great distance

prōcumbō, -cumbere, -cubuī, -cubitum: bend or fall forward

prōcurrō, -currere, -currī, -sursum: run forward; roll forth

prōdeō, -īre, -iī, -itum: come or go forward; advance

prōdō, prodere, prodidī, proditum: thrust out; give up, abandon, betray

proelium, -ī, n.: battle (sing. & pl.)

profānus, -a, -um: not dedicated to religious use; not initiated into a cult

prōferō, -ferre, -tulī, -lātum: bring forth; utter

prōficiō, -ficere, -fēcī, -fectum: make headway, gain results

proficiscor, proficiscī, profectus: set out, proceed

profundō, -fundere, -fūdī, -fusum: pour forth

profundus, -a, -um: deep, bottomless

prōgeniēs, -ēī, f.: offspring, progeny

prognātus, -a, -um: born, produced

prōiciō, -ere, -iēcī, -iectum: fling forth, throw forward; renounce

Promētheus, -ei, m.: the Titan who stole fire for mankind and warned Zeus not to have a child by Thetis

prōmissum, -ī, n.: a promise, assurance

prōmittō, -mittere, -mīsī, -missum: send forth; undertake, promise, guarantee

prōnus, -a, -um: leaning forward, angling or sloping toward the ground; sloping; face down, prone; flat

prope: adv. & prep. w/acc., near

properipēs, -pedis: swift footed

properō, -āre: hurry

propinquus, -i, m.: neighbor; kinsman, relative

prōpōnō, -pōnere, -posuō, -positum: expose to view, set forth, offer, propound, propose

Propontis, -idis, f.: the Propontis or Sea of Marmora, between the Black Sea and the Aegean

propriē: properly; particularly, especially; in the strictest or truest sense

propter: adv. & prep. w/acc., near

proscindō, -scindere, -scidī, -scissum: plow

prōsequor, -sequī, -secūtus: escort; chase after

prōsiliō, -īre, -uī: rush forth; jump up suddenly

prospectō, -āre: gaze out

prospectus, -ūs, m.: view, prospect

prosperus, -a, -um: agreeable to one's wishes, prosperous

prospiciō, -spicere, -spexī, -spectum: look forth or out

prosternō, -sternere, -strāvī, -strātum: lay low, strike down

prostituō, -stituere, -stituī, -stitūtum: to prostitute

prōsum, -desse, -fuī: to be of use, help, or profit

prōtēlum, -ī, n.: a team of draft animals such as oxen

prōtendō, -ere, -tendī, -tentum: stretch out; extend forward over a distance

Prōtesilāēus, -a, -um: of or belonging to Protesilaus

prōvincia, -ae, f.: province, a unit of Roman colonial administration, e.g., Bithynia

proximus, -a, -um: nearest

prūriō, -īre: itch, tingle; have a sexual craving, be sexually excited

-pte: emphatic particle

Pthīōticus, -a, -um: in or of Phthiotis, in southern Thessaly

pūbēs, pūbis, f.: the adult male population; manpower

pudens, -ntis: proper, decent, modest

pudenter: adv., properly, decently, modestly

pudeō, -ēre, -uī: to make ashamed, cause embarrassment

pudīcē: adv., decently, in a chaste manner

pudīcitia, -ae, f.: chastity, sexual fidelity

pudīcus, -a, -um: chaste, decent, sexually modest

pudor, -ōris, m.: a sense of shame; decency, modesty

puella, -ae, f.: girl; young woman; girlfriend

puellula, -ae, f.: dim. of *puella*, little girl; by extension, a maiden of marriageable age

puer, puerī, m.: boy; colloq., of a friend; slave;

puerpera, -ae, f.: a woman in childbirth

puerperium, -ī, n.: birth of a child; delivery

pugillāria, -ium, n. pl.: a set of writing tablets

pugnō, -āre: fight

pulcer, -cra, -crum, comp. pulcrior, -ius, sup. pulcerrimus, -a, -um: beautiful, handsome, lovely

pulcrē: beautifully, handsomely

pulvīnar, -āris, n.: a couch on which images of gods were placed at a banquet offered to the gods

pulvīnus, -ī, m.: cushion, pillow

pulvis, -veris, m.: dust; sand

pūmex, -icis, m. or f.: pumice or any similar volcanic rock, used to smooth the ends of book-rolls

puppis, -is, f.: the stern or poop of a boat; by meton., boat, ship

pūpula, -ae, f.: a little girl; the pupil of the eye

pūpulus, -ī, m.: a little boy

purgō, -āre: clean, clear out; (refl.) apologize, excuse

pūriter: in a pure manner

purpura, -ae, f.: a shellfish yielding a purple dye; purple dye; any purple-dyed cloth

purpureus, -a, -um: purple

pūrus, -a, -um, comp. pūrior: clean, pure; plain, unembellished

pusillus, -a, -um: puny

pūtidus, -a, -um: rotten; foul, stinking

putō, -āre: think

putridus, -a, -um: rotten, decaying, withered

quā: indef. adv. w/*lubet*, in whatever way; wherever

quācumque: adv., wherever

quadrāgintā: indecl. num. adj., forty

quadrivium, -iī, n.: a crossroads

quaerō, -ere, quaesīvī, quaesītum, iterat. **quaeritō, -āre**: ask, ask for, seek

quaesō, -ere: ask, pray, request; w/imper., please

quālis, -e: (interr) of what kind; (rel.) such as

quāliscumque, quālecumque: rel. adj., of whatever sort or quality; (in depreciatory sense) such as it is, for whatever it is worth

quālubet: adv., by any means at all; somehow or other

quam: interr. & rel. adv., to which extent or degree; how; as, than

quamquam: rel. adv., although

quamvīs: rel. adv., to any degree you like, as much as can be; concessive w/subjunctive, even though

quandō: indef. adv. following *si*, at any time

quandōquidem (2nd syll. short in dactylic verse): rel. adv., since

quantum, -ī, n.: indef. pron., whatever amount (with *est* + part. gen.) of all that exist

quantum: rel. adv., as much as

quantus, -a, -um: interr. or rel. adj., how much, how great, pl. how many

quantusvīs, quantavīs, quantumvīs: as much or as many as you could wish

quārē (from abl. *quā rē*): interr. & rel. adv., how? for what reason? on account of which thing; wherefore, therefore

quasi: conj. with subjunctive., as if

quassō, -āre (iterat. of *quatio*): shake repeatedly

quassus, -a, -um (pple. of *quatio*): shaken, battered

quatiō, quatere, quassum: shake

-que: enclitic conj., and

queō, quīre, quīvī: to be able

quercus, -ūs, f.: an oak tree

querella, -ae, f.: complaint, protest, lament

queror, querī, questus: complain, protest

questus, -ūs, m.: complaint, protest

quī, quae, quod: rel. pron. & adj., who, which; indef. adj./pron. after *si*, any

quī: interr. adv., how? how so?

quia: because

quicque: see *quisque*

quicum = *cum quo*

quīcumque, quaecumque, quodcumque: indef. rel. pron., whoever, whatever

quīdam, quaedam, quoddam: a particular –, a certain

quīdem: part., certainly, indeed

quiēs, -ētis, f.: sleep, repose

quīlubet, quaelubet, quidlubet: whoever or whatever you please; anyone, anything

quīn: adv., why not; conj., (w/expr. of no objection) that not; so as to prevent; (w/expr. of no doubt) that, but that

quindecim: indecl. adj., fifteen

quingentī, -ae, -a: five hundred

Quintilius, -a, -um: Roman *nomen gentile*, e.g., of Calvus' wife or mistress in poem 96

Quintius, -a, -um: Roman *nomen gentile*; see appendix A

quis, quid, interr. and indef. pronoun: who? what? anyone, anything

quisnam, quaenam, quidnam: pron. & adj., who/what, tell me?, who/what, finally

quisquam, quicquam: indef. pron., anyone, anything

quisque, quaeque, quidque or **quicque**: each one

quisquis, quidquid or **quicquid**: interr. or indef. pron., whoever, whatever

quīvīs, quaevīs, quidvīs: whoever or whatever you wish; anyone, anything

quō: adv., to which place, whither

quod: rel. adv., conj., with regard to the fact that; because

quondam: adv., once, formerly

quoniam: conj., as soon as, after; because, since

quoque: also

quot: indecl. adj., how many, as many

quotiens: rel. adv., as often as, whenever; **quotiens ... totiens**: as often as ... so often.

quotquot: indecl. adj., whatever number, as many as

rabidus, -a, -um: raging, ravening, frenzied, violent

rabiēs, -ēī, f.: savageness, ferocity; uncontrolled emotion, frenzy

rādīcitus: adv., by, from, or at the roots; roots and all

radiō, -āre: radiate light, beam, shine

rādix, -īcis, f.: root

Ramnūsius, -a, -um: of or native to Ramnus, a district of Attica (epithet of Nemesis, the *Ramnusia virgo*)

rāmus, -ī, m., dim. **rāmulus**: branch, twig

rapax, -ācis: predatory, rapacious

raphanus, -ī, f.: radish

rapidus, -a, -um: strongly flowing, swiftly moving, rapid; scorching, consuming

rapīna, -ae, f.: plunder

rapiō, -ere, -uī, raptum: seize and carry off

raptus, -ūs, m.: robbery, plunder; abduction

rārus, -a, -um: loosely woven; uncommon, rare; exquisite

rāsilis, -e: worn smooth, polished

rastrum, -i, n.: a type of hoe

ratiō, -ōnis, f.: account, reason; exercise of faculty of reason; business, matter, affair; method, means

ratis, -is, f.: raft; boat, ship

raucisonus, -a, -um: harsh-sounding

Rāvidus, -ī, m.: cognomen of a rival of Catullus; see appendix A

reboō, -āre: resound, re-echo

recēdō, -cēdere, -cessī, -cessum: draw back; extend backward, recede

recens, -entis: recent, fresh

recepso: see *recipio* and note to 44.19

recipiō, -cipere, -cēpī, -ceptum: receive, take in

reclūdō, -cludere, -clūsī, -clūsum: open; uncover, lay bare

recoctus, -a, -um: warmed-over, rehashed

recolō, -ere, -uī, -cultum: reoccupy; go over in one's mind

reconditus, -a, -um: hidden away, secluded

recordor, -ārī: call to mind, remember

recrepō, -āre: ring or sound in answer

rector, -ōris, m.: steersman, ruler

rectus, -a, -um: straight, erect, straight-limbed

recumbō, -cumbere, -cubuī: recline; settle

recūrō, -āre: restore

reddō, -ere, reddidī, redditum: give back, restore; repay (a debt, obligation, or vow); pay (honor, tribute, etc.); render, turn something or someone into

redeō, -īre, -iī, -itum: return

redimiō, -īre, -iī, -ītum: wreathe, encircle

reditus, -ūs, m.: return

redivīvus, -a, -um: reused, second-hand

redūcō, -ducere, -duxī, -ductum: bring back

redux, reducis: brought back, returned, restored

referō, -ferre, -tulī, -lātum: bring back; report; (reflexive) return; w/*in* + abl., write down; w/acc. & dat., put something down to, assign to a category

reficiō, -ficere, -fēcī, -fectum: restore

reflāgitō, -āre: demand repeatedly in a loud voice

reflectō, -flectere, -flexī, -flexum: bend back

refringō, -fringere, -frēgī, -fractum: break

refulgeō, -gēre, -fulsī: shine, gleam

rēgālis, -is: kingly, royal, regal

rēgia, -ae, f.: palace

rēgīna, -ae, f.: queen

rēgius, -a, -um: royal; princely, splendid; *carta regia*, a large size of paper

reglūtinō, -āre: unglue, unstick

regō, regere, rexī, rectum: direct, manage, guide, control

rēiciō, -icere, -iēcī, -iectum: throw back

relego, -āre: banish, remove from the scene

religiō, -ōnis, f.: religious scruple, taboo, or impediment; religious observance

religō, -āre: tie back, tie up; untie

relinquō, -linquere. -līquī, -lictum: quit, leave, forsake

rēmigium, -ī, n.: the action of rowing

remittō, -mittere, -mīsī, missum: send back, return

remoror, -ārī: wait, linger, dally

remōtus, -a, -um: removed, remote, distant

remūgiō, -īre: boom or bellow in reply

remūneror, -ārī: repay

rēmus, -ī, m.: oar

Remus, -ī, m.: brother of Romulus, legendary founder of Rome; see appendix A, Romulus

renīdeō, -ēre: shine; smile back, beam

renovō, -āre: renew, restore

reor, rērī, ratus: believe, think, imagine

repente: suddenly, immediately

reperiō, -īre, repperī, repertum: find, discover

repōnō, -pōnere, -posuī, positum: put back; put to rest

reportō, -āre: carry back, return

reposcō, -ere: demand back; claim as one's right, demand

requiescō, -quiescere, -quiēvī, -quiētum: rest, find relief

requīrō, -quirere, -quisīvī, -quisītum: try to find, seek, look for, ask about; need, miss

rēs, reī, f.: property, wealth; thing, matter

resideō, -sidēre, -sēdī: remain seated; persist

resīdō, -sidere, -sēdī: sit down, take a position

resolvō, -solvere, -solvī, -solūtum: loosen, undo

resonō, -āre: echo, resound

respectō, -āre: to keep on looking back at; wait expectantly for, count on

respergō, -spergere, -spersī, -spersum: sprinkle, spatter, splash

respondeō, -ēre, -dī, -sum: answer, reply

restituō, -stituere, -stituī, -stitūtum: rebuild; restore, cure; give back unharmed or in its original state

restringō, -stringere, -strinxī, -strictum: tie back, restrain with bonds

reticeō, -ēre, -uī: refrain from speaking, keep silent

retineō, ēre, -tinuī, -tentum: hold fast; keep

retonō, -āre: resound, reverberate

retrahō, -trahere, -traxī, -tractum: drag backwards; withdraw

reus, -ī, m.: a defendant in a trial

revertor, -vertī, -versus: return, come back

revinciō, -vincīre, -vinxī, -vinctum: hold down, attach, bind

revīsō, -visere: pay another visit; go back and see, return to

revocō, -āre: call back

rex, rēgis, m.: king

Rhēnus, -ī, m.: the river Rhine, often regarded as forming the border between Gaul and Germany

Rhēsus, -ī, m.: Thracian king, brother of Hecuba, ally of Priam in Trojan War killed by Diomedes and Ulysses

Rhodus, -ī, f.: the island of Rhodes

Rhoetēus, -a, -um: of Rhoeteum, city on the Hellespont near Troy

rictus, -ūs, m.: an open mouth

rīdeō, rīdēre, rīsī, rīsum: laugh

rīdiculus, -a, -um: funny

rigida, -ae, f.: the erect penis

rīsus, -ūs, m.: laugh

rīte: adv., properly, duly

rīvālis, -is, m.: orig. one who shares the use of a stream (*rivus*); a rival, esp. in love

rīvus, -ī, m.: stream

rixa, -ae, f.: quarrel, brawl

rōbur, roboris, n.: an oak tree, oak; the strongest element of anything

rōbustus, -a, -um: strong

rogō, -āre: ask, ask for

rogus, -ī, m.: funeral pyre

Rōma, -ae, f.: the city of Rome

Rōmulus, -ī, m.: eponymous founder of Rome; see appendix A

roscidus, -a, -um: dewy

roseus, -a, -um: rosy, red

rostrum, -ī, n.: the snout or muzzle of an animal; the beak of a bird or ship

rubeō, -ēre: to be or become red

ruber, -bra, -brum: red

rūbīgō, -inis, f.: rust; blight

rubor, -ōris, m.: redness, blush

rudens, -ntis, m.: rope, line

rudis, -e: still in its natural state; inexperienced, untried

Rūfa, -ae, f.: woman's cognomen in poem 59

Rūfulus, -ī, m.: dim. of *Rufus*; man's cognomen in poem 59

Rūfus, -ī, m.: man's cognomen in poems 69 and 77; see appendix A

ruīna, -ae, f.: uncontrollable forward movement; collapse, ruin

rūmor, -ōris, m.: rumor, gossip

rumpō, -ere, rūpī, ruptum: break, rupture, split, burst

ruō, ruere, ruī: rush

rūpēs, -is, f.: cliff, crag

rursus, rursum or **rūsum:** adv., back again; contrariwise

rūs, rūris, n.: country, boondocks

russus, -a, -um: red

rusticus, -a, -um: rustic; of the country, rural

rutilus, -a, -um: reddish, ruddy (inclining to gold or orange)

Sabīnus, -a, -um: from the Sabine country northeast of Rome

sacculus, -ī, m.: purse

sacer, sacra, sacrum: sacred, holy; accursed, detestable

sacrātus, -a, -um: sacred, holy

sacrō, -āre: consecrate; bind with an oath

sacrum, -ī, n.: a sacred object or observance, rite

saeclum, -ī, n.: a generation

saepe: adv., often

saepiō, -īre, saepsī, saeptum: enclose; surround with a wall or hedge

Saetabus, -a, -um: of or made in Saetabis, a town in Hispania Tarraconensis (cf. mod. Tarragona)

saevitia, -ae, f.: savagery, cruelty; violence, ferocity

saevus, -a, -um: fierce, savage

Sagae, -ārum, m. pl.: the Sacae, a Scythian people living east of Bactriana and Sogdiana

sagitta, -ae, f.: arrow

sagittifer, -era, -erum: arrow-bearing

sāl, salis, m.: salt; fig., of a quality that gives character and flavor, wit; meton., the sea

salapūtium, -ī, m.: unknown epithet said to refer to a person of short stature; perh. derived from *salio*, to mount or cover sexually (of male animals; OLD 4)

salax, -ācis: oversexed; lascivious (see *salio*)

salillum, -ī, n.: (dim. of *salinum*) a little saltcellar

saliō, -īre, saluī, saltum: jump, leap; mount for

sexual intercourse

Salisubsalus, -i, m.: a cult title, perhaps of Mars

salīva, -ae, f.: saliva, spit

salsus, -a, -um: salty, briny; witty, clever

saltem: adv., at least, anyhow

saltus, -ūs, m.: rough woodland broken with glades; a large country estate

salum, -ī, n.: swell, billow; the sea

salūs, salūtis, f.: safety, well-being

salvē, salvēte: greetings! hail!

sanctus, -a, -um: holy, sacred, inviolate

sānē: surely, decidedly

sanguis, -inis, m.: blood

sānus, -a, -um: healthy; sane; sober

sapiō, sapere, sapīvī: have a taste; have taste, sense, discernment

Sapphicus, -a, -um: of Sappho, the 7-6th cent. lyric poet

sarcinula, -ae, f.: a light knapsack

sat: adv., enough

satiō, -āre: satisfy

satis: indecl. adv., enough

Satrachus, -ī, m.: river in Cyprus, connected with the legend of Smyrna's son Adonis

satur, satura, saturum: well-fed; full

Sāturnālia, -ium, n. pl.: the festival of Saturn, beginning Dec. 17, a period of merriment and license

saturō, -āre: fill, satisfy, sate

Satyrus, -ī, m.: a Satyr, demigod of wild places, frequent companion of Bacchus/Dionysus

saucius, -a, -um: wounded, afflicted

saxeus, -a, -um: made of stone

saxum, -ī, n.: stone, rock

scaber, -ra, -rum: rough, scabrous from disease, scabbed

scabiēs, -ēī, f.: mange, scab (as term of abuse)

Scamander, -drī, m.: one of the two rivers of Troy

scandō, scandere: mount, climb, ascend

scelerō, -āre: stain or defile with wicked acts

scelestus, -a, -um: lying under a curse; (applied pityingly) wretched; wicked

scelus, -eris, n.: crime, iniquity; a wicked act

scīlicet (*scire licet*): clearly, evidently, no doubt

scindō, scindere, scicidī, scissum: split

sciō, scīre, sciī, scītum: know

scītus, -a, -um, comp. **scītior, -ius**: well-informed; clever, knowing, having *savoir-faire*

scomber, scombrī, m.: mackerel

scopulus, -ī, m.: a projecting rock or cliff

scortillum, -ī, n.: dim. of *scortum*, chippy, little bimbo

scortum, -ī, n.: skin, hide; prostitute, courtesan, bimbo

scrībō, scrībere, scrīpsī, scrīptum: write; mark up, inscribe with drawings

scrīnium, -ī, n.: a cylindrical wooden box for holding rolled books (*volumina*)

scripta, -ōrum, n. pl.: writings, works (in poetry or prose)

scriptor, -ōris, m.: writer

scurra, -ae, m.: a fashionable man about town

Scylla, -ae, f.: a cliff-dwelling monster in the Straits of Messina (between Italy and Sicily) who devours sailors on passing ships; Charybdis is on the other side of the strait

sē, sēsē: reflex. pers. pron., him/her/itself

sēcēdō, -cēdere, -cēssī, -cēssum: withdraw

secō, -āre: cut; (transf.) torment

sēcrētus, -a, -um: set apart, remote, secluded, secret

secta, -ae, f.: a line of movement or action; a line of teaching; way of life, occupation

sector, -ārī, -ātus: (freq. of *sequor*) follow constantly; pursue, chase

sēcubitus, -ūs, m.: a sleeping apart; the action of sleeping apart from one's spouse or lover

sēcubō, -āre: sleep apart (from one's spouse)

sēcum: (*cum se*) with himself, herself, itself, themselves

secundus, -a, -um: (early participial gerundive of *sequor*) going along with, following; hence (of a wind) favorable; second

secūris, -is, f.: axe

sed: disjunctive conj., but

sedeō, -ēre, sēdī, sessum: sit

sēdēs, -is, f.: seat; place, home

seges, segetis, f.: a field or crop of standing grain

sella, -ae, f.: seat; chair of office

semel: adv., a single time, once; once and for all

sēmen, -inis, n.: seed; semen, sperm

sēmihians, -ntis: half-open

sēmilautus, -a, -um: half-washed

sēmimortuus, -a, -um: half-dead

sēmirāsus, -a, -um: partly shaven

sēmitārius, -a, -um: of or associated with byways and alleys

semper: adv., always, forever

senecta, -ae, f.: old age

senectūs, -tūtis, f.: old age

seneō, -ēre: to be old

senescō, -escere, -uī: grow old, age

senex, senis, m.: old man, codger

sensus, -ūs, m.: sensation; any of the senses; consciousness

sentiō, -īre, sensī, sensum: perceive, sense, feel

septemgeminus, -a, -um: sevenfold; having seven mouths (e.g., the Nile)

Septimius, -ī, m., fam. dim. Septimillus: Roman *nomen gentile*

sepulcrētum, -ī, n.: cemetery, graveyard

sepulcrum, -ī, n.: tomb, sepulcher

sepultus, -a, -um: (part. of *sepelio*) buried

sequor, sequī, secūtus: follow

Serāpis, -is, m.: an Egyptian god popular in the Roman world; the temple of Serapis, where Romans went for faith healing

serēnus, -a, -um: clear, unclouded; calm, untroubled

sermō, -ōnis, m: talk, informal speech, conversation; topic of conversation

serō¹, -ere, sēvī, satum: sow, plant

serō²: adv., late

serpens, -entis, f. or m.: snake

serta, -ōrum, n. pl.: chains or festoons of flowers

serum, -ī, n.: whey; any fluid similar in appearance, e.g., semen

sērus, -a, -um: late

serva, -ae, f.: female slave or servant

serviō, servīre, -īvī, -ītum: w/dat., serve, be subject to

servus, -ī, m.: male slave or servant

sesquipedālis, -e: one and a half feet long

sessor, -ōris, m.: one who sits

sestertium, -iī, n.: (abbr. form of *milia sestertium*), a thousand sesterces

Sestiānus, -a, -um: of Sestius

Sestius, -a, -um: name of a Roman *gens* (see appendix A)

seu, sive: or if; whether ... or (see *sive*)

sevērus, -a, -um, comp. sevērior, -ius: austere, stern, strict, grave

sēvocō, -āre: call one apart from, draw aside; separate

sī: conj., if

sibi (final vowel may be long or short): dat. of the reflexive personal pron., to or for himself, herself, themselves

sībilus, -ī, m.: any sibilant sound; hissing, whistling

sīc: adv., in this way, so, thus

siccō, -āre: dry, drain

siccus, -a, -um, comp. siccior: dry

sīcine: *sic* + interrog. *-ne*: is this the way?

sīcula, -ae, f.: a small dagger; (metaph.) penis

sīcut: conj., in the same way as

sīdus, -eris, n.: star, planet, constellation

signum, -ī, n.: sign, signal

Sīlēnus, -ī, m.: an attendant of Bacchus, usually represented as old, fat, and drunken

silescō, -escere: become silent, grow quiet

silex, -icis, m.: any hard rock; flint

Sīlō, -ōnis, m.: cognomen of a pimp in poem 103

silva, -ae, f.: forest, wood

silvester, -tris: of the forest

silvicultrix, -īcis, f.: adj., living in the forest

similis, -e: similar to, like

Simōnidēus, -a, -um: of Simonides of Ceos (556-467 B.C.), famous for his poems of sadness

simul: adv., at the same time, together, as well; conj., as soon as

sincērē: adv., without impairment, falsehood, or dishonesty

sine: prep. w/abl., without

singulī, -ae, -a: one apiece; taken separately, individual

singultus, -ūs, m.: sob

sinister, -tra, -trum: left; harmful, perverse, misguided

sinistra¹, -ae, f. [sc. *manus*]: the left hand (traditionally used in thieving)

sinistrā²: adv., on the left

sinō, sinere, sīvī, situm: leave alone; allow

sinus, -ūs, m.: the cavity or fold produced by the looping of a garment (OLD); breast; bosom, refuge; a curved indentation in the coastline such as a bay or gulf

sīquis, sīqua, sīquid: *si* + indef. adj., if any

sīrīs: see *sino* and 66.91 note

Sirmiō, -ōnis, f.: mod. Sermione, a long promontory running out into Lacus Benacus (mod. Lago di Garda)

sistō, sistere, stetī, statum: (redup. *sto*) cause to stand, set; present, hand over

sitiō, sitīre: be thirsty

situs, -ūs, m.: stagnation, mold, rust, decrepitude

sīve, seu: conj., or if; whether ... or

soccus, -ī, m.: a loose shoe or slipper worn by women

socer, -erī, m.: father-in-law

socius, -ī, m.: partner, companion, colleague

Sōcration, -i, m.: dim. of Socrates; unknown addressee in poem 47

sodālicium, -ī, n.: club, fraternal organization; partnership

sodālis, -is, m.: crony, buddy, comrade
sōdēs: (*si audes*, lit. if you hear) if you please
sōl, sōlis, m.: the sun, sts. personified as *Sol*
sōlācium, -ī, n., dim. **solaciolum**: solace, comfort
solea, -ae, f.: sandal
soleō, -ēre, -itus: to be accustomed (to); (euphemistic, w/acc.) to "know," i.e., be sexually intimate with
solitus, -a, -um: accustomed
solium, -ī, n.: a high-backed chair, throne
sollers, -ertis: clever, skilled, ingenious, resourceful
sollicitus, -a, -um: restless, troubled, anxious
sōlor, -ārī: comfort, give solace to
solum¹, -ī, n.: base, floor; (sts. pl.) soil, earth, ground
solum², adv., only
sōlus, -a, -um: only, alone, lonely
solvō, -ere, -uī, -ūtum: loosen, untie, dislodge, cast off; discharge, fulfill (a vow)
somnus, -ī, m.: sleep, sts. personified as *Somnus*
sonipēs, -pedis, m.: (poet.) a horse
sonitus, -ūs, m.: sound
sonō, -āre: make a sound
sōpiō, -ōnis, m.: penis
sopor, -ōris, m.: sleep
sordeō, -ēre: be dirty; seem unworthy, not good enough
sordidus, -a, -um: dirty, squalid, shabby, unbecoming, tacky, sordid
soror, -ōris, f.: sister
sospes, -itis: safe
sospitō, -āre: preserve, defend
spatium, -ī, n.: racetrack; area, space, extent
spectō, -āre: look at, watch
specula, -ae, f.: look-out point
specus, -ūs, m.: cave or grotto
spernō, spernere, sprēvī, sprētum: scorn, spurn, reject
spērō, -āre: hope, hope for; anticipate
spēs, speī, f.: hope
spīnōsus, -a, -um: thorny, prickly
splendeō, -ēre: shine, be bright, glitter
splendidus, -a, -um: brilliant, bright, glittering
sponsus, -i, m.: a lover who has promised marriage; fiancé
spūma, -ae, f.: foam
spūmō, -āre: foam, froth
spūmōsus, -a, -um: foamy
spurcātus, -a, -um: morally contaminated, depraved
spurcus, -a, -um: filthy, foul, disgusting
squālidus, -a, -um: rough; filthy

stabulum, -ī, n.: stable, fold, shed; lair, den
stadium, -iī, n.: a running track
stāgnum, -ī, n.: any expanse of standing water: pool, lagoon, lake
statim: adv., immediately
statua, -ae, f.: statue
statuō, -uere, -uī, -ūtum: set up, set, stand; decide
stella, -ae, f.: star
sterilis, -e: incapable of procreation
sternuō, sternuere, sternuī: sneeze
stimulō, -āre: to goad on; incite, rouse, excite
stīpendium, -ī, n.: payment
stīpes, stīpitis, m.: tree trunk
stirps, stirpis, f.: stem, stalk, family, offspring
stō, stāre, stetī, statum: stand
stolidus, -a, -um: dull, stupid, inert
strīdō, strīdere, strīdī: make a shrill, strident sound
stringō, stringere, strinxī, strictum: bind fast; draw (iron) into bars, case harden
strophium, -iī, n.: a twisted band supporting a woman's breasts
strūma, -ae, f.: a swelling of the lymphatic glands; a person deformed by such swelling
studeō, -ēre, -uī: concentrate on
studiōsus, -a, -um: zealous, eager, diligent
studium, -ī, n.: zeal, ardor, eagerness, enthusiasm; pursuit, pastime
stultus, -a, -um: stupid, foolish
stultus, -ī, m.: a fool
stupor, -ōris, m.: numbness, lethargy, paralysis, torpor; (meton.) an insensate person, clod
stuprum, -ī, n.: dishonor, shame; illicit sexual activity, debauchery
Stymphālius, -a, -um: of Stymphalus, a territory in NE Arcadia, Greece
suāvior, -ārī, -ātus: kiss
suāvis, -e, comp. **suāvior, -ius**: agreeable, pleasant
suāvium, -iī, n., dim. **suaviolum**: kiss; the lips formed for kissing
sub: prep. w/acc. or abl., under
subdūcō, -ducere, -duxī, -ductum: draw up, raise; reckon, calculate
subeō, -īre, -īvī, -itum: go beneath
subitō: suddenly, at once, quickly
sublevō, -āre: raise, lift
sublīmis, -e: high
subrēpō, -rēpere, -rēpsī, -rēptum: creep up to, steal upon
subsellium, -ī, n.: a courtroom bench
substernō, -sternere, -strāvī, -strātum: lay or spread beneath; (of a woman) offer oneself

sexually to a man

subtegmen, -inis, n.: the woof or weft, cross-threads in a loom running at right angles to the vertical threads of the warp

subter: prep., below

subtīlis, -e: fine-textured, delicate

suburbānus, -a, -um: located close to the city

succipiō, -cipere, -cēpī, -ceptum: take up, take on, undertake to discharge (a vow or oath)

succumbō, -cumbere, -cubuī, cubitum: collapse; (w/dat.) "go down," lie under or submit to (a man) in the act of sex

sūdārium, -ī, n.: a cloth carried to wipe off sweat (*sudor*), also used as a napkin

sūdō, -āre: sweat, perspire

sūdor, -ōris, m.: sweat, perspiration

suescō, suescere, suēvī: become accustomed; in perf., be accustomed

Suffēnus, -i, m.: name of a Roman poet; see appendix A

suffīxus, -a, -um: attached beneath; attached up on

Sulla, -ae, m.: a Roman cognomen; see appendix A

sum, esse, fuī: to be (for alternative forms, see appendix D)

summissus, -a, -um: lowered, submissive

summus, -a, um: highest; the top of

sūmō, sumere, sumpsī, sumptum: take up

sumptuōsus, -a, -um, adv. sumptuōsē: expensive, lavish

sumptus, -ūs, m.: outlay, cost, expense

super: adv., over, above; more; besides; w/*est*, = *superest*; prep. w/acc., over

superbus, -a, -um: proud, haughty

supercilium, -ī, n.: eyebrow

superfluō, -fluere -fluxī: overflow; be or have more than enough

superō, -āre: surpass

supersum, -esse, -fuī: be higher; remain, be left over

supervehō, -vehere, -vexī, -vectum: (pass., w/acc.) carry or drive over

supīnus, -a, -um: lying on the back; facing upwards; flat; helpless

suppernātus, -a, -um (*perna*): having the leg cut from below; hamstrung; (transf.) felled

supplex, -plicis: making humble entreaty; suppliant

supplicium, -ī, n.: compensation offered to placate a person who has been wronged; reparation; punishment; **supplicium dare**: to pay the penalty, suffer punishment

suppōnō, pōnere, -posuī, -positum: put beneath, situate below

suprēmus, -a, -um: highest; final; decisive, critical, desperate

sūra, -ae, f.: calf of the leg

surgō, surgere, surrexī, surrectum: rise, get up

surripiō, -ripere, -ripuī, -reptum: steal

suscipiō, -cipere, -cēpī, -ceptum: undertake; perform

suscitō, -āre: rouse, dislodge

suspendō, -pendere, -pensī, -pensum: hang, suspend

suspicor, -ārī: guess, infer; suspect

suspīrō, -āre: sigh, pant

sustollō, -tollere, -tulī: raise

susurrō, -āre: whisper

suus, -a, -um: reflex. possesive adj., his/her/its own

Syria, -ae, f.: Syria, the region between Asia Minor and Egypt, usually including Phoenicia and Palestine (OLD)

Syrius, -a, -um: of or from Syria; Syrian

Syrtis, -is, f.: shoals on the N. African coast between Carthage and Cyrene

tabella, -ae, f.: board, placard, tablet; **liminis tabella**: portion of a double housedoor

taberna, -ae, f.: hut; inn, hostel

tābescō, -escere, -uī: waste away

tabula, -ae, f.: a flat piece of wood; a wax-coated writing tablet; pl., account books

taceō, -ēre, tacuī, tacitum: be silent, say nothing

tacitus, -a, -um: unspeaking; silent

taeda, -ae, f.: pinewood, esp. as used in torches; torch; marriage torch, by meton. wedding

taedet, taedēre, taesum est: impers., be sick or tired

taeter, -tra, -trum: foul, vile, horrible

Tagus, -ī, m.: the Tagus (mod. Tajo) river, which flows west through central Spain and empties into the Atlantic near mod. Lisbon, Portugal

Talasius, -ī, m.: a Roman marriage god (cf. Hymenaeus)

talentum, -ī, n.: a weight of silver used as a Greek unit of currency; a large sum of money

tālis, -e: such a, such

tālus, -ī, m.: anklebone; ankle

tam: adv., to such a degree, so; **tam ... quam**: as much as

tamen: however, nevertheless

tamquam: conj., as; just as if (it were)

tandem: adv., at last

tangō, -ere, tetigī, tactum: touch

tantillum, -i, n.: so little, so small a quantity

tantum, -ī, n.: pron., such a quantity, so much; acc.

as adv., to such a degree; only; **tantum ... quantum:** as much ... as

tantundem: adv., just as much

tantus, -a, -um: so much, pl. so many; so great, such

Tappō, -ōnis, m.: poss. a clown figure in poem 104

tardē: adv., slowly

tardipēs, -pedis: slow-footed, lame

tardō, -āre: delay, slow

tardus, -a, -um: slow, late, dull

taurīnus, -a, -um: of a bull

taurus, -ī, m.: a bull

Taurus, -ī, m.: a mountain range in the south of Asia Minor, directly north of Cyprus

tē: acc. or abl. sing. of 2nd personal pron, you

tectum, -ī, n.: roof; by meton., house

tēcum: = *cum te*

tegmen, -minis, n.: covering

tegō, -ere, texī, tectum: cover

tēla, -ae, f.: cloth on the loom; spider's web

Tēlemachus, -ī, m.: son of Odysseus (Ulysses) and Penelope

tellūs, -ūris, f.: earth, ground

tēlum, -ī, n.: spear, shaft, weapon

temere: adv., recklessly; without good cause

Tempē, n. pl.: valley of the Peneus R. between Mt. Olympus and Mt. Ossa, famous for its scenic beauty

tempestās, -ātis, f.: period, time, season; weather; storm

templum, -ī, n.: a consecrated area; a zone, space, region, or quarter

temptō, -āre: try

tempus¹, -oris, n.: time

tempus², -oris, n.: the side of the forehead, temple

tenax, -ācis: clinging, tenacious

tenebrae, -ārum, f. pl.: darkness; shade, shadow; place of concealment

tenebricōsus, -a, -um: shadowy, dark

teneō, -ēre, -uī, tentum: hold

tener, -era, -erum, dim. **tenellulus:** soft, tender, delicate; romantically tender (with ref. to love poetry)

tentus, -a, -um: taut; engorged, erect

tenuis, -e: thin

tenus: prep. w/abl. or gen., up to, as far as

tepefaciō, -ere, -fēcī, -factum: make warm

tepefactō, -āre: to be in the habit of warming

tepidus, -a, -um: warm

tepor, -ōris, m.: warmth

teres, teretis: smooth; rounded

tergum, -ī, n.: back; hide from an animal's back

terō, terere, trīvī, trītum: rub; tread, traverse repeatedly

terra, -ae, f.: earth; land

terror, -ōris, m.: extreme fear

tertius, -a, -um: third

testātus, -a, -um: well-attested; signed in the presence of witnesses

testis, -is, m. or f.: witness

tētē: emph. redupl. form of acc. or abl. 2nd pers. pron., you

Tēthys, Tēthyos, f.: a sea-goddess, wife of Oceanus, mother of Doris, grandmother of Thetis

Teucrus, -a, -um: Teucrian, Trojan

texō, texere, texuī, textum: weave

textum, -ī, n.: fabric; anything made of intercrossing materials, such as the framing of a ship; framework

thalamus, -ī, m.: bedroom

Thallus, -ī, m.: a *praenomen* in poem 25

Themis, -is, f.: Greek goddess associated with justice

Thermopylae, -ārum, f. pl.: Gk. "Hot Gates," the narrow passage between Mt. Oeta and the Malian Gulf, named after its hot springs, where the Spartans resisted the Persian invasion of 480 B.C.

Thēseus, -eī, m., acc. **Thēsea,** voc. **Thēseu:** son of Aegeus, seducer of Ariadne (later husband of her sister Phaedra), slayer of the Minotaur

Thespius, -a, -um: belonging to Thespiae, a Boeotian town at the foot of Mt. Helicon

Thessalia, -ae, f.: Thessaly, region of Greece south of Macedonia associated with Peleus and his son Achilles

Thessalus, -a, -um: Thessalian

Thetis, -idis, f.: the Nereid Thetis, wife of Peleus and mother of Achilles

Thīa, -ae, f.: wife of Hyperion and mother of Helios (the sun)

thiasus, -ī, m.: an orgiastic dance; a group that performs such dances

Thrācia, -ae, f.: Thrace, the land in southeastern Europe north of the Hellespont

Thyias, -adis, f.: a Bacchant or Maenad, orgiastic worshiper of Bacchus/Dionysus

Thȳnia, -ae, f.: the country of the Thyni; Bithynia

Thȳnus, -a, -um: Bithynian

Thyōniānus, -ī, m.: an adherent of Bacchus

thyrsus, -ī, m.: a pole tipped with a pinecone, ivy, or vine leaves, as carried by bacchants

tībia, -ae, f.: pipe, flute

tībīcen, -inis, m.: piper, a performer on the *tibia*

Tīburs, Tiburtis: of or belonging to Tibur (mod. Tivoli), about 18 miles ENE of Rome.

tigillum, -ī, n.: a small beam, e.g., the lintel or top of the doorframe

timeō, -ēre, -uī: be afraid; w/dat., fear for

timor, -ōris, m.: fear, anxiety

tingō, tingere, tinxī, tinctum: dip; dye

tinnītus, -ūs, m.: a ringing or clanging sound

tinnulus, -a, -um: making a jingling sound; high-pitched

tintin(n)ō, -āre: make a ringing sound

tollō, -ere, sustulī, sublātum: pick up, raise, take, carry off, steal

tondeō, tondēre, totondī, tonsum: cut (hair), clip, trim, shear

torōsus, -a, -um: knotty, bulging, muscular, brawny

torpeō, -ēre: be numb or paralyzed

torpor, -ōris, m.: numbness, paralysis

Torquatus, -a, -um: a Roman cognomen, e.g., of the groom in poem 61 (see appendix A)

torqueō, torquēre, torsī, tortum: twist, whirl, spin in an eddy

torreō, torrēre, torruī, tostum: scorch, parch

torus, -ī, m.: thong; bed

torvus, -a, -um: grim, fierce, stern

tot: indecl. adj., so many

totidem: indecl. adj., the same number, as many

totiēns: so often

tōtus, -a, -um: the whole, all

trabs, -bis, f.: tree trunk, timber; (by meton.) boat; penis, "shaft"

trādō, tradere, tradidī, traditum: hand down, consign, entrust, pass on

trans: prep. w/acc., across

transeō, -īre, -īvī, -itum: go across, pass on

transferō, -ferre, -tulī, -latum: transport; with two accs., move across

Transpadānus, -a, -um: from the region of northern Italy north of the river Po (*Padus*)

trecentī, -ae, -a: three hundred

trecentiēs: adv., three hundred times

tremebundus, -a, -um: shaking, trembling

tremulus, -a, -um: shaky, trembling; shaking (voluntarily, as one dandling an infant)

trepidō, -āre: panic; bustle, hurry; tremble with excitement

trepidus, -a, -um: fearful; shaking, trembling, quivering

trēs, tria: num. adj., three

tribuō, tribuere, tribuī, tribūtum: apportion, grant

trīgintā: indecl. numerical adj., thirty

Trīnacria, -ae, f.: Sicily, so-called because of its triangular shape

tripudium, -ī, n.: a ritual dance in three-step

tristis, -e: grim, fierce, gloomy; unhappy, sad

Trītōn, -ōnis, m.: Triton, a sea god; a river in Boeotia sacred to Athena/Minerva

trītus, -a, -um: worn

Trivia, -ae, f.: epithet of Diana, the triple goddess

trivium, -ī, n.: meeting place of three roads; street corner

Trōia, -ae, f.: the city and territory of Troy

Trōïcus, -a, -um: Trojan

Trōiugena, -ae, m.: a Trojan-born man; Trojan

Trōius, -a, -um: Trojan

truculentus, -a, -um: ferocious; n. pl. as subst., ferocity

truncus, -ī, m.: body, trunk, torso

trūsō, -āre (iterat. of *trudo*): keep pushing or thrusting; w/dat., of sexual intercourse.

trux, trucis: harsh, fierce, cruel, savage

tū (emphatic forms: nom. tūte, acc. & abl. tētē): second person sing. pronoun, you

tueor, -ērī, tutus: look at, view, observe

Tullius, -a, -um: Roman *nomen gentile*, e.g., of M. Tullius Cicero

tum: adv., then, at that time; tum denique: then only, not till then, in the last analysis

tumidus, -a, -um: swollen, bulging

tumulō, -āre: cover with a burial mound; bury

tunc: adv., at that time

tundō, -ere, tutudī, tunsum: beat repeatedly, buffet, pound

tunica, -ae. f.: tunic, a standard garment worn by both sexes

turbidus, -a, -um: turbulent, stormy

turbō, -inis, m.: anything that spins; whirlwind, tornado; maelstrom; a weight used in spinning (see n. to 64.312-5)

turgidulus, -a, -um: dim. of *turgidus*, swollen

turpiculus, -a, -um: somewhat ugly or indecent

turpis, -e: disgusting, repulsive, shameful, indecent

turpiter: adv., in an unbecoming or disgraceful manner

tussis, -is, f.: a cough

tūtāmen, -inis, n.: means of protection; bulwark

tūte: emphatic form of pron. *tu*

tūtus, -a, -um: safe; in tuto: safe and sound

tuus or tuos, -a, -um: poss. adj., your

tympanum or typanum, -ī, n. (as required by

meter): a small drum or tom-tom, usu. as used in the worship of Cybele or Bacchus

Tyrius, -a, -um: of Tyre, Tyrian; crimson (from the purple dye produced at Tyre)

ūber, ūberis: abundant; fertile; rich

ūbertim: copiously

ubi: (final vowel long or short) adv. where

ubicumque: (long or short *i*) rel. adv., wherever

ubinam: interr. adv., where in the world? just where?

ūdus, -a, -um: wet

ulciscor, ulciscī, ultus: take revenge on, punish

ullus, -a, -um: any

ulmus, -ī, f.: elm

ulna, -ae, f.: forearm, esp. the crook of the arm

ultimus, -a, -um: last, final, farthest

ultrā: adv., further

ultrō: adv., to a point farther off; of one's own accord, unasked

ultus, -a, -um: see *ulciscor*

ululātus, -ūs, m.: ululation, a howling or wailing in which the tongue is moved rapidly up and down to form the sounds

ululō, -āre: make an ululating sound with the mouth and tongue

Umber, -bra, -brum: Umbrian, from the region of Italy east of Etruria.

umbilīcus, -ī, m.: navel; the ornamental end of the cylinder on which a papyrus roll is wound

umbra, -ae, f.: shade, shadow

ūmidus, -a, -um: damp

ūmor, -ōris, m.: moisture

umquam: adv., ever

ūnā: adv., together; at the same time

ūnanimus, -a, -um: sharing a single attitude, like-minded

unctus, -a, -um, comp. **unctior, -ius:** greasy, well-oiled, rich

unda, -ae, f.: wave; waves of the sea, sea

unde: rel. adv., from which, whence

undique: from all directions, from everywhere; throughout

unguen, -inis, n.: aromatic oil, perfume, unguent

unguentātus, -a, -um: anointed or greased with ointments

unguentum, -ī, n.: a fragrant ointment, unguent, or perfume

unguis, -is, m.: fingernail, claw, talon

ūnicē: uniquely, particularly

ūnicus, -a, -um: one and only, singular, unique, special

ūnigena, -ae: born together with, twin; sharing a single parentage; (as substantive) brother

ūnus, -a, um: adj., one, alone, only; any, an ordinary

Ūrania, -ae, f.: muse of astronomy, mother of Hymenaeus in poem 61

urbānus, -a, -um: of the city, esp. Rome; having city manners, urbane

urbs, urbis, f.: city; often used as synonym for Rome

urgeō, urgēre, ursī: put pressure on; oppress

Ūriī, -ōrum, m. pl.: Italian town associated with the cult of Venus (see note on 36.12)

ūrīna, -ae, f.: urine

ūrō, urere, ussī, ustum: burn; pass., burn with anger or desire; keep alight

urtīca, -ae, f.: nettle

usquam: adv., anywhere

usque: adv., all the way (to), continuously, constantly; **usque altera mille:** still another thousand; **usque dum:** until

usquequāque: adv., everywhere; in every situation

ustor, -ōris, m.: a person employed to burn dead bodies

ustulō, -āre: char, burn

ūsus, -ūs, m.: use; habitual dealings between persons; requirement, need

ut, utī: adv., as, just as, like; when, where, how; conj. (in final clauses) so that, with the result that, that

uterque, utraque, utrumque: indef. adj. & pron., each (of two)

utinam: particle used to express a wish: would that, how I wish that

ūtor, ūtī, ūsus: dep. w/abl., use

utpote: part., as one might expect, as is natural

utrum ... an: whether ... or

ūva, -ae, f.: a bunch of grapes

ūvidulus, -a, -um: damp

uxor, -ōris, f.: wife

vacuus or **vacuos, -a, -um:** vacant, empty, empty-handed

vādō, vādere: advance (esp. with rapid or violent movement)

vadum, -ī, n.: a shallow piece of water, shoal; (pl.) the waters of the sea

vae!: interj., woe to, alas for

vagor, vagārī, -ātus: wander, roam

vagus, -a, -um: roaming, wandering, rambling. "*Vagus* is a favorite word of Catullus. ... Often, *vagus* is `always on the move': the idea conveyed is restlessness rather than unsteadiness or uncertainty." —Fordyce on 64.271

valdē: vigorously; strongly, greatly; very

valens, -entis: sturdy, robust, vigorous

valeō, -ēre, -uī, -ītum: have strength or health; be effective; **Vale!**: farewell

Valerius, -ī, m.: *nomen gentile* of Gaius Valerius Catullus

vallēs, -is, f.: valley

vānescō, -escere: vanish; become ineffectual

vānus, -a, -um: lacking substance, empty; vain, useless

vappa, -ae, f. or **m.**: flat wine; masc., a person who has gone flat, a nerd or dud

variē: adv., in different ways, variously

variō, -āre: adorn with contrasting colors; embroider; mottle, bruise

varius, -a, -um: different, various; many-colored; dappled

Vārus, -ī, m.: friend of Catullus. See appendix A

vastō, -āre: make desolate; destroy, sack

vastus, -a, -um: desolate, uninhabited, featureless, dreary, endless

Vatīniānus, -a, -um: of or pertaining to Publius Vatinius; see appendix A

Vatīnius, -a, -um: name of a Roman *gens*, and of Publius Vatinius; see appendix A

-ve: encl. conj., or

vēcors, -cordis: demented

vegetus, -a, -um: vigorous, active, energetic; fresh

vehō, vehere, vexī, vectum: convey, carry, transport

vel: part., or; even

vellus, velleris, n.: fleece; a piece of wool

vēlō, -āre: cover, clothe, veil

vēlum, -ī, n.: sail

velut, velutī: adv., just as

vēmens, -ntis: (*<vehemens*) violent, forceful, zealous

vēna, -ae, f.: blood vessel; vein of ore

venditō, -āre: offer for sale; prostitute

vendō, vendere, vendidī, venditum: sell

venēnum, -ī, n.: poison

veneror, -ārī: solicit divine good will by pleasing acts; worship, venerate

venia, -ae, f.: a favor, kindness

veniō, -īre, vēnī, ventum: come

vēnor, -ārī: hunt, hunt for

venter, -tris, m.: belly, stomach

ventitō, -āre: (freq. of *venio*) come frequently or habitually, keep coming

ventōsus, -a, -um: windy

ventus, -ī, m.: wind

Venus, -eris, f.: Venus or Aphrodite, goddess of love and charm

venustās, venustātis, f.: charm, grace, delightfulness

venustus, -a, -um, comp. **venustior, -ius**, adv. **venuste**: lovely, attractive, charming; graceful, pretty, neat

vēr, vēris, n.: spring

Vērāniolus, -ī, m.: dim. of *Veranius*

Vērānius, -i, m.: friend of Catullus; see appendix A

verber, -eris, n.: pl., an instrument used for flogging; blows, lashes

verbōsus, -a, -um: full of words, long-winded, talkative

verbum, -ī, n.: word

vērē: adv., truly

verēcundus, -a, -um: scrupulous; modest, honorable, restrained, seemly

vereor, verērī, veritus: show respect for; fear

vēridicus, -a, -um: truth telling

vernus, -a, -um: of spring, vernal

vērō: adv., part., in truth, indeed

Vērōna, -ae, f.: town in Gallia Transpadana, birthplace of Catullus

Vērōnensis, -e: belonging to, or native of, Verona; Veronese

verpa, -ae, f.: penis with foreskin drawn back; erect penis

verpus, -a, -um: having the foreskin drawn back

verrō, verrere, versum: sweep

versiculus, -ī, m.: dim. of *versus*, light verse, a short line of verse, epigrammatic verse

versō, -āre: keep turning; pass. w/middle force, toss and turn

versus, -ūs, m.: a line of verse; verse, poetry

vertex, -icis, m.: whirlpool, whirlwind; top of the head; summit

vertō, vertere, vertī, versum: turn; translate

vērum: adversative conj., assenting to what has been said but adding a qualification: but in fact, but, actually

vērus, -a, -um, comp. **verior, -ius**: true

vēsāniō, -īre: rage

vēsānus, -a, -um: frenzied, mad, wild

Vesper, -eris, m.: (Gk. Hesperos) the evening star

vester, -tra, -trum: 3rd pers. poss. adj., your, yours

vestibulum, -ī, n.: forecourt

vestīgium, -ī, n.: footprint, trail, track; mark, vestige; course; foot

vestis, -is, f.: clothing; any drapery, such as a bedspread or sail (cf. Eng. a *suit* of sails) veternus, -ī, m.: torpor, senility

vetus, -eris, dim. vetulus, -a, -um: old

vexō, -āre: buffet, harry, ravage, afflict

via, -ae, f.: way, path, route

viātor, -ōris, m.: traveler

Vibennius, -ī, m.: see appendix A

vibrō, -āre: shake, brandish

vicis (gen.), f., acc. vicem: a recurring occasion for action, turn; plight or situation

victima, -ae, f.: a living sacrificial victim

Victius, -a, -um: Roman *nomen gentile* in poem 98

victor, -ōris, m.: winner, victor; cognomen in poem 80

victoria, -ae, f.: victory

viden: abbr. form of interrogative *videsne?*

videō, -ēre, vīdī, vīsum: see, perceive; pass. seem, seem good or proper

viduus, -a, -um: deprived of a husband or wife, bereft, celibate; (of vines) unsupported by a tree

vigeō, -ēre, -uī: be vigorous and active, flourish

vigescō, -escere: grow strong

vigilō, -āre: stay awake; be awake (following sleep); be on the alert

vīlica, -ae, f.: the wife of a farm manager

vīlis, -e, comp. vilior, -ius: cheap; worthless, contemptible

villa, -ae, f.: dim. villula, -ae, f.; country house

vinciō, -īre, vixī, vinctum: fasten, tie, bind

vincō, vincere, vīcī, victum: conquer, beat, defeat

vinc(u)lum, -ī, n.: bond, fetter; any fastening device

vindex, vindicis, m.: guarantor, defender, champion; one who punishes a wrong or takes vengeance; adjectival in 64.192, avenging

vīnea, -ae, f.: grapevines

vīnum, -ī, n.: wine

violō, -āre: violate, defile

vir, virī, m.: man; husband; (poet.) manhood

vireō, -ēre, -uī: be verdant

virgātus, -a, -um: made of twigs; wicker

virgineus, -a, -um: of a virgin

virginitās, -ātis, f.: virginity

virgō, -inis, f.: maiden, virgin; the constellation Virgo

virgulta, -ōrum, n. pl.: brushwood, undergrowth

viridis, -e, superl. viridissimus: green

viridō, -āre: be green

virtus, -tūtis, f.: manliness, manly excellence (cf. Gk. *aretē*)

vīs, vis, f.: strength, force, violence

vīsō, -ere, vīsī: (freq. of *video*) go to see; look at, gaze at, view

vīta, -ae, f.: life; hyperb., as a term of endearment

vītis, -is, f.: vine

vītō, -āre: avoid, evade

vitta, -ae, f.: headband

vīvō, -ere, vīxī, vīctum: live

vīvus, -a, -um: living, alive

vix: adv., with difficulty; scarcely

vocātiō, -ōnis, f.: invitation

vocō, -āre: call, summon, invite

volātilis, -e: able to fly

volātus, -ūs, m.: flight

volitō, -āre: freq. of *volo*, fly about; move about rapidly; dart swiftly

volō[1], -āre: fly

volō[2], velle, voluī: wish, be willing

volturius, -ī, m.: vulture

voluntās, -ātis, f.: will, wish

voluptās, -tātis, f.: pleasure

Volusius, -ia, -ium: Roman *nomen gentile*; see appendix A

volvō, volvere, voluī, volūtum: cause to roll

vōmer, -eris, m.: a plowshare, the part of a plow that cuts the furrow

vorāgō, -inis, f.: a deep hole or watery chasm

vorax, -ācis, comp. voracior: ravenous, insatiable

vorō, -āre: devour, eat up

vōs: 2nd pers. pl. pron., you

vōtum, -ī, n.: vow, prayer

voveō, vovēre, vōvī, vōtum: promise, vow

vox, vōcis, f.: voice; word

vulgus, -ī, n.: (usu. pejorative) the general public, the rabble, riffraff

vulturius, -ī, m.: vulture

vultus, -ūs, m.: countenance, face

Zephyrītis, -idis, f.: title adopted by Arsinoë as deified and worshiped at a temple on a promontory named Zephyrium, east of Alexandria.

Zephyrus, -ī, m.: the west wind

Zmyrna, -ae, f.: Smyrna, city in Asia Minor (mod. Izmir); title of historical poem by C. Helvius Cinna (see poem 95)

zōna, -ae, f.: dim. zonula: a girdle or belt; as worn by unmarried girls, its removal signified loss of virginity